Nigerian History and Culture

**Edited by
Richard Olaniyan**

Longman

For J. L. Stanley

Longman Group Limited
Longman House
Burnt Mill, Harlow
Essex CM20 2JE, England
and Associated Companies
throughout the World

Longman Nigeria Limited
Ikeja, Ibadan, Owerri,
Zaria and representatives
throughout Nigeria

First published 1985

ISBN 0 582 64432 1

Library of Congress Cataloging in Publication Data

Nigerian history and culture.

   Bibliography: p.
   Includes index.
   1. Nigeria–History–Addresses, essays, lectures.
   2. Olaniyan, Richard.
DT515.57.N52   1982   966.9   85-812
ISBN 0-582-64432-1

Set in Times (Linotron)

Produced by Longman Group (FE) Ltd
Printed in Hong Kong

Contents

List of illustrations

Preface

Until now, no single volume has existed which encompasses within its pages the rich variety of topics on Nigerian history and culture dealt with in this book. The work has been motivated by the gnawing concern that historians of Nigeria have all too often paid greater attention to political and economic aspects of our past than to our cultural heritage. The attempt here has been to redress this imbalance by including contributions by experts in cultural studies in one compact volume. This comprehensive and interdisciplinary approach, as far as we know, is the first of its kind. It is hoped that this unique collaborative effort will appeal to university students and general readers.

The contributors are drawn from five Nigerian universities: Dr Ibrahim A. Gambari from Ahmadu Bello; Professor Tekena N. Tamuno and Professor S. H. Olu Tomori, from Ibadan; Professor I. A. Akinjogbin, Professor A. A. Akiwowo, Professor Olajide Aluko, Dr Biodun Adediran, Mr A. Adebayo, Dr Toyin Falola, Dr Akin Olorunfemi, Dr Fola Soremekun, Dr Leo Dare, Dr J. O. Kayode, Dr E. D. Adelowo, Dr Yemi Ogunbiyi, Dr Bade Ajuwon, and Dr Richard Olaniyan from Ife; Professor Akin Euba from Lagos; and Dr Nwanna Nzewunwa, from Port Harcourt. Sue Picton has worked in the National Museum, Lagos. They represent nine different disciplines. Without the co-operation and the sense of comradeship of all of them, for which the editor is profoundly grateful, it would have been impossible to bring out the volume in this form. Each of us is, of course, solely responsible for whatever errors may remain in our respective contributions.

It is a special joy to work with congenial and helpful publishing experts. Peter Warwick and Brian Willan of the Longman Group are a special breed. They have, with others, indefatigably and enthusiastically shepherded the work through the various stages of production. I am profoundly grateful to them. I am also deeply appreciative of the many kindnesses extended to me by several colleagues and friends, especially Professor R. S. Smith, formerly of the University of Ibadan: Professor Bisi Afolayan, Dean of the Faculty of Arts, University of Ife; Professor E. J. Alagoa, Deputy Vice-Chancellor, University of Port Harcourt; Professor Wole Soyinka; Mr S. O. Arifalo; Dr Yinka Bamiduro; Dr Segun Osoba; Dr G. O. Ekemode; Mr Ade Folowosele; Mr Ayo Oseleye; Mr F. O. Otuyemi; Abis Mejay and the families of Kayode Awe and Bola Pariola. Mr Fidelis Ogunsakin, who typed several of the chapters, deserves many grateful thanks.

Richard Olaniyan
Ile-Ife, 1981–2

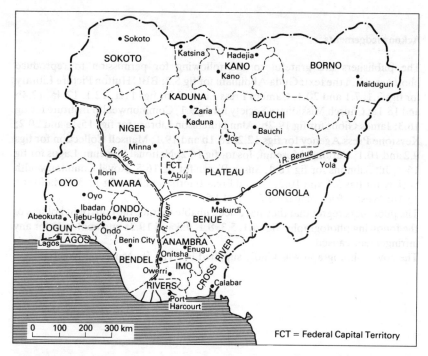

Political map of Nigeria

Acknowledgements

The publishers are grateful to the following for permission to reproduce photographs in the text: Guda Abdullahi for fig 5.2; BBC Hulton Picture Library for figs 3.1, 7.1 and 20.1; Camera Press Limited for figs 11.1, 12.1, 12.4a, 12.4b and 18.1a; Church Missionary Society for fig 9.1; Commonwealth Institute for fig 16.3; James Gibbs for fig 19.2b; Alan Hutchison Library for figs 15.1a and 20.2; Keystone Press Agency for figs 12.2, 18.1b and 19.1; Mansell Collection for figs 9.2 and 10.1; National Museum, Jos for fig 16.2; National Museum, Lagos for fig 16.1; Jill Salmons for fig 16.4; Susan Picton for fig 16.5; Royal Commonwealth Society for figs 5.1 and 10.2; United Press International for fig 12.3; Zefa for fig 15.1b; West Africa magazine for fig 12.5.
The publishers regret that they have been unable to trace the copyright holders of the following photographs: figs 4.1, 5.3, 8.1, 9.3 and 19.2a and apologise for any infringement caused.
The cover photograph was kindly supplied by: The Ife Museum, Nigeria.

1 Introduction: the relevance of Nigerian history

Richard Olaniyan

Although we must master science and technology as quickly as possible in order to make our political independence a reality, so we need the knowledge of our past and of our cultural attainments if we are to make our own distinctive contributions to world civilisation with confidence and success.

S. O. Biobaku[1]

But it . . . ought to be self-evident that any development planning which ignores or places too little emphasis on the study of our past, our society and our culture runs the risk of being meaningless in the end.

H. A. Oluwasanmi[2]

A nation which does not know what it was yesterday, does not know what it is today, nor what it is trying to do.

Woodrow Wilson[3]

All events of large significance take place within the setting of some culture, and indeed derive their significance from the culture in which they find themselves.

W. E. Abraham[4]

It is appropriate, indeed necessary, that we begin a discussion of the relevance of Nigerian history with an appreciation of what history is. There are of course as many definitions as there are schools of history, but two broad meanings are often associated with the word 'history'. It may be employed to mean 'the sum total of human acitivities in the past'; or, as is more commonly used, it may be considered as 'the record of events rather than the events themselves'.[5] In this second meaning, which is the more accepted usage, we can appropriately define history, to use Carl Becker's words, as 'the memory of things said and done'.[6] James Harvey Robinson's definition is similar but perhaps more comprehensive: he regards history as 'all we know about everything man has ever done, or thought, or hoped or felt'.[7] History is thus the memory of man, the way by which man knows himself. Just as man has his own individual memory, so also does a society have a collective memory. History as the record of all that human beings have thought and done tells of human glories and tragedies, triumphs and failures, hopes and aspirations, of the creative struggle of man to come to grips with the realities of his environment in the past.[8] It is a record of the evolution, growth and development of human society as reconstructed by the practitioners of the historical craft.

But can man know everything about his past? Man, by nature, constantly reflects on the meaning of his past, his achievements, and sufferings. Thus he desires a total comprehension of his own nature –

what man is. But a total or complete picture of the past may not in fact be desirable, and man almost instinctively tries to forget or misrepresent what he considers unpleasant, unsettling or inimical to his perception of himself. When that is done by an individual or by a society, a clear image of the past becomes impossible to obtain; reality has been falsified; and it becomes unhelpful, indeed dangerous, for the individual or the society to use such a distorted past as the basis for future action. A nation, like an individual, needs a correct perception, an unwarped memory of its past to make intelligent decisions, map out strategies and face the future with mature confidence.

Culture, too, is a product of man's past and his environment and therefore inextricably linked with his history. It is often popularly taken to mean such things as music, art, philosophy and literature. Admittedly these are all aspects of culture but they are by no means the whole of it. For culture has material as well as non-material components. The physical objects of a culture (e.g. technology) constitute its material component, whereas non-material culture consists of customs, ideas, beliefs, political and social structures and world views. Culture, then, is what Carroll Quigley describes as a 'complex medley of personalities, material objects, patterns of behaviour, subtle emotional relationships, accepted intellectual ideas and intellectual assumptions, and customary individual actions'.[9] In a sense, it is the dynamic social heritage, adaptive and persistent, transmitted from generation to generation. To speak of man's culture, therefore, is to speak of his total cumulative experience, with continuity and change as its intrinsic characteristics.

The question now arises: what is the use of history? Why study history? What relevance does it have to the socio-political development of any nation? We must say right away that in a practical sense history cannot be used in the way that physics or geology, for example, can be used. Its importance in this sense is limited: for history does not solve national or international conflicts; it does not show us how to avoid economic slumps, or provide certain means to progress. To be sure, history is not the only discipline that does not provide certain answers to questions posed. Certainly, too, society does not value only those things whose usefulness can be measured. Society has other ways, other yardsticks, for assessing usefulness. For how else could we account for the importance of music, philosophy, literature and poetry, to cite a few examples, in civilised societies the world over?

There must therefore be more to being *useful* than being of practical, measurable, quantifiable use. A music aficionado or a film buff derives some benefit, some pleasure or reward from his particular interest; so does history offer rewards, values or pleasures to those who cultivate an interest in it.[10]

In the first place history, as the memory of man, the way by which man knows himself by knowing his past, makes it possible for mankind to gain human self-knowledge. This is what the prominent English philosopher and historian R. G. Collingwood had in mind when he said:

Knowing yourself means knowing what you can do; and since nobody knows what he can do until he tries, the only clue to what man can do is what man has done. The value of history, then, is that it teaches us what man has done and thus what man is.[11]

We look to history for an illumination of human nature. This ability to gain self-knowledge is one of the essential values of history. Mature wisdom springs from self-knowledge based on critical self-appraisal. Generations which have gone before us have made contributions to the development of our cultures; the cultures have in turn been informed by certain values and shaped by certain forces. Our attitude and values have to a large extent been influenced by our cultures which are a product of our past. To examine these values and forces therefore is to become aware of our past. Out of that past we inherit some of our fears, beliefs, our hopes and limitations. The knowledge of our past can help us to understand our present.

There is another use for history which is perhaps more obvious: it adds new dimensions to our lives by immensely broadening our perspectives and enriching our experience. In this way, history produces what Herbert Butterfield calls 'a higher state of awareness and a greater elasticity of mind'.[12] What Hugh Trevor-Roper, a distinguished historian at Oxford University, calls historical imagination, that is 'the capacity to migrate into distant, foreign minds', makes the past 'fully intelligible to us, by enabling us to enter, as it were, into the minds and passions of people who, in some way, seem very different from us'.[13] History thus makes it possible for us vicariously to enter the past, to cast a beam of light over thousands of years and be 'participants' in or 'spectators' at great events.

History endows the elastic mind with a variety of experiences making us in a sense contemporaries, companions even, of great men and women who have gone generations before us. This is another vital value of history and one of its great pleasures. History allows students to enter the pleasant and immeasurably rewarding company of great minds, renowned statesmen, geniuses in the sciences and accomplished leaders in the humanities, visionaries, reformers and revolutionaries; and we can conjure up great debates, political conventions and diplomatic conferences, great battles, and manifestations of courage, which have affected the growth of civilisation.

Those who have developed more than a passing interest in history will agree that there are some significant similarities between history and travel outside one's country, or at least, outside one's immediate environment. The joy of knowing new places and experiencing new cultures is certainly one to be cherished. Both history and travel enrich the individual's experience by permitting him to go outside his own place. But history does more than that, for it also allows the individual to travel in the dimension of time. Since history is about time, places, change and peoples, it affords the individual the opportunity not only of visiting, for example, contemporary Sokoto but also the Sokoto of the era of the jihad; to be impressed today not only by the fast-modernising Benin city but also by its ancient artistic treasures; not only to admire the traditional architecture of the incumbent Alaafin's court but also the grandeur of the

3

NIGERIAN HISTORY AND CULTURE

court at the height of the Oyo empire. History permits us to go beyond the here and now of places, to delve into their past and see how the present is the logical heir of the past.

In other words, we need as good an understanding as possible of the past before we can begin to really understand the implications of the present. History thus serves as a bridge making the distant past accessible to the present; it serves as a lantern illuminating the present and future. Thus a knowledge of history can sharpen the consciousness of a nation by enabling it to appreciate its link with the past, cherish its continuity and help it chart, on the basis of its experience and hopes, a purposeful course of action to realise its potential and fulfil its historic destiny.[14]

The place of history in any country's educational policy should be of the utmost importance. It is no exaggeration to say that, except for religion, no other subject has been accorded more passionate homage by the most fertile and astute minds. Most of the statesmen, scholars and philosophers the world over from the times of the Greek and Roman civilisations to our own day have been nourished by the study of history.[15] Cultivated minds today find that history can and does provide the desirable qualities essential for the mind: variety, fecundity, intricacy and discernment.

Nigerian history, like other nations' histories, can provide us with all these rewards, and more. But can we really speak of Nigerian history? Should we not realistically be talking about the histories of the various ethnic groups? After all, the term 'Nigeria' itself, until 1914, remained a mere geographical rather than a political designation. Its birth was occasioned by the amalgamation in that year of the protectorates of Northern and Southern Nigeria into a political entity by Sir Frederick (later Lord) Lugard. The name 'Nigeria' had been earlier suggested for such a collectivity of British protectorates by Flora Shaw (who later became Lugard's wife) in an article for *The Times* of London, 8 January 1897.[16]

To be sure, Nigeria is a veritable mosaic of nationalities: all told, it has within its borders several hundred ethnic groups speaking different languages, and a wide variety of dialects. Its estimated population of eighty million makes it the most populous nation in Africa; one out of every four Africans is thus a Nigerian.

It is true that the history of Nigeria as a sovereign state is recent; it would, however, be totally misleading to say that there were no contacts between its many ethnic groups and states prior to 1914. In other words, the pre-amalgamation history of Nigeria is not just the individual stories of diverse groups but a credible story of meaningful contacts and dynamic relationships between these various peoples. These contacts and relationships came in many different forms: traders and scholars crossed frontiers; diplomats carried out their inter-state visits and, where appropriate, treaties were signed; wars were fought and prisoners or slaves taken; there was diffusion of political and religious ideas; there were also cultural borrowings.

These facts become clear when we consider the inter-state and inter-cultural influences both east and west of the Niger, and north of the

Niger–Benue. There is hardly any argument among cultural studies experts today about the significance of the Hausa peoples' cultural impact on the Yoruba; of the impact of the Igbo on the peoples of the Delta; of the societies of Kanem–Borno on the Hausa communities; of the Yoruba on Benin; of Benin on the Igbo societies. Hausa and Kanem–Borno cultural influences, too, are also noticeable among the Nupe and the Jukun.[17] What we are trying to emphasise is that there were a variety of links between the various communities which came to be known as Nigeria. These various states and peoples were also influenced at different times and in varying degrees by forces and developments outside Nigeria and indeed in some cases external to Africa – especially influences from Europe and the Americas. It is in the light of these shared experiences, cultural and political links and contacts – leaving no ethnic group completely isolated from its neighbours – that we can speak of a Nigerian history while, of course, recognising the individual pasts of Nigeria's diverse peoples.

Nigerians have always been conscious of their past. Their sense of history is inextricably entwined in their cosmology. History formed an essential ingredient in the process of socialisation in the pre-literate, traditional society. Children received their historical education from their parents and other adults who inculcated in them family traditions and societal values through story-telling, proverbs, myths and, when necessary, through direct instruction. Each community also had its own way of transmitting historical information; this could be done through priests and professional court historians such as the *arokin* in the palace at Oyo. There were occasions throughout the year, especially during religious and cultural festivals, when ancestral traditions were re-enacted ritually or symbolically to effect continuity or validate present realities or developments. Historical education was part of everyday life, manifesting itself in the peoples' socio-political and spiritual preoccupations, in their music, dance, art, poetry, literature and rituals.[18]

To the traditional society history was not a mere pastime indulged in by those who could afford such a luxury, it was not a mere abstraction contemplated by the gurus of the esoteric traditional arts; rather, history was conceived in the same way as it was seen by the French historians, Lucien Febvre and Marc Bloch, as the source of 'life in its most concrete, everyday, indestructible and anonymously human expression'.[19] This is the way history was studied and was seen as serving a variety of purposes. The values, norms, laws, institutions and the *Weltanschauung* (world view) of the society were understood and their import emphasised through the study of its history.

History helped to define the place, rights and duties of the individual within the community; historical education was also essential to the individuals who held traditional office – spiritual as well as temporal – for they were expected to be the custodians of the customs and traditions of their peoples and repositories of the ancestral wisdom. The traditional society also depended upon a knowledge of its history to affirm its origin, trace the course of its development, define its relationship with its neighbours, enhance its identity, and ensure group cohesion and solidarity.[20]

5

This traditional conception of history with its functional bias suffered a mild setback during the colonial era when the foreign rulers threatened our culture by seriously undermining the credibility, the integrity and relevance of our institutions, values and beliefs. Their objective was to establish and sustain the view that the British way of life was superior and more relevant. They needed this to promote their imperial interests. The effort failed to take root for several reasons: most young people in the various Nigerian communities did not attend the institutions where they would have been fed on a diet of western culture; the children who attended the Muslim religious schools remained untouched by the virus of the European culture; perhaps even more important, most of the population as a whole remained virtually unaffected by the invading colonial culture. The result was that the cultural institutions and ideas survived the threats and buffetings of the colonial period – admittedly, not without some scars. Of these, perhaps the most difficult to heal is what we have now dubbed the 'colonial mentality' – a state of mind and pattern of behaviour that make the culprits think and behave like foreigners in their own country, or make them look down on aspects of our culture because of an assumed cultural arrogance.

We should perhaps remind ourselves that the assault on our culture was a three-pronged one: first, the imperatives of colonialism; second, the challenge of Christian values; and third, the hostility of the Islamic religion and culture. The natural reaction from almost every quarter of the society was one of stout resistance. Acquiescence would have meant cultural suicide and annihilation of our collective personality.

There were several among the Nigerian literati of the colonial period who viewed the situation as inimical to our culture, or to what Professor Wole Soyinka calls our 'instruments of self-definition', or what Abraham calls 'the living being of a nation'.[21] It was partly in defence of the traditional culture and traditional forms of historical education that many volumes of local histories, relying heavily on oral traditions, were published in English in the various Nigerian languages (and in Arabic) during the colonial era. These works became important sources of information and inspiration to the political and cultural nationalists during the fight for independence from Britain; and they still remain valuable for our much-touted cultural revival.[22]

Our precolonial forebears had a clear conception of history, its function and place in the overall educational and development goals and strategies of their society. Today, we seem to be less clear in our perception of our past as a nation and we feel reluctant to recognise the past as our own. There is today, perhaps more than at any other time, an urgent need to achieve meaningful appreciation of our history. Ethnically heterogeneous and culturally pluralistic, Nigeria is a country that can boast of diverse cultural inheritances from its past; and it is history, better than any other discipline, that can define shared experiences and public identities as bases for defining our national identity. This is what Professor I. A. Akinjogbin is emphasising when he says: 'A nation is composed of people whose collective soul is their shared experience. The soul of a nation is its history.'[23]

Generally speaking, there is a broad consensus of agreement which allows us to describe, with a fair degree of confidence, how the various ethnic groups have come to be where they are, how their socio-political institutions evolved and matured to their present state. The pattern of meaning that emerges from a critically reconstructed account of our past can be summed up thus: that our past is a story of diversity, interaction and cross-cultural influences, moving towards integration and nationhood – albeit at times with faltering steps and blurred vision as if in bad weather; a story of 'continuing identity in the midst of change – indeed that is intimately linked with that change itself'.[24]

Once we are aware of and accept this bond uniting our many peoples, history can help us forge a sense of nationhood. One of the significant elements of nationalism is the memory of a common past, a common cultural heritage. For us to create a solid foundation for a modern nation out of our heterogeneous peoples, it is imperative that we let our history provide that element. And if we are truly and sincerely committed to building a united country and a common destiny, we will need a body of shared experiences, common heroes, a body of common references, set of assumptions, national instincts, prejudices, symbols and monuments. The study of a properly conceived Nigerian history can provide these essential ingredients with which the majority of our people can relate, as well as answers to certain fundamental questions which are important to gaining a deeper understanding of some of our contemporary national issues and preoccupations. This is the integrative nature of history – creating the basis for the acceptance of a common destiny, social accommodation and political tolerance, all of which are vital to societal harmony.

The historical perspective is vitally important to virtually all aspects of our national planning and socio-political development. A sound appreciation of the nature of historical process can equip a society with the prerequisite insight to the dynamics of change, be it social, cultural, economic or political. Such an insight is particularly valuable for assessing critically programmes of development with reference to their historical antecedents, their goals, the anticipated effects on the society, the extent to which such projects might be vitiated by cultural attitudes, and what lessons might be learnt from other countries' experiences.

The historical background is especially indispensable if contemporary events are to be properly understood. As Arnold Toynbee rightly states,

> If the historical background of the present is not kept in view, the present is likely to become an insoluble puzzle, and, in trying to cope with this unknown quantity, an unhistorical-minded man of action may get bogged in a rice-field or lost in a jungle.[25]

If we accept the analogy that the present is the child of the past, it would then follow that to understand the child properly it is important that we know something about the parents. For us to make any sense of the current events in Nigeria, we will need to have a clear grasp of the cultural inheritances that have continued to shape our attitudes as a nation. All of

7

us – from the highest public figure to the lowliest enlightened citizen – can benefit from the knowledge of our nation's past; for not only can it free us from the tyranny of provincialism by providing us with a frame of reference infinitely wider than our own, it can, in addition, enhance the sensitivity, intelligence, maturity and circumspection with which we must handle important public issues in our heterogeneous society.

Notes

1 Keynote address at an art festival, University of Ife, quoted in the *Daily Times*, 11 April 1981, p. 7.

2 An address delivered by the Vice-Chancellor at the opening of the 20th Annual Congress of the Historical Society of Nigeria, University of Ife, Ile-Ife, 19 December 1974, p. 3.

3 Quoted in T. N. Guinsburg (ed.), *The Dimensions of History* (Chicago: Rand McNally, 1972), p. 1.

4 W. E. Abraham, *The Mind of Africa* (Chicago: The University of Chicago Press, 1974), p. 11.

5 Harry E. Barnes, *A History of Historical Writing*, second revised edition (New York: Dover Publications, 1963), p. 1.

6 Carl Becker, *Everyman His Own Historian* (Chicago: Quadrangle Books, 1966), p. 235.

7 Quoted in Barnes, *A History of Historical Writing*, p. 1.

8 See the exchange of views in: David H. Donald, 'Our irrelevant history', *The New York Times*, 8 September 1977; and Edward L. Keenan, 'One Harvard historian to another', *ibid.*, 26 Sept. 1977.

9 Carroll Quigley, *The Evolution of Civilizations* (New York: The Macmillan Co., 1961), p. 20. See also Abraham, *The Mind of Africa*, pp. 12, 29.

10 This chapter benefits from Henry Steele Commager's admirable treatment of some of these pleasures in 'Why History', *American Education*, June 1965; Wilhelm Dilthey, *Pattern and Meaning in History*, edited by H. P. Rickman (New York: Harper & Brothers, 1962), 'General Introduction', pp. 59–61.

11 R. G. Collingwood, *The Idea of History* (New York: Oxford University Press, 1964), p. 10; see also Dilthey, *Pattern and Meaning in History*, pp. 13, 60.

12 Herbert Butterfield, *Man on His Past* (Boston: Beacon Press, 1966), p. 1.

13 *The Listener*, 27 February 1958; cited in Dilthey, *Pattern and Meaning in History*, p. 43.

14 See Allan Nevins, *The Gateway to History* (Garden City: Doubleday & Co., 1962), pp. 14–15.

15 For the importance of history in the development of leadership potential, see Frederick H. Schapsmeier, 'The study of history and its value in the development of student leadership', *College Student Journal*, Vol. VII (April–May 1973), pp. 34–37.

16 A. H. M. Kirk-Greene, 'Who coined the name "Nigeria"?' *West Africa*, 22 December 1956, p. 1035.

17 Thomas Hodgkin, *Nigerian Perspectives: an historical anthology* (London: Oxford University Press, 1960), p. 2.

18 S. O. Biobaku (ed.), *Sources of Yoruba History* (Oxford: Clarendon Press, 1973), *passim*.

19 This is the guiding principle of the *Annales*, the scholarly Paris review founded by Lucien Febvre and Marc Bloch in 1929; quoted in *Time*, 23 May 1977, p. 47.

20 See J. F. Ade Ajayi, 'Historical education in Nigeria', being the Presidential Address to the Nineteenth Congress of the Historical Society of Nigeria, meeting at Ife, December 1974, pp. 1–3; I. A. Akinjogbin, 'History and nation building', an inaugural lecture delivered at the University of Ife, November 1977, pp. 21–22; B. O. Oloruntimehin, 'History and society', an inaugural lecture delivered at the University of Ife, 1976, pp. 9–16.

21 Wole Soyinka, 'Theatre in African traditional culture: survival patterns', in Richard Olaniyan (ed.), *African History and Culture* (London: Longman, 1982), chapter 14; Abraham, *The Mind of Africa*, p. 39.

22 S. A. Akintoye, 'Nigerian contributions to black history', *Nigeria Magazine* (1975), Nos. 115–116, pp. 116–36; Hodgkin, *Nigerian Perspectives, passim*.

23 William H. McNeill, 'History for citizens', *American Historical Association Newsletter*, 14(3), March 1976, pp. 4–6. Even though Professor McNeill's concern is about 'a rationale of world history', some of his arguments could be used to make a case for national history; Akinjogbin, 'History and nation building,' p. 18.

24 R. J. Gavin, 'The historical profession: its place in Nigerian development', paper presented at the Nineteenth Congress of the Historical Society of Nigeria, Ife, December 1974, p. 11.

25 Arnold Toynbee, *Experiences* (London: Oxford University Press, 1969), p. 86; see also Hodgkin, *Nigerian Perspectives*, p. 52, for how the various Nigerian cultures 'have projected themselves into the present'.

2 The origins of Nigerian peoples

Biodun Adediran

It is common knowledge that Nigeria is peopled by many ethnic groups. There are perhaps over four hundred of them, each possessing a distinct language, social customs and belief. It is not possible here to refer to each of these ethnic groups; a representative sample will therefore form the basis of the discussion.[1]

First, a brief geographical survey. Nigeria can be divided into two broad geographical zones: the open savannah zone to the north and the southern forest zone. The area of the middle Niger and Benue rivers form a region of transition between the north and the south. It is often taken as a separate zone in itself and is commonly referred to as the 'middle belt'. The southern zone can further be subdivided into two, taking the lower Niger as a line of demarcation. This, however, is a matter of preference as the areas to the east and west of the lower Niger exhibit similar features.[2]

In Nigeria's northern zone, there are three major ethnic groups.[3] The Kanuri are to be found mainly in the north-eastern corner around Lake Chad; they are ethnically related to the Kanembu on the eastern side of the lake. The Hausa who form the dominant ethnic group north of the river Niger are to be found west of the Kanuri country. Their major concentrations are in the north-western and north-central parts of the region. The third major ethnic group, the Fulani, are to be found in scattered settlements all over northern Nigeria.

In the middle belt, there are clusters of small ethnic groups. These include the Jukun, Nupe, Bɔrgu, Igala, Tiv and Idoma. The concentration of ethnic groups in this region would appear to be related to the rugged topography. In the south the dense forest vegetation also allows for the existence of many ethnic groups, but we can identify only a few major ones for discussion. Thus to the east of the lower Niger are the Ibibio, Efik and Igbo, while to the west, the Yoruba and the Edo form the major ethnic groups.

Any discussion on the history and culture of Nigeria cannot but take adequate cognizance of the ethnic diversity sketched above. A few questions immediately come to mind. What are the origins of these peoples? When and how did they acquire their respective distinguishing characteristics? Have they always occupied the same areas or did their ancestors emigrate from elsewhere? Were there any links among these different ethnic groups who at the beginning of this century were brought together under a single political authority? These questions are significant to our understanding of the early histories of the peoples of Nigeria, especially the issue of ethnic differentiation.

Materials for our understanding of the issues raised above come mainly from two sources: oral traditions and ancillary studies like archaeology and linguistic studies. It must be pointed out that the evidence so far assembled from these sources is not comprehensive enough for a definitive reconstruction of the early histories of Nigerian peoples. Nevertheless, from a review of the materials available, it is possible to reconstruct the outlines of these histories.

Oral traditions

Among the peoples of Nigeria, there are various legends that seek to explain the processes by which their ancestors came to the areas which they now occupy.[4] These legends can be classified into two. In the first category are traditions woven around culture-heroes who migrated at the head of groups of people from somewhere outside the area covered by present-day Nigeria; Arabia and the north-eastern part of Africa have always been pointed out as likely sources of these migrations. These types of traditions are the more widespread and until quite recently were very popular among academic scholars.

The second category of traditions of origins of Nigerian peoples are those which do not remember a time when the area now occupied by any of the ethnic groups was entirely unpeopled. These latter traditions refer to autochthonous inhabitants whose traditions and culture are continuous with those of the various peoples who now inhabit Nigeria.

Thus unlike the first group which explains the peopling of Nigeria in terms of external migrations, the second group of traditions suggests that the process of ethnic formation took place within the area of present-day Nigeria and that the peopling of the country had little, if anything, to do with external migrations. For quite some time a silent battle has been going on between exponents of the two views. The two views may look contradictory, but as we shall see presently they are not irreconcilable.

Of the three major ethnic groups north of the Niger–Benue rivers, one is certainly not indigenous to Nigeria. The Fulani traditions of an ancestral migration from the Senegambia region in the western Sudan are well established.[5] Though the question of the ethnic origin of the Fulani is still a subject of controversy, it is beyond doubt that by the time they entered the present area of Nigeria, they had acquired an ethnic identity which distinguished them from other peoples. In fact the advent of the Fulani to northern Nigeria is part of a general migration which started between the twelfth and thirteenth centuries and took the Fulani to virtually all parts of the West African savannah region.

But the story of the peopling of northern Nigeria began thousands of years ago, certainly long before the advent of the Fulani. This fact can be gleaned from the traditions of various Kanuri and Hausa communities. Among the Kanuri,[6] the belief in an ancestral migration from Arabia is very strong. According to the legends the culture-hero of the Kanuri was one Sayf b. Dhi Yazan who migrated across the Sahara and successfully imposed his authority on pockets of autochthonous inhabitants on the eastern shore of Lake Chad. The advent of this culture-hero led to the unification of some pre-existing pockets of settlements and the rise of a central dynasty. According to the legends, these developments sparked off the process of the formation of the Kanuri as a single ethnic group identifiable from other ethnic groups in the vicinity.

For the Hausa, the culture-hero was one Bayajida, a prince of Baghdad in Arabia. Versions of the traditions of migration of this legendary hero vary in detail from one Hausa community to the other, but the outlines are the same.[7] After some quarrels not unrelated to the rise of Islam, Bayajida fled his country of origin, crossed the Sudan and eventually settled in Kanem among the Kanuri. There he married a daughter of the ruler and gradually built up a large following to the displeasure of his father-in-law. To avoid the wrath of the Kanem authorities, Bayajida fled westwards with his followers. He entered present-day Hausa country first settling at Biram where he left his wife. At Gaya, his next place of settlement, Bayajida met a community of blacksmiths who made a special sword for him. Next at Daura, he met another settlement and here he did what made him a hero in Hausa legends.

The people of Daura had a central well from which they drew water. By the time of Bayajida's coming, an evil snake had taken possession of this well, scaring away the people from drawing water except on Fridays. Efforts made to kill the snake failed until Bayajida came and slew it with the sword he got at Gaya. As a reward Bayajida was offered the hand of the queen of Daura in marriage and from the union emerged the seven principal Hausa states to which every Hausa man traces his origin. According to the legend, Bayajida had seven other children from illegitimate affairs. These latter children were the progenitors of Zamfara, Kebbi, Gwari, Yoruba, Jukun, Nupe and Yauri – all southern neighbours of the Hausa.

The belief in external migrations is also strong among the peoples south of the Kanuri and Hausa countries. One of these well-known bodies' tradition is the Kisra tradition[8] by which the Borgu seek to explain their origins and the peopling of their country. The Borgu believe that their ancestors migrated under the leadership of Kisra, a prince fleeing from the reforms of Prophet Mohammed. Similarly, some versions of the Yoruba traditions of origins refer to Oduduwa (their culture-hero) as a prince who migrated from Arabia[9] after the establishment of the Islamic religion. According to the Yoruba legend, after crossing the Sudan and the Hausa country, Oduduwa eventually settled in Ile-Ife which subsequently became the dispersal centre for the Yoruba people.

Following the archetype found in the preceding traditions, other ethnic groups south of the Niger have accounts of ancestral migrations from the east. But there are some ethnic groups which have no tradition of external migrations. As pointed out earlier, Hausa traditions maintain that some of the ethnic groups in the south of their country are descended from illegitimate sons of Bayajida. This seems to imply that the ethnic groups in this region emerged as a result of less exposure to external influences.

Recent studies of Igbo traditions are emphatic that until recently the Igbo had no tradition of external origin.[10] The Ibibio who live in the south-eastern corner of Nigeria have two popular traditions, both of which emphasise that the ancestral origin of the people could not be traced beyond the Benue valley. It has in fact been suggested that the

Ibibio have occupied their present habitat for a very long time and that other neighbouring ethnic groups like the Efik, Eket and Anang, ethnically related to the Ibibio, were derived from them.[11]

Some other ethnic groups explain their origins only in terms of local migrations. Thus the Ijo traditions only refer to movements within the Niger Delta.[12] A few of these traditions are clear enough for one to see the process of ethnic differentiation by which the various ethnic groups emerged. For instance, the Igala claim ancestral connections with the Yoruba, Edo, Nupe and Igbo. Their legends talk of series of migrations in the area of the Niger–Benue confluence resulting in the separation of these ethnic groups.[13] The Igala actually believe that their progenitor was a prince who migrated from the principal Edo settlement of Benin to found Idah which became the nucleus of their state and their dispersal centre.

Similar traditions of ethnic differentiation resulting from local migrations are found among the Tiv[14] and the Nupe. The Nupe, for instance, look towards the Igala state as the source of their migration. According to Nupe legends, Tsoede or Edegi (their culture-hero) was an Igala prince who migrated to the region north of the Niger presumably in the fifteenth century. Tsoede's unification of the acephalous (chiefless) communities in the area under his leadership marked the beginning of the Nupe ethnic group.[15]

A few comments can be made on these traditions of migrations. Firstly, one can see that the events narrated are concerned with the emergence of dynastic states among the ethnic groups now identifiable in Nigeria. Secondly, most of the traditions refer to events in relatively recent times especially after the rise of Islam. Thirdly, virtually all the traditions refer to some pre-existing communities in the areas which became the nuclei of the formation of the ethnic groups. It is this last observation that makes it possible to reconcile the traditions of migrations with those that talk of autochthonous origins. In fact, some evidence to buttress the second category of traditions referred to earlier on come from the traditions of external origins themselves. Both the Kanuri and the Hausa legends of emigration from Arabia refer to identifiable pre-existing communities.

The Kanuri legends record clearly that the emergence of the ethnic groups was due to the fusion of the aboriginal inhabitants of the Lake Chad region with the immigrants referred to in the traditions. The traditions make it explicit that for a long time after the arrival of the immigrants, the aborigines maintained a separate identity. Similarly, the Bayajida traditions give the impression that the emergence of common ethnic identity in the establishment of the seven 'legitimate' Bayijida dynasties resulted from the co-operation of migrant groups and aboriginal settlers.

South of the Hausa country where the legends of external migrations are less popular, virtually all the traditions of ethnic migrations make clear reference to pre-migration communities which formed the bases of the formation of the present ethnic groups. The Nupe, for instance, talk of five original groups of inhabitants in their country before the arrival of Tsoede and the emergence of a distinct Nupe ethnic group.[16]

The major questions are on the identities and origins of the pre-migration peoples that existed in Nigeria before the emergence of the present ethnic groups. To answer these questions one has to turn to the traditions of autochthonous origins.

Apart from reference to aboriginal communities in the Kanuri and Hausa legends, there are many other legends which make it possible to discern a pre-migration layer of peoples in northern Nigeria.[17] Among the Kanuri the remnants of such people locally referred to as 'So' are still identifiable. In Hausaland, there are many legends of 'giant hunters' associated with mounds scattered all over the region. Kano traditions still remember that a pre-Bayajida settlement of blacksmiths existed on Dala hill. In Kano today, there is a group called 'Abagayawa', said to be descendants of these early settlers. Though these traditions are silent on the questions of the origins of these predecessors of the Hausa, they are emphatic enough on their antiquity in the region.

However, there are some traditions which attempt to answer the question of the ultimate origins of the peoples of Nigeria by reference to the issue of creation. The Nri traditions among the Igbo indicate that the heartland from where the Igbo dispersed was the area of the Niger–Benue confluence where the first man 'father Nri' descended from the sky.[18] Both the Yoruba and the Edo still cling to the belief that it was at Ile-Ife and Benin respectively that the first man was created. According to the Yoruba genesis Ile-Ife was not only the centre of Yoruba civilisation but also that of creation.[19] The legends of how Ile-Ife was created are many and varied; they agree, however, on the process and the personalities involved. Before the creation of Ile-Ife, the whole world was covered by water. God then sent out a party to create land out of the water. They were given pieces of iron, a handful of soil and a five-toed cockerel. Under the leadership of Oduduwa, the party descended at the present site of Ile-Ife by means of a chain. Here they set out to perform the task of creating land. The pieces of iron were placed on water, the soil placed on them and the five-toed cockerel made to spread the soil. The water receded and so the earth was created. It was from Ile-Ife, the first land created, that all Yorubaland and indeed the whole world was peopled!

The immediate implication of the traditions explaining the formation of some peoples of Nigeria in situ is that the hitherto heavy reliance on the traditions of external origins has to be critically re-examined. This is not to deny the possibility of external migrations into some parts of the country or to dismiss outright a suggestion that external influences might have contributed to the emergence of some of the ethnic groups. It should be clear from the existence side by side of traditions belonging to the two categories among the various ethnic groups that there are two distinct periods involved in discussing the peopling of Nigeria. The first and the earlier period was that of the early settlers depicted in the traditions as 'giants' or as coming directly from the skies. The second and relatively recent period was that of the differentiation of the ethnic groups identifiable in the country today.

The inferences drawn from the oral traditions above have some support from the ancillary studies. Information relating to the early histories of Nigerian peoples have been derived from three major sources: archaeology, geology and ethno-linguistic studies.

Archaeological evidence

In using archaeological evidence, a major fact that has to be borne in mind is that the human development of early man did not take place evenly all over Nigeria. At any given time, one finds men living on different points of the archaeological time-scale. The implication of this to our discussion is that the formation of the various ethnic groups could not have taken place at the same time. Furthermore, archaeological evidence available is not even for the whole of the country. This again is a great handicap in a comprehensive understanding of the process of ethnic formation in Nigeria.

One safe inference that can easily be drawn from the few available pieces of archaeological evidence is that the region of Nigeria had for long been inhabited by man. Archaeological works have discovered sites of Stone and Iron Age cultures in different parts of Nigeria.[20] Although the evidence on Stone Age habitation so far assembled is scanty, it is clear enough for us to draw a picture of what the region looked like thousands of years ago. In one of the archaeological sites at Iwo Eleru in western Nigeria, the discovery of a human skeleton dated to some 10 000 years old is suggestive of the antiquity of man in the area. From the same site, radiocarbon dates ranging from 9000 to 3000 BC were obtained from remnants of some occupational materials.

Excavations carried out in various parts east of the Niger indicate also that there had been human habitation of the region for thousands of years. At Ukpa rock shelter near Afikpo, an extensive stone industry with pottery was unearthed. Interpretations of the artefacts from this site establish that by 3000 BC stone implements and pottery were already being made.

North of the Niger–Benue, evidence suggesting early human occupation has also been found. In the north-east around Lake Chad stone works associated with the peoples of early Kanuri traditions were unearthed. There is also evidence that Stone Age men lived on the Jos plateau. The Nok culture which developed around the plateau is very well-known to students of West African history. Although some controversy still exists on the correct interpretation of evidence from Nok sites, it is beyond doubt that by 500 BC there was already a people with a rich and dynamic culture living on the plateau.

Of great significance is the discovery of evidence suggesting knowledge of iron-working technology by the early peoples of Nigeria. At Taruga, near Abuja, iron-working furnaces have been discovered in a site which give radiocarbon dates ranging from 580 to 200 BC. Other iron-using sites have been excavated in Daima near Lake Chad. It has also been suggested that the Nok culture is to be associated with the use and working of iron in spite of the assemblage of stone implements and utensils from that culture-area.

All these archaeological finds not only confirm the antiquity of man in Nigeria, they also demonstrate cultural developments before the migrations related in the traditions. Inferences drawn from other studies further indicate that the process of formation of some Nigerian peoples took place earlier than suggested in the traditions of migrations.

Geological and climatic evidence

From a study of geological and climatic changes in the Sahara region and northern Nigeria,[21] inferences have been drawn of ancient demographic upheavals which could have set in motion the process of ethnic formation. According to this hypothesis, the Sahara was once a region of dense forest. During that era known as the wet Makalian phase, the northern part of Nigeria was covered by a forest type of vegetation. There were some large rivers, and Lake Chad was then much bigger than it is now. Then there began drastic climatic changes as a result of which the Sahara became drier. The details of these changes are not yet well known. What seems certain is that between 5000 BC and 2000 BC conditions in the Sahara region became unbearable. As a result, the inhabitants began to move into the West African subcontinent and a few found their ways into present-day northern Nigeria.

The process of desiccation reached northern Nigeria. Lake Chad became smaller, most of the rivers dried up and the vegetation became more open. This further added to the population movements already set in motion by the desiccation of the Sahara desert. People moved into the few relatively fertile areas mostly in the basins of Lake Chad and of the rivers. Thus in place of the scattered settlements of the pre-desiccation era, there were now a few relatively densely populated settlements. In these developments are probably to be found the origins of the ethnic groups in northern Nigeria. East of Lake Chad, the settlement of northern immigrants led to a concentration of peoples who fused together, producing the Kanuri. Likewise, the concentration of peoples west of the Lake Chad was the spring-board for the formation of the Hausa people.

Ethno-linguistic studies

Evidence from linguistic studies buttresses the above speculation regarding the emergence of the Kanuri and Hausa. The various ethnic groups in Nigeria can be classified into three broad linguistic families: Nilo–Saharan, Afro–Asiatic and Niger–Congo.[22] The first two linguistic families to which the Kanuri and the Hausa belong respectively include various ethnic groups across the Sahara and North Africa. The implication of this is that both the Kanuri and the Hausa presumably belonged to the same parent stock as the respective Saharan ethnic groups to which they are linguistically related.

Linguistic studies also give a clue on the process of ethnic differentiation south of the Hausa country. In the middle belt there is a concentration of ethno-linguistic groups. Most of these groups are closely related to the larger ethnic groups in the forest region. In fact the Niger–Congo family to which most of these groups belong can be sub-divided into clusters of closely related languages.[23] For instance, the Yoruba, Edo, Igbo and a host of middle-belt ethnic groups like the Igala, Idoma and Nupe form a cluster within the 'Kwa' sub-group of the Niger–Congo family. This indicates that the ancestors of the speakers of these languages separated from the same parent stock. By a method of dating called glottochronology, possible dates of separation have been suggested for the speakers of these languages. Furthermore, it can be inferred from the linguistic evidence that the emergence of these closely related ethnic groups took place in or near the areas they now occupy. As the late Dr R. E. Bradbury put it,

> there is no reason to suppose that the divergence of these languages from a parent stock has not taken place side by side more or less *in situ*. Any theory which would derive the carriers of one of them *en masse* from far afield, when the others were established in the area raise historico-linguistic difficulties of great magnitude.[24]

What we can suggest for the peopling of Nigeria's middle belt and the forest zone, therefore, is a process of slow separation of the various ethnic groups presumably from the same parent stock. When exactly this process began we do not know. If one goes by the evidence from the linguistic studies, it would be suggested that it started thousands of years ago.

Conclusions

Summing up the fragments of evidence from the ancillary studies, it is clear that different parts of Nigeria had been continuously inhabited from a very early time. The emergence of the various ethnic groups now identifiable in the country is the result of a long process of cultural differentiation.

What then are we to make of the various traditions of origins? The traditions of 'giants' and men who descended from the skies are testimonies of the antiquity of man in Nigeria. These types of traditions suggest that the questions of the origins of these early peoples are beyond human understanding. The traditions of external migrations of Nigerian peoples from Arabia or the north-east are certainly concerned with relatively recent events. At best, they are twisted memories of ancient migrations from the Sahara or simply attempts at self-glorification by linking the peoples concerned with Islam or the better-known civilisations of the Nile valley.

The hypothesis that can be put forward here is simply that the peopling of Nigeria began thousands of years ago, perhaps before man could be distinguished from his ape-like ancestors. The whole country was peopled by autochthonous inhabitants in scattered settlements. As population expanded through natural means of procreation and the influx of migrants from the Sahara area, there was a demographic upheaval during which the process of ethnic separation began.

The process was conceivably intensified by the geographical variations noted at the beginning of this chapter. Man is greatly influenced by his environment. The climatic changes and the subsequent demographic upheavals necessitated modifications in the ways of life of the peoples concerned. The point being made here is that ethnic diversity is only to be expected where there are environmental variations and constant climatic changes. It would be wrong to assume that the diversity was a result of different waves of migrations. Neither can one explain it in terms of an age-long isolation of one ethnic group from the others. As we shall see in subsequent chapters, in spite of the fact that the process of ethnic differentiation started in Nigeria thousands of years ago, the different ethnic groups that emerged at various times had never been completely isolated from one another.

Notes

1 Problems of precision arise in this regard because some of the ethnic groups are little known. See A. L. Mobogunje, 'The land and peoples of West Africa', in J. F. A. Ajayi and M. Crowder (eds), *History of West Africa* (Longman, 1971), p. 5.

2 R. K. Udo, *Geographical Regions of Nigeria* (University of California Press, 1970), pp. 1–9.

3 'Major', purely on the basis of population.

4 Some of these are in T. Hodgkin, *Nigerian Perspectives: an historical anthology*, second edition (Oxford University Press, 1975), pp. 74–86.

5 Mabogunje, 'The land and peoples', pp. 26–27.

6 Hodgkin, *Nigerian Perspectives*, pp. 77–78.

7 *Ibid.*, pp. 74–76.

8 A. B. Mathews, 'The Kisra legend', *African Studies*, 9, 1950; J. Lombard, 'Chieftaincy among the Bariba of Dahomey' in M. Crowder and O. Ikime (eds), *West African Chiefs* (University of Ife Press, 1970), pp. 125–28.

9 Hodgkin, *Nigerian Perspectives*, pp. 78–83.

10 V. C. Uchendu, *The Igbo of Southeastern Nigeria* (New York: Holt, Rinehart and Winston, 1966), pp. 2–3; E. Isichei, *A History of the Igbo People* (Macmillan Press, 1976), pp. 1–7.

11 D. Forde and G. I. Jones, *The Ibo and Ibibio-speaking Peoples of South-eastern Nigeria* (London: International African Institute, 1962), p. 68.

12   E. J. Alagoa, *A History of the Niger Delta: a historical interpretation of Ijo oral traditions* (Ibadan University Press, 1972), p. 3.

13   J. S. Boston, *The Igala Kingdom* (Ibadan: Oxford University Press, 1968).

14   Rupert East (translator), *Akiga's Story: the Tiv tribe as seen by one of its members* (Oxford University Press, 1965), pp. 15–17.

15   S. F. Nadel, *A Black Byzantium: the kingdom of Nupe in Nigeria* (Oxford University Press, 1961).

16   *Ibid.*, pp. 72–76. The aboriginal settlements are Ebe, Beni, Dibo (Zitako); Ebagi and Bataci.

17   See G. T. Stride and C. Ifeka, *Peoples and Empires of West Africa* (Nelson, 1971), pp. 86–131.

18   M. D. W. Jeffries, 'The Umundri tradition of origin', *African Studies*, vol. 25, 1956.

19   E. B. Idowu, *Olodumare: God in Yoruba belief* (Longman, 1962), pp. 18–29.

20   T. Shaw (ed.), *Lectures on Nigerian Prehistory and Archaeology* (Ibadan University Press, 1969). Also his 'The prehistory of West Africa', in Ajayi and Crowder (eds), *History of West Africa*, I, pp. 33–77.

21   A. Smith, 'The early states of the central Sudan', and L. Mabogunje, 'The land and peoples' in Ajayi and Crowder (eds), *History of West Africa*, I, pp. 158–64, 1–32.

22   J. H. Greenberg, *Languages of Africa* (Indiana University Press, 1966), pp. 45–48, 130–33.

23   J. H. Armstrong, *The Study of West African Languages* (Ibadan University Press, 1966); also his 'The use of linguistic and ethnographic data in the study of Idoma and Yoruba history', in J. Vansina *et al* (eds), *The Historian in Tropical Afriea* (Oxford University Press, 1964), pp. 127–44.

24   R. E. Bradbury, 'The historical uses of comparative ethnography with special reference to Benin and the Yoruba', in Vansina *et al* (eds), *The Historian in Tropical Africa*, p. 150.

19

3 Pre-colonial Nigeria: east of the Niger

Nwanna Nzewunwa

Introduction

A survey chapter such as this does some injustice to the large and diverse area covered within it. This is not only because it touches on a number of things superficially but also because inevitably it leaves out quite a number too.

This chapter covers what was formerly the Eastern Region of Nigeria but which is now broken into four separate states – Anambra, Cross River, Imo and Rivers. After a preliminary survey of the environmental setting and present-day economic practices the chapter treats the indigenous peoples of the region, their early history, their traditional social organisation, political structure and finally examines the factors and processes of the socio-political developments before the colonial period. In order to make possible comparisons and to amplify continuities and discontinuities over space and time it has been found necessary to adopt a thematic approach as set out above.

The environmental setting

An understanding of the environmental milieu in which the peoples of the area lived is important for a fair assessment of their reaction to situations of change and their general world view. Geologically speaking, the area rests upon a basement complex made up of metamorphic rocks with intensive granite bodies overlain by much younger cretaceous and tertiary sedimentary strata both of marine and continental origin. There were three tectonic (structural) phases coupled with transgressive and regressive movements of the ancient sea. The Niger Delta started growing in the later period of the second phase but its configuration was confirmed in the third.

There is a conspicuous absence of major hills and mountains except for the eastern uplands around Obudu and Oban and the Nsukka–Udi plateau and escarpments. This has made for ease of mobility of men, materials and ideas. There are numerous streams emptying into the Cross River which, along with the Imo, Anambra and Orashi, form the largest drainage system after the river Niger.

Rainfall is high in the south and decreases northwards. There is marked seasonality, and intensity in the falls. The crop calendar reflects the rainfall regime. Temperatures are uniformly high with very little seasonal variations, giving a mean annual of over 24°C. The relative humidity is high all over but much higher along the coast.

The soils follow the general pattern of the geology, landforms and climate. The vegetation is equally a reflection of the soil pattern. In the southern extremity of the area under study the juvenile soils support the freshwater raffia swamps, the mangrove swamps and the sandy beach ridges fronting the Atlantic coast. Human settlement here is sparse, and there is a lack of drinkable fresh water. The main human activity is fishing although hunting and salt-making are also pursued.

On the ferruginous soils (impregnated with iron) in the Cross River and Obudu plateau, population is sparse and the vegetation is dense forest. Agriculture is the major economic activity although fishing is practised on the Cross River.

More than 50 per cent of eastern Nigeria is covered by ferrolitic soils (containing iron) which are rated poor agriculturally. It is remarkable, however, that these 'poor' soils support the highest densities of rural population in Anambra and Imo states, which produce yams, cassava, beans, vegetables and oil palms. In contrast the hydromorphic soils (water-bearing) of the Anambra valley, Nsukka escarpments and Abakaliki areas are sparsely populated but very rich agriculturally.

Economic activity dependent on natural resources may either be terrestrial or marine/riverine oriented. Beyond farming and fishing and hunting there is a good measure of food collecting in the wild – especially palms, fruits, and vegetables in the hinterland and shellfish in the delta.

The peoples and their early history

All the peoples east of the Niger speak languages which belong to the Niger–Congo family. But they subdivide into two sub-family groups. The peoples of the Cross River basin – Annang, Efik and Ibibio – belong linguistically to the Benue–Congo sub-family while their immediate Igbo and Ijo neighbours belong to the Kwa sub-family of the Niger–Congo family. Current research points out that the peoples of the Cross River basin are linguistically closer to the Bantu of central, eastern and southern Africa than to other Nigerians to their immediate west. The languages of peoples east of the Niger show various directions of movement or migration to their present location and various levels of cultural contact in their history. Beyond the Efik–Ibibio, the Igbo and the Ijo-speaking peoples there are also the Khana (Ogoni), the Andoni, Odual and small groups of other Benue–Congo speakers all found in the present Rivers State. If in the course of this chapter mention is made mainly of the Efik–Ibibio, the Igbo and the Ijo it is only because the other small groups fit into the pattern being discussed, not that they are being neglected.

A common factor in the history of all these peoples is that the story of their origin as a people or as peoples has been lost. What exists in the oral traditions is mainly speculative, non-definitive and lacking in time-depth, although, as we have seen in the previous chapter, some important conclusions can be drawn. In some cases current political situations have influenced traditional histories to a point of absurdity. One outstanding fact in the oral histories is the level of continued interaction in varied ways between these different peoples. It is this long

21

period of interaction that accounts for the diffusion of ideas and materials as a result of human mobility.

Prehistoric research east of the Niger has made remarkable progress and has contributed immensely to the peoples' awareness of their culture and early history. Unfortunately there has been an uneven distribution of this work leading to a position in which some parts are well studied while other areas remain a virgin field. On the whole there are still many places waiting for archaeological prospection, even within areas where much is already known.

Prehistoric studies have been slow east of the Cross River because of the lack of field archaeologists. As a result comparative data in the form of radiocarbon dates and evidence of material culture or economic residue are lacking. From ethnography and oral literature it is proper to suggest that the Cross River was one of the earliest occupied sectors east of the Niger. Archaeological studies in Afikpo, west of the Cross River, indicate that there was early occupation and village farming well before the sixth millennium BC. The southernmost and delta Efik-Ibibio no doubt subsisted partly on cultivation and partly on marine resources like their delta Ijo counterparts.

In the Niger delta, archaeological research has made a tremendous contribution to a clearer understanding of the prehistoric developments and the time-depth involved. Recent radiocarbon dates suggest that the area was inhabited well before the beginning of the Christian era. Conclusions that can be drawn from the state of prehistoric research are, firstly, that the initial occupation of the east Niger Delta was motivated by economic considerations based on the more gainful exploitation of the abundant natural food resources of the mangrove ecosystem; secondly, that the primary occupants were fishermen, shellfish collectors, hunters and salt processors; thirdly, that there was a systematic and gradual spread of the initial populations and the acceptance of new immigrants leading to the eventual occupation of the entire east Niger Delta; fourthly, that there was an economic symbiosis between inhabitants of the Niger Delta and their immediate hinterland neighbours based on the exchange of delta protein resources for inland carbohydrate products; and lastly, that a shift in emphasis was initiated from the late fifteenth century with the advent of external visitors by the sea route. This last factor brought about accelerated transformation not only in the internal cultural patterns of the delta, but also affected their world view and their relationships with their immediate neighbours. Some of these consequences will be treated in a later section.

Igbo are the indigenous inhabitants of the present Anambra and Imo states and are also found in the eastern parts of Bendel State and northern parts of Rivers State. One common cultural factor pervading the Igbo culture area is language which, though it has dialectical variations, is mutually intelligible among people within the Igbo culture area.

Prehistoric research has brought about an acceleration of people's awareness of their past and has given the Igbo their rightful place in the culture history of Nigeria. Radiocarbon dates obtained from archaeological excavations confirm that the Igbo were in their present location by 250 000 BC with a stone-using culture; that they had progressed to the village farming stage before 3000 BC and were using iron by the beginning of the Christian era; and that they had perfected their art in noble metal working by the ninth century AD, as the bronze objects of Igboukwu demonstrate. Like the other peoples east of the Niger the Igbo were affected by both internal and external stresses to which they reacted by adjusting their ways of life. The Igbo subsistence economy was based on yam cultivation with occasional fishing in the rivers, hunting and collecting food in the wild. There were specialised craftsmen practising blacksmithing, clay and wood work.

The social structure

The peoples living east of the Niger, like other African societies, were and are organised in kinship and lineage systems. The nuclear family is the lowest unit within the lineage system. The nuclear family was made up of a man, his wife – but usually wives – children and his slaves. While among most groups a man lived with his nuclear family within a defined compound, the southern Igbo preferred a system whereby several men (and their families) – sons of the same father – lived together in one compound sharing one gate. A number of nuclear families or compounds made up a family group, which consisted of men, their wives and children, sons' wives and their children. A number of family groups made up the lineage or extended family, a group of which again made up the village or what has been called the maximal lineage. The last unit was the village group or town, which was a collection of related villages.

The table below shows that there were five basic social units:

English	Efik-Ibibio	Igbo
Village group	Oduk (Iman)	Mba (Obodo)
Village	Obio	Mbam (Ogbe)
Lineage (extended family)	Ekpuk	Onumara
Family group	Ufok	Umunna
Nuclear family	Ikip Ete	Umunne

It must be observed at this point that there are differences of opinion over the correct English terminological equivalents of local units. However, a few points stand out although local differences and peculiarities may be observed. Each lineage was a land owning, land allocating and settlement unit with a head. According to the genealogical history of these peoples they are predominantly patrilineal. However, among the Ijo of the east Niger Delta the lineage organisation followed the two systems of marriage by which a low bridewealth made an offspring matrilineal while a high bridewealth made the other patrilineal in descent and inheritance. Among the Cross River Igbo of Ohafia a matrilineal descent system operated. Among the Cross River Igbo of Afikpo the double descent system operated. That is, descent could be patrilineal; patrilineal and matrilineal at the same time; or simply matrilineal. A man's jural rights – political, religious and inheritance rights – were determined within his

23

descent group.

It has been argued at times that the simple nature of these peoples' organisation denotes the absence of social stratification. This view stems from a superficial look into their social systems. The fact is that just as there exists a hierarchy from the village group down to the nuclear family so is there a hierarchy within each unit. The head of each unit was usually chosen from among a family whose ancestors were responsible for the founding of the settlement or the unit. If nothing else he enjoyed a right of first among equals and his position also carried religious status.

Social stratification ensured the smooth functioning, in socio-political terms, of the unit. Among the Annang, for instance, a village was primarily stratified along sexual lines – male and female – each of which was further divided into age grades as follows:

Male	Female	English equivalent
Ndem Isong	Akani Iban	Elders
Nka Ikpo Owo	Nka Ikpo Iban	Middle aged
Nka Mkparawa	Nka Nkaiferi	Youth
Ndito Owon	Ndito Owon	Children

Age grades, apart from performing social functions, were for the men principally a forum from which to enter or progress within the political, military, economic and social hierarchy. In fact among the Ijo of the delta the age-grade system was the most certain forum from which to launch into the politics of the units.

Among the Igbo inequality was recognised in age, status, wealth, religion, birth, descent. Royalty was in name and not in fact, as the Igbo recognised achievement rather than hereditarily-bestowed greatness. In the same manner social status was viewed from one's origin and upbringing – depending on whether one was freeborn or slave (*Ohu*) or cult slave (*Osu, ume*), a legitimate child or one born out of wedlock, or 'native' or stranger (immigrant). In like manner, delta society from the sixteenth century distinguished between royalty, freeborn and slaves born within the community and slaves bought from outside who could be sold in times of financial stress. The northern Igbo also recognised titled men as being very high in the social set-up. This class constituted the nobility. For the southern Igbo, titles were in the form of *Oha* which accepted only one member from one family group on account of his age and/or vacancy. This was in principle similar to the Efik–Ibibio political set-up called the *Ubong* Order, identified by its raffia-string cap, *Ntinya*.

The traditional political structure

Legislative

The underlying need for a political structure at whatever level and of whatever degree of simplicity or complexity appears universally to be the maintenance of law and order and the demand for the efficient execution of policies affecting the people within the structure. Government is therefore for the management, direction and control of public affairs of any given group. The components of a political structure are political and administrative activities.

In the study of the political structure of Nigerian peoples two systems have been identified – monarchical and non-monarchical. The levels of 'civilisation', progress in material culture and the degree of organisational ability and efficiency attributed to these two have been the point at which most scholars miss the mark. A political structure is not necessarily good or bad because of its elaborate and complicated processes. Definitions and descriptions of political systems of Nigerian groups have not been sharp and clear enough even in the few isolated studies of traditional political structures. Whether a polity is described as a kingdom, monarchy, city state, republic or what have you, four criteria appear to define a state clearly – a permanent population, a defined territory, a government, and a capacity to enter into relations with other states.

It is at this point that it becomes meaningful to probe the traditional political organisations of the peoples east of the Niger and observe the points at which they begin to impinge on, or be impinged upon their by, immediate neighbours and distant visitors alike, and to understand the various adjustments they made in the process of their development.

The nuclear family is the smallest or lowest unit of political organisation. The father or the oldest male member is the head politically, socially, economically and religiously. Family headship follows the rule of primogeniture. As the custodian of the family traditions and ancestral cults the head acted as the intermediary between the family's ancestors and the living members. Normally his old age kept him free from the influence of other old members of the village, of sexual desires, of jealousy and greed and he was expected to be a man of wisdom acquired from long experience in the religious, political and social life of the people.

It is at the lineage or village level that political organisation proper can be said to begin. Each village was a state in the sense defined above. Each village was independent in every sense of the word, maintaining its territorial integrity, tolerating no interference in its internal affairs and recognising no other authority except that within its territorial framework. Because of some difference in points of detail we will now discuss the different peoples separately below.

The Annang and the rest of the Efik–Ibibio recognised a major family, *Ekpuk*, from which the rest of the village formed. This nucleus they called *Itibe Ekpuk*, meaning literally the royal family – similar to the founding family among the delta and Igbo peoples. While the founding family among the *Itibe Ekpuk* and delta peoples produced the *Okuku Obong Obio* or *Idung* and *Amanyanabo* respectively, whose office was marked by elaborate investiture, their Igbo counterpart in most cases exercised a headship carrying honorific and religious status but hardly any political influence.

Generally, government at the village level was the joint

responsibility of lineage heads or elders of the lineages but among the peoples east of the Cross River the *Okuku* directed other lineage heads like the *amanyanabo*. Both offices have been said to have been autocratic and from time to time exercised the right of life and death.

Between the *Okuku* and the lineage heads was the office of the *Ayara Ufot* or *Akpan Okuku*, a kind of middle man whose responsibilities were those of communication between the two groups but who on occasions presided over the village council in the absence of the *Okuku*. The *Ayara Ufot* was usually the most senior member among the *Ekpuk* heads in the village council. Although his appointment was subject to ratification by the *Okuku*, the *Ayara Ufot* held his post partly for his popularity among the different families making up the lineage. As the president of the village council he had executive, judicial and administrative powers. The Annang traditional village system of government did not allow anybody to rise to prominence as nobody could possess power beyond his *Ekpuk* (lineage).

The political process of the Efik–Ibibio appears to have differed in terms of the distribution of power. While the *Obong Obio's* or *Idung's* main function was religious, other functions – political and judicial – were handled by men specially appointed. Hence one can regard them as ministries and their incumbents as ministers. Such ministries included poultry, livestock, oil palms, raffia palms and palm wine, yam and fisheries. The ministers were appointed from a special class, the *Ubong* Order, made up of royal members of the village council. With the *Ekpuk* heads and the *Ubong* members, the *Obong Obio* formed the village council, *Esop Idung*.

The lineage head in the east Niger Delta was elected and he sat in court with adult male members of the group. Among the Efik–Ibibio, the bond of the lineage and the village did not lie strictly in kinship or blood ties as among the Igbo and the Annang, because the lineage and village members were of diverse ancestry who had moved into the site from different settlements. Unity lay, however, in the political autonomy, obligations of mutual aid and the territorial isolation of the lineage or village.

In the delta, the lineage of fishermen was loosely knit as a result of the constant movement of its members in chase of shoals and new fishing grounds, and this was reflected in the marriage and descent systems and the traditional political structure. It is no wonder, therefore, that lineages usually split and new ones came into being. The *amanyanabo*, or village head, came from a lineage that was reputed to have founded the settlement. The village assembly was composed not of lineage heads as in the Igbo, Annang and Efik–Ibibio villages but of members of a few adult age grades who initiated decisions on most matters and over whom the *amanyanabo* presided.

The Igbo traditional political system, like those of other peoples east of the Niger, was based on the lineage structure. It consisted of flexible democratic political systems characterised by autonomous federations of lineages or villages organised through lineage heads, age grades and title societies. Age grades and title societies cut across lineage lines. The policy-making body was composed of representatives of lineages within the autonomous political groups.

From a close study of the power base (decision-making) in the Igbo political system, five categories may be identified. 1) The first is the traditional archetype whereby decisions are reached by consensus among the lineage representatives among whom age, wealth or privilege have no overriding influence. It would appear that the other categories are later developments from this archetype. 2) The second category, which is a slight modification of the first, is found among the Awka Igbo where members of title societies and lineage elders constitute the political decision-making group. 3) The third is found among Cross River Igbo in Abriba, Ohafia and Arochukwu where secret societies dominate the political scene. 4) Among the Asaba, Aguleri and Abriba Igbo, the fourth category operates where age grades and lineage heads form the decision-making body. 5) The fifth is found among those people Nzimiro has identified as 'Niger Ibos' (Ogbaru, Oguta, Aboh, Onitsha and Osomari) where the political structure is hierarchical. In all these categories the essence of government remains the same. Even in the fifth category the checks and balances are so employed that autocratic tendencies do not exist. There will be further comment on these developments in a later section.

Executive

In executing the decisions and policies of any lineage or village a number of elements are employed – some human, some supernatural. One phenomenon common to the traditional political structures of these peoples is the absence of total segregation of powers. For instance in the systems employed by the Annang, Efik and Ibibio, although functions were distributed among members of certain classes, other organs and individuals were used who were hardly a party in the decision-making process.

Age grades were employed in the legislative, executive and judicial processes of the lineage and village. The oldest grade was co-opted into the village council when the need arose. In most cases its function was the administration of ceremonial – administering oaths, offering sacrifices, initiating male members into exclusivist clubs. The middle-aged grade was made up of successful business people who offered financial help and directed the next grade – the youth – in military and social services. The lowest grade – the children – was used for public sanitation. Beyond these functions, the age grades organised public entertainment from time to time and took an active role in the system of social control.

Exclusivist clubs, otherwise called secret societies, operated among all the peoples of south-eastern Nigeria. The most prominent were the *Ekpe* and *Ekpo* of the Cross River (*Ekpe* – leopard, *Ekpo* – ghost). The clubs were graded, each grade having its peculiarities in dress, dance and ritual. Admission and promotion into and within any club involved elaborate ritual and monetary investment.

Among the Igbo the masquerade (*Mmuo*) clubs operated while the delta and other riverine people used the *Owu*. Again membership was restricted. The Ibibio *Ekpo* was decentralised, each village possessing a lodge and membership open to all – freeborn, slave and stranger. The Efik *Ekpe* was open only to freeborn people, and this accounts for why the *Ekpe* was fiercer and more repressive than the *Ekpo*. As of rule masquerade and exclusivist clubs were open only to the men as the women played no political role in the society.

The *Ekpe* or *Ekpo* was the supreme authority in the maintenance of law and order. The societies/clubs were a form of insurance policy for living members and a source of elaborate funeral ceremony for dead members. The *Ekong* club added intelligence and security duties to those of law and order.

Judicial

In the judicial system the nuclear family was the first court over which the head presided, settling minor cases between members. The lineage heads settled cases involving fighting, assault, petty theft, family disputes, adultery and even divorce. The village court handled inter-lineage cases over which the lineages involved could not reach agreement. Both plaintiff and defendant paid settlement fees in kind although the plaintiff paid the summons fees. The innocent party had a part of its settlement fees refunded while the guilty party forfeited its fees and was subject to further fines in line with the gravity of the offence. Part of the settlement fees and fines were turned over to the village revenue while part went for the payment of allowances to court members. The right of appeal was always upheld. In some cases divination could be employed to establish a person's innocence or guilt. In such an instance a reputed diviner, or oracles like the *Ibini Ukpabi* (Long Juju) of Arochukwu, or the *Igwekala* of Umunoha, were consulted. Judgment here was final.

The Efik–Ibibio employed trial or ordeal (*Afia* or *Ukang*) which included the use of boiling oil, eggs, and water in a plate to determine a person's guilt or innocence. The most notorious was the use of the *Esere* beans, which in 1919 were reputed to have claimed 550 lives. The injustice in ordeals lies in the fact that most innocent persons were punished.

Social control

The peoples east of the Niger employed various methods in maintaining social order. These differed in their effectiveness from group to group. Social control techniques, as these methods may be called, are processes by which a society induces or compels its members to act according to its wishes even when the members' interests are not safeguarded. Traditional social control was based on customs and traditions, and techniques of social control included laws, creeds, sanctions, customs, traditions, socialisation and even mores. Religion was the pivot on which the system of social control rested for its effectiveness. The concept of life among peoples east of the Niger is mirrored in their idea about God, spirit, deities, ghosts and witches. All laws have supernatural sanction because the lineage heads and elders derive their authority – political, legal and social – over other members from invisible ancestors.

Popular social control techniques were the use of exclusivist clubs from which females were barred, folk play in which young men and women entertained the public and used satirical and abusive songs against social deviants. Oath-taking, divination and ordeals were forms of social control designed to serve as deterrents. The use of significant symbols such as the palm-frond to summon meetings; court warrants to place a ban on disputed property, to restrict movement over private property or the misuse of public property; the use of other leaves or herbs to place a ban on the use of any property; or the Efik–Ibibio use of the sheepskin among the Uruan villages as a symbol of injunction – all were forms of social control. It is also known that the rites of passage were a technique of social control. For instance, the puberty rites of the Annang *Mbobo* was aimed at ensuring that no teenage girl had sexual experience before this ceremony which led to marriage. It can be seen, therefore, that where institutionalised systems stopped, social control began in the effective maintenance of law and order.

Later developments

As a result of varying degrees of interaction between the different villages and village groups within each of the linguistic groups identified at the beginning of this chapter, and inter-linguistic group interactions, the socio-political systems of the peoples east of the Niger remained dynamic. While conservative in a sense they were nevertheless sensitive to situations around them, at times peacefully accepting change, at times being forced to accept changes, at times also innovating their systems from within. A few of these changes have been noticed in the systems already discussed. Overall, it would appear that economic factors played the major role in transforming the socio-political systems of the peoples east of the Niger.

A major development in the traditional political system of the peoples of this region was the personification of power. This factor had a tremendous impact on political authority in Nigeria as a whole. This phenomenon had been gradually evolving even in the archetype of the traditional systems, but could not find full expression because of the numerous checks on individualism (as opposed to the society as a monolithic group). Its emergence may be attributed to the economic transformation of the societies as a result of European contact with the coast from the late fifteenth century AD onwards.

The changing economic situations bred a new class of rich men who owed nothing to land or the sea and their fruits for their wealth. In short, they owed no obligation for their progress to the elders who controlled these traditional bases of wealth. This development tore into shreds the bonds of society. It gave birth to a new generation – a generation rich in money, material goods and even human beings (slaves) acquired through trade with men of foreign lands. As will be seen shortly the different peoples responded differently to this development, thereby bringing about permanent change in a number of respects.

The origin of sacred or divine kingship among peoples east of the Niger is still unknown, although this phenomenon is prevalent among the Nri Igbo, the Kukun, the Ekoi and the Ibibio not to mention the elaborately studied polities of the Yoruba, the Edo and the Igala, who were in close contact with the east Niger peoples.

The Efik differ from other Cross River peoples in their development of a monarchical political system. It should be pointed out that the Efik settlements were similar to those of Bonny and Opobo and were based on the House system, a feature of the east delta. The use of the term 'King' in Old Calabar by the seventeenth century appeared to be purely honorific, conveying no idea of monarchy. It referred to leaders of Old Calabar, and possibly some others engaged in European trade. Barbot's record shows that at no time was any one person the paramount head. By the time of Antera (Ntero) Duke in the eighteenth century the term applied not only to local community heads but also to the office or rank in the *Ekpe* society. But by the end of the eighteenth century some sub-cultural changes had taken place in Efik political organisation. From the memoirs of Captain Hugh Crow, Ephraim (Efiom), the head of Duke Town who came from the Ephraim branch of Duke Town, preferred the title Duke to King as he considered it higher than that of King. By this time it was possible to recognise someone as the head of Duke Town. During the last quarter of the eighteenth century, as Captain Hall observed, Calabar had three kings, who reigned respectively in the realms of religion, law and civil affairs.

The *Oku Ndem*, the cult priest of Ndem Efik, was connected with the traditional fishing occupation of the Efik. Taboos kept their members from new sources of wealth acquired through trade. The office thus lost favour after 1850 when it became difficult to fill it at the death of the incumbent. Even when it was revived the *Oku Ndem* had no place of precedence.

The *Eyamba* was the president of the *Ekpe*, the exclusivist club that performed religious, civil, political, judicial and commercial functions. The third functionary was the *Obong Isong* (sub-chief), who was the chairman and spokesman of the community council which dealt with matters of general interest to the entire settlement. The building and strengthening of the Efik political organisation in the late eighteenth and early nineteenth centuries involved the *Eyamba* and *Obong Isong*, the latter having become important in trade and negotiation with Europeans.

As a result of marriage the office of *Eyamba* had moved from the original Ambo Ward of Creek Town to Eyamba Ward. Thus Ekpenyong Offiong (Egbo Young) of Eyamba ward became *Eyamba* after the death of his father-in-law. In short, from the late eighteenth century onwards the same ward provided both *Obong Isong* and *Eyamba* – as was the case, for example, when Ekpenyong Offiong became *Eyamba* in the 1770s and *Obong* in 1786 after the death of Edem Ekpo (Ephraim I). Ekpenyong Offiong became the most important personality in Efik affairs – the principal trader and chief in Calabar. He became *Ebunko*, the

Fig. 3.1   A Niger Delta war canoe on its way to attack the Royal Niger Company's post at Akassa

vice-president of Ekpe, about 1767. He caused the *Ekpe* to be invoked on his only rival, Eyo Nsa (Eyo Willy Honest I), a former slave of Ambo ward of Creek Town, in about 1805. The heavy fines imposed on Eyo Nsa broke his power. A significant stage was reached when Effiong Edem (Duke Ephraim II) of Duke Town became *Obong* and purchased the title of *Eyamba* in about 1819–20. Because Eyo Nsa died about this time Ephraim II had no rival in the Efik community. He proceeded to consolidate his power and influence. This was highly advantageous to the institution of kingship but did not really mean the emergence of a single king for the Efik communities during the nineteenth century. The selection of kings of Old Calabar in the nineteenth century remained similar to that in the Igbo, Ibibio or Efik communities. Although one House (Ward) now provided the king he was expected to be the head of the maximal lineage, or a close relative.

Earlier, we observed how the delta fishing village developed. From the late fifteenth century there was a shift in emphasis from the mangrove resources sent to the interior to the supply of other materials to the Portuguese at the coast. The most significant was the lucrative trade in slaves from the sixteenth century. An adjustment was again made from the nineteenth century, followed the abolition of the slave trade in 1807, to the trade in local produce – palm. The period of European contact was the most revolutionary in delta society, in terms of its economy and social structure as well as its political organisation.

The first major change in social relationships, and consequently in

31

political organisation, followed the switch in economy from fishing and salt-making to slave trading. This switch resulted also to a switch from the lineage to the 'House'. Generally the House was made up of a successful trader, who became its head, his immediate family, and slaves who came from different linguistic groups. In contrast to the loosely knit lineage, the House was a close-knit trading and fighting corporation capable of manning and owning a war canoe.

The elected head of a House was in theory an absolute ruler with power of life and death over its members. He was the guardian of its property and finances which in his own interest he invested to promote and increase the trade of his people. Because good government and peace were prerequisites of a flourishing trade, the House heads used their absolute power with restraint. The House was a unit of local government for law and order, the responsibility for which fell on its head.

The Houses were in constant competition, and stronger ones usually absorbed the weak ones. Successful Houses took every opportunity to increase their membership by acquiring slaves. Similarly, Houses split in their evolution as a result of mismanagement of their affairs or poor leadership, resulting in conflicts and quarrels.

The *amanyanabo*, or king, resolved inter-House disputes, confirmed the election of new House heads, determined the hierarchy of the heads, was in control of foreign affairs, and initiated commercial policies in his capacity as the chief merchant as well as that of chief priest.

Initially, the founding of Houses was the prerogative of royal princes. By the eighteenth century the emphasis on trade made it imperative that only the most successful traders be elected to the headship of Houses so as to control the inter-House rivalry. It was this factor that decided the future course of delta political development. It was in this situation that gradually successful and able slaves in the Houses rose to ranks of prominence. By the early nineteenth century the heads of Houses were still royal princes chosen by the *amanyanabo* on grounds of ability and success in trade. But in the course of the century, however, freeborn, commoner and slave could rise to the headship of Houses. Despite the prejudice that barred them from becoming kings, their political standing had so much improved that by the mid-nineteenth century they participated in the election of kings. In short they had become kingmakers. The effect was very remarkable. Amongst other things it meant that the wealthiest and most prosperous prince was no longer automatically elected king. This weakened the monarchy considerably and forced it to depend more and more on European support. This was the situation in Bonny and Kalabari, and it led to civil wars and their eventual split into two and three respectively.

Among the Igbo, socio-political developments were in the main internal. But it would appear that from about the fifteenth century AD onwards increased Igbo activity beyond their homelands brought about the incorporation of new elements into their system. It should be noted, however, that the archaeological excavations in Igboukwu confirm the existence in Igboland of a 'monarchy' or 'ritual head' with elaborate and highly regarded ceremonial and paraphernalia. The use of Nri ritual symbols for the institution of *Eze* and the presence of secret societies and the cults of *Ezeoguda* and *Agbala* among the Nsukka Igbo show Nri influence.

Intrusive phenomena also emanated from Igala on communities in modern Nsukka. The rise of Ida as the powerful capital of the Igala led to wars of conquest; and the diplomatic activities that followed resulted in the adoption of Igala political symbols – as is evident in the religious title *Atama* bestowed by the Igala. Of course, Igala migrations into northern Igboland were absorbed linguistically. The use of secret societies or exclusivist clubs in other Igbo communities must be seen in the light of wilful adoption, as is the case with the Cross River Igbo. The existence of monarchical institutions among the 'Niger Igbo' is definitely a borrowed phenomenon. Its origin is not exactly known but some have attributed it to the influence of the Benin empire. In this system the remarkable development is that there is an *Obi* (king) with a court and a state council. The state council is the decision-making body, with legislative, judicial, executive and military functions. As noted earlier – and consistent with traditional Igbo democracy – there are a number of checks and balances to prevent autocratic tendencies within the monarchical structures.

Conclusion

This chapter has surveyed the traditional social and political organisation of the different peoples east of the Niger. It has also put into focus the dynamic properties within each system which made it possible for the peoples to interact with each other, bringing about restricted or at times large-scale absorption of external elements. These external elements constituted the primary catalysis in internal development. This was the stage at which the Annang, Efik, Ibibio, Igbo and Ijo-speaking peoples adopted or intensified the use of new socio-politico-religious symbols and paraphernalia. It largely involved peaceful borrowing, hence was an addition to existing situations and not a total replacement. The accommodation of the new elements within the existing system ensured the survival of these systems even under severe stresses.

From the late fifteenth century onwards these peoples were subjected to new pressures. The peoples immediately fronting the Atlantic seaboard first felt this impact. It gradually spilled into the communities squatting along the banks of the major rivers, which also became commercial highways, and thence to others very close to them. The peoples right in the interior were less accessible to the direct impact of the foreign trade. Even though they produced the articles of trade – slaves and later palm produce – their homes were hardly the arena of direct activity, especially as the traders travelled long distances to dispose of their wares. Their traditional, or pre-sixteenth century, socio-political systems appear not to have been badly disrupted even in the era of the slave trade, contrary to widely held opinions. The pressing need to evolve new systems did not therefore arise. In short the peoples of the interior, while very receptive to the economic benefits of trade, remained largely conservative or minimally dynamic in their socio-political development. It is in this light that one can appreciate the retention of the traditional democratic institutions within a large corpus of the Igbo socio-political systems.

Elsewhere, overseas trade brought about disruption in the relationships between peoples within the same political unit and was to encourage, and later institutionalise, the personification of power. It is still not clear what time-depth and motivating force lay behind this process among the Annang. The possibilities are the result of an internal evolutionary process over time; the result of contact with other Nigerian groups in the Benue valley; and the results of the impact of the Atlantic slave trade; or an amalgam of all three possibilities. Among the Efik–Ibibio and the delta Ijo, where there is some documentation from the late fifteenth century, the process of personifying power is much easier to perceive. It started about the early sixteenth century and was consolidated and institutionalised before colonial rule. The dominant if not sole causative factor was economic – the trade in slaves and palm produce. Although the impetus was external, the new socio-political systems utilised known elements and symbols within the various societies, and acquired some from the trade itself. In sum, therefore, in the course of their history the peoples east of the Niger retained, or modified or in some cases evolved new administrative, judicial, executive and religious processes of government and social structure which were adequate for their needs.

Further reading

E. J. ALAGOA, *A History of the Niger Delta* (Ibadan: 1972).

K. O. DIKE, *Trade and Politics in the Niger Delta* (Oxford: 1956).

D. FORDE AND G. I. JONES, *The Ibo and the Ibibio-speaking Peoples of Southeastern Nigeria* (London: 1950).

ROBIN HORTON, 'From fishing village to city state', in M. Douglas and D. Kaberey (eds), *Man in Africa* (London: 1969).

OBARO IKIME (ed.), *Groundwork of Nigerian History* (Ibadan: 1980).

ELIZABETH ISICHEI, *A History of the Igbo People* (London: 1976).

G. I. JONES, *The Trading States of the Oil Rivers* (Oxford: 1963).

K. K. NAIR, *Politics and Society in South Eastern Nigeria* (London: 1972).

N. NZEWUNWA, *The Niger Delta: aspects of its prehistoric economy and culture* (Oxford: 1980).

THURSTAN SHAW, *Igbo-Ukwu: an account of archaeological discoveries in eastern Nigeria* (2 vols, London: 1970).

V. C. UCHENDU, *The Igbo of Southeastern Nigeria* (California: 1965).

4 Pre-colonial Nigeria: west of the Niger

I. A. Akinjogbin and Biodun Adediran

The region west of the river Niger exhibits a variety of physical features which have allowed for a great degree of experimentation in social and political developments. From a low-lying coastal belt in the south, the terrain rises gently towards the north with the highest peaks in the north-east and north-west. The region is well drained by many rivers, such as the Ogun, Osun, Oluwa, Siluko and Ethiope. Although there is no evidence that any of them was used extensively for transportation, it is certain that none of them was a hindrance to population movements; they are of moderate size and during the dry season which comes up annually from about August to April they could be easily forded.

The region is the home of the Yoruba and Edo peoples, two ethnic groups famous in West African history for their works of art. The Edo occupy the eastern part of the region, while the Yoruba, the more populous group, occupy the western and northern parts. Apart from these two groups who live mostly on the mainland, there are other ethnic groups found along the coast and in the Niger Delta. These are the Itsekiri, Ijo, Urhobo, Igbo and Egun. The western Igbo found on the western banks of the lower Niger, and the Ijo, are extensions of the main groups east of the Niger. Likewise the Egun, found mainly in the south-western corner of the region, are a sub-group of the Adja ethnic group found mainly in modern republics of Benin and Togo.

While each of these ethnic groups can be identified as being distinct from the others, they are not in watertight compartments. There are continuous interactions among them; and they have certain cultural traits in common. They all share, for example, such traits as respect for age, the inseparable nature of religion and temporal affairs, patrilineal descent, age-grade and family organisations. There are, of course, regional differences between, for example, the city-dwelling and state-forming Yoruba and Edo peoples and the village-dwelling Urhobo and Ijo. Even though the languages spoken in the region are not all mutually intelligible, they form a cluster of closely related languages classified under the 'Kwa' sub-group of the Niger–Congo family of languages. Beyond this, the relationship between these peoples is clearly explicable in historical terms. The Yoruba have fairly well-authenticated traditions of ancestral links with the Edo, Itsekiri and the Egun. So do the Edo with the Igbo, Urhobo, Ijaw and Isoko.

It is now fairly certain that before the emergence of each ethnic group (a development which presumably took place with the process of state-formation) there were aboriginal inhabitants who lived in communities scattered all over the region.[1] Remnants of these aboriginal inhabitants have been identified in various places which served as the nuclei of the respective ethnic group. Around present-day Benin, they were known as the *Efa*; in Ife they were called *Igbo*. In other places they were known by various local names. If inferences from linguistic and ethnographic studies are anything to go by, these scattered communities would appear to be similar in nature. In fact there is a strong belief in scholarly circles that the whole region formed a single cultural continuum. These aboriginal elements formed the bedrock for the formation of the various ethnic groups.

The first group to emerge from this cultural continuum would appear to be the Yoruba, who occupy a prominent position both in terms of population and culture. Although they can be differentiated into many sub-groups, they are culturally homogeneous and possess a strong tradition of historical consciousness which traces their origins to Ile-Ife.

According to Yoruba traditions, Ile-Ife was the place where the ethnic group emerged from the undifferentiated layer of aboriginal inhabitants. It was also from Ile-Ife that the salient aspects of Yoruba civilisation diffused to other parts.[2]

Although the process of the formation of the Yoruba ethnic group is not yet clear, it is not impossible to sketch an outline of the developments. Oduduwa, the putative founder of Ile-Ife, played a leading role. Most of the legends of Ife concerning the roles of Oduduwa are too well known to require a recapitulation here.[3] Suffice it to say that before the advent of Oduduwa the region of Ile-Ife was occupied by about thirteen semi-autonomous settlements organised into a loose confederacy. It would appear that Oduduwa did not belong to this confederacy. According to the traditions, Oduduwa's settlement was on one of the hills which surrounded the thirteen settlements that made the confederacy. It is in fact said that on his descent from the hill, Oduduwa and his followers were settled at a strangers' quarter allocated to them, presumably by the head of the confederates.

Then Oduduwa embarked upon a series of activities which led to the subjugation of his hosts and the imposition of his political authority over the thirteen pre-existing settlements. The cumulative effect of all these was the fusion of the thirteen settlements into a single settlement. There began a series of constitutional experimentations in which some of the displaced heads of pre-existing communities were given certain roles to play in the new administration. The overall result was the emergence of a monarchical form of government with the *Ooni* as the central figure and the heads of the aboriginal communities as ritual or administrative chiefs.

This transformation of the loose alliance of the pre-Oduduwa era into a permanent feature brought into existence the first dynastic state or kingdom in the region west of the river Niger. Unlike the pre-existing form of organisation, leadership was not rotated among the heads of the pre-dynastic groups but was now monopolised by the Oduduwa group or dynasty. The new group further enhanced its power by installing itself within a walled enclosure or palace and preventing others from enjoying certain privileges such as the use of beads or crowns.[4]

Various other experiments at consolidation took place following the Oduduwa revolution. For instance, some of the pre-existing groups formed themselves into a resistance group known as the *Igbo* and continued to trouble the new settlement, scattering markets and putting the *Ooni* himself to flight on many occasions. It was only during the reign of the fourth *Ooni* Obalufon Alaiyemore that the *Igbo* menace was solved.

The means by which the *Igbo* menace was overcome has gone down as one of the best-known examples of feminine heroism in Yoruba history. According to the traditions,[5] the *Igbo* used to disguise themselves so as to look like spirits and in such a way that usually instilled fear into the people who, on seeing them, took flight without offering much resistance. However, Moremi, a woman of uncommon beauty, allowed herself to be taken captive on one occasion and later absconded back to Ife to organise a confrontation with the *Igbo*. During the confrontation that followed, the *Igbo* were overpowered and the recalcitrant elements were brought back into the fold to contribute to the building of the new settlement.

While attempts at consolidation were going on, groups of individuals began to leave Ile-Ife to set up themselves elsewhere. The movement out of Ile-Ife was intensified when, as a result of population expansion, Ile-Ife was hit by a prolonged drought which, in spite of many supplications, continued for many years, causing famine and malnutrition. In fact a decision was taken that the best way to solve the problem was for some people to emigrate.[6] A meeting was summoned at a place which still bears the name of *Ita Ijero* (place of deliberation) where a decision was taken as to what direction each party should take, and how future contacts were to be made with Ile-Ife and among the migrants, who were led by princes who belonged to the Oduduwa group.

Some of the decisions taken at the meeting are still remembered in Ife traditions. First, in addition to crowns beautifully adorned with beads, the leader of each group was given a symbol which became his totem of authority. For instance, the leader of the group that founded Oyo received a special type of sword called *Ida Ajase* (sword of victory), while the prince that led the Owu group got a chain called *Epe*. The Igbomina group was given a special type of cutlass called *Ogbo*. While the crowns were given as signs of authority for each prince to carve out a kingdom in the same way that Oduduwa had established the Ife kingdom, the totem was important as a reminder that the ultimate source of the group was Ile-Ife. Consequently, in spite of the fact that each kingdom was to be independent, it was clear before the *Ita Ijero* conference broke up that they were to regard themselves as kinsmen and to look up to Ile-Ife as their 'home'.

It is not now known for sure how many kingdoms emerged as a result of the *Ita Ijero* conference. However, Benin's link with the Ile-Ife was documented as early as the fifteenth century by European visitors to the coast of Benin, and by European administrators at the beginning of the century.[7] It would appear that Oyo and Benin acted as centres of dispersal from which other kingdoms were established on the Ife model. Whether established directly from Ile-Ife or indirectly through another kingdom, states founded on the Ife model had to be confirmed by reference to Ile-Ife. Thus not fewer than sixteen kingdoms are known to have been formed after the Ife model in various parts of Yorubaland.[8]

It is difficult to establish in detail the historical development of most of the kingdoms, but it would appear that the process was similar and involved the displacement of pre-existing heads of settlements and the combination of many such settlements to form a single settlement which invariably became the nucleus of a sub-group.[9]

In Ile-Ife itself, after the dispersal, there were successive attempts to consolidate the position of the *Ooni* vis-à-vis those of the pre-dynastic groups. First the palace was moved to a more central location and the *Ooni* surrounded himself with many royal servants (*Emese*) recruited from certain lineages sympathetic with its cause. Secondly, the new settlement was surrounded with town walls, giving it a more permanent look. Thirdly, the new settlement was divided into quarters under loyal lineage-heads who became civil chiefs responsible to the *Ooni*. This was a double-edged innovation as it made the *Ooni* less involved in the daily affairs of the settlements. Fourthly, possibly taking a cue from the sufferings brought by the drought and famine, another chieftaincy system, the *Isoro*, was instituted specifically to propitiate the gods of the various pre-dynastic settlements. Thus the *Ooni* was able to emerge as a central force but not without making some concession to the pre-dynastic groups who organised themselves into a powerful cult known as *Imole* (Ogboni).

With peace and stability achieved at Ile-Ife, the people could embark on patronising art and culture. As early as the reign of Obalufon the art of brass-casting was initiated and many Ife artists went to other Yoruba kingdoms to teach it. During the reign of Luwoo, a female *Ooni*, all the streets in Ife were paved with potsherds. The Ife developed various other art-forms such as terra-cotta, bronze figures made through the 'lost wax' method, wood-carving, beads and glass manufacture. The *Ooni* became great patrons of art, and in fact a royal courtyard, in which many of the Ife masterpieces were stored, was created within the precincts of the palace.

However, it was in the process of state-formation that Ile-Ife became very important. In essence, taking the Ife model, the political organisation of each Yoruba kingdom exhibits only slight variations in details to suit particular localities and circumstances. Though autonomous, the kingdoms were bonded closely together and continued to share ideas. Because the founders were all sons or grandsons of Oduduwa, there arose a situation in which succeeding rulers of the kingdoms (and their subjects) looked at one another as relations (*Ebi*).[10]

The gathering at *Ita Ijero* seems to have laid down responsibilities, or a code of conduct, for each departing prince. From some re-enactment ceremonies performed at the death or enthronement of kings an outline of the decisions could be sketched. Firstly, it appeared that the departing princes agreed on a periodic renewal of their contact with the ancestral spirit at Ile-Ife. In the religious aspect, this took the form of sending to Ife items for the worship of certain important 'national' deities, such as Oduduwa, Ogun and Oranmiyan. In the political sphere, it took the form of renewing the original symbols of royalty. Another important agreement reached appears to be that the departing princes should maintain the family link through inheritance. This practice of inheritance

(*Ogun pinpin*) is perhaps the strongest evidence that the rulers of Yoruba kingdoms continued to regard themselves as kinsmen; for in Yoruba custom, only immediate relatives could inherit the movable property of a deceased person. Until about three decades ago, it was the accepted practice that whenever any *Oba* regarded as a direct descendant of Oduduwa died, his movables, particularly his dresses, were divided among his living 'brothers'.[11]

Of the kingdoms founded by Ife princes, Oyo became the latest and most powerful. Its dynastic founder, Oranmiyan, was Odudwa's youngest and most adventurous son. However, Oyo had very humble beginnings as a state and would appear to have been initially tributary to Owu,[12] another major Yoruba kingdom whose founder, according to traditions, was the first to receive the mandate to establish a kingdom. In fact one account of the foundation of Oyo records that while other princes received valuable legacies such as money, women, cattle, beads, garments and crowns, Oranmiyan inherited only a bit of rag containing earth, twenty-one pieces of iron and a cock.[13] The story of how Oranmiyan eventually turned this pittance of heritage into a large fortune is told in various ways, all of which agree on one thing: that Oranmiyan was adventurous.[14]

There is a consensus in the traditions that after the meeting at *Ita Ijero* Oranmiyan led a group eastwards towards Benin where, as we shall see later, he laid the foundations of the Benin kingdom. Apparently, Oranmiyan then returned to Ile-Ife where he spent a short time before leading another party northwards towards the river Niger, where he ran into trouble with the Nupe who were then attempting to found a kingdom on the Niger. However, Oranmiyan received the sympathy of a Bariba king, possibly the ruler of Bussa, who pointed out a suitable site to the group.

Even at the site, the task of building a kingdom was not easy as many pre-existing groups prevented the immediate settlement of Oranmiyan. He had to embark on a series of conquests before he could found Oyo, which was surnamed Ajaka. Although Oyo Ajaka later became the capital of a kingdom, Oranmiyan did not himself live there for long. He founded another settlement at Oko, where he remained for a short time before returning to Ile-Ife where he became the third *Ooni*.

The task of building a solid foundation for the Oyo kingdom fell on two of the early *Alaafin*, Ajaka and Sango. There were threats from Oyo's neighbours, especially the Owu, Nupe and Bariba. The problems were such that the young kingdom needed an active and tactful leader. Ajaka, who succeeded Oranmiyan, did not prove equal to the task. His main interests were the pursuits of peaceful occupations like agriculture. Consequently, he was deposed and his more valiant younger brother, Sango, ascended the throne. The choice of Sango was probably a diplomatic move. Sango's mother was a Nupe princess and his choice appears to have been a deliberate attempt to stem the tide of hostility from the Nupe.

Sango took adequate advantage of the situation. Being aware of the circumstances which led to his brother's deposition, he was determined to establish Oyo as an independent kingdom. His ambitions soon brought

39

him into conflict with the Owu kingdom, which he destroyed. Next he embarked on establishing a strong central administration. To do this, he removed the seat of government from Oko to Oyo Ajaka. The removal of the capital could be seen in two ways. Firstly, it could be seen as a tactical measure, for the new site was more easily defensible. More importantly, it was possible that Sango wanted to court the friendship of the king of Bariba who had pointed out the site of Oyo Ajaka to Oranmiyan's party in the first place. In any case, in spite of his warlike nature, Sango continued to show filial piety towards the Nupe, apparently buying time to lay a solid foundation before embarking on territorial expansion.

Sango never had the opportunity of expanding the kingdom, though he succeeded in making it very strong. His people soon grew tired of his wars. In another *coup d'état*, Sango was deposed and Ajaka was recalled in the hope that he would bring some peace. But Ajaka himself had changed. He waged a successful war against the Nupe, pushing the frontiers of Oyo across the Niger. He then embarked on a series of internal reorganisations, at the end of which the *Alaafin* emerged as the undisputed leader of the people.

The next four *Alaafin* made whatever contributions they could to the political development of the kingdom.[15] Though the close of Aganju's reign was marked by domestic troubles, it was on the whole peaceful and prosperous. Kori's reign began with a constitutional problem. At the death of his father he was a minor and until he was old enough his mother, Iyayun, acted as regent. When he assumed full powers, one of the memorable acts he performed was the founding of Ede as Oyo's boundary town with the Ijesa. Oluaso's reign is remembered as the longest, most peaceful and most prosperous since the foundation of the kingdom. Generally the atmosphere was peaceful and it can be presumed that the Oyo seized the opportunity to embark on gainful economic pursuits such as agriculture, trading and artistic ventures. Oluaso himself engaged in building palaces, said to have numbered fifty-four.

However, all was not smooth sailing. During the next reign, that of Onigbogi, disaster struck. The Nupe, who had been defeated by Ajaka, had successfully consolidated themselves on the Niger and were extending southward into the Yoruba country.[16] They took advantage of an internal crisis in Oyo-Ile to invade the kingdom. They destroyed the capital and put its inhabitants to flight.[17] The *Alaafin* himself took refuge in Gbere, apparently a town under the Bariba king of Bussa. The sojourn outside Oyo-Ile took a fairly long time. Onigbogi died in the Bariba country and was succeeded by Ofinran, an ambitious youth whose restless nature soon brought him into conflict with his hosts. Following a dispute between the *Alaafin* and the Bariba king, the Oyo refugees were forced to retrace their steps into the Yoruba country. The main group under Ofinran passed through Kisi and settled at Kusu, a few kilometres north-east of Saki. Here Ofinran died and his successor, Eguguoju, continued the journey, passing through Iju Sanya, Saki and finally founding Igboho which became the seat of four *Alaafin*: Eguguoju, Orompoto, Ajiboyede and Abipa.

The occupation of Igboho was not, however, the end of troubles. At the time the Oyo were leaving Borgu, the region was being invaded by the

Songhai under Askia Dawud.[18] This unleashed a series of political upheavals which put the Bariba in hot pursuit of the Oyo. Thus during the reign of Orompoto, the Bariba attacked Igboho. The Oyo appeared to have regained their fighting spirit for they successfully resisted the attack. During another fierce encounter with the Nupe, *Alaafin* Ajiboyede's forces were victorious. This military resurgence of Oyo paved the way for the reoccupation of Oyo-Ile. In spite of opposition from the chiefs and elders at Igboho, *Alaafin* Abipa succeeded in reoccupying Oyo-Ile in about the first decade of the seventeenth century.

The experience of Oyo between the evacuation of Oyo-Ile and its re-occupation was not an entirely negative one. There was some institutional growth. While in exile, the *Alaafin* was initiated into the *Ifa* mysteries and Egungun cult. Also, the Oyo learned that they had to depend more upon their fighting strength and on diplomatic alliances. Thus by the time of the reoccupation of Oyo-Ile, Oyo forces had undergone a complete reorganisation. In the process of fighting and seeking refuge, their cohesiveness grew, as often happens to people who pass through the same danger. Furthermore, the power of the monarchy appeared to have been greatly increased, for the *Oba* continued to lead his subjects to war, and as such, effectively controlled the army. During this period also, large towns such as Igboho, Ede, Ikoyi, Igbon and Iresa were founded. The internal organisation and system of government also evolved, having stood the test of troubles. Oyo traditions suggest that by the time of the reoccupation of Oyo-Ile all the *Oyo Mesi* chieftaincy titles and most of the *Eso* (military) titles were already in existence.

Thus the kingdom of Oyo at the beginning of the seventeenth century was poised for imperial expansion.[19] The *Alaafin* who started this movement was Obalokun. He extended Oyo's influence southwards to the coast and started the colonisation of Egbado. Ajagbo, who succeeded Obalokun, further strengthened the Oyo army by a massive reorganisation and the introduction of new military tactics, which made the Oyo army the most impressive military machine in West Africa at the time. With a strong army Oyo easily expanded, recording one military success after another. By 1750, the *Alaafin* was emperor of a territory which included the Oyo kingdom, the whole of Egba and Egbado, some parts of Igbomina, the kingdoms of Ajase (Porto Novo), Weme, and Dahomey (modern Republic of Benin) and parts of Nupe and Bariba countries.[20]

In contrast to the large state-formation of the Oyo, there were small states formed by the other sub-groups of the Yoruba. Of these, the Ekiti provide a good example. It may be pointed out that the terrain of the Ekiti country allowed for the emergence of many foci of power which eventually developed into independent states; and in fact many Ekiti towns and villages claim autonomous status. Some of the kingdoms were actually made up of the principal town and a few outlying villages. Ado, which was presumably the largest of the Ekiti states, was made up of only about seventeen settlements. In all, there were about twenty Ekiti kingdoms of which sixteen are traditionally recognised as having crowned rulers. In actual fact, however, only a few of them, namely Ado, Ara, Ijero, Ikole, Otun and Oye, have credible traditions of being founded by children or grandchildren of Oduduwa.

What is certain is that in spite of the differences in size of the states, the political developments in the Ekiti country followed the pattern in Ile-Ife and Oyo. In each case, the group which built the kingdom displaced heads of pre-existing communities. The formation of the Ado kingdom, as recorded by Father Oguntuyi,[21] exemplifies the pattern. The progenitor of the *Ewi* (*Oba* of Ado-Ekiti, was one of the sons of Oduduwa who left Ile-Ife after the *Ita-Ijero* conference. He took an easterly route which led him to Benin. Later he left Benin and took a circuitous route which took him to the site of present-day Ado. There the migrant group, now under Awamaro, met a community called Ilesun under the *Elesun* (*Olu* or chief of Ilesun). The new arrivals initially lived amicably with their hosts, but after a whole a power tussle arose between Awamaro and the *Elesun*. In the confrontation that ensued, the Ilesun were defeated and their leader was assassinated. Awamaro then took over the leadership of the settlement and established the *Ewi* dynasty which gradually built the Ado kingdom from the remnants of the Ilesun and other aboriginal groups in the area.

The early history of Ado saw progressive attempts by successive *Ewi* to consolidate and expand their political authority. In its expansion, Ado gradually subdued many pre-existing settlements. This expansionist tendency led some of the neighbouring states, who were much alarmed, to seek the assistance of the Edo of Benin to curb what to them was the *Ewi*'s excesses. Apparently seizing the opportunity to settle an old score, a Benin army invaded Ado, then under *Ewi* Ata, Awamaro's immediate successor. Ewuare, the Benin king under whom the expedition was sent out, was an imperialist to the core. It is not surprising therefore that Benin did not limit itself to the subjection of Ado but took the opportunity to overrun most of Ekiti. In some places, such as Ikere, the ruling dynasty was replaced. It was only a mutual agreement with Oyo that checked the expansion of Benin and fixed its western boundary at the northern Ekiti town of Otun. Nevertheless, Benin continued to be a major factor in the politics of Ekiti and the more easterly Yoruba kingdoms of Akure, Ondo and Owo.

The placid internal development of Ife, and the turbulent development of Oyo, with that of the Ekiti coming in between, were probably representative of the developments of the other sub-groups. But kingdoms did not emerge in every part of Yorubaland. In the north-eastern extremity of Yorubaland, among the Akoko, Ijumu, Abunu, Yagba and Oworo, the level of socio-political organisation remained simple. Here, as Daryll Forde rightly remarked, 'no right or authority beyond that of the village is recognised, and each village or quarter of a village has its own particular tract of land, the boundaries of which are jealously guarded'.[22]

In spite of the variation in size and complexity that existed between the political organisation of one sub-group and another, the political system of all the sub-groups was, in broad outline, similar. The basic political unit was the town (*ilu*). Each *ilu* was made up of lineages. A typical Yoruba kingdom was made up of many towns, villages, markets and farmsteads. One of these, as the capital town where the king (*oba*) lived, was the focus of attention of all inhabitants within the kingdom.

Each settlement, whatever its size, was organised in a hierarchical form. The component lineages were headed by male adults called *Baale* (father of the house). Some of the *Baale* were appointed as chief (*ijoye*) who saw to the governmental affairs of the town. At the apex of these was the head-chief whose status as a ruler depended on the status of the town. There were four categories of Yoruba rulers. The head of a kingdom was an *oba*. Claiming descent from Oduduwa, he lived in a palace and had, as his symbols of authority, beaded paraphernalia of office such as crowns, slippers, fly-whisks and sceptre. Under the crowned *oba* were *oba* of lesser rank who were often provincial governors or members of the royal family ruling over outlying settlements of the kingdom. Below these were *Baale* who ruled various towns and villages. A fourth category of local rulers was that of the *Oloja* who was in charge of a market town.

Within his sphere of authority, the *oba* or head-chief was the head of government and was politically supreme. As the executive head of the government, he exercised considerable powers; he could arrest, punish or reward any of his subjects. In practice however, the *oba* or head-chief was not an absolute ruler. His powers were checked in a number of ways and, most importantly, he did not rule singlehandedly but in conjunction with a council of chiefs known generally as the *Iwarefa*. The chiefs on the council were usually grouped into two parallel lines representing princely interests and commoners' interests. The chiefs representing commoners' interests were particularly important as they were potential rallying points of civil intrigues. In Oyo, for instance, the *Oyo Mesi*, council of chiefs, was the actual machinery of government and its leader, the *Basorun* (prime minister), was one individual whose position the *Alaafin* could not discountenance. In addition to the secular chiefs, there were religious chiefs representing the main religious interests in the town or kingdom. These two sets of chiefs (secular and spiritual), together with some prominent citizens, were brought together in another powerful organisation (or cult) known variously as Ogboni, Osugbo or Imole in different parts of Yorubaland.

Whether organised into an empire, kingdom or city-state, the internal organisation of Yoruba political communities was on the pattern outlined above. It was only in the administration of outlying settlements that differences existed. Thus while large kingdoms were sub-divided into provinces (*ekun*) headed by provincial *oba*, the towns of the smaller kingdoms were directly responsible to the crowned *oba* through their respective *Baale* or *Oloja*.

While up to the end of the eighteenth century it was possible to talk of a 'Yoruba type' of political organisation, the situation changed drastically in the nineteenth century when various types of constitutional arrangements emerged in different parts of the Yoruba country. The roots for this were laid in the eighteenth century.

The large territorial acquisitions of the *Alaafin* created more problems than they had bargained for. There were the problems of maintaining peace and order and of preventing secession. The intensity of these problems depended on the personality of the reigning *Alaafin* and the state of affairs in the capital. Until the nineteenth century these problems did not come out into the open. As long as Oyo's army remained strong there were no threats of secession. The administrative problem was also resolved by the appointment of the *Ajele* or 'colonial governors' without whose consent local rulers could not take any major political or economic decision and through whom annual tributes were sent to Oyo-Ile.

But the most persistent problem was how to distribute among the ruling circles in the capital city the power and economic resources which accrued from the acquisition of the empire.[23] The constitution of Oyo, like those of all the other Yoruba kingdoms, was carefully balanced in its distribution of power between the *Alaafin* and his chiefs, prominent citizens as well as the young men in the capital. The acquisition of the empire resulted from the combined efforts of all these elements, but tended to tip the balance of power in favour of the *Alaafin*. The *Alaafin* appointed the *Ajele* to the conquered territories which thus became a vast source of patronage for the monarchy. In some cases, the *Ajele* appointed were of non-Oyo origin and were therefore directly dependent on the *Alaafin*.

It is in the light of this increasing power of the king and the desire of the chiefs to curtail that power and prevent despotism that the quarrel between the *Oyo Mesi* and the *Alaafin* in the eighteenth century must be understood. Undoubtedly there were other causes besides this main political issue. There were, for instance, the personal failings of individual *Alaafin* and issues of economic expediency. The quarrel continued prominently below the surface of Oyo's political ascendancy, and the problems created were never really solved but contributed to the dissolution of the empire at the end of the eighteenth century.

In 1754, Gaa, the *Basorun*, successfully supplanted the *Alaafin* as the *de facto* ruler of Oyo. Twenty years later, after four puppet kings, *Alaafin* Abiodun (1774–1789) was able, through popular support, to restore the monarchy to its traditional position.[24]

But shortly before Abiodun's death the empire began to disintegrate. First, in 1783, the Bariba declared their independence from Oyo overlordship. They were followed shortly after by the Egba. In 1791, the Nupe also threw off the Oyo yoke and were followed in quick succession by the coastal dependencies.

Awole, Abiodun's successor as *Alaafin*, aggravated the already poor relations between the *Alaafin* and his chiefs; in the end he brought chaos which led to the final collapse of the central administration. With this, various local rulers started to reduce areas under themselves to order. Afonja at Ilorin and Opele at Gbogun were perhaps the most prominent of such leaders. In 1818, Dahomey, the only remaining important tributary state, declared independence. Around 1823, Afonja put himself at the head of all Hausa slaves in the neighbourhood of Ilorin and declared the settlement a republic. Afonja's attempt misfired. The strangers he had invited to aid him turned against him in battle and turned the movement into the thrust of the Fulani jihad into Yorubaland.[25] This event awakened the quarrelling Oyo chiefs to the real dangers they were now facing. But various attempts made to dislodge the Fulani from Ilorin failed.

These troubles in Oyo reverberated in other parts of Yorubaland. From the closing years of the eighteenth century there had been gradual movements of northern Oyo people southwards. By the third decade of the nineteenth century this had become a mass movement as thousands of Oyo citizens fled to Osun, Ibarapa, Egba, Ife, Ijesa and Ekiti countries.[26] Meanwhile, the Fulani, using Ilorin as their base, continued to put pressure on the northern Yoruba and systematically brought many Yoruba settlements under their control. Eventually Oyo-Ile, the capital of the *Alaafin*, fell to the jihadists. Atiba, the reigning *Alaafin*, attempted to re-establish the grandeur of the old capital at Ago, a market town south of Oyo-Ile which he renamed Oyo.[27] In spite of the accommodation of the Oyo in some towns, many Oyo refugees continued to roam the countryside and took to a life of pillaging, thereby increasing the insecurity. This provoked a series of wars in central and southern parts of Yorubaland.

The most devastating of these wars was the Owu war.[28] The turmoil which started as a minor affair between the Ife and Owu kingdoms had by 1821 become a major war. By 1826 both the Ijebu and the Egba had been dragged into it. The war did not abate until 1828 after the Owu and Egba kingdoms had been completely destroyed.

Out of the ruins of the destructions, new settlements emerged from about 1830. Of these, New Oyo, Ibadan, Abeokuta and Ijaye were to become popular as the century wore on. New Oyo, as pointed out earlier, was established to accommodate the *Alaafin* and the bulk of the inhabitants of Oyo-Ile. Ibadan, formerly an Egba village, became a settlement accommodating the Ife, Ijebu and Oyo elements after the Owu war. Abeokuta developed as a cosmopolitan settlement in which various Egba sub-groups and the Owu who escaped the ravages of the Owu war settled.

One significant by-product of the regrouping of people was the emergence of new political systems and the evolution of new constitutions.[29] At Ibadan, a military aristocracy emerged in about 1830. This was a direct result of the open door policy of Ibadan which encouraged the settlement of diverse peoples. Since it started as a war camp, military ability rather than hereditary nobility had become the main criterion for recognition. In essence therefore, military leaders, irrespective of their origin or birth, were the *de facto* rulers. At Ijaye, which was founded about the same time as Ibadan, a military absolutism emerged. Kurunmi, the founder, was of the opinion that power shared as in the old Oyo empire was bound to lead to political instability. Thus he became the personification of the state till it was destroyed in a war with Ibadan in 1862. A third type of new constitution was operated by the Egba at Abeokuta. This system, which could be called a military federalism, took into cognizance the fact that the new settlement was made up of at least four originally independent states – Ake, Gbagura, Oke-Ona and Owu. Thus it was not easy for one group to lord it over the others. What was fashioned out was a system where a council of leading warriors of each group was delegated to ruler. In face of continual threats from Dahomey, which wanted to control the Egbado region adjacent to the Egba state, the war veterans continued to dictate the pace of development in Abeokuta for most of the century.

However, not all the Yoruba states fashioned new constitutions. The Ife, Ijebu, Ijesa and Ekiti, who were not much affected by the demographic upheavals, continued to operate the old system in which the respective *oba* was regarded as the paramount ruler within his kingdom.

All over Yorubaland, variations of these forms of constitutional arrangement were experimented with. What was common to all was the emphasis upon military factors. Although the Fulani and Dahomean incursions into Yorubaland were eventually checked, there were incessant struggles for power among the new states. It is no surprise therefore that in spite of the fact that all the new constitutions had been fashioned by the middle of the nineteenth century, civil wars continued to plague Yorubaland till the end of the century.[30] The rivalry was first demonstrated in 1845 in the Batedo war, followed by a cold war between Ibadan and Ijaye which led to the Ijaye war (1860–65).

From the struggles, Ibadan emerged the great military power in Yorubaland. It soon embarked on a career of imperial conquests which brought a greater part of the territories of the old Oyo empire under it. Ibadan also acquired territorial possessions in Ife, Ijesa, Ekiti and parts of Akoko; and it continued to exploit these areas till the Ijesa and Ekiti revolted in the Kiriji (Ekitiparapo) war, 1878–1893.[31]

The political tumult provided an excuse for the British to extend their influence beyond the coast where, till the second half of the nineteenth century, their activities had been confined. Gradually, they extended their influence from Lagos (which they invaded in 1851) to the interior of Yorubaland, paving the way for British colonisation of the area.

The rise of the Edo kingdom of Benin as a political power in the West African forest region dated to about the thirteenth century with the establishment of the Eweka dynasty over the semi-autonomous settlements of some pre-dynastic groups known as the *Efa*. The emergence of this dynasty was accompanied by the emergence of the Edo as an ethnic group distinct from their neighbours.

Before the emergence of the Eweka dynasty, there had been attempts by the multi-village communities of the Ogiso at a form of political centralisation. Some Benin traditions about this early period connect it with the Yoruba and the founders of the Ogiso settlements are said to have passed through Ile-Ife.[32] What is certain is that on the eve of the emergence of the kingdom of Benin, a number of Ogiso settlements formed a confederacy enclosed by walls, remnants of which can still be seen today.[33] But like the pre-Oduduwa confederates in Ife, each settlement retained its characteristic features and was autonomous under a leader who had a hierarchy of subordinates. Apart from the number of the Ogiso who ruled Benin, very little is remembered of the political activities during this period. It is known, however, that at the end of the period, the rulers tried a republican form of government which they found unworkable.

If the tradition that the Ogiso passed through Ife is accepted, then it is more than conjectural that their previous connection with Ile-Ife was partly instrumental in their sending to Ife to ask for a prince to rule them.[34] Benin and Yoruba traditions are in remarkable agreement that the second period of Benin history owed a lot to ideas from Ile-Ife. In spite of recent speculations to the contrary, concrete historical evidence confirms the traditions almost to the detail.[35] This is borne out by the adoption of the Yoruba title of *oba* for the ruler of Benin; references to the *Ogane* (*Oghene, Ooni*) in early Portuguese accounts; the practice of giving a new *oba* Yoruba facial marks at his installation, and that of symbolic burial of his remains at Ile-Ife.

Furthermore, both Benin and Yoruba traditions are emphatic on Oranmiyan's career in Benin.[36] It is stated that Oranmiyan left Benin to found the *Alaafin* dynasty at Oyo-Ile. According to this tradition, when in Benin, Oranmiyan first stayed on the outskirts of the town and got married to a daughter of the *Ogiego*, one of the pre-existing heads of settlements. The marriage was a diplomatic manoeuvre which ensured the acceptance of the new leadership by the Ogiso. Before he left Benin for Oyo, Oranmiyan had a son by his Edo wife. This son, Eweka, he designated as his successor.

Eweka systematically eliminated the *Onogie* of Ego and gained control of settlements in the neighbourhood.[37] Gradually he extended his influence beyond Use, his base. Although he started his reign as a minor, Eweka later assumed full powers and built up government institutions which were similar to those of Yorubaland. He is remembered for having created the *Uzama Nihinron*, a council of seven high-ranking chiefs who had the responsibility of running the affairs of the state. What exactly their power was at initiation is not clear, but it would appear that they enjoyed privileges which put them on a par with the *oba*.

The next two successors of Eweka remained at Use and were probably too weak to control the whole of Benin territory or assert their authority over the pre-existing groups. It was Ewedo, the fourth *oba* of the new dynasty, who successfully established the ascendancy of the monarchy. He conquered a local resistance under the leadership of

Fig. 4.1   Benin city as seen by a European visitor in the seventeenth century

Ogiamwen. Next, he built a palace for himself away from the rest of the *Uzama*. He then concentrated into the hands of the monarchy many of the powers which the *Uzama* had been exercising. Henceforth, only the *oba* could confer titles, and have a state-sword (*ada*) carried in front of him. No *Uzama* could sit down in the presence of the *oba*. However, the *Uzama* retained the right to install a new king, and the *Oliha*, their leader, continued to crown him. The next reign, that of Oguola, saw the conquest of the ruler of Udo, who was apparently the last of the Benin opponents of the new dynasty.

With the establishment of a strong monarchy and the defeat of most of the original opponents, Oguola and the next five kings after him appear to have consolidated the powers of the monarchy and to have introduced more peaceful arts. This interpretation is supported by the absence of any stirring events in the traditions remembered for the period. Oguola, according to an account, sent to Ile-Ife to learn the art of brass-casting and Udaegbedo is said to have encouraged agriculture. At the same time, it appears that a limit was being set to the power of the monarchy. This comes out clearly in the traditions associated with Ohen who became paralysed after a fairly long time on the throne. He continued to hide his infirmity until the *Iyase* (his premier chief) decided to find out. This enraged the king, who had the *Iyase* beheaded; but the chiefs would not have that and they in turn stoned Ohen to death. Egbeka, the successor of Ohen, got into trouble with the *Uzama* who found him incompetent. In general, however, it seemed that during these reigns the new monarchy had become generally accepted and the Benin kingdom was gathering internal strength.

When Ogun ascended the throne and took the title Ewuare towards the end of the fifteenth century, Benin was set for expansion. Ewuare had to fight his way to the throne. Probably as a result of that, he needed to broaden the base of his authority in order to be secure. He therefore organised the town chiefs into an order, similar to that which already existed in the palace. But he kept power firmly in the hands of the monarchy by making the titles non-hereditary and completely at the behest of the king. To make succession less disputable, he instituted the *Edaiken* (Crown Prince) by which the reigning king designated his eldest son as his successor.

Ewuare then harnessed the energy of his people towards imperial conquest. He waged successful wars against some Ekiti towns, Owo and Akure. He extended Benin City itself, made wide roads and new earth-works for defence. It is probable that the vigour of external wars and civil construction combined to force the inhabitants of Benin to emigrate in order to secure some repose, though tradition relates that people left Benin City because of the stringent laws he made.

From then on till about the end of the sixteenth century, Benin arms were carried far and wide despite sporadic and persistent internal dissensions. The result was that Benin influence was felt in large parts of Yoruba country. Benin traditions claim imperial authority over large areas of Ekiti, Akure, Owo, Ondo, Ijebu and Lagos. But, with the immediate areas surrounding Benin itself not securely held during this period, it is difficult to see how the empire could be more than informal.

There can be no doubt, however, that in the late fifteenth and early sixteenth century the power of Benin was sufficiently great to compel respect in the coastal areas from about Lagos to the river Niger, and for the limit of its influence to extend to the boundary of the Idah kingdom in the north and Oyo territory in the north-west. During this period too, and indeed from the very beginning of the Eweka monarchy, the practice was maintained of sending princes to the nearby villages to reign as *Ogie* or *Ovie*.

In the seventeenth century the expansionist momentum was lost and, by one of the internal constitutional changes which has not yet been fully explained, the law made by Ewuare in favour of primogenitive succession was revoked, thus making the throne open to all princes of the blood. This probably had the effect of strengthening the power of the *Uzama* against that of the kings. But it may also be responsible for the lack of distinction of most of the seventeenth-century Benin *obas*. At the end of the century or the beginning of the eighteenth century, the rule of primogeniture was restored by Oba Ewuakpe, Akenzua I, who succeeded to the throne after Ewuakpe had to fight the town chiefs to secure his right, for in spite of Ewuakpe's law, they had tried to maintain their position by appointing a prince younger than Akenzua.[38] For the rest of the eighteenth century and the first half of the nineteenth, Benin appeared wealthy and reasonably stable, with the exception of sporadic revolts in the dependent towns.

From about the end of the fifteenth century, European merchants started to visit Benin: first the Portuguese, then the English, the Dutch and the French.[39] They engaged mainly in trade although they attempted unsuccessfully to convert the *oba* and his nobles to Christianity. Unlike the situation on the coast of modern Ghana and the Republic of Benin, the European traders in Benin did not build any permanent buildings nor did they ever acquire the kind of influence that the Portuguese acquired in the court of the *Manikongo*. Still, a continuous contact of over four hundred years before British encroachment must have had some effects, but these are still to be studied.

The political development of the ethnic groups that share contiguous territories with the Edo was undoubtedly influenced by developments in Benin. As pointed out above, Benin political influence at one time or another extended north-eastwards to the banks of the Niger and southwards to the delta region. The traditions of the Igbo, Urhobo, Isoko, Itsekiri and Ijo show traces of socio-political interactions with the Edo.

One of the offshoots of the Benin monarchy is the Itsekiri kingdom in the Niger Delta. According to traditions, it was founded towards the end of the fifteenth century by Igunwa (Ginuwa), a son of *Oba* Olua of Benin.[40] He was sent out of Benin because he was unpopular in the city. Itsekiri traditions imply that before the coming of Ginuwa the area was not inhabited, or was only inhabited by *Imale* (ghosts). Other traditions also tend to reveal that Ginuwa's settlement was on only one of the many Itsekiri settlements founded at about the same time. The others, such as Gborodo, Omadina and Ureju, were founded by Yoruba elements who probably migrated from the Ijebu area. The preponderance of

Yoruba-speaking elements as well as the fact that Yoruba was probably the dominant language, even among the Edo-speaking peoples of the region, would probably account for the emergence of the Itsekiri dialect of the Yoruba language. Ginuwa probably established hegemony over all the other settlements because he was the son of an *Oba* of Benin. He became the first ruler of the Itsekiri, taking on the title of *Olu* in memory of his father, *Oba* Olua.

Ginuwa was succeeded by two of his sons, Ijijen and Irame, under whose reigns the new kingdom expanded through the establishment of settlements near and around Ode Itsekiri, the capital. It is known that Ode Itsekiri came into contact with European traders and missionaries as early as the sixteenth century. In the seventeenth century, a prince who later became an *Olu* was educated in Portugal while another Itsekiri prince was trained to become a bishop. During the same century, the land of the Itsekiri appears to have become an enthusiastic little Christian kingdom, friendly towards Portugal from where the *Olus* were always asking for missionaries, whom they never got. Because of the economic advantages which the kingdom derived from its trade with Europe, and perhaps trusting in its friendship with the Portuguese monarchy, the *Olu* appears to have been fairly independent of Benin control at a very early date.

The evidence we have is still insufficient to enable us to trace the evolution of the Itsekiri monarchy, but it is reasonable to presume that the general pattern would not be too different from the Yoruba and Edo picture, though its special characteristics must be looked for in Itsekiri history when detailed research is done.

Other groups of people closely connected with both Benin and the Itsekiri were the Urhobo and the Isoko. Here, however, we move away from societies that had centralised political institutions to those that had none, except in so far as it was under the dominance of the Benin kingdom. Indeed, perhaps one of the best ways to see Urhobo's political development is in relationship with either of its two neighbouring monarchies, and not much research has really been done to make such a treatment possible. The only thing possible at this stage, therefore, is to trace their story of origin, and such political organisation as existed among them before the British colonial administration.

The Urhobo and Isoko peoples fall broadly into three migratory groups.[41] There are those who claim to have migrated from Benin to their present homes. Benin traditions also substantiate this claim. These people include the Iyede, Uzere, Owe, Emevo, Ozoro, Aviara, Abraka, Olomu, Ikpe and Agbon. The second group claims traditional links with the Ijo. These include Ewu, Ughienvwe and Ughelli. The third and latest arrival has been attributed to Benin through the western Igbo settlement of Aboh. The people of this third group include Evreni, Igbide, Enwe and Olomu. The details of these migrations need not detain us. Suffice to say that more work will have to be done before the routes or the periods of migration can be known with any degree of accuracy.

What emerged after the migration was a large number of clans made up of groups of villages, all of which traced their origin to a common ancestor through the male line. A village might comprise one single family or might be joined by other families with the permission of the original settlers. In that case, the village began to have wards, each being settled by various families, but with the ward of the original family being given a special recognition. Some of the clans possessed *Ovie* (a priest-king) and some even had kings. These were the people who were probably much more under the influence of Benin. Although the power of Benin is not too clear, those *Ovie* were required to go to Benin to have their titles conferred; without this they would not be recognised by their own people. The clans who had kings went to Aboh for confirmation of their own titles. But these incipient monarchical institutions never really grew to become a potent political force. There were two types of *Ovie*, one being in a real sense the head of his people, and the other being essentially a priest.

Effectively, however, the most important political unit remained the village. Here the whole population was divided into age grades (called *Otu*). The youngest, the *Otu Imitete*, was largely unorganised and had no well-defined jobs, but was expected to help in keeping village streets clean. It was made up of people between one and fifteen years of age. The second grade, the *Otu Evrawa* or *Otu Evbie*, made up of people between fifteen and thirty-five years old, formed the labour corps. They had a chairman and spokesman (the *Otota*) and could deal with the village head as well as with the next senior rank above them, the *Otu Iletu*. The *Otu Iletu* was made up of men aged between thirty-five and fifty years and constituted the executive and military class, as well as supervisors of the junior grade, the *Evrawa*. Their head, who was also the commander-in-chief, was the *Olotu-Olugbo* or *Olotu-rode*. They also had the right to try minor cases and send their verdicts as well as the fines they collected to the next higher rank, the *Ekpako*, who shared such fines out. The fourth and highest rank was the *Otu-Ekpako* whose members were usually aged fifty and above. They, being mature men, formed the village council and also exersised final judicial authority over the village. The head was usually the oldest man in the village and was called *Okpako-Ewo* or *Okaroro*. There were also titled societies to which belonged fairly rich people from all the age grades. The only authority higher than the village council was the clan, but the powers of the clan council were never formally defined and the clan meeting was usually infrequent.

Like the Urhobo and the Isoko, the Ijo also did not develop great centralised kingdoms.[42] Here also we can only talk about dispersals and settlements and not much of stirring political developments. The Ijo claim four different sources as their origin. Some of them claim to have always been in their present country. A second group, typified by the *Ikitiri*, claims to have come from Egypt through Benin. This is probably the group that also claims connections with Ife and Itsekiri. A third group claims to have migrated from Ogobiri and Opreza. The most important Ijo group, the Brass-Nembe Ijo, claims to have migrated from Benin. According to their traditions, an unnamed *Oba* of Benin sent out an expedition which was accompanied by his son without his knowledge. The son got killed, and so the soldiers were afraid to return home. But there is another tradition with Benin connection which would tend to make the Ijo the autochthones (original inhabitants) of the present Edo

51

country. According to that account, the Ijo who migrated from Benin gave the Edo their form of greeting – *do*. In their migrations, the various Ijo groups probably encountered other peoples such as the Andoni with whom they formed such new groups as the Kalabari and Ibono (Bonny).

The political organisation of the Ijo did not go beyond the village level. Each village was headed by the eldest man called *ama okosowei*, who was chairman at all village meetings. He was assisted by the spokesman called *ogulasowei* and a priest called *orukarowei*. In addition, each group of villages claiming the same ancestry was collectively called *Ibe* and had a high priest called the *Pere*. These were the people who took all the decisions on behalf of the village community, saw to defence and security and made all social laws.

The Ijo were, and still are, a water people, much renowned for their prowess and feared by their neighbours. They came early into contact with Europeans but precisely how the contact affected their organisation and migration remains to be studied. But we know for certain that as the nineteenth century opened, there was an overall decline in the Niger Delta trade with the Europeans. This brought a series of squabbles which involved all the delta peoples – Itsekiri, Urhobo, Isoko, Ijo and of course the Edo of Benin.[43]

One of the major reasons for the decline of the Niger Delta trade was that Lagos became the popular port for European commercial transactions. Moreover, the British prohibition of the overseas slave trade and the subsequent operations of the British naval squadron in the delta region brought a series of economic problems for the peoples who, by the nineteenth century, relied substantially on the coastal trade.

The Itsekiri typify the problems faced by the other delta peoples. In an attempt to maintain a viable economy the *Olu*, Akengbuwa, ran into trouble.[44] His attempt to keep the little trade on the delta in his hands brought him into open conflict with the *Oba* of Benin. At home, powerful and ambitious individuals resisted his rule, fell out with him and moved out of areas under his jurisdiction to found new settlements in parts of the delta favourable to commercial activities which they kept to themselves. The result was that by 1848 when *Olu* Akengbuwa died, what was left of the Itsekiri kingdom was hardly more than the capital city of Ode Itsekiri. The death of Akengbuwa produced more commotion in the kingdom and brought further migrations from the capital. The situation was such that for the whole of the period between 1848 and the fourth decade of the twentieth century no *Olu* could be installed. The kingdom was virtually broken up, and opposing factions of the royal family continued in fierce opposition. As there was no *Olu*, successful traders took over control in different parts of the delta and new trading centres which were also powerful political bases grew. These include Jakpa, Batere and Ebrohimi.

For the Benin kingdom, the situation was equally bad. The major problem was that of the decline of coastal trade. In addition to this, the civil wars in Yorubaland affected the economy of Benin, for much of its internal trade was through the Yoruba and Nupe countries. This economic decline affected the political status of Benin. By the mid-nineteenth century, the empire had receded to the core of the kingdom. Even at the metropolis, Benin suffered a series of troubles. The death of *Oba* Osemuede in 1851 was followed by succession disputes which sapped the energy of the empire considerably. Internal dissension continued throughout the reign of Adolo and attempts by *Oba* Ovonramwen to restore the grandeur of the monarchy and bring some stability failed.

All these developments from the early years of the nineteenth century could be seen as prelude to the subjugation of the Edo, Urhobo, Isoko, Itsekiri and Ijo by the British before the close of the century.

Notes

1 A. Obayemi, 'The Yoruba and Edo-speaking peoples and their neighbours before 1600', in J. F. Ade Ajayi and Michael Crowder (eds), *History of West Africa* (London: Longman, 1976), I, Ch. 6.

2 See for instance Samuel Johnson, *The History of the Yorubas* (Lagos: CMS, 1921), ch. I; S. O. Biobaku, *The Origin of the Yorubas* (Lugard Lectures) (Lagos: 1956).

3 See, however, Biobaku, *The Origin of the Yorubas*; and M. A. Fabunmi, *Ife Shrines* (Ile-Ife: University of Ife Press, 1970).

4 A. A. Adediran, 'A descriptive analysis of Ife palace organisation', *The African Historian*, vol. 8 (1976), pp. 3–28.

5 J. O. Abiri, *Moremi: an epic of feminine heroism* (Ibadan: 1970).

6 I. A. Akinjogbin and E. A. Ayandele, 'Yorubaland up to 1800', in O. Ikime (ed.), *Groundwork of Nigerian History* (Ibadan: Heinemann, 1980), pp. 123–24.

7 De Barros Joao, *Da Asia*, discussed in S. O. Biobaku (ed.), *Sources of Yoruba History* (Oxford: Clarendon Press, 1973); Akinjogbin and Ayandele, João 'Yorubaland up to 1800', *Groundwork*, p. 133.

8 W. R. Bascom, *The Yoruba of South Western Nigeria* (New York: 1969), p. 11.

9 A. Obayemi, 'The Yoruba and Edo-speaking people', *History of West Africa* I, pp. 208–40.

10 I. A. Akinjogbin, *Dahomey and its Neighbours 1708–1818* (London: Cambridge University Press, 1967), pp. 14–17.

11 Akinjogbin and Ayandele, 'Yorubaland up to 1800', *Groundwork*, pp. 131–32.

12 Samuel Johnson, *The History of the Yorubas*, p. 149.

13 *Ibid.*, pp. 8–9.

14 For a summary of the Oranmiyan traditions and a general account of early Oyo history, see *ibid.*, pp. 8–12, 143–54.

15 *Ibid.*, pp. 155–59.

16 S. F. Nadel, *A Black Byzantium: the kingdom of Nupe in Nigeria* (Oxford: Clarendon Press, 1942), pp. 72–76; R. C. C. Law, *The Oyo Empire c.*

1600–1836: A West African imperialism in the era of the Atlantic slave trade (Oxford: Clarendon Press, 1976), p. 38.

17 For the general account of the period, see Johnson, *The History of the Yorubas*, pp. 161–67; R. S. Smith, 'The Alafin in exile: a study of the Igboho period of Oyo history', *Journal of African History*, 6(1), 1965, pp. 61–62; S. O. Babayemi, 'Upper Ogun: a historical sketch', *African Notes*, 6(II), pp. 77–79.

18 N. Levtzion, *Muslims and Chiefs in West Africa: a study of Islam in the Middle Volta Basin in the pre-colonial period* (Oxford: Oxford University Press, 1968), p. 173.

19 I. A. Akinjogbin, 'The Expansion of Oyo and the Rise of Dahomey 1600–1800', in Ajayi and Crowder (eds), *History of West Africa*, I, pp. 385–89, 395–99.

20 Law, *The Oyo Empire*, pp. 237–41.

21 A. Oguntuyi, *A Short History of Ado-Ekiti* (Akure: 1957).

22 D. Forde, *The Yoruba-speaking peoples of Southwestern Nigeria* (London: 1951), p. 60.

23 Akinjogbin and Ayandele, 'Yorubaland up to 1800', *Groundwork*, p. 137.

24 For the account of the period see Johnson, *The History of the Yorubas*, pp. 178–87.

25 *Ibid.*, pp. 206–07.

26 Ajayi, 'The aftermath of the fall of Old Oyo', in Ajayi and Crowder (eds), *History of West Africa,* II, pp. 145–52.

27 J. A. Atanda, *The New Oyo Empire: indirect rule and change in Western Nigeria 1894–1934* (London: Longman, 1973), pp. 39–40.

28 J. F. A. Ajayi and R. S. Smith, *Yoruba Warfare in the Nineteenth Century* (London: Cambridge University Press, 1964); A. L. Mabogunje and J. Omer-Cooper, *Owu in Yoruba History* (Ibadan: Ibadan University Press, 1971).

29 J. F. A. Ajayi and S. A. Akintoye, 'Yorubaland in the 19th Century', in Ikime (ed.), *Groundwork*, pp. 285–88.

30 Ajayi and Smith, *Yoruba Warfare.*

31 Ajayi and Akintoye, 'Yorubaland in the 19th century', *Groundwork*, pp. 289–93.

32 J. U. Egharevba, *A Short History of Benin* (Ibadan: Ibadan University Press, 1968), pp. 1–6.

33 G. E. Connah, 'New light on the Benin walls', *Journal of the Historical Society of Nigeria (JHSN)*, 3(iv), 1967, pp. 593–610.

34 Egharevba, *A Short History of Benin*, p. 6.

35 Obayemi, 'The Yoruba and Edo-speaking peoples', *History of West Africa*, I, pp. 246–47.

36 For the Benin account see Egharevba, *A Short History of Benin*, pp. 6–7.

37 *Ibid.*, pp. 8–19.

38 *Ibid.*, p. 39.

39 A. F. Ryder, *Benin and the Europeans 1484–1897* (London: 1969).

40 Egharevba, *A Short History*, pp. 20–23; W. Moore, *History of Itsekiri* (Stockwell: 1936), *passim*.

41 For the socio-political organisation of the Urhobo and Isoko, see O. Ikime, *Niger Delta Rivalry* (London: 1969), pp. 6–10, 19–29; and his *The Isoko People: a historical survey* (Ibadan: 1972), pp. 1–18, 28–42.

42 On the Ijo, see E. J. Alagoa, 'Ijo origins and migrations', *Nigeria Magazine*, No. 91, Dec. 1966, pp. 279–88; and his 'The Western Ijo 1900–1950: a preliminary historical survey', *JHSN*, 4(1), Dec. 1967, pp. 70–72.

43 For the 19th-century account see Ikime, 'The Western Niger Delta and the hinterland in the 19th century', in Ikime (ed.), *Groundwork*, pp. 262–79.

44 For details, see Ikime, *Niger Delta Rivalry*, pp. 35, 39–41.

5 Pre-colonial Nigeria: north of the Niger–Benue

Toyin Falola and Akanmn Adebayo

Introduction

The region north of the rivers Niger and Benue to the fringes of the Sahara desert was the home of a large number of ethnic groups, living in different states. The most important of these were as follows: first, the Kanuri empires in the Lake Chad basin, which were the earliest of these states, second, the Hausa city-states and third, a conglomeration of different communities in and around the rivers Niger and Benue. All these states were so fluid that they shaded into each other, and they also interacted with one another on the basis of trade, diplomatic and cultural relations, and war.

All the various states owed their rise and development to similar factors which included, among others, physiographic and economic reasons, the emergence of strong dynasties and rulers and the introduction of Islam. They all occupied the savannah, an area favourable to human habitation and socio-political experimentation. The savannah encouraged both the domestication of animals and of plants, and it has been suggested that the use of iron and the practice of agriculture probably began in this region. The valleys of Lake Chad and the rivers Niger and Benue, together with their tributaries, are areas that could support a large population and encourage the development of a complex civilisation. The region also had minerals such as salt, copper, tin and iron which were worked and used to manufacture hundreds of tools for domestic and industrial use. The output of industries and agriculture were produced in large quantities and this made internal trade possible. Trade was also carried on with North Africa across the Sahara and this contributed immensely to the wealth and prosperity of the various societies. Wealth is important to all societies, ancient or modern; it creates ambition and power, both of which contribute to the emergence and downfall of states. These contacts also led to the diffusion of foreign ideas from southern Europe, North Africa and Asia. One of the most important products of this contact was the introduction and spread of Islam, which revolutionised the socio-political system and brought many aspects of Arabic culture, such as the art of literacy and Arabic names and dresses. Finally, there emerged very strong and able leaders in the various societies who were able to turn the geographical and economic advantages they enjoyed to good use by embarking on vigorous political centralisation, consolidation and expansion. The Kanuri were the first to benefit from a combination of these factors and were thus the first to build an empire, north of the Niger–Benue.

The Kanuri empires of Kanem and Borno

In the ninth century AD, the Kanuri succeeded in imposing their authority on the politically disunited and scattered communities of the Lake Chad basin. The *girgam* – Kanuri's oral traditions – credit this achievement to Say'f b. Dhi Yazan (or simply Saif) who established the Sefawa dynasty, the longest-lived in Africa. Saif's political experimentation began in Kanem, east of the Chad. Using Kanem as a base, Saif gradually integrated a number of other smaller communities, notably Tomagra, Tubu, Kayi, Ngalaga and Kaguwa. Saif became the overall leader of all these integrated places, thus laying the foundation of a state.

From the ninth to the eleventh centuries, Saif's successors (all now bore the title *Mai*) continued with the programmes of political centralisation and consolidation. The *Mais* annexed to Kanem many of the neighbouring nomadic and semi-nomadic groups. In the second half of the tenth century, the *Mais* embarked upon the integration of a number of city-states, notably those of the So and other settled populations. By the eleventh century the Sefawa had succeeded in incorporating many scattered communities into the Kanem empire, and they also provided the necessary leadership.

There were at least three reasons why the Sefawa were able to establish an empire and a dynasty. Firstly, the Sefawa leaders were great warriors. Military ability was an important factor in welding together diverse groups and in imposing a recognised authority. Secondly, the Sefawa made use of religion, both indigenous and Islamic, to reinforce their authority. The *Mais* were sacred and they also became the custodians of sacred objects which the Kanuri and others associated with their prosperity. An Arab writer, al-Muhallabi, wrote in about 985 that the Kanuri:

> exalt and worship him [i.e., the *Mai*] instead of God. They imagine that he does not eat for his food is introduced into the compound secretly, no one knowing whence it is brought. Should one of his subjects happen to meet the camel carrying his provisions he is killed instantly on the spot. . . . Their religion is king-worship, believing that it is they who bring life and death, sickness and health.[1]

Lastly, the Sefawa deliberately inter-married with the women in the conquered ares in order to minimise feuds and rebellions. A number of the products of such marriages became members of the ruling dynasty.

A significant development in the post-eleventh-century era was the acceptance of Islam by the ruling dynasty.[2] *Mai* Hume was the first Muslim ruler and his devoutness was not in doubt. He employed a learned Mallam, the privileged Muhammad Ibn Mani. He also undertook the pilgrimage to Mecca, although he did not return. Hume's pilgrimage reveals two significant developments in the history of the Kanem empire. In the first place, it shows that the empire had become politically stable enough to survive even in the absence of its key executives. Secondly, it shows that strong links had already been established with North Africa and the Middle East.

The empire continued to grow until it reached its zenith during the career of Dunama II (1221–1259), who excelled all previous rulers in imperial ambition and Islamic piety. The basis of his power was the army, which he enlarged and improved both in mobility and striking capacity.[3] Dunama employed this strong army to expand the empire's influence and territory. His conquest of Fezzan further strengthened trade relations with North Africa while his wars to the east established Kanem's influence to as far as the east of the Upper Nile. Kanem's neighbours, notably the Hausa and Bulala, were also subdued. These various wars brought more territories, people and tribute, and made possible the peaceful exchange of goods over a wider region.

Dunama also concentrated on the purification and spread of Islam. He converted many non-Muslims, including the rulers, in the conquered territories, enforced the use of the *Maliki* law, went on pilgrimage and built a hostel in Cairo for students and pilgrims. In his over-zealousness, Dunama II tried to destroy part of Kanuri religion by opening the *múné* ('the ark of convenant'), 'whose nature was known only to God most high'. The *múné* was believed to contain the spirit-force of victory in war and success in all undertakings, and it was forbidden for anybody, no matter how highly placed, to open it. As Sir Richmond Palmer pointed out, 'The factor regarded as essential to preserve the efficacy of the Mune and similar *sacra* . . . is "covering" '.[4]

The sacrilegious act of opening the *múné* was a political miscalculation and a diplomatic blunder.[5] It set Kanem on a path of disintegration as loyalists of the indigenous religion correctly interpreted it as an open invitation to rebellion as well as a deliberate act of provocation and alienation. Dunama unwittingly failed to realise that the survival of the empire depended very much on the support of his subjects whose religious faiths should be secondary to him as long as they accepted his leadership. The anti-Islam members of the ruling dynasty, the nobility, commoners and those in the non-metropolitan area, particularly the Bulala, found an excuse to unite against Dunama. Socio-political crises began to brew in the empire and Dunama only just managed to cope with the situation until his death in 1259.

The post-Dunama era was marked by upheavals, rebellions and a struggle for power which brought the decline of the first Kanuri empire. Perhaps the most fatal of the series of upheavals was the struggle for power within the Sefawa dynasty, mainly between the descendants and followers of two previous rulers, *Mai* Dawud b. Nikalle and *Mai* Idris. This struggle was eventually won by the Idrisids in the 1460s but considerable damage had been done to the stability of the political system. The nobles also fought against the *Mais* and against themselves in their bid to increase their wealth and power. In the process, two provincial governors, the *Kaigama* and *Yerima*, encouraged rebellions in their provinces and became independent of the *Mai*.

The tributaries of Kanem were able to declare their independence because the hold on them had become very loose and the empire's army had become a shadow of its former self. Fezzan was lost and the route to North Africa became unsafe, thus bringing a decline to the trans-Saharan trade. The So engaged the Kanuri from 1342 to 1352, during which four years successive *Mais* were killed. The Bulala also launched military offensives, killing two *Mais* and gaining control of Kanem, the core of the empire.

In 1388, the Sefawa left Njimi, the capital, together with hundreds of Kanuri and migrated westward to Kaga in the region of Borno. But their problems were yet to end. For almost a century, the Kanuri lived an insecure, nomadic life. Their enemies, the So, Bulala, Hausa and, in the fifteenth century, nomadic Arabs, continued to invade them. The crises among members of the dynasty and the nobility continued. Two *Mais* were assassinated by the *Kaigama* in the last years of the fourteenth century while nine *Mais* ruled in quick succession in the first half of the fifteenth century. Nevertheless, the empire never completely fell and the weak *Mais* continued to govern the Kanuri.

In 1470, the *Mai* who was to build the second empire at Borno emerged. This was the famous 'Ali Ghaji who reigned till 1506. As a first step, 'Ali Ghaji reasserted the *Mai*'s authority over all other dignitaries. Through the use of diplomacy, force and wealth 'Ali Ghaji reduced the power of the councillors, thus minimising power rivalries and conflicts among the élite.

The second step which he took was to put an end to the nomadic and semi-nomadic tendencies of the Kanuri by building a new capital at Birni Ngazargamu.[6] The capital became a safe place for people to live in as well as a strong military base for defence and offence. This capital attracted many people and traders.

Finally, 'Ali Ghaji made use of Islam to consolidate his bureaucracy and strengthen ties with North Africa. He never used force to spread Islam but tried to abide by Islamic preachings, and employed Islamic advisers and the *shari'a* in the administration of justice.

All these measures brought the Kanuri together once again. They were now willing to defend themselves. The Kanuri army became a match for those of the So, Bulala, Hausa and Jukun. 'Ali Ghaji extended his authority over the whole of the Borno region which became the core of the empire, subdued Borno's frontiers and undertook a military thrust in the desert, conquering Tibesti, thus securing a safe route to North Africa.

By the time 'Ali Ghaji died in 1503, the second Kanuri empire had emerged. His successors continued to expand the empire further. In 1572, *Mai* Idris Alooma, the greatest ruler of the second empire, came to the throne and ruled till 1603 during which time Borno reached its apogee. Alooma was a devout Muslim, a gifted administrator, an able leader and a skilful diplomat. Though he came to the throne when the economy was bad and when there were hostilities from the So, Ngizim, Bulala and Hausa, Alooma not only solved these problems but also contributed immensely to the empire's territorial expansion, diplomatic relations and prosperity.

He built an effective and efficient military machine. An able warrior himself, he appointed dedicated commanders to man the various units of the army. The army was also considerably improved by importing firearms from North Africa and Arab and Turkish soldiers to give training and advice on how to use them.

With a strong army, Alooma was able to undertake a vigorous

imperial policy.[7] All pockets of resistance emanating from the So, Maghi and Mandara were suppressed. The Bulala were checked, and Kanem, their major centre, was partitioned into two, the bigger half falling under Borno's control. The Hausa and Tuareg were also subdued, thus further expanding the tributaries.

Alooma was also famous as an Islamic leader; indeed, J. S. Trimingham concludes that he 'is more significant from the Islamic viewpoint than as a genuine emperor'[8] and his chronicler, the famous Ibn Fartuwa, eulogised his devotion by describing him as 'the learned, just, courageous and pious Commander of the Faithful'.[9] Alooma's devotion as a Muslim cannot be doubted; he carried out all the five pillars of Islam to the the letter. He encouraged others to take to Islam by building more schools, mosques and a hostel for Bornoan pilgrims and students in Mecca. He also converted members of the ruling dynasty and many great men. Finally, he integrated many aspects of Islamic practices into his bureaucracy. For instance, he substituted the *Shari'a* for *ada* (customary law) and he divorced the judiciary from the executive by setting *qadi's* courts with wide powers.

Alooma's death in 1603 has sometimes been seen as the beginning of the end of Borno empire. Trimingham, for instance, concluded, *inter alia*:

> Although we know so little about them none of his successors seem to have had his ability, and the tendency of the following centuries was towards stagnancy and decline.[10]

However, the available evidence does not support Trimingham's assertion.[11] Borno remained strong till the first half of the eighteenth century. It is true that no new areas were conquered but the empire consolidated all its gains, retained its dominance in the Lake Chad basin and the hold on the tributaries, and successfully resisted the Kona, Agades, Tuaregs and Jukun. The political system continued to work, trade still flourished, Islam and education thrived and contacts with North Africa remained unbroken.

The career of 'Ali b. Dunama (c. 1750–1791) really marked the beginning of Borno's decline as a power. From Dunama, it would appear that the *Mais'* leisurely living and elaborate court rituals constituted obstacles to good government. It allowed the nobility to resume their competition for power, fiefs and wealth, and this tended to erode the *Mais'* power and control over the citizens. The *Mais* were also unable to solve the economic problems of famine, decline in the trans-Saharan trade and massive population movements to fertile areas. The population movements and the demographic changes that accompanied them brought, in turn, political crises of a great magnitude. The movements into the fertile areas on the shores of the Chad, Fombina, the plains of Kilba and the slopes of the Mandara hills led to tensions among the Fulani, Shuwa Arabs and the Kanembu. These areas and many others became centres of resistance to the Sefawa authority. Between 1747 and 1794, Bagirmi, the Mandara, Tuaregs, Beddo, Ngizim and Agades secured their independence of the empire. Early in the nineteenth century, the Fulani in the southern part of the empire joined in the jihad against Borno. The jihad eventually brought the Sefawa dynasty to an inglorious end and its replacement by the al-Kanemi dynasty.

The Kanuri empires, the first at Kanem and the second at Borno, survived for almost ten centuries because of a number of factors. Firstly, the Sefawa provided a strong leadership in men such as Saif, Dunama II, 'Ali Ghaji and Idris Alooma. Secondly, the empire encountered only small-scale, uncoordinated resistance from its neighbours, many of which were weaker communities. Lastly, the empire enjoyed a workable and dynamic political system. By the seventeenth century, the structure of Kanuri administration had become clear. It was, however, never static and it owed its origin and changes to at least four sources. In the first place, the Kanuri absorbed the socio-political features of the pre-dynastic (i.e. pre-ninth-century) inhabitants. There is evidence to suggest that the institution of the sacred monarch and the paraphernalia of office in the Lake Chad region were older than the Sefawa dynasty. Secondly, the customs of the Kanuri became part of the political system of the empire. Thirdly, new reforms were introduced whenever there were major socio-political problems. Finally, the introduction of Islam brought about many notable changes.

The political organisation operated at two levels, central and provincial. The *Mai* towered above everybody else in the empire. He was sacrosanct. He was also the personification of the empire, and the well-being of his subjects was identified with his state of health. Besides a few councillors who held their titles as hereditary rights, the *Mai* appointed court and state officials and assigned responsibilities to them. All important activities of state culminated in his palace.

However, like other sacred monarchs in other Nigerian states, the *Mai* was not an autocrat. He had to take cognizance of the existence of two bodies of title holders. The first was the council of state, made up of twelve men selected from the nobility and great men of servile origin. These twelve dignitaries, together with the *Mai*, formed the supreme ruling body. It was very unlikely for a *Mai* to take any decision without consulting them. The second body comprised three women title holders: the *Gumsu*(*Mai*'s first wife), the *Magara* (*Mai*'s senior sister) and the *Magira* (the Queen Mother). These three women performed important activities in the palace and they trained the princes. They exercised great influence in the politics of the empire and they also wielded wide powers during an interregnum or when there was a weak *Mai* on the throne.

The provinces were placed under four governors chosen from among the twelve councillors. The *Galadima* was in charge of the west, the *Kaigama* the south, the *Yerima* the north and the *Mestrema* the east. These governors defended their areas against attack, prevented them from secession, mobilised their citizens for war and saw to the collection of taxes. The governors, except for the *Galadima*, did not, however, live in the provinces and had to appoint representatives known as the *Chima Gana* to perform their functions. The day-to-day administration of the provincial villages and towns was left in the hands of their hereditary rulers, an arrangement which made it possible to govern indirectly and reduce instability.

The organisation of the army and the imperial treasury was administered by both the central and provincial authorities. The army had two divisions, each under twelve commanders (the *Kacella*). All the *Kacella* were in turn placed under an overall commander, the *Kaigama*. The first division was the 'home front' based in the capital and made up of professional warriors. The second was the 'bush division' comprising able-bodied males mobilised by the governors.

The revenues of the state came principally from tolls and dues collected from traders, tributes from vassal states, presents, spoils of war, profits of justice, harvests from slave villages and taxes. Finally the economic foundations of the empire rested firmly on a sound agriculture, virile industries and a well-developed exchange system.

Borno under the al-Kanemi dynasty

The jihad in Hausaland spread to Borno at a time when the Sefawa were not strong enough to withstand a strong military opposition. A number of Fulani warriors obtained flags from dan Fodio, signifying their intention to spread the jihad. Three of these men, Ardo Lerlima, Gwoni Mukhtar and Ibrahim Zaki, became very successful and they carved out four emirates in the west of Borno (Gombe, Missan, Hadejia and Katagum). The capital of Borno was attacked in 1808 and the Sefawa had to flee to Kanem. A number of Borno's vassal states seized the opportunity to declare their independence (e.g., Zinder) while Wadai, an emergent state in this region, also attacked Kanem and Bagirmi.

Realising the danger which the various wars posed to Borno's survival, *Mai* Ahmad solicited the support of al-Kanemi, a distinguished warrior-cum-scholar living at Ngala, south of Lake Chad. Al-Kanemi had little or no sympathy for the Fulani. Indeed, he believed that the attack on Borno was unnecessary since it was not a pagan state. To him, the attack was only political; and as he later told Bello, dan Fodio's son:

> Tell us therefore why you are fighting us and enslaving our free men. If you say, 'We have done that to you because of your heathenism', then I say, 'We are innocent of heathenism and it is far from our court-yard'. If the performance of prayer, the giving of alms, knowledge of the unity of God, fasting [in] Ramadan and the building of mosques is heathenism what is Islam then? These buildings in which you have said the Friday prayer, are they churches, or synagogues or fine temples? If they were not for Muslim rites, then why did you perform the prayer in them when you captured the capital? This is nothing but sheer contradiction!
>
> Among your greatest arguments for associating believers· in general with heathenism is the practice of the emirs riding to some places for the purpose of offering sacrifices . . . . But those who are guilty of it are not to be branded as heathens since not one of them claims that it is efficacious or intends by his act to associate other gods with God . . . . There is Damietta, a great town among the Muslim towns between Egypt and Syria, a place of learning and Islam; in it

there is a tree to which the common people go as did the Ajam [non-Arabs]. Nevertheless, none of the 'Ulama [learned men] rose to eight them and none attributed heathenism to them.[12]

In another letter, he told the Fulani that no society could comprise only Muslims; rather there are always four groups, made up of unbelievers, apostates, nominal Muslims and devout ones.

Al-Kanemi's education was not his only qualification. Perhaps of more importance was his military ability. He had once defeated a small Fulani army at a time when it was believed they were invulnerable. He also had extensive connections with rulers and peoples in Kanem, Fezzan, Egypt and Arabia which were great assets in securing military and diplomatic assistance and in obtaining weapons.

Al-Kanemi's assistance saved Borno. In 1809, he recaptured Ngazargamu and dispersed the Fulani. This was, no doubt, a considerable achievement which traditions credit to his magical power and which H. Barth, the well-known European traveller, attributed to his 'inspiring fanaticism . . . the courage and valour of his Kanembu spearmen'.[13] For his success, the *Mai* rewarded him with cattle, money and slaves, and he returned to his base at Ngala.

The Sefawa again became the rulers of Borno. This was, however, not to last because the Fulani again attacked and sacked the capital in 1811, driving away the Sefawa to Birni Kafela which became their new home and capital. *Mai* Dunama, who was now on the throne, was too weak to deal with the Fulani and he was forced to call on al-Kanemi for help. Al-Kanemi now exploited the crisis by demanding land and fiefs in Ngurno (where the Kanembu inhabited) before he could render any assistance. The helpless *Mai* Dunama conceded, promising him as much as half the total revenues of all reconquered places. Al-Kanemi agreed once again and he drove out the Fulani, who never succeeded in any of their subsequent moves to conquer Borno.

The leadership which al-Kanemi provided was the major factor for the failure of the jihadists in Borno. Consequently, al-Kanemi became an acknowledged leader and hero. He was now the overall military commander and his charismatic leadership attracted more and more followers to him.

Instead of returning to Kanem, al-Kanemi decided to stay in Borno and he built a cantonment at Ngorno. In 1814, Ngurno was renamed Kukawa and it became the new capital of the empire. Birni Kafela was, however, still inhabited by the *Mai* but it was now more of a ceremonial capital while Kukawa became the real administrative and military centre. Al-Kanemi was now a man of great influence, and many people saw him as their leader. At Kukawa, his followers and soldiers increased and his fief brought substantial wealth in the form of tax.

Al-Kanemi became not only Borno's military commander but the religious leader and the chief justice of his followers. He rejected all titles, however, and was simply referred to as Shehu. A dual leadership was thus inevitably created in Borno. Al-Kanemi became the power behind the throne and the most effective authority in the empire. In 1813 he deposed *Mai* Ngilemma, who had earlier driven out *Mai* Dunama, and re-installed

Fig. 5.1 The Mai *of Borno holding court in 1821. Real political power had by this time passed to al-Kanemi.*

the latter. Al-Kanemi's power and influence brought more than half of Borno under his influence. He built a strong body of scholars and advisers drawn from his friends and relatives among the Shuwa Arabs, Kanembu and Fezzani. This body rapidly became Borno's leading élite in the army and administration. He derived revenues from tributes to the vassal settlements holding allegiance to him.

Al-Kanemi operated at Kukawa as if he was the legitimate head of Borno. He made efforts to expand the empire by conquering Zinder and Kanem and by regaining old vassals in the north-west, notably

Damagasam and Tesawa. But he met with little success. He was forced to recognise Fulani authority in the west and that of the Tuareg in the north-west. What remained of Borno enjoyed peace, and trade flourished once again after the disturbances of the first decade of the century. Borno's trade with Hausaland resumed in 1826 and the trade with North Africa, especially with Fezzan, also resumed in the 1830s.

Finally, al-Kanemi promoted the spread of Islam. Within the walls of Kukawa, Islam was successfully transformed into a state religion. Like the *emirs* of the Sokoto caliphate, he endeavoured to discourage prostitution, corruption, drunkenness, gambling and inefficiency among administrators. He promoted Islamic education and tried to reorganise the collection of revenues according to Islamic principles. The administration of justice followed the *shari'a*. Al-Kanemi supervised the courts and insisted on the correct interpretation of Islamic laws.

Al-Kanemi's contributions were without doubt immense. His fame, greatness and popularity were also recognised by many of his contemporaries. Louis Brenner, a renowned scholar of Borno history, describes him thus:

Al-Kanemi was a man of exceptional political insight and intense religious devotion. He was also a man of passion. He engaged his battles with ferocity, whether these conflicts were military, political, or intellectual .... Al-Kanemi captivated those around him. Not only was he ferocious in battle, brilliant in debate, astute in politics, fervent in religious devotion, and encompassing with his love, but his mere presence was commanding .... Perhaps above all else al-Kanemi possessed the strong determination to fulfil the fate which he felt God has assigned to him.[14]

The fame of al-Kanemi and his contributions to Borno undermined the power, and threatened the existence, of the Sefawa. The Sefawa hardly anticipated this development. Thus, *Mai* Dunama, in collaboration with Kanuri nobility, began to scheme for the liquidation of al-Kanemi. In 1814 and 1817 he tried to expel al-Kanemi but the plans failed and the *Mai* retained his title at the mercy of al-Kanemi. In fact, al-Kanemi could have capitalised on the two futile rebellions to terminate the Sefawa dynasty. Though he did not succeed in this, the *Mais* became puppet kings, deprived of all power. In 1820, Dunama again attempted to gain control by conspiring with Bagirmi against al-Kanemi. The plan failed, Dunama lost his life and al-Kanemi presided at the installation of a new *Mai*, thus signifying a total shift of political power.

In 1837, al-Kanemi died and his son Umar succeeded him as the ruler of Kukawa. *Mai* Ahmad also died and was succeeded by *Mai* Ibrahim. These two rulers saw themselves as political opponents; the *Mai* no longer wanted al-Kanemi and his group, while Umar was too ambitious to adopt his father's quiet and subtle diplomacy in dealing with the *Mai*. Umar took measures to raise himself far above the *Mai* and to make himself the leading power in the empire. The struggle for power between both of them led to an open war in 1846, and Umar's success put an end to the one-thousand-year-old Sefawa dynasty and the decimation of its leading members.

A new dynasty, the al-Kanemi or Shehu dynasty, now governed Borno. Umar adopted the title of Shehu but retained all other titles in the Sefawa dynasty for his officials. His sister was now the royal senior wife and his mother the 'Queen Mother'. He retained the council of six (the *nokena*) and the palace officials bore ancient Borno titles. All other titles were given to Umar's friends and relatives. Like the *Mai*, Umar lived a life of ritual seclusion in the palace. He delegated wide authority to the *Waziri*, al-hajj Bashir, his principal adviser and prime minister. Islam remained as important; officers of state were expected to be Muslims and the *shari'a* was still used as the basis of law. On the whole, the Shehu did not introduce radical changes to the political system; no new order nor an Islamic state emerged. There were, however, two differences. In the first place, the empire became more centralised than before. Secondly, a new set of rulers came into being. Most of them were drawn from the Shehu's friends, slaves, family and followers. These men were new to Borno politics and a number of them were inexperienced. Consequently, there were some cases of resistance by the governed, and a number of these new rulers were alleged to have displayed high-handedness in administration and greed in the collection of levies.

From 1884 onwards, the empire entered upon a gradual path of decline. A number of factors were responsible for this . Firstly, there were internal disputes within the al-Kanemi dynasty. Umar was weak, indecisive and slow. He delegated much power to slaves and courtiers who combined to circumscribe his power and who also weakened the empire by their incessant and vicious power conflicts. A period of *malaise* set in with the result that Borno's external power deteriorated to a considerable extent. Secondly, Borno experienced grave economic difficulties arising from plague, famine and dwindling revenues. Thirdly and most importantly, the greatest threat to the empire came when the ambitious state of Wadai and the military adventurer, Rabih b. Fadlallah, began the struggles to control the Lake Chad basin and the trans-Saharan trade. Wadai was the first to gain an upper hand and by 1890 had become the strongest power in this region. Wadai did not, however, enjoy its dominance for long because of the military exploits of Rabih from the Sudan. In 1893, he conquered Wadai, Bagirmi and Borno and set up an empire with its capital at Dikwa, south-east of the Chad. Like Wadai, Rabih could not consolidate his gains because of the advancing imperialist armies of Britain, Germany and France. Rabih's attempt to defend his empire failed when he was killed by the French in 1900, an event followed by the European partition of the Lake Chad region.

The Hausa states

The western part of the Central Sudan is the home of a fairly large number of people of distinct ethnic groupings. The most numerous of these, and the one which occupies the greater part of the territory, is the Hausa. Others are the Ngizim, the Manga, the Buduma, the Margi, the

Kotoko and the Bolewa. This territory, which lies historically between the great empires of Kanem–Borno to the east and the Songhai to the west, is well drained by rivers which flow either south-westwards from the Azben and the Jos plateau to the Niger, or north-eastwards fromthe Bauchi highlands to the Chad, or south-eastward from the Azben, also to the Chad. The region is believed to have supported a parkland flora merging into denser vegetation in the south-west during the palaeolithic period. However, in about 7000 BP (Before Present), the whole of the Central Sudan began to witness dramatic climatic changes. This subsequently affected the conditions of human life in the area. According to Smith:

> the great Chad began to dry up ... the dense vegetation of the southern edge of (the) region retreated to leave in its place the Guinea savanna ... the northern half ... suffered extreme desiccation to produce a desert of sand dunes stretching from near Agades eastwards into the Jurab depression which had once been the deepest part of the Mega–Chad.[15]

One important effect of this desiccation was the concentration of population in the southern part of the Central Sudan as a result of the migration of the Sahara-dwellers in a southward direction. In fact, the northern part was so dry that the roughly triangular stretch of country, the Azben–Borku–Chad, was practically uninhabitable. The movement of people away from this area of declining rainfall to the more humid lands of the Chad basin and the well-watered landscape between the Chad and the great bend of the Niger represents the migration preserved in the traditions of origin of the people of the western and eastern-central Sudan.

The Hausa version of this legend of origin, as preserved in the Daura Chronicle, tells of

> a stranger coming to (Daura) and asking an old woman for water for his animal, which was like a horse and yet was not a horse. Though warned that no water could be drawn from the well except on Fridays because of the presence there of a snake called 'Sarki', he was not afraid to let down a bucket. At once the snake sprang up out of the well to kill the stranger, who quickly cut off its head – and it was like the head of a horse. The queen was so pleased at the news that she sent for this hero intending to give him half her town. But the stranger said that he wished to marry her, and she consented. Their son, Bawo, begat the first rulers of the seven Hausa states who were the origins of the Hausa race.[16]

Since this legend has become popular among historians in explaining the origin of the Hausa states, it is necessary here to dwell upon it in more detail. This stranger, Abuyazidu (or Bayajida), regarded as the son of the king of Baghdad, had a quarrel with his father, left Baghdad, crossed the desert and settled temporarily in Borno. At Borno he married the *Mai's* daughter. But when he discovered the *Mai's* plan to kill him, Bayajida fled west to Daura, stopping briefly at Biram–Gataba for his Borno wife to deliver, and at Gaya to collect a knife being made for him by a blacksmith. Bawo, the fruit of Bayajida's marriage to the queen of Daura, gave birth to six children. These were Bagauda, who became the king of Kano; Kazuru, the king of Daura; Duma, king of Gobir; Kumayo, king of Katsina; Zamagari, king of Rano; and Guguma, king of Zaria. Bayajida's son, Biram, born by his Borno wife, became king of the seventh Hausa state, Garim Gabas (or Gabas ta Biram).

It is obvious from the content of this tradition that this migration and the subsequent events do not actually relate the origin of the Hausa people themselves, or even the inauguration of the states. All that they relate is the foundation of the ruling dynasties; and this suggests that there were already people in these towns before the arrival of the Bayajida groups. It is not possible to give the exact date of the arrival of the first Bayajida group. But if the claim of the chronicle that Bagauda, the first dynastic king of Kano, came to power in about AD999 is true, then the history of the Hausa people and states is a very ancient one indeed. In fact, we can hazard the suggestion that Borno and the Hausa states developed in parallel, as evidenced by the effects of the desiccation.

The movement of the northerners to the south in the Central Sudan also raises the question of what happened to the people originally living in the south. The continuous arrival of people resulted in conflicts which produced the Kanuri people, while in the western part of the Chad no such conflict was recorded in the traditions. An explanation for the lack of conflict in the west has been put forward. It is suggested that the area of Hausaland was very sparsely populated before the immigration of the northerners, and the Chadic-language-speaking peoples therefore did not precipitate any substantial displacement of people by their coming. The immigrants settled among the indigenous population, absorbing the latter by their large number. This settlement was dated between the last millennium BC and the first millennium AD.[17]

Origin of the Hausa people and states

There are various postulations on the origin of the Hausa people. Those by M. G. Smith, S. J. Hogben, A. H. Kirk-Greene and H. A. S. Johnston tend to suggest that the Hausa people were formed at the beginning of the second millennium AD by a mixture of Berber immigrants from the Sahara with a Negro population of the savannah.[18] However, there is no evidence for any Berber (Tuareg) penetration into the western Central Sudan before the latter part of the fifteenth century. Moreover, linguistic evidence has not indicated that the Hausa language is a mixture of the Tamesheg and Sudanic elements developing less than a millennium ago. In any case, the above postulate represents a variation of the discredited Hamitic hypothesis.

The Hausa people appear to have existed from time immemorial and to have occupied this zone for a very long time. There is also no evidence of formation of any new people. The people had been Hausa before their southward migration, a migration which was internal rather than international.

Communities of Hausa-speaking peoples were established probably early in the first millennium AD. However, by the beginning of the present millennium state-like political organisations among the people began to appear. Hausaland, as defined in this chapter, covers the area bounded by a line running from Azben southwards as far as the Jos plateau, from there westwards to the Kaduna River, and from there to Azben through the valley of Gulbin–Kebbi. These frontiers were occasionally adjusted by the intrusion of other people and empires, like the Tuareg, the Kanuri, the Fulani and Songhai. Fluctuation in frontiers has also been occasioned by the formation of Hausa colonies in the territories of the Kambari, Acipawa, Dakarkari, Gwari and Kamuku, though the frontiers have been largely maintained up to the present.

In this region there emerged not a single great centralised state, but various centres of political organisations of varying sizes and power. The emergence spanned a long period, and passed through many stages. At first, there developed centres of power, the capitals of the states of the future, called *birane*. The *birane* (singular, *birni*) concept is so important in this discussion that we can talk, as Smith has done, of the pre-*birni* and the *birane* eras.

In the pre-*birni* era, an era that came immediately after the desiccation, there emerged small agricultural communities known as *unguwoyi* (singular, *unguwa*). These were nucleated settlements which consisted of family groups who organised themselves for crop production. Overall leadership in these communities was vested in a ruler called the *sarki*, whose main duty was the maintenance of communal discipline, transcending the family group. In most cases, he was the *sarkin noma*, the king of farming, whose duty was to organise agriculture. Authority also resided in the family heads, the *maigida*, who maintained discipline within his family and organised farming. In practice, the *maigida* had more power than the *sarkin noma*. This is because allegiance of members of a community was primarily to the head of the family.

Hausa society even at this pre-*birni* era did not consist of nucleated hamlets alone. Given the right conditions, larger settlements soon started to appear where distantly related family groups and strangers who pursued non-agricultural occupations all congregated. This gave rise to the emergence of the *gari*, town. The growth of the towns seems to have been aided by the introduction of the use of iron, and by the religious factor of contiguous communities belonging to the same cult. Within these *gururuwa* there developed established political authority vested in the *sarkin gari*. His authority, however, did not extend beyond the boundaries of the farmlands of the *gari*. We can say, therefore, that the pre-*birni* era was characterised by 'agricultural settlements of varying sizes, some with markets and the workshops of artisans and some without, but all mutually independent of each other in the political sense'.[19]

The *birane* era was born out of a revolution that substituted the political system based on kinship relations with one based on control of territory. The revolution also substituted the numerous small and independent communities by fewer, larger (though still independent) political aggregates with centralised institutions. The *birane* became large capital cities, and they became cosmopolitan in character as a result of the addition of many more immigrants.

Among the conditions that favoured the rise of these *birane* in Hausaland were geographical location, trade and strategic factors. It can be assumed that large urban populations developed where the necessary agricultural and industrial goods were available. For instance, Birnin-Kano was located in the fertile region where, apart from food, industrial raw materials like cotton and iron-stone were available. Birnin-Kano also lay on the great convergence of major trade routes. Strategic factors relate to the defensibility of the *birni* from attack. Each of the *birane* was fortified, always a walled city. The walls were strong, and they were built to encircle the *birni* as well as the farmlands around it. This meant protection against external attack and made possible survival in a period of protracted siege.

It is essential at this stage to differentiate between the *gururuwa* of the pre-*birni* era and the *birane* of the latter period. First, the *birni* was cosmopolitan, providing shelter for people of different ethnic origin and who lacked kinship relations with each other, while the *gari* was peopled by members of the same, or closely related families. Second, while the *gururuwa* might or might not be walled, the *birane* were of necessity walled cities. Third, the *birni* was the seat of a new type of government not based on kinship relations as is observable in the *gari*.

What were the essential features of this new government? First, there was the *sarki* who was the overall authority in the city as well as in the countryside. He was no longer the *sarkin birni*; he had become the *sarkin kasa*, king of the country. The 'country' as used here refers to the territory under the *sarki*'s authority which comprised the *birni*, the farmlands and the surrounding parcel of land where there were many *gururuwa* and *unguwoyi*. The *sarki* was assisted by a wide range of specialised officials. These officials and their titles have been preserved in the local government of the Hausa right up to the present day. There were the *magajin gari*, a general administrator who was regarded as heir apparent; the *sarkin kasuwa*, the king of the market; the *sarkin kofa*, the gate keeper; the *sarkin turawa*, chief of the white (Arab) group; and a host of others which we shall soon consider.

This new form of government substantially reorganised the Hausa society. It succeeded in giving birth to new territorial groupings in the form of 'states', and in them, new classes also emerged. In the pre-*birni* era, there was no permanent class distinction; there was o1t1ntnerentiation by age. In the new states, however, a sharp distinction was drawn between the rulers and the ruled, between the *masu sarauta* or fief-holders and the *talakawa*, those who held no official position. It was quite difficult for the *talakawa* to move vertically into the fief-holding class, except when rewarded for outstanding military service. Even then, he could only be *barde*, cavalry man, or *jarumi*, brave man, titles with very little significance. With the development of the *sarki's* court, there emerged a class of palace officials, the *fadawa*, and palace slaves recruited from the *talakawa*.

From the foregoing discussion, it is obvious that the establishment of the Hausa states was a lengthy process. It was also complicated, as some claims in the existing body of tradition do not seen to fit. For instance, the story of the establishment of the dynasties as contained in the Daura tradition of *Hausa Bakwai* is of very little significance, though it is most popular. As we have already pointed out, the Bayajida immigrants might well be founders of some of the dynasties in Hausaland; but the process of state formation had been set in motion before their supposed arrival.

We shall now examine the early history of some of the major states. It is necessary to note that it is difficult to give exact dates of events that preceded the fifteenth century in these states. This is mainly because the traditions often attribute very long reigns to early rulers. For instance, Daura quotes 150 years for Bayajida, 90 years for Bawo, and 110 for Gazaura. Some king-lists, like those of Zazzau, do not give regnal years for the first seventeen rulers.[20] The errors the historian can make through using these traditions are compounded by the lack of archaeological information on the *birni*-type sites in Hausaland. One therefore cannot determine precisely the antiquity of the states and dynasties.

Daura

Bayajida, the mythical hero of the snake-killing episode, arrived in Daura and met (probably) Shawata, the eighth queen who reigned in Daura. Daura itself was founded by a queen by that name who was the ninth in her line. Before this founding, the earlier queens had resided in a *birni* called Tsofon Birni, about 9 kilometres north of modern Daura. It is tempting to accept the Tuareg meaning of Daura – blacksmith – because of the importance of iron at this age of Daura history. It is also tempting to accept that the word and title *sarki*, evolved in Daura from *Sare-Kia*, the snake-slayer. Nevertheless, it is indisputable that Daura kept custody of the ancient well mentioned in the legend beside which has been inscribed the following words:

> This is the well at which, according to ancient legend, Bayajida, son of the King of Baghdad, slew the fetish snake known as Sarki and afterwards married the reigning Queen of Daura.[21]

Very little can be said about Daura before Usman dan Fodio. There were king-lists which we can only accept with caution since some of them ascribe to some rulers reigns of over one hundred and even two hundred years. It seems plausible, however, to accept the Tuareg story that the people of Daura came under the authority of Kanem. It was also conquered by Gobir at the height of the latter's power.

The story of the jihad and the parts played by flag-bearers is the subject of another chapter in this book. What is of relevance here is that in the nineteenth century Daura became an emirate in the Fulani Caliphate being created by the jihadists. The revolt in Daura was sparked off by Malam Ishaku, who had once been a herdsman to the king of Daura. In July 1805, and with the aid of Dan Tunku and Malam Musa from Zaria, Ishaku attacked Daura; and *Sarkin* Gwari Abdu presented a bold front.

Fig. 5.2   The Gobirau minaret in Katsina

But he, Abdu, was not strong enough to withstand the long siege that followed. He actually died in 1809 and when the jihadists finally took the town they captured many slaves from the 'pagan' community.

Daura and its immediate surroundings quickly came under Malam Ishaku. But the Hausa community in Daura who were loyal to Abdu and who had settled in Zango came under Abdu's successor. There were splinter groups of these Zango settlers and the title *Sarkin* Daura was claimed by many in the course of the nineteenth century. Late in the century, the *Sarkin* Daura of the Abdu line received assistance from the *Sarkin* Damagaram at Zinder, the *Sarkin Kano at Maradi and the Sarkin*

Katsina at Maradi in order to try to dislodge the Fulani in Daura. The attempt failed; and Daura continued to suffer raids as it lay between Kano and Damagaram.

Gobir

This is the most northerly of the Hausa states. Because of this position, its duties according to legend were to guard the others from the fierce attacks of the Sahara nomads. From the beginning, therefore, Gobir has been forced to be powerful. Gobir traditions remember over 125 kings, the earliest said to have lived in Gubur in the Yemen. The Gobirawa were also said to have lived in Azben, probably between the twelfth and fourteenth centuries. In the same region occupied by Gobir was Zamfara, one of the *Banza* states. In about 1715, during the reign of Babba, Zamfara became so strong as to break away from the domination of Kebbi. It later became drawn into wars with Gobir. The eighteenth century was remembered as the golden age of Gobir. It was at this time that Gobir, under *Sarki* Soba, infiltrated into Zamfara, Kebbi and across the Niger into Ilorin. Soba later besieged Maradi in Katsina, though without much success. Soba's successors from Uban Ashe to Babari also led raids to Katsina, Kano and Shira in Katagum. It was Babari who in 1757 forced his way into Zamfara and completed Soba's infiltration into friendly territory. Babari raided as far south as the Nupe territory where Etsu Ma'azu was recorded as sending 10 000 slaves to Bawa, the Gobirawa capital. Among Babari's achievements was the building of a new capital at Alkalawa. He died in 1770 and was succeeded by Bawa Jan Gwarzo. Bawa was defeated by the Katsinawa in 1795 and he died of grief 40 days after the battle. Yakuba, his brother and successor, was killed six years later in another battle in the Katsina–Gobir war. In 1801 Yakuba was succeeded by Bunu Nafata who reigned for only two years. In the reign of his son and successor, Yunfa, the Fulani jihad began.

It is interesting to note that Gobir was the state of Usman dan Fodio. It is therefore important to draw attention to the introduction of Islam into Gobir (see below). Suffice it to say here that the allegations levied by Usman dan Fodio against the practice of Islam in Hausaland were probably drawn from his experience of Islam in Gobir.[22]

Katsina

The history of Katsina started at Durbita Kusheyi, located at a distance of about 27 kilometres south-east of present-day Katsina. Here, the *Sarkin* Durbawa was overthrown by the legendary figure to whom the founding of the dynasty was ascribed. This was Kumayo, a grandson of Bayajida. In the early stages the *sarki* was chosen from the two houses – houses of the *Sarkin* Durbawa and Kumayo – alternately. This shows that the overthrow of the ruling dynasty by Kumayo was not complete. The Kumayo group was known as Larabawa. It seems that Durbi was evacuated later and another settlement was founded at Bugaje, 20

73

kilometres west of Katsina. The evacuation of Durbi was put at some time in the fifteenth century. The *Sarkin* Katsina at this time was divine and his person was surrounded with many taboos. He was not allowed to die a natural death because rainfall and the fertility of the land depended on his physical well-being. As soon as he gave signs of failing in health, he would be strangled by an official called *hayar-giwa*, the elephant breaker. A new *sarki* was chosen after the performance of a rite involving the throwing of a spear. A candidate's name was called and the spear was thrown. If it stood upright in the ground the candidate was the new king. He would then be bathed in the blood of a black bull. The old king would then be wrapped in the bull's hide, slapped and dragged to be buried in an upright position.

The first Muslim king of Katsina was one Muhammadu Korau, descendant of Korau who overthrew the Kumayo dynasty by murdering the last king in the line, Sanau. He reigned from about 1492 to 1542. Muhammadu Kumayo probably became a Muslim through conversion by al-Maghilli, who visited Katsina in 1493. In 1512–13, however, Katsina was conquered by the Songhai forces and it was brought into the orbit of Gao for over 40 years. It is therefore plausible to suggest that what Maghili was unable to do peacefully was subsequently done by conquest. His successor, Ali Murabus, who reigned for about 26 years, was credited with building the first mud walls round the city. It was during Ali's time that the famous Kano–Katsina wars were fought. They were wars that ended in favour of the Katsinawa. It was also at this time that Katsina faced odds on all sides, with wars and raids threatening from Songhai and Borno, both of them at the peak of their power, and Kano, Kebbi and Gobir, all hostile Hausa states. When, in 1591, Songhai fell, Katsina quickly chose Borno as its overlord without fear of reprisal from Songhai, and thenceforth every *Sarkin* Katsina on his accession sent 100 slaves to the *Mai*. This practice continued until the end of the eighteenth century, though Katsina still remained strong among the Hausa states. At the opening of the nineteenth century, the *Sarkin* Katsina, Bawa dan Gima, insisted on breaking open a sacred room which had always been kept closed in a covering of red leather. Thousands of egrets flew out and filled the town, and this was interpreted as an impending disaster. The disaster was the Fulani jihad which sacked Katsina in 1806.

Zaria

The ancient name of Zaria is Zazzau, meaning sword. Variants of the name include Zakzak, Zukzuk, Zegzeg, Zazzagawa and Zage-zagi. It was, however, in the sixteenth century that Queen Zaria gave her name to a new capital, Zazzau, and Zaria has since remained the name of the state. The *Zaria Chronicle* recalls about 60 rulers of Zazzau before the Fulani conquest of 1804. The first was Gunguma, a grandson of Bayajida. The Zazzagawa were said to have lived in Kawar, Rikoci, Wucicerri and Turunku. Bakwa Turunku, the 22nd ruler (as recorded in the *Chronicle*) was the one who moved the Zazzagawa away from the dry Turunku to Jufena, near the river Galma. The movement took place in about 1536.

Bakwa's daughter and successor, Queen Amina, was very popular in Hausa history. She was famous for the walls she built during her extensive travels over Hausaland. The original wall around Zaria is called after her. Bakwa's second daughter was Zaria, who gave her name to the state. Amina fought many wars and, according to the *Kano Chronicle*,

Zaria under Queen Amina conquered all the towns as far as Kwararafa and Nupe. Every town paid tribute to her. The Sarkin Nupe sent 40 eunuchs and 10 000 kola nuts to her. She first had eunuchs and kolanuts in Hausaland. Her conquests extended over 34 years.[23]

That she died at Atagara near Idah is a pointer to the extent of her conquests.

After Amina, there were no strong-willed kings or queens to continue their conquests or maintain the states she had. The history of Zaria in the seventeenth and eighteenth centuries was one of domination by the Borno empire. Because of these long centuries of Borno domination, Zaria bore quite a close resemblance to the Borno political structure, and people of Borno origin were given influential positions; for instance the *Limamin Kona* was given to a family of Borno origin. Before its conquest by the jihadists, the capital of Zaria was moved to its present position near Kubani River. The town has a wall of about 16 kilometres in length with eight gates; the ninth gate, now filled in, was said to have been taken to Abuja by the *Sarkin* Zazzau when he fled from the Fulani in 1808.

The introduction of Islam to Zaria occurred in the sixteenth century, and one Muhamman Abu (1505–1530) is presumed to have been the first Muslim *sarki*. The fortunes of Islam in Zaria, however, were not stable. There were periodic lapses into the old *bori* cult. Jatau, who reigned between 1786 and 1806, was converted to Islam and built a mosque. But his son and successor, Makau, reverted to pagan rites and demolished the mosque.

Kano

The *Kano Chronicle* lists 48 kings and pushes the date of the founding of Kano back to the tenth century. It also tells the legend of the foundation of the state by a black man of great size called Barbushe, descendant of one Dala who settled on Dala hill. He was a hunter, 'who killed elephants with his stick and carried them on his head about nine miles'. He had a god, Tsumbur-bura, which he stationed under a tree, Shamus, in a grove called Kurmin Bakin Ruwa. It was said that none but he could enter and remain alive. Sometime around the tenth century, the *Chronicle* claims, certain immigrants from the north and the east came to Kano. The first Kano king was Bagauda. His son, Gajamasu, succeeded him and built the city walls which was completed by the fifth king, Yusa, who died in 1194. Naguji who succeeded him introduced the *gaudu* tax which demanded one eighth of every farmer's crops.

By the fourteenth century Kano was coming increasingly into

contact with Muslims from Mali. The first step towards acquiring religious power by any *sarakuna* of Kano was taken by the ninth king, Tsamiya (1307–1343) when he forced his way through the crowd of the worshippers of Tchibiri and chased out the priest. He was initiated thereafter into the cult and accepted as priest. The *kakaki* (long trumpets) used during his reign played the tune *Zauna daidai, Kano garinka ne*, or Stand firm, Kano is your city. It was possible thenceforth for any Kano king to make a religion the state religion. Islam was made the state religion in about 1349–1385 in the reign of Yaji. During this period, a group of 40 Muslim missionaries came to Kano and converted Yaji, built a mosque beneath the sacred tree of the Tchibiri cult, and asked the towns in Kano state to observe the hours of prayers. His successor, however, reverted to the old paganism when he could not bring the Zazzagawa into his orbit. A wave of Muslim scholars came from Mali to Hausaland and Borno as a result of Sunni Ali's antagonism towards the Muslim community in Gao and Timbuctu. We can assume that these scholars contributed to the spread of Islam in Kano. Towards the close of the fifteenth century, the famous Mohammed Rumfa ruled in Kano. He gained fame not just because of his wars but also because of the place he accorded Islam. Al-Maghili must have been impressed by Rumfa's religious piety, for he wrote a *risala* on Maliki law for Rumfa titled *The Obligation of Princes*. In this essay, al-Maghili advocated strong rule for the prince in the classical Machiavellian manner. He left Kano but left his three children behind. One of them (Isa), with whom he left his rosary, sword, kettle, Quran, staff and scales, founded a dynasty that provided the sherifs of Kano. Rumfa built a mosque and introduced the eastern custom of the harem – he was recorded to have had a thousand concubines. He also started appointing eunuchs to political office and made use of such regalia as *kakaki* (long trumpets), *figini* (ostrich fans) and *dokin zage* (a spare horse) as kingly costumes.

Rumfa's reign started the series of wars between Kano and Katsina. His son and successor, Abdullahi, defeated both the Katsinawa and the Zazzagawa, but he was humbled by Borno whose forces advanced on Kano to support a revolt by the pro-Borno settlement of Dagaci. Abdullahi's son and successor, Kisoki (1509–1665) had a very long reign which was dominated by wars with Zaria, Katsina, Borno and Songhai. From about 1570 to 1650 there were constant; devastating wars between Kano and Katsina; and from about 1618, the Zamfarawa also entered the incessant wars with Kano. In 1653, in the reign of Kukuma (1652–1660), the Kwararafa under Adashu invaded Kano. This invasion was repeated in 1671 and this time they sent the *Sarkin* Kano on a flight to Daura. During the eighteenth century, the fortunes of Kano improved slightly through its good relations with Borno and the attendant trading benefits. The invasions of Katsina and Zamfara still continued, and new weapons – muskets and gunpowder – were brought into the wars.

Reasons for the lack of unity among the Hausa states

From the brief survey of political developments in the major Hausa states presented above, it is clear that the states lacked any form of political unity. All along, we have been talking about wars between the Gobirawa and other states, or between Katsinawa and the Kanawa. We have not encountered evidence of such developments as the temporary alliance of two or more states against an external body; or a willing and conscious effort to create a confederation by the states. In the face of the Fulani attack in 1804, the *Sarkin* Gobir was said to have made a last-minute effort at calling on all Hausa states to unite and present a common front against the jihadists. His call went unheeded. An attempt will be made here to isolate the factors responsible for this lack of unity among the Hausa. It is important to state, however, that this condition of lack of unity, oddly enough, did not affect the economic and cultural relations which the Hausa states maintained with each other. They shared the same language and applied a similar system of political organisation in the day-to-day running of the states.

One major reason for the lack of unity was the desire by each of the states to continue the process of state-formation and state-building which definitely took precedence over good neighbourliness.[24] This process of state-building was not regarded as completed in a state 'A' until such states contiguous to it, say states 'B', 'C' and 'D', had been brought under its rule. What was, therefore, paramount in the mind of the state-builders was the desire to acquire territories and to adjust boundaries to suit their search for political and economic survival. This had always been the source of constant conflicts and feuds; and the possession of superior military capability was often a temptation to use such power against a less fortunate neighbour. One can therefore reject the Biram tradition that the Hausa states of Zaria and Katsina, Kano and Rano, Gobir and Daura (all listed as twin brothers) were each given duties to perform for the corporate survival of all. It could be true, for instance, that Gobir was the *Sarkin Yaki*, the war lord, because it was positioned to defend the northern frontiers of Hausaland. But the duty was not assigned, and the assumption was not based on any assistance given to it by the other states. The same tradition ascribes to Katsina and Daura the title of *Sarkin Kasuwa*, responsibility for trade and commerce. This title, as we shall soon see, is claimed by all the states in their struggle to gain control of the trade routes.

The conflict between the states was more pronounced in the two centuries that preceded the Fulani conquest. Kano, Katsina, Kebbi, Zamfara and Gobir had tried at one time or another to conquer other Hausa states but none of them was strong enough to do this. They did not possess the right military strength and their conception of war was not one of total annihilation but one of fighting to acquire spoils. Queen Amina of Zaria, for instance, was reputed to have raided as far south as the Nupe country, but she failed to establish hegemony over the areas she conquered. The lack of strength to subdue all the other states by any of these developing states therefore constitutes another factor responsible for the absence of political unity among the Hausas. The dominant theme in Hausaland before the Fulani conquest was not one of total defeat of an enemy but one of frequent wars leading either to periods of stalemate or those of a tenuous hold of one state over another.

Thirdly, the states were often divided in their loyalty to a foreign power. This was true particularly of the era of the Songhai–Borno infiltration into Hausaland. Kano, Katsina and Rano had their brief spells under Borno while Gobir, Kano, Zaria and Zamfara were all under the control of Songhai for some time. It was therefore difficult for states loyal to two different foreign lords to unite against either or both of them.

A fourth factor is the concept of balance of power in Hausaland, where the rise of a state to political prominence was often seen and interpreted as a threat to the political survival of each of the states. The rise of Zamfara and Gobir in the eighteenth century was seen by the other states not as something that could provide experience in cooperative state building, but rather as something which gave an indication of the accentuation of inter-state political conflict. Kano and Katsina both took up arms against Zamfara and Gobir for reasons of self-defence and the preservation of their states. None of the other states rose to the defence of Zamfara and Gobir.

The desire to control the east–west and north–south trading routes was another factor that made the establishment of a strong and united Hausa state impossible. In fact, many of the conflicts and intrigues between the states arose as a result of the desire of each of them to gain control of the lucrative trade between the north and the south. Important Hausa states that were right on these routes were Kano, Katsina and Zaria. They all became important centres where North African goods were exchanged for products of the forest region. As we shall soon observe in our discussion of the economy of the Hausa states, not a single state, even those that were not on the trading route, wanted to be excluded from this trade, which boomed in the seventeenth and eighteenth centuries as a result of the fall of Songhai and the diversion of the trading centres to the east.

Hausa economy

Like most indigenous economies, the economy of the Hausa states involved a division into broad categories of agriculture, manufacturing and trading. According to G. O. Ogunremi, the economy of the Sahel region to which Hausaland belongs rested largely on land and household labour and comprised the production of agricultural and non-agricultural products and their distribution.[25]

The agricultural implements consisted of hoes and cutlasses of various sizes. These were the implements with which large tracts of land were cultivated. Ploughs were unknown until they were introduced during the colonial era. The types of crops grown by each farmer depended on the vegetation of the area. Food and non-food crops were grown. Sokoto, Gando, Zamfara and Katsina were areas where rice, corn and onions were cultivated. Millet and rice were the products of Kebbi, Katsina and Sokoto. Root crops were quite uncommon for reasons of vegetation, though yam and cassava were known to have been cultivated in areas close to Borguland. Cotton, tobacco and indigo, among the non-food crops, were produced in the states. Richard Lander and Ajayi

Crowther were both impressed by the cotton grown in Hausaland,[26] and in 1906, when the British Cotton Growing Association opened a ginnery at Lokoja, it had no problem in obtaining adequate supplies of cotton. Tobacco was also important and European travellers all commented on the tobacco grown in Katsina and other parts of Hausaland in the nineteenth century. Indigo, an industrial raw material used in dyeing cloths, was also grown widely in Hausaland. Its cultivation was particularly extensive in Sokoto and Bauchi. Fishing and animal-rearing were further aspects of the agricultural pursuits of the Hausa states.

The Hausa people were also engaged in manufacturing, especially mining and processing of raw materials. They could be carried out as industrial projects; they could also be engaged in the form of craftsmanship. There were those engaged in salt-mining, tin-mining, blacksmithing, pot-making, etc. Three major manufacturing businesses were cloth-making, leather-working and salt-mining. Cloth-making involved integrated stages from cotton cultivation, through yarn-making and dyeing to weaving. What is remarkable about this industry is that the raw materials and the equipment employed were all obtained locally. The cotton and indigo were grown locally, and the major equipment for weaving – the looms – were made by craftsmen. Kano was the biggest centre for the industry. The state was reputed to have clothed more than half the population of the Central Sudan.[27] Tailors in Kano and other important centres engaged in making ready-made embroidered clothes such as robes, tunic shirts, caps and pants. They produced for both local consumption and export, and Hausa cloths were famous in the Sudan. Leather work was also widespread. The raw material, hides and skin, were produced locally from the herds. Some sections of the population specialised in curing, tanning and dyeing animal skins; and like the cloth-dyers, skin-dyers depended on home-made dyes. Heinrich Barth was highly impressed by the quantity and quality of the leather and the art of tanning in Katsina. Among the products from the leather industry were bags, sword-cases, saddle-covers, sandals, cushions, boots, mats, aprons and large skin vessels. Salt was a very significant mineral in West African history. It was one of the major articles of trade across the Sahara. In areas such as Kebbi and Keana north of the river Benue, the soil was impregnated with salt. When the water collected in these places during the rainy season was evaporated, salt was left abundantly on and near the surface of the ground and this was collected and distributed.

These agricultural and non-agricultural products were exchanged and the machinery of distribution in Hausaland was very efficient. In fact, even though the quest for control of trade was one of the factors responsible for the internecine wars in Hausaland, the wars did not actually affect its volume and direction. One important item of the distribution system was the trans-Saharan trade. Kano and Katsina were adequately exposed to this trade from their founding. These two centres were linked with the all-important centres in the west (Timbuctu, Gao and Jenne) and the east (Kukawa and Ngazargamu) by the major routes from across the Sahara. They were also linked by a network of trade routes with other Hausa states and communities contiguous to them. Large markets developed in the cities and it was here that most of the exchanges took place. The commodities that entered Kano market, for instance, included copper, zinc, needles, gunpowder, salt, sword-blades, mirrors, red coral beads and Arab dresses. The currencies used as means of exchanging these goods varied from place to place. They ranged from tiny plates to iron, shirts, and slaves to cowries and foreign coins. The cowrie became widely used in the nineteenth century. Though it had the disadvantage of being cumbersome to carry about, it nevertheless promoted an easy means of exchange, bearing in mind the peoples' dexterity in reckoning large sums of money.

The most important means of transport employed in this trade was by animals. Of these, the donkey was the most important. The donkey had the advantages of easy breeding, cheap maintenance and hardiness. Donkeys were bred in Kano and Katsina districts; and traders could buy or hire donkeys at very low prices. Polly Hill gives a picture of what the donkeys did in the nineteenth century.[28] They carried large quantities of tobacco to a place about 250 miles northward for storage until the prices went higher. On their return journey, they carried natron to Katsina and thence southwards to Ilorin or Ibadan. On their northward journey again they carried kolanuts to Katsina and Kano. This clearly depicts the hardiness in the donkey. There were, however, traders who employed water transportation where there were navigable rivers, especially in the rainy season. A few others employed human porterage.

Islam in Hausaland

The religion of Islam first appeared in Hausaland via the western, and later the eastern, routes. Kano and Katsina traditions claim that Islam was introduced through the eastward migration of the Wangara people. Wangara is a well-known region where ancient Ghana and Mali derived their gold wealth. It was therefore probable that the Wangarawa had accepted Islam through contacts with Muslim traders involved in the gold trade. The date of their migration into Hausaland, however, cannot be fixed. Muhammad Korau, one of the *Sarakuna* of Katsina and founder of the Korau dynasty, was a Wangara man. It is therefore probable that Islam was in Katsina in the fifteenth century. The *Kano Chronicle* states that the Wangarawa came to Kano in the reign of Yaji dan Tsamiya in the second half of the fourteenth century. One can assume that Islam came to Hausaland in the fourteenth century. But events in later years seem to point to the fact that the Muslim community in Kano was essentially a foreign one, living separately and outside the Hausa settlement. *Sarki* Kanajeji, for instance, reverted to the Tsumburburai cult to which he attributed his success over the Zazzagawa.[29] Against this background, we can justifiably see Sarki Muhammad Rumfa as the developer of Islamic society and life in Kano.

Rumfa was the first *sarki* to apply himself seriously to ruling the people in accordance with Islamic laws. He consulted Muhammad al-Maghili who was impressed by Rumfa's performances and wrote a *risala* for him on the art of government. Rumfa built mosques and ruled according to the treatise handed him by Maghili. Similar developments took place in Katsina under Muhammad Korau and his immediate successors, Ibrahim Sura and Ali Murabus. In fact, the al-Maghili treatise was meant for Katsina as well. It would seem, however, that the religion of Islam at this stage was that of the court, not that of the general populace in the states.

Over the years, many more people began to accept the new faith. By the seventeenth century, Islam had made significant incursions into the ranks of the general masses. In fact, the fall of the Songhai empire at the end of the sixteenth century caused fleeing *mallams* to seek refuge in Hausaland and to start propagating their religion. Katsina and Kano again were the cities to which these Muslim immigrants flocked. This immigration led, further, to the emergence of villages to which zealots flocked. In fact, we can hazard the suggestion that the beginnings of the process which was to develop later in the eighteenth century in the way of the spread and purification of Islam in Hausaland can be found in the seventeenth century, particularly with regard to intellectual awareness and the growth of evangelisation.

Intellectual awareness, as distinct from irrational belief, led directly to the questioning of the traditional beliefs and practices. Earlier questionings, addressed especially to the traditional political system by the new religion, was not fully grappled with because Islam was still in its infancy in Hausaland. But with the spread of education and the growth of intellectual awareness, religious educational propaganda was vigorously pursued. Schools and colleges were opened, and a considerable volume of writing was done.

From about the second half of the eighteenth century these writings came to be directed towards social criticism. Muslims were called upon to follow the right path as laid down in the Quran and the Shari'a. Muslim scholars travelled far and wide and preached sermons (*wa'z*). Students changed from one master to another in order to benefit from their specialised knowledge. People began to take to itinerant preaching as a full-time occupation. Learned men proliferated and conflicts often arose between them, often helping to sharpening their criticism of the society. The end-result of all these developments was that leadership of Islam in the states shifted from the kings to the religious leaders. The kings could not keep pace with the speed of intellectualism in Islam. Like their ancestors, they took out of Islamic teachings and culture only those aspects that would add to their power and the economic well-being of their states. They did not make any bold departure from the traditional practices. They therefore could be said to be syncretising Islam with 'pagan' practices. These 'pagan' practices were those abuses pointed out by Usman dan Fodio in his *Kitab al-Farq*.

It was alleged that the *Sarkin* Kano, Kumbari dan Sharefa (1731–1743) levied illegal taxes in the Kurmi market and imposed *jizya* on learned men. Baba Zaki (1768–1776) was also accused of oppressing his subjects, including the nobles whom he made to fight his battles. Hausa kings all over were charged with practising or at least condoning polytheism. In fact, a Katsina talisman similar to the sacred Mune of Borno was opened towards the close of the eighteenth century by Bawa dan Gima and this was regarded as a sacrilegious act by the believers in the cult.[30] The Hausa people had such deities as Uwandowa, goddess of agriculture. They offered sacrifices to these gods. Some communities believed in a water-spirit, the *Sarkin Rafi*, to whom a virgin was usually sacrificed. It was these abuses that the intellectuals criticised and fervently hoped to reform.

The demands of these leaders and preachers for reform was justified under the Islamic law that stipulates that one is not a Muslim who is subjected to 'pagan' laws. They called for a total reform, which would not end at the level of the individual or group. The number of these Muslim zealots is not known. Probably they were not many, in proportion to the population as a whole. But they could count on the support of a cross-section of the community in the event of a clash. For instance, Usman dan Fodio in 1788–89 is said to have had 1 000 *mallams* on his side. His own *jama'a* was only one of many in the period.

The preachings and criticism of the zealots allured the Fulani especially. As aliens in the politics of Hausaland, and as highly Islamised and learned men, they were drawn into the *jama'as* by the veracity of the criticisms. There, they almost naturally became leaders. When Usman dan Fodio launced his jihad, it was they who led the army and took the flags from the Shehu. This is probably why the jihad was characteristically a Fulani jihad.

Political organisation of the Hausa states

The Hausa states did not form any single empire, neither did they work together in a confederation. The political organisation of each of the states, however, followed the same pattern. As we have pointed out, in the *birni*, capital of the state, resided the *Sarki* who was the descendant of the founder of the state. Authority resided in him, or devolved on the body of state officials who ministered to him. These courtiers or palace officials were given titles and assigned duties. The administration was financed by custom duties, spoils of war, market dues and tributes from vassals.

With the introduction and adoption of Islam the structure of the political organisation underwent some changes. First, a new class was added to the earlier four. This was the class of the *ulama*, the learned men, who now served in the courts of the *Sarakuna* as advisers, scribes and finance ministers. Secondly, the *Sarki* acquired more power in accordance with Islamic practices, though he was no longer considered as divine.

Hausa government could be seen as operating at two levels. The first level was the capital city where the *Sarki* and his courtiers and officials resided. Among his officials were the *Galadima*, who had the power of deputising for the *Sarki* in Zaria; the *Madaki*, the commander-in-chief of the army who was actually next in power to the *Sarki*; the *Magaji*, who was in charge of finance; the *Sarkin Yan Doka*, who headed the police; and the *Sarkin Dogari*, who was the head of the palace body-guards. These were all trusted friends and relatives of the *Sarki* and they held their positions as long as their loyalty was not questioned.

The second level was the provinces. Here the administration was in the hands of the village *Sarakuna*, usually referred to as *maiunguwoyi*. Their appointment was confirmed by the *Sarki* and this gave him room to appoint trusted members of thesarki ruling house or use some members of his own royal house.

Judicial proceedings at the *Sarki's* court, prior to the introduction of Islam, put the *Sarki* in the centre as the chief judge. His court was both the court of the first resort for those living in the capital, and the court of appeal for those who lived in the districts. With the coming of Islam, a *Qadi* was appointed. This *Alkali* administered the Maliki law. He was a man versed in Islamic laws as contained in the *Shari'a*. Appeals could be made from the *Alkali* courts in the districts to the chief *Alkali* courts at the capital. The decision here would be final.

This system was very efficient. It is remarkable that the Fulani jihadists preserved it and the British colonialists adapted it to form the basis of 'indirect rule'.

The states of the middle belt

The Nigerian middle belt stretches between the rivers Niger and Benue, covering the land mass on both banks of the rivers in varying depths. The greatest depth to the north and south is located in and around the confluence of the two big rivers at Lokoja. This belt accommodates various ethnic groups, which, because of their varying sizes and complexity, are regarded in modern-day parlance as 'minority ethnic groups'. Each of these ethnic groups is small in population, and, compared with their neighbours to the north, covers smaller areas.

It was not possible for the peoples of this zone to unite and form a centralised state for three major reasons. First, the topography of the Nigerian middle belt is rugged. Second, and closely related to the first reason, the existence of two large and various other small rivers made the task of state formation quite difficult. Third, their neighbours to the north and south were not only more powerful but also hostile.

In spite of these handicaps, some people within the zone succeeded in establishing centralised states which, by the beginning of the nineteenth century, were quite well known. These were the Borgu, Nupe, Igala and Jukun. They owe their emergence to a number of factors.

The first was geographical location. It is true that the topography of the area was quite rugged; but there are advantages as well as disadvantages that came from this. The area was most suited for the practice of agriculture, for the rivers Niger and Benue not only brought richness and fertility to the soil through their annual floodings but also provided adequate drainage for the land. Apart from farming, fishing and other occupations were pursued, all on large scale. In addition, the two rivers were navigable and trade could be carried on up and down the rivers on a very large scale. In fact, the middle belt was the centre at which the trade routes from the north and the forest region terminated. Most of the exchanges took place in this belt and the people therefore benefited from this important commercial position. The Borgu example can be cited to demonstrate how advantageously these middle-belt states were placed. Here, Bussa, Borgu's principal settlement, was situated on the important caravan routes from the coast through Yorubaland to Hausaland and from Asante and Gonja in the west through the West African middle belt to Hausaland and Borno. It was also located on the waterway along the Niger from Gao southwards to the delta. One can well imagine the economic benefits that accrued to Bussa from this position.

Secondly, the Nigerian middle belt offered the security that was necessary for the emergence of strong, though small, states. The terrain was hilly and the rivers served as natural defence barriers. Against each other, the states in the middle belt were well defended by the hills and the rough terrain. This was one of the reasons why they were not united – no one state was strong enough to bring the others under it. Collectively, against external foes, the middle belt was impregnable. This probably explains why, despite continual and persistent external pressures, the states were not brought under foreign domination for long. The security afforded the states by the geographical factor, however, ended in variegating the states of the middle belt. A strong spirit of ethnic patriotism was encouraged by this security, and in the end all the middle-belt states coincided approximately with distinct ethnic groupings.

Though differentiated and claiming independence from each other, these states interacted with each other to a large extent. They maintained commercial relations with each other and developed important market centres. Raba, Egga, Funda and Ikiri centres were frequented by middle-belt peoples as well as their Kanuri, Hausa, Igbo, Edo and Yoruba neighbours. Among the articles that changed hands in these centres were horses, asses and silk which came from the north, yams, onions, corn, millet and other grains produced in the middle belt, and kolanut, gold and other fruits and minerals that were brought from the south.

At this stage, it is essential to examine the traditions of origin[31] of these states, not only to prove the relations between them but also to see how historically connected these states were in the beginning. All the traditions relate the migration of groups of people either from a distant land or from nearby. Among those that relate traditions of long-distance migration is the Kisra legend, which has variants among the different peoples of the middle belt. The Borgu variant claims that Kisra migrated westwards from Arabia following the emergence of Islam. He wandered to the Lake Chad region, stayed there for a brief period, and later migrated southwestwards to the banks of the Niger River. According to the Jukun version, the migrants from Mecca were led by 'Agadu' and he also lived briefly in Borno before founding the Jukun state. It is obvious from these legends that migration from Arabia seemed to be fashionable and widespread among the people. This could be traced to the influence of Islam right from the time of Songhai's domination of the West African middle belt.

Traditions of local migrations, however, seemed to have been inspired by a more recent development dating from about 1500 – the domination of some groups in the middle belt by their neighbours to the north and south. First, there was the Hausa–Fulani tradition born out of their claim to the domination of the middle belt. This body of tradition refers to the Bayajida legend of origin of the Hausa states where the Nupe and Jukun were mentioned as one of the *banza bokwoi* states. Other variants of traditions of local migration inspired by domination of the middle belt by their more powerful neighbours included those that claim that ancestral concentrations existed between the Igala and the Nupe on the one hand and the Yoruba, the Edo and Igbo people on the other. For instance, one version of the Igala tradition recorded in the mid-nineteenth century by the Rev. Samuel Crowther states that a Yoruba *Oba* travelled to Raba on the Niger from where he settled at Idah, which became the capital of the Igala state. The Nupe tradition also relates that Tsoede, the Nupe culture-hero, was an Igala prince who migrated from Idah to establish the Nupe civilisation. Further discussion on the traditions of origin of each of the middle-belt states is offered later in this chapter, when the political developments of the states are treated in turn.

Another aspect worth emphasising in this general discussion is the political structure of the states in the middle belt. Available evidence points to the fact that the emergence of each middle-belt state was the result of a long and intricate process of cultural hybridisation involving two major phases. There was the pre-dynastic era, when political power within each of the states was shared by chiefs who had equal access to power. These chiefs belonged to a council, at the head of which was one of them, collectively chosen by them. If he was a charismatic figure, this chief would be *primus inter pares*; if he was not, then he just occupied the position without real powers. This phase was eclipsed in each of the states, giving way for a second phase – the dynastic era. The process by which the pre-dynastic era passed on to the dynastic era varied from state to state; but traditions are quite clear on how this was achieved. In most cases, the transformation was as an answer to the immediate need of the state either to fight wars of expansion, or to repel external attack. The emergency situation called for a military leader, who very soon arrogated to himself political as well as ritualistic powers.

When this stage has been achieved, the state exhibited a political system that was monarchical with a semi-divine ruler at the apex. The degree of sacrosanctity attached to each ruler and the amount of initiative allowed him varied from state to state. The *Aku Uka* of the Jukun was the most divine of all the heads of the middle-belt states.[32] He was the personification of the state, and his person and court were surrounded with many rules. He had palace officials, notable among whom were the *Aku Nako* (chief steward), *Kundushishi* (put in charge of the king's wives), the *Ankwshi* (official queen) and *Angwu kaku* (head of the queens). These officials were not so influential as to overrule the *Aku Uka*, who was even believed to control his subjects' destiny.

Though he had wide powers over his subjects, the *Aku Uka* himself was subject to sacred regicide. Because he personified the state and held his subjects' destiny in trust, and because his success was judged by the state of affairs in the kingdom, the *Aku Uka* was expected to be in a healthy state at all times. An ailing *Aku* was quickly put to death; and if there was an epidemic or bad harvests, the *Aku* had to commit suicide – all adversities were interpreted as a rejection of the reigning *Aku* by the ancestors.

Apart from these limitations due to sacred beliefs, the *Aku* was also subject to the opinions of the priests of the state cult and a body of high-ranking state officials. The priests could reject an unpopular *Aku* by threatening to destroy the ritual basis of his royalty. They could invite the *Aku* to commit suicide, through a careful interpretation of the wishes of the cult of the ancestors. The influential state officials were the *Aku*'s councillors; but they could precipitate crisis for him either by boycotting the palace or by declaring the *Aku*'s condition, and therefore the affairs of the state, as unwell. The *Aku* therefore always placated these two groups of people by fat concessions, including gifts and privileges.

The Jukun monarchy could be regarded as the most thoroughly divine. Approximating this were those of the Nupe and Igala. Here, the kings were divine, even objects of reverence. They were, however, not autocratic and their powers were hedged in by constitutional checks and balances. The Borgu system exhibited two stages – first, the relation among the four principal Bariba states of Bussa, Nikki, Illo and Wawa; and second, the organisation of each of these states.[33]

With regard to the former, the Borgu state was a confederacy of smaller states. These states were rivals and they were often at each other's throat on matters of privileges and trading rights. Bussa and Nikki, the leading Bariba states, exercised weak control over their provinces, and often these provinces gained their independence or came under the overlordship of some other Borgu state. Despite this rivalry and seeming lack of unity, Bussa especially nurtured the ancestral ties that existed between these states and often intervened in disputes that occasionally arose between the states. In fact, the Borgu states always united solidly against any external attack.

The internal administrations of the Bariba states were similar in many respects. For the purpose of this brief analysis, Bussa administration will be examined in detail, not only because it typified the Borgu administration but also because Bussa was regarded as the head of all Bariba states. At the head of this administration was the *Kibe,* who towered above everyone else in the kingdom. Political power was, however, exercised by three groups of office holders. First, there were the members of the royal family, or the *wasangari.* From among this group was chosen the official queen, the *Yon Magara,* usually the daughter of a previous king. She was in charge of naming the king's children and looking after the princesses. The *Kiwotede* or *Yerima* was also chosen from this group. He was the heir apparent, responsible for the administration of Bussa township.

Second, there were the king-makers. They were nine in number. The first four – the *Bakarabonde, Bamode, Badaburude* and *Beresuni* – were descendants of the original indigenes of Bussa. The remaining five – the *Batafu, Beresondi, Bamarubere, Madoko* and *Zhinkina* – were members of the free Borgu citizens.

The third group of state officials was made up of the prime minister (the *Batafu*), the *Yon Magara*, the *Kiwotede* and other princes.

The Borgu succession system was complex and brewed clashes and disputes. The throne passed from the king to his brothers in rotation in order of birth and then returned to his first son. Those unsuccessful contestants often set themselves up as independent foci of authority in the outlying parts of the state. They thus reduced the area of effective jurisdiction of the incumbent *Kibe*.

The history of the major states: Igala, Borgu, Nupe and Jukun

The Igala

The Igala were located on the river Niger, close to the confluence of the Niger and the Benue rivers. This location was of great economic advantage to the people, who benefited both from the fertility and richness of the soil and from contacts with other groups to their north and south, including the Edo, Igbo, Jukun, Nupe and Yoruba.

The Igala traditions of origin did not exhibit any unity – they were conflictive as well as reflective of the series of migrations that might have taken place in the early history of the area.[34] One tradition assigns an oriental origin to the Igala, another says that they were descended from the Jukun, and a third claims that Queen Amina of Zaria founded the Igala kingdom. Furthermore, a tradition traces the origin of the Igala to the Yoruba; and yet another tradition states that Idah, the capital of Igala, was founded by a son of Eri, an Igbo ancestral father. These conflicting traditions suggest that the Igala were related to these other Nigerian groups and that no single group could lay claim to being the founder of this state.

In spite of the conflicting traditions of origin, it is, however, clear that the Igala society passed through two phases in its political development before the colonial era. These were the pre-dynastic and the dynastic eras.

From a remote time in the past, there was a gradual infiltration of people into the Igala area and this infiltration led to the establishment of nine settlements in Igala. These were referred to as *Igalamela*.[35] In the initial stages, each of these settlements was independent and was under the leadership of a patriarch assisted by other elders. But as time went on, it became necessary to have closer relations in economic and military matters. For instance, the expansionist activities of the Jukun and the Hausa state of Zaria pushed some peoples to the south and into Igala territory, while the Benin empire also initiated ripples into the Igala area. These new groups would then want to gain access to the river Niger trade. In this time of troubles – probably between the twelfth and fourteenth centuries – meetings were held among the *Igalamela*. The meetings were presided over by the representative of the strongest Igala settlement which also provided the leadership against external invaders. He was referred to as the *Ata*, or father; and he was allowed to oversee the general welfare of the *Igalamela*. As already pointed out, the strong-willed *Ata* with charisma would wield substantial powers while a weak one would only be seen as occupying a position without commensurate powers.

The genesis of kingship in Igala is still being debated even among the Igala themselves. It is, however, certain that the Igala state was created by a surrendering of sovereignty by the indigenous population to a foreign immigrant of royal descent. Before then, the *Ata* had advanced from a *primus inter pares* to a monarch-like institution. This transitional period also witnessed the emergence of the position of *Achadu*, who was the second most influential figure in the *Igalamela*, later to become the prime minister.

It is still not certain whether the Igala monarchy was inspired by the Yoruba. But it is not doubted that the Igala had their earliest contact with the Yoruba. It is, however, generally believed that Benin gave the Igala its monarchy and the first real monarch.[36] According to Igala traditions, a Benin man of royal birth came to settle at Idah around the mid-fifteenth century. He had magical powers and was generous to the people of Idah. They therefore made him *Ata*. By this single act, the *Ata* assumed a new meaning – significantly that of a monarch. The traditional authority vested in the *Igalamela* was reduced, though the right to choose and install the *Ata* was retained. Also, the *Achadu* kept his position as prime minister.

Why the Idah accepted this Benin prince as *Ata* is still not clear. Traditions do not assign it to physical conquest. But there is reason to believe that all was not well with the internal politics of Idah and the people were ready to accept a foreign prince as a redeemer. What is not doubted is that the new dynasty paid tribute to the *Oba* of Benin for some time after its inauguration.

Among the changes introduced by the new dynasty were the *Ata*'s mask (the *Eju beju ailo*), the practice of wearing beads on the wrist, keeping secret the death of an *Ata* for a while, payment of tributes by lesser chiefs to the royal court and a royal stool (the *Akpa Ayagba*).[37]

During this period some wars of expansion were fought. After having been checked by the Benin in the Igala–Benin war of 1516, the Igala direction of expansion was shifted to Lokoja, Idoma territories and northern Igboland. This dynasty was, however, toppled around the middle of the seventeenth century by another immigrant group led by Princess Ebulejonu of the Jukun. She was the daughter of Prince Abute Eje who, having lost the contest for the Jukun throne at Wukari, settled and died at Amagede. It was from here that Ebulejonu travelled to Idah, and, like the Benin prince, was installed *Ata*. She thus became the first Igala queen.[38]

This new dynasty embarked in the seventeenth century upon a series of campaigns, first to detach the Igala state from foreign overlordship, and second to further extend the frontiers of the state. Traditions record that these developments took place under the *Ata*-ship of Ayagba. Ayagba was credited with mystical powers; he combined this with subtle diplomacy and military prowess.

Ayagba fought many wars to maintain the territorial integrity of the Igala state. The most celebrated of these was the war he fought against the Jukun. Apparently, the Jukun dynasty to which Ayagba belonged was still paying tribute to Wukari, and Ayagba determined to end this. When he stopped paying, the Jukun went to war; Ayagba won the war and achieved independence for the Igala state, an independence that endured until the British conquest.[39]

Ayagba achieved this success in his foreign relations because he had reformed the administrative machinery of the Igala state. He had inaugurated a corporate body of officials comprising the *Achadu* and the nine traditional elders of the *Igalamela*. This body served as advisory council to Ayagba in his capital. To the interior, he sent his relatives and trusted friends, who established fiefs over which they presided. These *Ata*'s representatives were conferred with the title *Onu* or *Akomu Ata*.

This constitutional arrangement was further strengthened by Ayagba's successor, Anocheje. In fact, Anocheje was more revolutionary. Where Ayagba soft-pedalled, Anocheje went all the way. For instance, while Ayagba still retained the traditional *Igalamela* in the advisory council, Anocheje excluded them. The advisory council which Amocheje created was constituted by members of the royal family. Only the *Achadu* was retained; and with the overwhelming majority of the royalists against him, one can well imagine how little his power was.

The newly constituted royal council became the most important organ of government in the Igala state. It held daily audience with the *Ata* and performed high judicial and executive functions. The members resided permanently at Idah. They therefore appointed *Onus* who ran the affairs of their fiefs on their and *Ata*'s behalf.

In the end, the Igala monarchy developed into a cult. The *Ata* was conceived as divine and he lived in complete seclusion. He was supposed to have power over agriculture, soil fertility and fecundity of women. He rarely appeared in public. In fact, the monarchy developed to the extent that Anocheje boasted to Captain Trotter, leader of the 1841 expedition, that 'I am all same as God'.[40]

The Borgu or Bariba

The Borgu state was situated on the Niger River. The area was extensive, fertile and well drained by the Niger. This location was of immense economic importance; it was a major junction for the north–south and east–west trade routes. By taking full advantage of this trade, the Borgu succeeded in establishing four closely related states: Nikki, Bussa, Wawa and Illo. It is not now known for certain when each of these states was established. Traditions, however, claim that in the sixteenth century the Borgu states successfully repulsed a Songhai army. This could mean that by the end of the fifteenth century, the process of state formation had been completed. In fact, Bussa state seemed to have been formed earlier than any of the other Borgu states, for the tradition is widespread among the Bariba and the Yoruba that the foundation of Oyo received some assistance from a Bariba king.[41]

Bussa was the traditional city of the Bariba, just as the Yoruba view Ile-Ife. Though other Bariba cities were occasionally more powerful and more influential than Bussa, the traditional position which Bussa occupied as the earliest Borgu state never declined. This position was further reinforced by the Kisra tradition of origin to which all the Bariba states subscribed. We have referred to this tradition once. What is of significance here is that the kings of Bussa had personal charge of the Kisra relics, which included the chains and spears of Kisra, the *gangan kisra* (Kisra drum), Kisra kettle drums and state trumpets.[42]

The Bariba states exhibited similar patterns in their foundation. Usually, there was a group of indigenous landowners. This group welcomed a migrant group represented by the Kisra tradition. Bussa, for instance, was founded after a peaceful arrangement between the indigenous landowners and the migrant group. This resulted in a pact that stipulated that the newcomers must respect their host's customs and position as landlords. During the coronation and interment ceremonies at the court of the king of Bussa, leaders of the indigenous land-owning group played a prominent role. Two of them, the *Badaburude* and the *Bakaranbonde*, were incorporated into the new administration.

From these humble beginnings, the Bariba states developed into a strong force on the Niger. By 1505, Borgu had become one of the major impediments in the expansionist activities of the Askia of Songhai.[43] The Bariba soon grew to become the terror of their neighbours, particularly the Oyo-Yoruba to the south. For most of the sixteenth century, Borgu remained a principal factor in the political development of the Oyo empire. It established royal dynasties over some existing Yoruba towns and founded new ones. When Oyo emerged as a strong political force in about 1610, the activities of the Bariba in northern Yorubaland were reduced, so much so that Oyo controlled some towns in southern Borguland. Later, in the latter part of the eighteenth century, when Oyo imperial power started to wane, the Bariba renewed their pressure and in 1783 started to assert its independence successfully. In fact, the Bariba intervened in the internal politics of the Oyo empire.

From the records, the eighteenth century was the 'golden age' of Borgu history. Its position was confirmed as lord of the middle Niger when, in about 1750, Yerima Bussa defeated a neighbouring Habe state in a war.[44] It was during this century that such smaller Borgu states as Nikki and Kaiama rose to paramountcy.

An important factor that aided the rise of Borgu and gave it its striking force was the development of cavalry. It has been claimed that the horses and camels needed for this all-important force were received from Borno.[45] This could mean that, apart from the military factor, Borgu's rise was also due to its early integration into the trans-Saharan trade. In fact, virtually all the important routes from Badagry, Oyo, Asante and Gonja passed through one of the Bariba states before continuing further to the north or east.

Until the nineteenth century, when the jihads brought Borgu into the orbit of the Fulani Caliphate, the Bariba state could not be said to have been Islamised. The Muslim preachers who came to Bussa shortly after its establishment achieved little success.[46] Then there was the war which the Bariba fought against the Songhai empire, and in which the Bariba successfully checked the incursion of Songhai. This put an end to

Fig. 5.3   The chains of Tsoede, given to him by his father, which became symbols of royalty

any inroads Islam would have made into the Borgu society. Though there were Muslims in Borgu before the jihad, they were few in number and had little influence at the courts.

The Nupe

Oral traditions of the Nupe people credit the foundation of the Nupe state to *Etsu* Edegi, or Tsoede. Before him, there apparently existed in the area a number of states that were not only very small but also semi-autonomous. Among them were Ebe, Gbidye, Kusopa, Benu, Beni, Dibo, Kede, Ebagi, Batsoi, Kupa, Cekpa and Gwagba.[47] Some of them were very strong, and traditions occasionally referred to some forceful characters in some of them. However, only two of them, Kede and Beni, made any concerted attempts to form an extensive state. Kede was an important fishing and trading centre and asserted its influence along the

Kaduna River. The Beni state went further by establishing a closely knit confederacy over the settlements between the Kaduna and the Gbako rivers. These Beni settlements included Bida, Esa, Doko, Tafie, Towagi, Gada, Eda, Egbe, Nupeko, Ewu, Panjuru and Yesa. They paid tribute to the leader of the confederacy, the chief of Nku.

During this pre-Edegi period, the Nupe states acknowledged the political overlordship of the *Ata* of Igala and paid tribute to him, which included male slaves.[48] When the Nupe emerged into a strong, united state, this Igala burden was thrown overboard.

Tsoede, to whom this emergence was credited, was regarded as an Igala prince. His mother was the daughter of the chief of Nku, leader of the Beni settlements. He spent his formative years at the court of the *Ata* of Igala (he had been sent there as one of the items of annual tribute given by one of the *Igalamela*). There, he was exposed to the administrative set-up of the court of the *Ata*, and when he eventually left, the *Ata* gave him gifts, including the insignia of kingship which later became symbols of royalty among the Nupe. These were one bronze canoe, long bronze trumpets, state drums hung with brass bells and heavy iron chains and setters.

Tsoede's arrival in his maternal land was not met with easy and ready acceptance. In fact, the imposition of Tsoede's authority over the semi-autonomous Nupe states was not achieved by peaceful means; rather, it was brought about by conquest. Tsoede first established himself at Nupeko. From here, he started methodically to subjugate the whole of Nupe. He installed his followers from Igala over the conquered settlements and made his own settlement, Nupeko, the nucleus. He also adopted the title *Etsu*.

Soon afterwards, Tsoede embarked upon a series of wars to consolidate the state. These wars surpassed those of the pre-Tsoede era in ferocity and scale. Two sub-groups of the Yoruba close to Nupeland, notably the Yagba and the Abunu, soon fell victim to this military activity. The Ebe, Kamberi and Kamuku peoples to the north also felt the impact of this strong state. The Nupe later penetrated deep into Yorubaland, sacking Ede on the Osun River and raiding some Ijesha villages.

Though oral traditions tend to credit these successes to Tsoede's magical powers, we can identify three factors as responsible. One was Tsoede's determination, which could be related to the circumstances of his flight from Idah. Another was the relative weakness of the settlements on the Niger–Benue confluence. These settlements were not only weak, they were also so disunited that they could not present a common front against what then amounted to a foreign invasion. Lastly, Tsoede's grand design was aided by the adoption of cavalry, for, like the Bariba, horses and camels which they imported made their movement swift and their attack ferocious. *Etsu* Edegi himself was remembered in tradition as having 5 555[49] horses, indicating that it was quite a fantastic number. A settlement, Dokomba, was later established as a royal stable.

Tsoede introduced important cultural and economic reforms into Nupeland. Some of these he had learnt from Igala. Among them were the introduction of smithery, bronze-casting and glass-making. With these,

Nupe became an important centre for these industrial products and craftwork. It also became prosperous as an important market centre on the trade routes. Apart from industrial goods, Nupe exported eunuchs, who were in high demand in the harems of the Habe rulers north of Nupeland.

The history of Nupe in the early part of the nineteenth century was one of crisis. *Etsu* Muaazu was succeeded by Mamma, who reigned for only a year. Mamma, however, had the notable achievement of establishing Raba as another capital. But in 1796, two rival *Etsu*, Jamada and Majiya II, claimed the throne, the former at Jimi and the latter at Raba. This diarchy and the crisis it created were settled once and for all by the Fulani flag-bearers who carried the jihad to Nupe.

The Jukun or Kwararafa

Agadu, the founder of the Jukun, was said to have migrated from Mecca in the Kisra style. The Daura chronicle, however, mentions Kwararafa as one of the 'banza' states. These traditions, despite the conflict, point to one factor – that the ruling dynasty in Jukun was founded by a migrant group by their imposition over an indigenous people in a manner so common elsewhere.

It is not clear when the Jukun state was founded. A Katsina account states that one Kwarau, the king of Katsina in about 1260, waged a war against Kwararafa.[50] If this is taken as authentic, then the Jukun state had already been in existence by the mid-thirteenth century. It is, however, certain that from this early period to the sixteenth century the history of the Jukun was one of vassalage to the Hausa states. In the middle of the fourteenth century, for instance, Jukun was under Kano. When Jukun refused to pay the usual tribute, Yaji, the *Sarki* of Kano (1349–1385) attacked and forced it to resume payment, and at the time of Kanajeje (1390–1410) the tribute paid by Jukun included some 200 slaves. Zaria, under Queen Amina, forced the Jukun to pay tribute to her for most of the fifteenth century.

Jukun, however, rose to prominence in the second half of the sixteenth century. Its rise has been attributed to the following three factors. First, the Hausa states were not united, nor were they a conquering group. Only on a few occasions when the Hausa states had forceful rulers did they engage in wars of conquest, and even then only to raid for spoils and slaves. Moreover, the Hausa states themselves were subjected to incessant attacks from Songhai and Borno. Furthermore, Queen Amina's death left a big vacuum which no Hausa state could moderately fill. The Jukun were therefore left alone to recoup at the end of the fifteenth century.

Second, the creation of the *Aku Uka* of the Jukun in the sixteenth century as the king of Igala, and the semi-divine concept attached to this creation, made the Jukun state highly centralised. The *Aku Uka* was believed to have magical powers and this made him feared and respected by neighbouring groups over whom he established his authority.

Third, the adoption of cavalry afforded the Jukun the opportunity of having a strong fighting force. They soon became prominent in the politics of Hausaland and Borno – they probably acquired their horses

93

from Borno. With this cavalry, the Jukun began wars to assert their independence and then to embark upon conquest. They turned first to Zaria which they reduced to tributary status. Then Kano was attacked under Muhammed Zaki (1582–1618). By the end of the sixteenth century, the Jukun had acquired political influence on the middle Benue over the Idoma, Igala and Nupe peoples.

The Jukun state reached the peak of its glory in the seventeenth century.[51] They waged wars over important Hausa cities and returned home with big spoils and slaves. Kano was attacked twice – in 1653 and 1671; while Katsina was attacked, between 1670 and 1684. In 1680, Birni Gazargamu, the Borno capital, was attacked though the Jukun army was swiftly repulsed. This unsuccessful bid against Borno in fact marked the beginning of Jukun's decline. The *Mai* of Borno not only checked the Jukun army, he also reduced the hitherto powerful state into a vassal.

A number of reasons can be identified as accounting for the decline of the Jukun state after the seventeenth century. Firstly, the Jukun army was concerned mainly with plunder and effective occupation of places attacked and conquered was not made. The subjects therefore owed very weak allegiance to the *Aku*.

Secondly, the Jukun state was on the periphery of the trade routes. It therefore did not control any part of the trans-Saharan trade routes, or the coastal waterways. Though the Jukun did not neglect trade as such (after all, they manufactured salt locally and exchanged it together with slaves for horses supplied by Borno), they nevertheless could not take an active part in it.

Thirdly, the constitutional set-up of the state, and the divine position occupied by the *Aku Uka*, made the *Aku* pay much attention to rituals at the expense of politics. The day-to-day running of government was left to non-royal officials who often sought personal gain. Apart from this, there were dynastic disputes arising over lack of clearly defined succession law.

The Jukun state therefore collapsed in the face of attacks from the neighbouring Tiv and Chamba peoples, and the Fulani in the nineteenth century.

Notes

1 Cited in J. S. Trimingham, *A History of Islam in West Africa* (Oxford: 1965), p. 111.

2 See J. E. Lavers, 'Islam in Borno Caliphate', *Odu: Journal of West African Studies*, No. 5, 1971, pp. 27–53.

3 H. R. Palmer, *The Bornu, Sahara and Sudan* (London: 1936), p. 29.

4 *Ibid.*, p. 185.

5 A. Smith, 'The early states of the Central Sudan', in J. F. Ajayi and M. C. Crowder (eds), *History of West Africa*, Vol. 1, (Longman, 2nd ed., 1976), p. 171.

6 See A. D. H. Bivar and P. Shinnie, 'Old Kanuri capitals', *Journal of African History*, III, 1962, pp. 1–10.

7 His wars are recorded by his chronicler, A. Fartuwa; see his *Ta'rikh Mai Idris wa ghazawa tih* (Kano: 1932).

8 Trimingham, *A History of Islam*, p. 123.

9 Fartuwa, *Ta'rikh*, p. 2.

10 Trimingham, *A History of Islam*, p. 124.

11 See, J. E. Lavers, 'Kanem and Borno to 1808', in O. Ikime (ed.), *Groundwork of Nigerian History* (Ibadan: Heinemann, 1980), pp. 198 ff.

12 Cited in C. C. Ifemesia, 'Bornu under the Shehus', in J. F. Ajayi and I. Espie (eds), *A Thousand Years of West African History* (Ibadan University Press and Nelson, 1969 ed.) pp. 291–92. See also D. M. Last and M. A. Al-hajj, 'Attempts at defining a Muslim in 19th-century Hausaland and Bornu', *Journal of the Historical Society of Nigeria*, Vol. III, No. 2, Dec. 1965.

13 H. Barth, *Travels and Discoveries in North and Central Africa* (New York: 1859), Vol. I, p. 600.

14 L. Brenner, *The Shehus of Kukawa: a history of the Al-Kanemi dynasty of Bornu* (Oxford: 1973), pp. 45–47.

15 A. Smith, 'The early states of the Central Sudan', p. 155.

16 S. J. Hogben, *An Introduction to the History of the Islamic states of Northern Nigeria* (London: O.U.P., 1967), p. 73.

17 Smith, 'The early states', p. 158.

18 See M. G. (now A.) Smith, 'The beginnings of Hausa society', in Vansina, Mauny and Thomas (eds), *The Historian in Tropical Africa* (London: 1964), pp. 338–45; S. J. Hogben, and A. H. Kirk-Greene, *The Emirates of Northern Nigeria* (London: 1966), pp. 145–50; H. A. S. Johnston, *A Selection of Hausa Stories* (London: 1966), pp. xiv–xvii.

19 A. Smith, 'The early states', p. 181.

20 *Ibid*.

21 S. J. Hogben, *Introduction*, p. 73.

22 See R. A. Adeleye, 'Hausaland and Borno, 1600–1800', in Ajayi and Crowder, *History of West Africa*, Vol. 1, pp. 584–89.

23 Hogben, *Introduction*, p. 117.

24 This view is expressed by R. A. Adeleye, 'Hausaland and Borno', p. 593.

25 G. O. Ogunremi, 'The pre-colonial economy and transportation in northern Nigeria', in I. A. Akinjogbin and S. O. Osoba (eds), *Topics on Nigerian Economic and Social History* (Ile-Ife: Univ. of Ife Press, 1980).

26 See Lander, *Journals*, Vol. II, p. 122, and S. Crowther, *Church Missionary Gleaner*, Dec. 1858, p. 138.

27 See C. H. Robinson, *Hausaland or Fifteen Hundred Miles Through the Central Sudan*, London: 1896, p. 113.

28 Polly Hill, *Studies in Rural Capitalism in West Africa* (Cambridge University Press, 1970), pp. 141–45.

29 S. J. Hogben, *Introduction*, pp. 99–100.

30 *Ibid.*, pp. 86–87.

31 See J. S. Boston 'Oral traditions and the history of Igala', *Journal of African History*, X, No. 1, 1969, pp. 29–43; S. J. Hogben and A. H. Kirk-Greene, *The Emirates of Northern Nigeria*, pp. 579 ff.; S. F. Nadel, *A Black Byzantium: the Kingdom of the Nupe on the Niger* (London: 1942), pp. 19–26; and A. Obayemi, 'States and peoples of the Niger–Benue confluence', in O. Ikime (ed.), *Groundwork of Nigerian History* (Ibadan: Heinemann, 1981).

32 Information on the *Aku Uka* of the Jukun can be found in C. K. Meek, *A Sudanese Kingdom* (London: 1931).

33 See N. Levtzion, *Muslims and Chiefs in West Africa* (Oxford: 1968).

34 See J. S. Boston, 'Oral tradition and the history of Igala', *Journal of African History*, X, No. 1, 1969, pp. 29–43.

35 *Ibid.*

36 'The rise and fall of the Igala State', in *Nigeria Magazine*, No. 80, 1964, pp. 17–30.

37 P. E. Okwoli, *A Short History of Igala* (Ilorin: 1972), pp. 28–30.

38 See J. S. Boston, *The Igala Kingdom* (Ibadan: 1968).

39 See Okwoli, *Short History of Igala*, pp. 28–30.

40 *Ibid.*

41 Samuel Johnson, *The History of the Yorubas* (C.M.S. Bookshops, 1976), p. 11.

42 D. F. Heath, 'Bussa regalia', *Man*, Nos 90–91, May 1937, pp. 77–88.

43 N. Levtzion, *Muslims and Chiefs in West Africa*, p. 173.

44 S. J. Hogben and A. H. Kirk-Greene, *Emirates of Northern Nigeria*, p. 579.

45 M. Crowder, *Revolt in Bussa* (Faber and Faber, 1973), p. 29.

46 N. Levtzion, *Muslims and Chiefs*, pp. 174–78.

47 S. F. Nadel, *A Black Byzantium*, pp. 19–26.

48 S. F. Nadel, 'Nupe state and community, *Africa*, Vol. III, 1935, pp. 257–303.

49 S. F. Nadel, *A Black Byzantium*, p. 74.

50 C. K. Meek, *A Sudanese Kingdom*, p. 26.

51 A. Obayemi, 'States and peoples of the Niger-Benue confluence', in O. Ikime (ed.), *Groundwork of Nigerian History*.

6 Nigeria's indigenous economy

Toyin Falola

An understanding of the economic systems of the pre-colonial Nigerian communities sheds a great deal of light on the economic foundations of the various states described in the preceding chapters, on what the majority of the people did for a living and on how they interacted among themselves. The economy of all Nigerian communities can be divided into two major sectors, namely, production and distribution, both of which attained different levels of development in the various communities. In the discussion that follows, emphasis is placed primarily on the salient features of these two sectors of the economy.

Production

The majority of people in the different societies of Nigeria participated in various occupations ranging from agricultural and allied activities to craftsmanship, manufacturing and trading. Many tilled the land as farmers, many hunted for game, many fished the sea and rivers, and many others made use of the resources within their localities and imported items to produce other goods. Consequently, there was a diversity of economic activity in almost every society, so the conclusion that people in the pre-colonial Nigerian societies were engaged exclusively in farming is wrong.

Basic to all these occupations were the availability of land and labour, and the organisation of both for production. Scarcity of land was an uncommon feature, though there were a few areas where the land was poor due to excessive use over time, as was the case in northern Igboland, or where unfavourable geographical and natural features like drought, experienced in some parts of northern Nigeria bordering on the Sahara, reduced the amount of land which could be used. Every society had its laws and regulations on access to, and distribution of, its land, and how to settle disputes over land. Though these laws varied from one community to another, there were some characteristic underlying concepts or features common to all of them.[1] Land was corporately owned; it was the cohesive force which united all the members of a community. This communal land was administered on behalf of the community by the rulers or the village leaders. The rulers or leaders had to defend their peoples' right, fight against aggressors who wanted to dispossess them of their land and see to it that nobody was unjustifiably denied land. The communal ownership of land and the rights of rulers remained important in almost all the communities, irrespective of the political changes or upheavals they might have experienced. Even when a ruler died or was replaced by another, and in cases where a new dynasty or a set of rulers replaced another through conquest – as happened, for example, in early nineteenth-century northern Nigeria when the successful jihad led to the establishment of the chieftancy institution of the *emirs* – land was still vested in the new rulers who held it as trustees on behalf of the community.

Every family or descent group in the community was entitled to a portion of land. Irrespective of the political control exercised by a ruler, no family or descent group could be denied its share. In most of the communities, the rulers were just overseers without power over ownership of land; it would be illegitimate for them to tamper with or trespass onto the land of any family besides theirs. Even in the nineteenth century, when the new Fulani overlords in northern Nigeria introduced the Muslim Maliki law of land, which meant that all conquered lands were now treated as *wakfs* and *kharaj*, that is, land dedicated to religious use and lands on which tributes may be collected, the land still continued to remain in the hands of the families who had been the original owners although they were forced to pay tax on them.

It was through the membership of a family that every individual in the community had a right to a piece of land which could be used for any legitimate economic undertaking. To dispossess a person of land was synonymous with excommunicating him from the society; and this was rarely done.

A family or an individual could not alienate the land. Land was not a negotiable commodity and any commercial consideration whatsoever was ruled out by the communal ownership of land and the rule of non-alienability. There were religious beliefs and sanctions to back the land tenure system. Land was deified and selling it was sacrilegious. Among the Igbo, the earth-deity or the spirit-force of the land was the 'fount of all fertility and the guardian of public morality'.[2] This was true of most other communities. There was also the universal belief that land belonged to the ancestors and the living person only held it in trust. To part with it was to invite the wrath of the ancestors.

Nevertheless, there were rules and practices which made it possible for strangers to obtain land and for members of the community to get additional land. A person could borrow land from another family. Nominal or token gifts like kolanuts could be made by the borrower for the land. Thereafter, the borrower could pay tribute at intervals. But even this was voluntary. If the borrower did not acknowledge the right of the owner there were many social sanctions to prevent the ungrateful borrower from making further use of the land. As for strangers, the usual thing to do was to take up abode in, and request land from, a family of their choice. Some strangers might be given part of the unappropriated land of the community.

The organisation of land described above shows that there were no hindrances on access to land. To make use of this land, each family constituted the primary working unit or the labour force. A family was an operative economic entity which produced goods together and shared the fruits of their labour. Many researches on the organisation of the family as an economic unit have shown convincingly that this economic unit was very efficient and that it suited the economic system of the Nigerian societies. Generally, a man exercised control over his wife or wives, children and close relatives, and organised all of them for work. No wages were paid for this labour but the man was expected to cater for their needs. This system encouraged a man to have many wives, for each additional wife and child increased the number of hands working in an economic enterprise.

There were, however, a number of ways of getting additional labour besides those members of the family. First, through cooperative work groups, a person could benefit from the labour of many others. A cooperative work group was usually organised when farm work was heavy, when a specific project like building a workshop was urgent and whenever a task demanded more hands than could be provided by a family. The organisation of the cooperative work group was not uniform throughout Nigeria. But in all communities it generally involved the pooling together of members of the same age grade, friends, kinsmen or all the female or male members of a village.

Secondly, there was a system of peonage in many communities. Some people, especially the wealthy, had others working for them as pawns. These pawns served as the collateral security for, and as interest on, loans borrowed by their parents or themselves. The pawns continued to work for the creditor until the loan was paid.

Thirdly, the system of clientage provided another means of providing labour from outside one's family. Wherever it operated, and especially in the big states like the Oyo empire, Ibadan and the northern emirates in the nineteenth century, this system usually operated in favour of the political élite. Ordinary, powerless citizens voluntarily attached themselves to a chief whom they chose as their patron. The clients offered their labour and services in return for protection. In some cases, the choice of a patron was not voluntary but compulsory for, as in the case of Ibadan, it was important for every citizen to have a patron.

Finally, the institution of domestic slavery enabled slave owners to exploit the labour of their slaves. These slaves were obtained as captives in wars or raids, as gifts and as commodities bought in the market. Slaves were used for different purposes: they could work as priests, diviners or prophets in the service of gods or cults like the *Osu* among the Igbo;[3] they could be employed as domestic servants, soldiers, farmers, traders and, in short, in any work assigned to them by their masters. The majority of slaves were integrated into the society and to the respective families of their owners in order to obtain their loyalty, prevent rebellion and get the best out of them. The slaves were free to some extent; they could inter-marry among themselves, own property and redeem themselves if they had the means.

The various methods of securing labour developed in the Nigerian communities at different periods and over time. It is, however, difficult at this stage of knowledge to trace the origins of the various methods in each Nigerian community. Another point worth emphasising is that the use each community made of pawns, clients and domestic servants differed. While further research is necessary on this, it can be tentatively concluded that the military, imperial and highly centralised societies made greater use of slaves as soldiers and farmers than the small-scale societies.

It was by combining and exploiting the land and resources of labour that the people engaged in many activities to produce different kinds of goods. Farming was the most important occupation in many communities. The history of agriculture in Nigeria is one of continuity, change and adaptation to the environment. The archaeologists have maintained that there was a time in the history of Nigeria and other African societies when the people depended on food-gathering and hunting. This economy was replaced by stock-raising and farming, a revolution of which historians still know little, such as where and when it started. Since this revolution, farming has remained essential and a primary economic activity in most communities.[4]

Every community tried to adapt to its environment. The agricultural year followed a regular pattern. During the dry season, the bush was cleared in preparation for hoeing and planting which usually began with the earliest rains. Weeding at regular intervals followed. The last stage was harvesting and the time to do this depended on the crop. The harvesting of the major crop of an area, like yam in the south, was usually heralded by celebrations, festivals and religious ceremonies.

Farming operations were conducted on the basis of mixed cropping, shifting cultivation, rotational bush–fallow, permanent cultivation and irrigated farming. All these systems were adopted and conditioned by the land tenure system and physiographic factors. Of all the farming systems, shifting cultivation was the most predominant. Under this system, a plot of land was cultivated for three to four years before it was abandoned for another piece. The abandoned land was left to go into fallow during which it regained its fertility. This system had a number of advantages: it conserved the soil and prevented widespread diseases.

Whatever the system adopted, Nigerian farming was efficient, being able to produce more than enough to feed the population. It was also intensive; simple tools like the hoe and the cutlass were used to clear extensive land. It was ritualised. Rituals were performed at the beginning and end of a farming season. Crops had their spirit-force. Among the Igbo, for example, the spirit-force of yam was the venerated *Njoku* or *Ihiejioku*. The god was alleged to punish those who committed crimes which involved yam, like defecating on a yam farm, and cooking yam and cassava in the same pot.

The crops grown in each community depended on its geographical location. Two broad geographical zones can be identified: the tropical rain forest to the south and the savannah or sahel region to the north. Those in the south cultivated staple root crops, yams of different species being the most important. Yam was cultivated along with other crops like cowpeas, calabash gourd, spinach, melon, pumpkin, bambara groundnut and guinea corn, which was replaced by maize at a time which is not yet known.[5] Tree crops were also cultivated and the important ones included the ancient and commercially valuable kolanut trees, oil and raffia palms. Also planted were akee apple, locust bean and bitter kola. The farmers in the savannah specialised in the production of cereals which included a variety of wet and dry rice, sorghum and pearl millets. Other important crops in this area included groundnut, yams, indigo and cotton.

The type of crops cultivated in each region was not, however, fixed;

new crops were tried and if successful became a part of the agricultural economy. New crops were acquired through being introduced or borrowed from other places – from communities within and outside Nigeria, within and outside Africa. Unfortunately, little is at present known about how certain crops spread from one part of Africa to the other. However, there is some information, though it is somewhat controversial, on how some crops spread from Asia and South America to Nigeria and other parts of Africa. Africa is said to owe its cocoyam, banana, plantain and some species of yam to Asia. Also from South America, beginning from the fifteenth century, came crops like cassava, peanuts, sweet potatoes, tobacco, rice, a variety of fruits and vegetables, and probably maize. Some of these crops were adopted with success in different communities and at different times. The introduction and adoption of these crops had far-reaching consequences. It increased the choice of crops open to farmers and also enabled them to earn more income and produce more surplus. In addition, the crops 'offered the means of improving nutrition ... reduced the risk of famine, and ... made it possible to support a larger population'.[6]

There were many part-time activities carried along with farming. These included keeping livestock, small-scale fishing and hunting, protecting trees and collecting such products as mushrooms, snails, insects and edible fruits. These products were consumed in the households and some were sold in the markets. However, some of these activities, which were part-time in many communities, were full-time, highly specialised occupations in many others. Three of these, hunting, fishing and livestock rearing, were dominant in the economy of several communities. Hunting was not restricted to any particular area or culture but there were more professional hunters in the savannah region. Though hunting activities were carried out throughout the year, it was during the dry season and the off-farming period that the search for game became important. It was easier to hunt in the dry season when the bush could be burnt, and when hunters could penetrate deep into the bush.

Fishing was more developed than hunting. Fishing dominated the economy of communities living along the coast, lagoons and delta and the big rivers. In the south, many people in the Niger Delta, the Yoruba along the lagoon and the riverine Igbo on the Niger were professional fishermen. In the north, there were professional fishermen among the Nupe, Hausa and Borno. The Wurbo and Jukun on the Benue, the Kede and Kakande on the Niger can also be mentioned. Professional fishermen could leave their localities for distant areas to obtain fishing rights. For instance, the Gunyawa and Sarkawa left their Kebbi homeland for four months every year to go on fishing expeditions. The Ijo could also be found in Epe, Lagos and Badagry on fishing expeditions. Besides searching for fish, many professional fishermen engaged in allied activities like making or repairing nets and canoes.

The most important implements used to catch fish were traps of different types, nets, paddles and dugouts. Most of these implements were manufactured in the fishing communities. The major techniques used involved setting and throwing lines and nets, poisoning the fish and using traps of many sorts. The catches were sold to traders who in turn sold them to consumers. Those not eaten fresh could be smoked, dried or salted to preserve them.

Animal husbandry was important in the north. It was difficult in the south to rear large herds because there was no abundant pasture and, secondly, the tse-tse flies posed a great menace to the animals. Unlike in the south where there were no professional rearers, the Fulani cattle herders in the north were famous for the milk, butter and skins which they provided. Like farming, cattle-rearing depended on family labour, each pastoral family minding its cattle. The herds were usually large and the herders drove the cattle to where they could get food and trade in cattle products. In places where the occupation was well established, the supply of cattle was usually high. That of Sokoto province was reckoned early in this century to be close to 100 000 head of cattle and 40 000 sheep at any given time.[7]

One feature which distinguished animal-rearers from others was their migration from one place to another. They migrated in search of pasture and water, and to exchange their animal products for foodstuffs. It was the scarcity of pasture for the animals that always kept them on the move. As soon as the cattle finished the grass of an area, the herders had to move lest they lose their cattle. Except in full migration when the pastoralists transferred to a new area, the movement was usually from their homes in the Sahara margins to the savannah, up to areas below the Niger.[8]

Not everybody in a community took part in agriculture and its allied activities. Every community had its craftsmen who manufactured different kinds of goods for consumption and for sale to other communities. There were well-organised industries for the production of cloth, war implements, tools of various kinds, household utensils, food products and a hundred other goods. Some of these goods could be manufactured by most people in the society (e.g. basket-making, food-processing), some only in restricted families within a town or village (e.g. smithing) and some only in a few communities where raw materials were available (e.g. salt- and canoe-making).

In many communities, the craftsmen organised themselves into guilds. These guilds recruited and trained apprentices, disciplined members, controlled the production of goods, set the standards of goods, made laws against undercutting and inflationary prices and fixed prices of goods. These guilds were famous among the Hausa, Yoruba, Nupe and Benin. Nadel has provided information on the Nupe guilds.[9] According to him, there were guilds of carpenters, masons, wood-workers, potters, weavers, glass-makers, iron ore miners, blacksmiths, brass- and silver-smiths. Each guild was composed of members of the same family but others in the society who applied could be considered. These guilds were controlled by the state. Every guild had a leader who was a member of the king's council. This made it possible for the Nupe rulers to monitor the activities of the guilds, and obtain revenues and goods from them. Similarly, the guilds controlled all the important crafts in Benin.[10] There were guilds of carpenters, wood and ivory carvers, brass-workers, pot-makers, weavers, leather-workers, butchers, ritual specialists, cattle-keepers and doctors. New guilds were created as new crafts became important. As in other communities, the guilds were organised on a family basis, a son belonging to his father's guild. All the various guilds were interdependent; the blacksmiths supplied the hunters and carpenters with tools, the carpenters supplied wood to carvers, and the hunters supplied skin to leather-workers. All the guilds were affiliated to the *oba*'s (chief's) palace and this helped to facilitate communication between the rulers and members of the guilds and the collection of manufactured goods and fees from title holders among guild members.

Though all the crafts and manufacturing industries were well developed, only a few can be used as illustrations to show how specialised they were and how resources were combined to manufacture goods. One highly specialised and restricted industry was the production of minerals, among which were salt, iron, gold, silver, copper and tin. Salt-making was restricted to areas where brine water was available. Boiling the brine in special pots to evaporate the water and leave the crystals was the most common process. Salt was manufactured from the sea water in the lower Niger Delta by the Benin, Itsekiri, Ijo and Ilaje. There were major salt centres in the salt-bearing springs, pools and marshes in northern Nigeria. Areas of production were in the northeast, on the banks of Lake Chad and at Awe in Adamawa, and in Kebbi in the northwest. But by far the largest centre was in the area of the alluvial swampy land on the north bank of river Benue. In this area, Keana produced the best and cheapest salt.

Pig iron was produced in many places in Nigeria. From the archaeological discovery at Nok near Jos, it has been suggested that iron was being smelted in Nigeria around 500 BC. From Nok and a few other places, the knowledge of iron-working diffused to many parts of Nigeria with the result that each region had its famous centres of production. Among the Igbo, for example, there were three main production centres. The first was at Awka, which served the needs of the Igbo in the north and west, the Isoko, west of the Niger and the Igala and Idoma in the middle belt of Nigeria. The second was at Nkwerre from where pig iron was distributed in southern Igboland, Ijo and Ogoniland. The third was at Abiriba, which benefited the people of the Cross River area.[11]

The process of producing pig iron was common throughout Nigeria. It involved, firstly, digging iron-stone from pits and quarries and secondly, subjecting the iron-stone to continuous heating in specially designed clay furnaces. The methods of doing both varied from place to place. Among the Yoruba, three types of iron-stone were smelted to produce iron ore. With the aid of cutlasses, baskets, pickaxes, hoes, ladders and lamps, the miners dug up the area suspected to contain iron-stone. The extracted stones were later washed and dried before being smelted in the factories located at the outskirts of the towns. Inside these factories were the smelting plants and the furnaces. To make the fire generate the heat needed by the domed furnaces, horse dung was mixed with charcoal. The ore would be put inside the furnace and fired at a temperature of about 1 500° centigrade for three consecutive days. It would be left to cool down for another two to three days. The pig iron and the slag would then be removed from the furnace.[12]

The pig iron was sold to the blacksmiths who used it to forge iron objects such as axes, javelins, arrows, knives, cutlasses, hoes, anklets, adzes, bells, hairpins, needles, daggers and bracelets. Blacksmiths were found in most Nigerian communities, forging new implements, repairing and re-shaping old ones.

There were smiths for other metals. There were casters in different communities working in the non-ferrous metals like lead, silver and copper. They cast in bronze, an alloy of copper and tin, and in brass, an alloy of copper and zinc. These metals were used to cast objects like animal figurines, human heads, brass emblems, religious objects, swords, bracelets, anklets, necklaces and other ornaments of metal. All these were popular objects sought after by many people, and the constant demand for these products always kept the casters busy. Some areas like Benin and Ile-Ife were famous production centres. The brass and bronze works that made these two places well known are today scattered all over the world in different museums. There were also highly skilled producers on the Bauchi plateau. Here iron and tin were produced in large quantities. There was also a high degree of specialisation; smelters separated tin ore from the earth in their furnaces while the brass-makers used the straw tin to manufacture bracelets, bowls, jugs and other objects. Other famous producers included the Baushe and Bargami of the Kano area, the Ankwai, Jari and Angas of Bauchi, the Beriberi and Shuwa of Borno.

Other groups of professionals were not engaged in the production of minerals but in the equally important industries of woodwork, leatherwork, carving and the ceramic and cloth industries. All these industries were widespread. Leatherwork, for instance, was popular throughout northern Nigeria, where it was possible to get skins. Many people specialised in curing, tanning and dyeing animal skins. The skins were used to make bags, saddle-covers, sword-cases, cushions, aprons, mats and large skin vessels. Specialists in this industry could be found in Bauchi and especially in Katsina, which Barth, the famous nineteenth-century European traveller, described as indisputably the leading centre for leather and tanning in the whole of Africa.

The cloth industry was, however, the most widespread and the one that attracted a large number of people who produced dyestuffs, yarns, thread and cotton. There were other people who dyed cloth, sewed and wove thread. The cloth industry was an ancient craft. Even before the discovery of cotton, other materials had been used. The Igbo, for instance, made cloth from the fibrous bark of trees. The use of cotton was revolutionary; it popularised the use of cloth and the techniques of production over a wide region where cotton could be grown. There were only a few communities where cloth was not made. In the southeast, cloth-making was done in fattening rooms by young girls and old women. In the southwest both sexes were engaged in it, and in the north the industry was also well established.

Like the other industries, there were renowned and famous cloth production centres in Nigeria. These were among the Yoruba, Igala, Nupe and Hausa. One of these centres was the commercial city of Kano in the north. Barth, who visited Kano in the nineteenth century, was highly impressed by the Kano cloth industry. He enumerated no less than twenty different types of cloth produced in Kano, and he also described how the industry employed hundreds of people. Barth estimated the cloth which Kano exported annually at 3 000 million cowries.[13] Another European traveller said that the cloth produced in Kano alone could meet the demands of half the population of the Central Sudan. Nupeland was another well-known centre where cloth was made by 'well-trained craftsmen'.[14]

Though the methods varied from place to place, the stages in the making of cloth were uniform. These included ginning, carding and spinning, dyeing and weaving. The way in which this was done in southwestern Nigeria is used here as an illustration. Ginning, carding and spinning belonged to the same yarn-making industry. Ginning was done by rolling a cylindrical iron rod over the cotton placed on a wooden block. The main instrument for carding was the carding-bow. The bow string would be snapped so that the string could vibrate through the cotton and by so doing the ginned cotton became carded. For the spinning, a carding-bow and a spindle were used. The yarn produced was sold to dyers.

To dye cloth, the indigo was first obtained from the indigofera trees by processing the leaves to get the blue dye-stuff. The leaves of the wood climber (*Lonchocarpus cyanescens*) were also sun-dried or pounded and fermented to get indigo. The dye was put in a big vat, and thread, cloth and other materials were dipped into it. The dyed materials were then sun-dried in an open space to complete the process.

The dyed thread was in turn sold to weavers. Male weavers used the horizontal loom while the women used the vertical. Weaving was the most specialised activity in the cloth industry and it flourished best and survived for long in areas where cotton was abundant.

Distribution

Most of the goods produced were sold in the markets. The craftsmen had to sell their products to buy foodstuffs and the farmers too had to sell in order to buy tools, cloth and other necessities. This made trading an important sector of the economy. Every community engaged in both internal and external trade.

Internal trade involved the exchange of goods within each community. Every village and town had markets which were attended in the morning or evening and in some cases, throughout the day. These markets were held either daily or periodically. The daily markets were local exchange points where producers, traders and consumers met to sell and buy. The periodic markets were organised on a cyclical basis of every three, four, five and sixteen days to feed the daily markets. Every community had a market cycle which enabled traders and buyers to attend different markets on different days.[15]

Selling and buying were also done in private houses, in the homes of brokers and chiefs, in farms and along trade routes. Among the Hausa, for example, there was the 'hidden trade' which allowed women who were forbidden by religious custom from being seen in the public to sell goods in their husbands' houses.[16]

A market occupied an open space where trees, stalls or tents built of thatched roofs provided shade. The traders sat on stools made of wood, raffia-poles or stones with their wares placed before them. The goods were put inside baskets, calabashes, on trays or leaves or on the bare ground. Traders selling similar commodities sat close together. This arrangement had a number of advantages. It made it convenient for buyers to locate the regular selection of each commodity, to choose from a wide variety of goods and to buy at a fair price since the traders had to compete with one another at the same time.

The markets were well organised. Every market had officials who settled quarrels and differences and supervised transactions. The traders, too, formed guilds which saw to the cleanliness of the markets, resolved disputes among members and agreed on prices.

Currency was used for transactions. It is true that there was a time in the history of the different communities when goods were exchanged for goods in a barter economy but this was replaced by the use of money. This happened at different times which we do not know at the moment. By the fifteenth century when the Europeans arrived at the coast, the use of money had been firmly established. Before this time, money had been used in transactions between Nigerian traders and their North African counterparts. However, exchange units were still based on produce in some communities despite the existence of money. Among the Jukun, for example, an *agi*, a standard calabash of corn, was reckoned as a standard of value; an *agi* was equivalent to a large manilla. Salt was another standard of value; five cup-shaped receptacles known as the *Kororo* or *baha* were equal to one *agi*. Cloth, salt, horses and slaves were used in many other places.

There were different types of currencies in Nigeria. The most important ones consisted of iron, copper and brass objects and cowries. Iron currencies were used in the north, the middle belt, the southeast and part of the southwest. For example, in Logone near Lake Chad, small, thin plates of iron were used and were counted in parcels of ten to twelve plates. Thirty of these plates were reckoned in the nineteenth century to be equivalent to a dollar.[17] In the Benue valley, there were iron currencies of two types. The first resembled the hoe and were tied up in bundles of about twelve. According to Meek, the money was used by the Jukun and Idoma, who called it *akika*, by the Hausa, who called it *agelema*, and by the Tiv, who called it *ibia*. Meek also described the second type as 'pointed towards the extremities, but thicker in the middle'.[18] It was as popular as the first.

Manilla was another popular currency, particularly in the Niger Delta and the Cross River from where it probably got to the Benue valley. The Jukun, Igala and Igbo made use of the manilla.

The most universal was the cowry (*cyprae moneta*). It was also an ancient currency, antedating the fifteenth century, and it continued to be in circulation up till the first few decades of this century. The cowry was known in many parts of Nigeria. Most of the European travellers in the nineteenth century observed that cowries were spent in the places they visited. Baikie, for example, mentioned the Niger Delta, Yoruba, Benin, Igbo, Igala, Nupe, Hausa and Fulani territories as among the places where cowries could be spent. The cowry had a number of advantages. Its units of counting were uniform in many regions. In the south-west, cowries were counted singly and in multiples of 20, 200, 2 000 and 20 000. It was uni-denominational; traders did not have to understand one another's language before they could use it. The cowry was very efficient for small transactions. Another advantage which the cowry had was that it could not be forged or counterfeited.[19]

Besides the internal trade within each community, there also took place external trade between a community and other places within and outside Nigeria. Ecological differences, production of surpluses of certain goods in some communities and the inability to produce certain goods in others were amongst the reasons for the development of external and long-distance trade. For instance, only limited areas could produce salt and natron, and to distribute these two articles there had to be commercial cooperation on a wider territorial level.

Every community had its long-distance traders who made it possible for articles of diverse origin to get to the consumers. These long-distance traders required more working capital than the internal, local traders. They needed capital for credit advances in goods and in cash to their customers, to purchase goods needed for transportation like canoes and slaves. They obtained their capital by raising loans, by saving and by reinvesting their money.

Through trade, nearly all the Nigerian communities were linked together. The geographical setting of Nigeria and the absence of many natural barriers allowed for a free movement of traders within and outside it. The trade contacts were important in many ways. They allowed for a free flow of goods from one area to another. Farm products, manufactured goods, basic necessities and luxury articles were taken from where they were cheap and abundant to where they were dear and scarce. Articles like dried fish, salt and, from the fifteenth century onwards, European goods like tobacco, arms and ammunition and spirits were taken from the coastal area to the hinterland. For instance, the Ijebu and Egba traders bought coastal goods which they sold to traders from the Yoruba hinterland. The Benin traders went to eastern Yorubaland for the same reason. The coming of the Europeans from the fifteenth century stimulated the Benin–Yoruba trade. Through it, European articles like cloth, red caps, brandy and firearms got to Yorubaland. The traders in the Niger Delta did the same thing. In addition to goods earlier mentioned, they sold brass rods, manilla and copper wire to traders from the interior.

The coastal traders were not the only middlemen and agents. Middlemen and agents could be found everywhere buying goods in one market and selling them to another group of traders who again sold the goods elsewhere. The system of middlemanship contributed immensely to the exchange of goods throughout Nigeria and led to the development of a complex market system.

Goods moved up and down from the southern to the northern part of Nigeria. Yoruba traders carried articles like kolanuts and salt to Nupe and Hausaland. The Nupe and Hausa traders, too, went to the south to sell natron, horses, leather goods and cattle products, Sokoto and Kano cloth and Bauchi metal goods. Slaves were also exchanged, their value and price tending to increase the further they were taken from their homes. Goods went in many directions: suffice it to say that goods of different origins could be found in places where there were consumers.

North African and Mediterranean goods also reached Nigeria through the trans-Saharan trade. Nigerians, Arabs and North African traders met in the commercial centres of northern Nigeria to transact business. Traders in Kukawa, Kano and Katsina had been participating in this trade before the fourteenth century.[20] Among the articles which the trade brought to Nigeria were Arab dresses, coral beads, copper, zinc, needles, mirrors, swords, blades, horses and salt from places such as Fezzan, Malta and Italy. This trade remained important in Northern Nigeria long after the coming of the Europeans. As late as 1895, more goods came through the trans-Saharan trade than through the coast. The volume of this trade was high. For example, about four thousand camels entered Borno annually carrying mainly salt.

Besides the trade link with North Africa, trade also went westwards to link Nigeria with other West African states. Hausa traders left Nigeria for the forest region, especially Gonja in Ghana, to buy kolanuts and sell cloth. Professional long-distance Hausa traders could also be found in Salaga, Timbutu, Kintampo, Segu, Darfur and other communities south of the Niger. Borno and Katsina were the major centres for this trade until the nineteenth century, when Kano became the leading commercial centre in northern Nigeria.

The advantages of trade were not restricted to the circulation of goods. More than anything else, long-distance trade promoted inter-group relations and interactions among the various Nigerian communities.[21] Through trade, people shared, exchanged and borrowed ideas on cultural, economic, political and religious institutions. It is a well-known fact that trade routes and traders served as carriers of culture and civilisation and they provided the avenue for the intermingling of peoples and the exchange of ideas. For instance, the trade routes provided the lines of communication for the spread of Islam in Nigeria, and in the nineteenth century the routes also became the channels used by the Christian missionaries to spread the gospel. Trade also contributed to the growth and development of towns and villages. Kano, for instance, owed its size, wealth and population to trade. The same is true of most trade termini–like Lagos, Onitsha, Aba and Gboko, to mention a few examples. It should, however, be noted that trade also caused wars and hostilities among different communities. The struggles for the control of trade in many communities, especially in the nineteenth century, is a case in point.

A primary requisite for long-distance trade was transportation. There were two major means for this – by land and water. Both of these were well organised. The earliest form of transportation was probably through the relay system from one place to another but this gave way to highly organised commercial highways with the emergence of a class of non-agricultural professional traders. There were hundreds of trade routes. There were those which linked one settlement with another and these were as old as the settlements. There were also inter-state trading routes. In fact, Nigeria was crisscrossed by a network of routes. Important routes started in the coastal area, passed through the hinterland and went through to the northern part of the country. A few routes also had their termini in the west and ran through to the east. The south–north routes were the most important. For example, trade routes began in Badagry, Lagos and Porto Novo, passed through places like Egbado and Oyo and continued through Raba on the Niger to Kano. From Kano, routes went northwards, across the Sahara to the Mediterranean littoral. Other international routes connected Borno and Hausaland with Gonja and other Western Sudanese states.

Transportation on the land routes were chiefly by head porterage and pack animals. The traders carried the goods themselves or made use of their family labour or slaves. Slaves were commonly used. Many long-distance traders were also slave dealers. The slaves were self-transporting and they also carried articles of trade. Many traders would not sell their slaves until they disposed of their goods. The distance from one place to another was reckoned in days and hours, and the average rate of travelling was five kilometres an hour. A trader could carry between eighty to one hundred and twenty pounds of load.

Pack animals were used in the north where it was easier to breed the animals. The most suitable of all the pack animals was the donkey because it was the easiest to breed, the cheapest to maintain and the most hardy. The donkey was capable of travelling great distances at a stretch. It was a patient animal which could endure bad weather, heavy loads and insufficient food. There were other pack animals like the camel, mule, bullock and ox. The camel could carry more loads, travel faster and do without water for many more days than the donkey. Bullocks were used less frequently than the camel and donkey because they were more expensive, difficult to breed and they had little stamina and resistance to diseases. The mule, like the bullocks, was also difficult to breed.

The use of pack animals had some advantages over human porterage: animals could carry more loads; traders could travel with ease and at a faster rate. The disadvantages of these animals were that, unlike porters, they were more useful during the dry season and they were susceptible to diseases, especially to trypanosomiasis.

One aspect of the organisation of trade related to transportation by land is that traders travelled in caravans. This made the journey less boring and it reduced the risks of losing trade routes and falling prey to marauders. The caravan moved at a slow pace, and stopped to rest and sleep in well-known places. To pass through a town, the traders had to pay the customary toll. The tolls were collected by the representatives of the rulers of each community and the amount collected varied from place to place and also depended on the commodities involved. Articles like cloth, horses and slaves attracted higher duties.

The waterways provided the second means of transportation. In the coastal area to the south, the lagoon was navigable from Lagos to Sapele. In the Niger Delta, there is a mass of waterway which also led to the Imo River, the lower bank of which was navigable. The Niger–Benue system encouraged water transportation over a long distance. It also has subsidiary rivers to the north like the Gongola, Kaduna and Rima, all of which made communication possible, especially in the wet season. There were many other rivers in Nigeria though only parts of their course were free of snags and were navigable.

Though many methods and crafts were used in navigation, the canoe was the most popular. The canoe could be used to transport bulky goods like yams and onions, and many passengers, over a long distance. It was cheaper than head porterage and pack animals. Like the modern-day vehicle, the canoe had its builders, its repairers and its drivers.[22]

The land and waterways were safe for traders' use except during wars and hostilities. In fact, for trade to survive, there had to be security for life and property. This was achieved in a number of ways. The rulers in the respective communities tried to establish control over the economy and this included taking care of the trade routes and traders that passed through their domain, and doing everything possible to encourage trade to flourish. It was not unusual for armed guards appointed by rulers to accompany traders or to patrol trade routes.

Other informal sanctions and customs made it possible for traders to travel with ease. The custom in every community forbade killing, molestation and kidnapping of fellow village or town dwellers. Thus, trade within the same community was assured. In inter-community trade, there were some established institutions which promoted peace. Some communities entered into mutual agreement never to attack one another. Marriage ties cemented the relationship between many places. Many traders deliberately chose wives in commercial centres and towns along the trade routes and this strengthened the relationship between communities. Finally, religion was used to promote trade. For instance, Muslim traders regarded themselves as brothers who must not harm one another. Among the Igbo, the oracle system helped to promote trade. The Eze Nri, the Awka and the Aro were the three most successful groups of Igbo long-distance traders who manipulated the oracle for economic reasons. The Eze Nri and Awka travelled as priests, doctors and craftsmen without fear of molestation. The Aro succeeded more than the others in building a network of trade routes and in establishing depots in many parts of Igboland. The Aro traders were feared because of the powerful charms which the people believed they had. It was an offence against the gods and man to hurt, molest, kidnap or kill any Aro trader or his agent.[23]

Conclusion

From the foregoing discussion, it can rightly be concluded that the Nigerian pre-colonial indigenous economy was highly developed, well organised and efficient. In the sphere of production, the various communities were able to produce agricultural and industrial goods in large quantities and good quality, and highly skilled professionals were able to render their invaluable services to the benefit of the society.

Production went far beyond subsistence level and surpluses had to be sold. The exchange sector was also efficient enough to distribute the products from the farms and the factories. No community was self-sufficient and every community relied on others for some necessary and luxury goods. There were astute, efficient and hard-working traders who transported goods from one place to an other. Trading activities were facilitated by the extensive network of land routes and waterways, and general-purpose currencies.

The economy was not static as alleged by some writers. Rather, it exhibited a great deal of change and innovation. For instance, the transition from vegeculture to agriculture and the introduction of Asian and South American crops brought about revolutionary agricultural changes. Other sectors of the economy also underwent notable changes. Finally, the economy was capable of adapting to changes from within and without. Some of the factors responsible for the changes, such as the Atlantic slave trade and the British imposition of colonial rule, are discussed elsewhere in this book.

Notes

1 Only a few studies on the land tenure system of Nigerian societies can be cited here: C. K. Meek, *Land Tenure and Land Administration in Nigeria and the Cameroons* (London: 1951); L. T. Chubb, *Ibo Land Tenure* (Ibadan: 1961); C. W. Cole, *Report on Land Tenure, Zaria Province* (Kaduna: 1952), and *Report on Land Tenure, Niger Province* (Kaduna: 1952); T. O. Elias, *Nigeria Land Law and Customs* (London: 1953); C. W. Rowling, *Report on Land Tenure, Kano Province* (Kaduna: 1949); P. C. Lloyd, *Yoruba Land Law* (Ibadan: 1962).

2 Meek, *Land Tenure and Land Administration in Nigeria*, p. 113.

3 See, for example, R. Horton, 'The Osu system of slavery in a northern Ibo village-group', *Africa*, Vol. XXIV, No. 4, 1952, pp. 311–36.

4 An extensive discussion of the importance of agriculture in Nigeria is provided in H. A. Oluwasanmi, *Agriculture and Nigerian Economic Development* (Ibadan: Oxford University Press, 1966).

5 See details in P. A. Allison, 'Historical references to be drawn from the effect of human settlement on the vegetation of Africa', *Journal of African History (JAH)*, Vol, III, No. 2, 1962, p. 27.

6 A. G. Hopkins, *An Economic History of West Africa* (London: Longman, 1973), p. 31.

7 *Northern Nigeria Colonial Report*, 1900–1911, p. 251.

8 A most interesting study on this is D. J. Stenning, *Savannah Nomads* (London: 1959) and his 'Transhumance, migratory drift, migration: patterns of pastoral Fulani nomadism', *Journal of the Royal Anthropological Institute*, 87, 1957, pp. 57–73.

9 S. F. Nadel, *A Black Byzantium, the Kingdom of the Nupe in Nigeria* (London: 1942), p. 257 ff.

10 P. A. Igbafe, 'The pre-colonial economic foundation of Benin', in I. A. Akinjogbin and S. O. Osoba (eds), *Topics on Nigerian Economic and Social History* (University of Ife Press), pp. 45–48.

11 See A. E. Afigbo, 'The economic foundations of pre-colonial Igbo society', in Akinjogbin and Osoba (eds), *Topics on Nigerian Economic and Social History*, pp. 27–28; and M. W. Uzomaka, 'Trade and politics in pre-colonial Nkwerre', Special final year project, Department of History and Archaeology, University of Nigeria, Nsukka.

12 For details, see D. Adeniji, *Ise Irin Wiwa ati Sisun – Iron mining and Smelting*, translated and edited by R. G. Armstrong (University of Ibadan, Institute of African Studies, Occasional Publications, No. 31, 1977).

13 H. Barth, *Travels and Discoveries in North and Central Africa* (New York: 1859), Vol. III, p. 85; I, p. 512.

14 H. Bindlois, *In the Niger Country* (London: Frank Cass, 1968), p. 317; also C. H. Robinson, *Hausaland or Fifteen Hundred Miles Through the Central Sudan* (London: 1896), p. 113.

15 For details, see B. W. Hodder and U. I. Ukwu, *Markets in West Africa* (Ibadan University Press, 1969).

16 P. Hill, 'Hidden trade in Hausaland', *Man*, Vol. IV, No. 3, Sept. 1969, pp. 392–409.

17 See M. Johnson and Sven-Olof, *Nigerian Currencies, Manillas, Cowries and others* (Sweden, 1967); and H. M. A. Kirk-Greene, 'The major currencies in Nigerian history', *Journal of the Historical Society of Nigeria (JHSN)*, 2, 1960, pp. 132–50.

18 C. K. Meek, *A Sudanese Kingdom* (London: 1931), p. 452.

19 M. Johnson, 'The cowry currencies of West Africa', *JAH,* Vol. XI, 1970, pp. 17–44, 331–53.

20 Cf. Ibn Battuta, *Travels in Asia and Africa 1325—1354,*, translated by H. A. R. Gibb (London: 1929), p. 336.

21 J. Goody and T. M. Mustafa, 'The caravan trade from Kano to Salaga', *JHSN*, Vol. III, 4, 1967; also J. F. A. Ajayi and E. J. Alagoa, 'Nigeria before 1800: aspects of economic developments and inter group relations', in O. Ikime (ed.), *Groundwork of Nigerian History* (Ibadan: Heinemann Educational Books Ltd., 1980), Chap. 12.

22 R. Smith, 'The canoe in West African history', *JAH.*, II, 1970, pp. 515–33; also S. F. Nadel, 'The Kede: a riverine state in Northern Nigeria', in M. Fortes and E. E. Evans-Pritchard (eds), *African Political Systems* (London: 1940).

23 For more information see U. I. Ukwu, 'The development of trade and markets in Iboland', *JHSN*, Vol. III, No. 4, 1967; A. E. Afigbo, 'The economic foundations of pre-colonial Igbo society', in Akinjogbin and Osoba (eds), *Topics on Nigerian Economic and Social History*, Chap. 1; and F. I. Ekojiuba, 'The Aro system of trade in the nineteenth century', *Ikenga: Journal of African Studies*, Vol. I, No. 1, Jan. 1972, pp. 11–26.

7 The Atlantic slave trade

Richard Olaniyan

The Atlantic slave trade constituted without doubt the greatest forced migration in the history of mankind. It involved four continents and has left its permanent imprint on the histories and cultures of these lands. How has it affected Nigeria? This question is our main concern in this chapter.

The socio-economic development of Nigeria was to be dramatically and immeasurably affected by the arrival of the Portuguese in Benin in the last two decades of the fifteenth century. They began paying regular visits to the rivers west of the Niger Delta from about 1480, carrying slaves in their ships to the Gold Coast to be exchanged for gold. In 1485 they established contact with the kingdom of Benin and later set up a trading post at Ughoton on the Benin River. This facilitated the development of a thriving slave trade in the Itsekiri and western Ijo territories. From there, they soon developed a direct trade in slaves with the Ijebu kingdom to the west; and the Portuguese colonies on the islands of São Tomé and Príncipe also established trade links with the delta.

The Ijo of the Niger Delta were the first Africans to participate in the slave trade. It is most likely that they obtained the first slaves they sold to the Portuguese from two sources, namely, from amongst the prisoners captured in the inter-community conflicts; and from people in the hinterland north of the delta, with whom they were traditionally in commercial contact for foodstuffs. It is reported by an eye-witness that the Ijo possessed large canoes, which greatly facilitated commercial interaction between the creek and the interior. In exchange for yams, slaves, cows, sheep and goats, and other items which they could not themselves produce in the swampy delta terrain, the Ijo offered fish and salt which they produced in large quantities. When the Portuguese arrived, they were buying these products that the Ijo brought from the hinterland for copper bracelets.[1] The expansion of trade caused by the Portuguese demands for slaves and foodstuffs tremendously aided the expansion of salt production. The salt was used in paying for the products from the interior. It must be emphasised, however, that it was the Ijo communities of the eastern delta, with their better-developed trade systems, who benefited more readily from the expanding commercial transactions. Where the necessary support-systems, or what Professor E. J. Alagoa calls the 'basic internal superstructure for trade consisting of institutions, trade routes and relations with producing communities and market',[2] were inadequate or non-existent, the slave traders took the initiative to establish direct links with the sources.

This was the case in the western delta where the Portuguese travelled up the rivers in their ships to establish direct trade contacts with the Ijebu from whom they bought slaves and ivory. When they visited Ijebu-Ode, they discovered that this principal Ijebu town, ruled by the

Awujale, was 'surrounded by a very large ditch' which was probably used for defence. Further inland, they found the kingdom of Benin to be constantly 'at war with its neighbours'. The captives taken from such wars were sold to the Portuguese for brass or copper bracelets.[3] For 'a considerable time', a thriving trade in slaves developed between Benin and São Jorge de Mina (Elmina in modern Ghana). [4] Thus, initially, the slaves who came principally from the coastal region of the 'five slave rivers' (i.e. Primeiro, the Benin River, the Escravos, the Forcadis and the Ramos) and Ijebu were carried either to the Gold Coast or to the Portuguese colonies in São Tomé and Príncipe. The island colonies soon became, certainly after the end of the opening decade of the sixteenth century, the slave depot or barracoon for the Portuguese since slaves meant for the Gold Coast had now first to go to these islands. This practice continued into the 1520s when slaves were no longer carried via Europe to the New World.

The use of these islands, especially São Tomé, as slave depots, where slaves were also put to work on the sugar plantations, had a major impact on the direction of the expansion of the trade. The Cross River area, by the 1520s, became a busier slave-trading centre than Benin. It is possible that this eastward shift of the trade was due to the ban in Benin on the sale of male slaves to Europeans from 1516 until the close of the seventeenth century – a policy arising apparently from religious considerations which was observed for almost two centuries. This ban greatly limited Benin's involvement in the slave trade; and when the ban was lifted in the eighteenth century, the Europeans had found more attractive markets elsewhere. The result was that the area around the Benin River could only sell about one thousand slaves a year made up of war captives or political prisoners, most of whom were Itsekiri, at the height of the trade boom in the late eighteenth century. All along, the trade in products like pepper, ivory, beads, and locally-woven cotton textiles had developed. By the early nineteenth century, Benin had completely ceased trading in laves. This had little impact since the slave trade was never a major commercial concern, as was the case in the states of the Niger Delta whose origin antedated the slave trade but whose influence and growth had much to do with it.[5]

It is also possible that the eastward shift became necessary because the prices of slaves in the region of the Benin River and Ijebu had become high and the Portuguese were naturally looking for cheaper new markets. Thus, by the middle of the sixteenth century, the area east of the delta and the Cross River became the chief sources of slaves for the Portuguese slavers. The English and the Dutch entered the scene in the second half of the sixteenth century looking for non-human commodities like pepper, ivory, timber, and so on. This soon changed. The new development which dramatically changed the pattern of the commercial relations between the Europeans and the West Africans occurred on the other side of the Atlantic.

The rapid expansion of what was hitherto a limited commercial transaction in human cargoes between the southern coast of Nigeria and the Portuguese island colonies of São Tomé and Príncipe began with the emergence of sugar plantations in the West Indies in the mid-seventeenth century. The production of sugar demanded the right type of labour on a large scale to be provided by people who were capable of surviving the rigours of plantation life and the dangers of tropical diseases in the Caribbean. The Amerindians (the 'native' Americans) could not cope since they were gravely affected by the new diseases introduced by the Europeans; and the voluntary European emigrants' labour was scarce, and when found, too expensive. What the planters wanted was a steady supply of cheap labour. African slave labour was found to be especially suitable: the mortality rate of the African slaves was low because of their higher resistance to tropical diseases such as malaria and yellow fever; and the slaves could be obtained cheaply from West Africa. The Europeans did not establish sugar plantations in Africa where sugar-cane could grow and where African labour would be readily available, although this would have saved them the high cost of transporting Africans to the New World, and, several reasons can be adduced for this irrational and seemingly uneconomical arrangement. In the first place, the mortality rate of Europeans in Africa due to attacks of malaria and yellow fever was higher than their death rate in the West Indies. Secondly, more suitable land for sugar cultivation was available in the New World than in Africa. Thirdly, European labourers were too few for the labour-intensive sugar plantations; they were also very expensive. The African slaves, on the other hand, could be obtained at low prices and the effective supply system guaranteed availability of cheap labour. We must also add that the African rulers greatly cherished their independence, and European attempts to establish permanent settlements in their domains were resisted. Furthermore, to protect their political and commercial interests as middlemen the Africans restricted the European traders in West Africa to the waterside and prevented them from moving into the interior. It would seem that the Europeans were not at this time in a militarily strong position to dictate to the Africans; the reputation of West Africa as 'the white man's grave' also provided little attraction for European occupation. The only practical solution was to carry the Africans to the New World.[6]

The islands of the West Indies, led by Jamaica and St Domingue, utilised the labour of the African slaves on the sugar plantations and in the sugar industries to meet the increasing demand of the tea and coffee-drinkers of Europe. Sugar dominated the economic intercourse between England and the West Indies in the eighteenth century, and the region became the most important commercial life-line to the British empire. Its commercial importance is aptly encapsulated in the observation that the British empire was a 'magnificent superstructure of American commerce and naval power on an African foundation'.[7] Our main concern in this chapter is to examine the Nigerian aspect of that 'African foundation' in its many ramifications.

The increased demand for slaves occasioned by the establishment of Dutch and English sugar plantations in the Caribbean in the first half of the seventeenth century led to a new rush for slaves, no longer by the Portuguese merchants alone but also by the English, the French, the Dutch, the Spanish and Swedish traders. The trade was now concentrated on New Calabar River with the Kalabari dominating the trade for much of the seventeenth century. They were able to tap the human resources from the slave markets far into the hinterland much more easily than the Bonny merchants. However, by the close of the century there is sufficient evidence to show that Bonny, too, had acquired the trading strategies of using large canoes, and its merchants had been successful in securing more trading routes and markets far into the Igbo areas.[8] The upshot of the keen commercial rivalry was that Bonny surpassed its competitor before the end of the eighteenth century – at the expense of the Igbo whose population was immensely affected. For example, as Captain John Adams observed in 1822, Bonny was a leading slave emporium where

> not fewer than 20 000 are annually sold ... 16 000 of whom are natives of one nation called Heebo [Igbo], so that this single nation has not exported a less number of its people, during the last twenty years, than 320 000; and those of the same nation sold at New and Old Calabar, probably amounted in the same period of time to 50 000 more, making an aggregate amount of 370 000 Heebos. The remaining part of the above 20 000 is composed of natives of the brass country ... and also of Ibbibbys [Ibibios] or Quaws [Ibibio Kwa].[9]

Adams's figures appear to be confirmed by another witness, Macgregor Laird, who maintained that between 1827 and 1834, the delta exported 'at the lowest calculation', about 200 000 slaves.[10] Adams's report makes it clear that the Igbo constituted by far the majority of the slaves sold at Bonny, followed by the Ibibio. The expansion of the trade in the delta also caused an expansion of what we may call the 'catchment area', with the result that slaves from ethnic groups north of the Igbo areas began to show their appearance among the slaves sold in Bonny in the first half of the nineteenth century.

The ascendancy of the Bight of Bonny as the leading exporter of slaves for about a century after 1750 can better be appreciated if we consider the development in the area of a network of commercial systems. The phenomenal growth was greatly helped, first, by the emergence of commercial houses which sustained the expansion of the city states; second, by the effective Aro commercial system which extended to the Cross River, the Niger Delta and to the northern hinterland, thus dominating the commercial activities in the Igbo region; third, the founding at Calabar of the Ekpe Society which set up and enforced commercial codes and payment of debts; and finally, the establishment of spheres of influence in the Niger River trade by different communities. All these taken together constituted a veritable economic system which made the production and export of slaves a flourishing business. Bonny and Calabar, by their strategic location, became the two leading ports which handled the export trade.[11]

Developments elsewhere also contributed to the expansion of the slave trade in the delta states. For example, the conquest by Dahomey of the great slaving ports of Allada, Whydah and Jakin within a dozen years after 1720 forced many European slavers to go eastwards to the ports in the delta for their human cargoes.[12]

As a result of the response of the delta peoples to the European

Fig. 7.1   Conditions on a European slave-trade ship

contact and the economic transformation that resulted from it, certain socio-political and institutional changes became inevitable. A new class of rich businessmen emerged who, by their wealth, power and prestige, were able to control the economy and manipulate the political developments in the society. The change from traditional fishing and production of salt to slave trading led to the change from the lineage to business firms, or 'canoe-houses' as they came to be known.

Canoes became very vital instruments in the commercial competition and, in fact, were often armed for military encounters with rivals. Usually, a 'house' consisted of a successful merchant who headed it, his immediate family, his slaves, guards, oarsmen, and other traders. They worked together as a corporate, close-knit organisation, ready and willing to promote the commercial and political interest of the 'house'. It was possible for successful and prominent slaves to rise to the headship of 'houses'.[13] What is important to note in this whole structure is the evolution of new patterns of leadership and economic structure in response to the increasing commercial activity with the European slavers.

The 'house' system became the institution through which the Europeans carried out major financial transactions like the giving of credits. In turn, the canoe-houses served as guarantors of credits, and saw to the prosecution of defaulting parties. Thus, the 'houses' played an enormous role in the economic life of the delta.

In political matters, the 'house' was a force to be reckoned with in local government; it served as an agent of law and order. In other words, the 'house' was both a political and an economic force in the delta society.

The Aro of Arochuku, a sub-section of the Igbo, dominated the slave trade through their commercial network between the delta, the Cross River and the interior grasslands to the north. They combined commercial and organisational acumen with their control of the widely and highly respected oracle known as the Long Juju. This combination proved to be of great advantage to them: they enjoyed protection of their properties and persons throughout the territories in which they did business. They were good in the use of firearms, maintained groups of mercenary soldiers for purposes of acquiring slaves, established trading settlements and markets, and long-distance routes in the Igbo country, held periodic market fairs, and gave out contracts for the purchase of slaves to local merchants. With good business relations with Calabar, the Aro were able to obtain credit facilities used in their commercial operations. They used religious sanctions to maintain discipline and preserve their own commercial interests.[14]

The development in Calabar of the Ekpe secret society made it possible for the Calabar merchants to monopolise the slave trade east of the Bight of Bonny during the last half of the eighteenth century. Controlled by the heads of the influential Efik lineages, the society was used as an agency for the collection of debts and the regulation of credit facilities. They used it to maintain their vast economic and political influence. A remarkable degree of trust developed in the financial transactions between the European merchants who made available credit advances and the leading indigenous captains who organised the supply of slaves. The trade along the river Niger was dominated by different groups: the Aboh businessmen controlled the trade north to Onitsha; the Igala, up to the Niger–Benue confluence; the Nupe, from there to Bussa, while the Jukun and Idoma controlled the Benue trade.

In the Yoruba country, the powerful Oyo empire did much to organise and promote the slave trade by establishing commercial centres on routes to the coast, especially in Egbado; collecting taxes and fees to control trade in the dependencies, and controlling the passage of northern merchants in its domain. The Oyo imperial preponderance probably owed much, among other factors, to the effective production and delivery system so adroitly utilised by the Alafins during the late seventeenth and throughout the eighteenth centuries.[15]

The Yoruba had been sold into slavery and sent to the New World as early as the seventeenth century through the Dahomean ports of Allada and Whydah but the late eighteenth century marked the beginning of the large export of Yoruba slaves. The increase in the volume of Yoruba slaves exported, beginning at the close of the eighteenth and the opening decade of the nineteenth century, could be attributed to, first, the development of Badagry and Lagos as active slaving ports – the former, about the middle of the eighteenth century, and the latter later in the same century; and second, the upheavals, or what Akintoye calls 'revolution and power politics', in the Yoruba country following the collapse of the Oyo empire.

By the first decade of the nineteenth century Lagos had become the leading outlet. It was about this time too, that is, the late eighteenth and early nineteenth century, that the Hausa and other groups from north of the Niger began to be exported as slaves in large numbers through Porto Nova, Badagry and Lagos.[16]

In most parts of Nigeria affected by the slave trade, slaves were produced through warfare, raiding, kidnapping, payment of tributes by vassal states, gifts, manipulation of the judicial process, and purchasing. The procuring and marketing of slaves required large capital outlay and entrepreneural ingenuity. It was not a business that could be successfully embarked upon by the weak, the timid, the artless or the poor. At every stage of the slave-capturing and marketing process, a great deal of energy and money had to be expended. It was the business of the rich, the influential or of the state. Without the active participation by the Africans at every stage, the Europeans alone would have found the execrable business daunting. It is therefore important to realise that, as Hopkins put it, the 'Atlantic slave trade was made possible by an alliance of two groups, European shippers and African suppliers'.[17] Perhaps not an alliance but rather a coincidence of economic interests bestially egged on by man's inhumanity to man.

The total number of slaves exported from Africa in the Atlantic slave trade, according to Professor Philip D. Curtin, was about 11 million. It has been argued that Curtin's figure is rather low and that the growing weight of evidence would support an addition of 40–60 per cent to it, thus raising the overall total considerably. It may well be that a total of between 15 and 20 million would not be an unreasonable estimate for the continent. It has been estimated that rather more than half of Curtin's figure were exported from West Africa.[18] Here again, the actual number might be several millions more than this. Not included in these figures are the many lives lost during the wars or raids or in the process of kidnapping. The rigours of long treks to the entrepôts and the harsh living conditions in the coastal waiting camps would surely have contributed to the pre-shipment fatalities. Perhaps we can better appreciate the magnitude of the losses if we realise, as Curtin contends, that the number of pre-shipment fatalities added to the deaths during the transatlantic passage would be almost equal to the numbers that actually made it to the American destinations.[19]

The exact number of peoples of Nigeria sold into slavery will probably never be known. However, historians have identified some patterns. From about 1480 to 1630, it is likely that up to about 2 000 slaves annually were taken from the Nigerian shores 'in exceptional years'. From 1630 to 1730, the number would depend on the prevailing conditions in the producing areas in Nigeria, in Europe and the New World; it is possible that the number might have exceeded 5 000, but the average would be much lower. Finally, beginning with the opening of the

Yoruba coastal outlets and the flourishing trade in Bonny to the closing years of the Atlantic slave trade, 'the overall total for all ports in the period must have approached an annual peak of 30 000'.[20] In exchange for the slaves and other non-human products exported by the Africans, they imported such goods as textiles, firearms, gin, brandy, beads, bar iron, salt, tools and utensils.

In assessing the impact of the Atlantic slave trade on the Nigerian societies, it is strongly tempting to think largely of the quantifiable, tangible costs – the number of prime-age individuals forcibly removed, for example – leaving aside the intangible social, psychological and political effects. No account of the costs would be correct without a special underscoring of these intangible costs. And even then, it is highly doubtful, as Gann and Duignan rightly maintain, that any 'balance sheet can ever present the full debt account of the slave traffic'.[21] Both the victims and the beneficiaries of the nefarious traffic suffered from it; as Professor Ryder holds, 'on those who lived by it as well as those who suffered it the slave trade wrought havoc and debasement'.[22]

Thousands of people in their prime, the productive sector of the population, were sold into slavery. This population loss inevitably affected the productive capacity and the real cost of production, especially in the food-producing areas. Raids and warfare for the purpose of gathering slaves disrupted social and economic life and survival became of a greater value than anything else. Inter-state commercial rivalry often grew into open confrontations which further promoted untold cruelty among the warring groups and enslavement of the captives. Even though inter-state wars might be caused by factors other than the slave trade, nevertheless, most wars did indeed contribute to the increase in the volume of the slave traffic. The weapons of war introduced by the Europeans were employed to stage more raids or fight wars to produce more slaves, or to resist attempts at enslavement. Thus the availability of firearms contributed to the climate of fear, social insecurity and political instability. It was a legacy of violence and destruction. The emergence of rich merchants as heads of 'houses' and political 'power-brokers' who could trade with the Europeans on acceptable terms reduced others to mere participants in a controlled economy, almost entirely dependent on the slave trade, and caused loss of freedom to many in the society, created a 'middleman' economy and dependence mentality.

Perhaps on the positive side was the introduction of cassava and maize from the New World – two crops which have become very important in the nation's food resources.[23] The general insecurity and social dislocation caused by raids and wars retarded the expansion of domestic and inter-regional trade, and made the development of local technology or the acquisition of relevant European technology for the benefit of the Nigerian peoples virtually impossible. It is safe to say that the Atlantic slave trade, considered in all its multifarious ramifications, helped to initiate the process of Nigeria's underdevelopment.

Notes

1 Duarte Pacheco Pereira, *Esmeraldo de Situ Orbis*, edited by R. Mauny (Bissau: Centro de Estudos da Guiné Portuguesa, 1956), No. 19, pp. 130–47, translated in T. Hodgkin (ed.), *Nigerian Perspectives: an historical anthology* (London: Oxford University Press, 1960), pp. 92–95.

2 E. J. Alagoa, 'Development of institutions in the states of the eastern Niger Delta', *Journal of African History*, XII (2), 1971, p. 273.

3 Pacheco Pereira in Hodgkin, *Nigerian Perspectives*, pp. 92–93.

4 De Barros on the arrival of the Portuguese in Benin, in *Nigerian Perspectives*, p. 88.

5 See Alan Ryder, *Benin and the Europeans 1485–1897* (London: Longman, 1977), pp. 88–93, 168, 196, 198; Obaro Ikime, *Niger Delta Rivalry: Itsekiri-Urhobo relations and the European presence, 1884–1936* (London: Longman, 1969), pp. 50–59. It should be pointed out that even after the ban was lifted, the sale of male slaves in Benin remained strictly the prerogative of the Oba of Benin. See also Captain John Adams' *Remarks* in Hodgkin, *Nigerian Perspectives*, p. 176.

6 Actually, African slave labour had been introduced into the Americas from Spain as early as 1501; the first direct shipment from West Africa to the New World was in a Spanish ship in 1518. It was the Dutch who deposited the first 20 African slaves in Jamestown, Virginia, in 1619 – a year before the *Mayflower*. See D. A. Farnie, 'The commercial empire of the Atlantic, 1607–1783', *Economic History Review*, 15, 1962, pp. 205–18.

7 Quoted in Eric Williams, *Capitalism and Slavery* (New York: Capricorn Books, 1966), p. 52.

8 G. I. Jones, *The Trading States of the Oil Rivers* (Oxford: Oxford University Press, 1963), pp. 91–92.

9 James Adams, quoted in Hodgkin, *Nigerian Perspectives*, p. 178.

10 Cited in K. O. Dike, *Trade and Politics in the Niger Delta* (Oxford: Clarendon Press, 1966), p. 29.

11 See Jones, *The Trading States of the Oil Rivers*; E. J. Alagoa, *A History of the Niger Delta* (Ibadan: Ibadan University Press, 1972); E. J. Alagoa, 'Long distance trade and states in the Niger Delta', *Journal of African History (JAH)*, II (3), 1970, pp. 319–29; S. J. S. Cookey, 'An Igbo slave story of the late nineteenth century and its implications', *Ikenga*, I(2), 1972, pp. 1–9; F. I. Ekejiuba, 'The Aro trade system in the nineteenth century', *Ikenga* I(1), 1972, pp. 11–26; F. I. Ekejiuba, 'The Aro system of trade in the nineteenth century, Part II', *Ikenga*, I(2), 1972, pp. 10–21; A. E. Afigbo, 'The Aro of southeastern Nigeria: a socio-historical analysis of legends of their origins', *African Notes*, 6(2), 1971, pp. 31–46; *African Notes*, 7(1), 1971–1972, pp. 91–106; A. E. Afigbo, 'Trade and trade routes of nineteenth century Nsukka', *Journal of the Historical Society of Nigeria (JHSN)*, 8(1), 1973, pp. 77–90; A. F. C. Ryder, 'The trans-Atlantic slave trade', in *Groundwork of Nigerian History*, Obaro Ikime (ed.) (Ibadan: Heinemann, 1979); A. J. H. Latham, *Old Calabar 1600–1891: the impact of the international economy upon a traditional society* (London, 1973).

12 I. A. Akinjogbin, *Dahomey and its Neighbours 1708–1818* (Cambridge: Cambridge University Press, 1967), pp. 91–92. It was also as a result of

developments following these conquests that Badagry and Porto Novo received the influx of refugees; the former also soon became a flourishing slave market frequently patronised by European slavers.

13 For further details on the 'house' system, see Alagoa, 'Long Distance Trade', pp. 322ff.; Cookey, 'An Igbo Slave Story', p. 4; Dike, *Trade and Politics*, pp. 34–37.

14 Ekejiuba, 'The Aro Trade System', pp. 13–15; Afigbo, 'The Aro', p. 41; M. Crowder, *The Story of Nigeria* (London: Faber and Faber, 1962), pp. 72–73.

15 Peter Morton-Williams, 'The Oyo Yoruba and the Atlantic Slave Trade, 1670–1830', *JHSN*, 3(1), 1964, pp. 25–46; also R. C. C. Law, *The Oyo Empire c. 1600–1836, A West African imperialism in the era of the slave trade* (Oxford, 1977).

16 Ryder, 'The Trans-Atlantic Slave Trade', p. 243; S. A. Akintoye, *Revolution and Power Politics in Yorubaland 1840–1893* (London: Longman, 1971), pp. 39, 40, 60.

17 Hopkins, *An Economic History of West Africa*, p. 106.

18 Philip D. Curtin, *The Atlantic Slave Trade: a census* (Madison: University of Wisconsin Press, 1969), pp. 86–87; J. D. Fage, *A History of West Africa* (Cambridge: Cambridge University Press, 1969), pp. 84–88. Fage estimates 6 300 000 as the total from West Africa. See recent discussions of the estimates of slave exports from West Africa in J. Inikori, 'Measuring the Atlantic slave trade: an assessment of Curtin and Anstey', *JAH*, 17(2), 1976, pp. 197–223; 'Measuring the Atlantic slave trade once again: a comment by Philip D. Curtin', *JAH*, 17(4), 1976, pp. 595–605; also, 'Measuring the Atlantic slave trade: a rejoinder', by J. E. Inikori, *ibid.*, p. 605.

19 Philip D. Curtin, *Economic Change in Precolonial Africa* (Madison: University of Wisconsin Press, 1975), p. 182.

20 Ryder, 'The trans-Atlantic slave trade', p. 243; Hopkins, *An Economic History of West Africa*, pp. 101–104.

21 L. H. Gann and P. Duignan, *Africa and the World* (San Francisco: Chandler, 1972), p. 339.

22 Ryder, 'The Trans-Atlantic Slave Trade', p. 245.

23 *Ibid.*, pp. 244–46. The suggestion that maize might have been introduced to West Africa as early as AD 1100 (based on an impression of maize on a piece of pottery found at Ife, Nigeria), would seem to contradict the hypothesis of Portuguese introduction of maize to Africa. See Marvin P. Miracle, *Maize in Tropical Africa* (Madison: University of Wisconsin Press, 1966), p. 89.

8 The Fulani Jihad and the Sokoto Caliphate in the nineteenth century

Akin Olorunfemi

Causes of the Jihad

The origin and nature of the Islamic revolutions commonly referred to as the 'Fulani Jihad' in the Hausa states during the early years of the nineteenth century have been so thickly overlaid with interpretations which later generations have given to them that there is today some difficulty in seeing the Jihad as it appeared to contemporaries. The simple idea that the word *Jihad* itself means 'holy war' aimed at religious reforms – as Usman dan Fodio himself would probably have conceived it – has been submerged and its place taken up by conflicting ideological interpretations based pre-eminently on socio-economic and political theories.

The religious theme, of course, still has some respectable disciples in the 'Bello school of thought', which believes that 'the story of Usman dan Fodio is the story of the religious war or Jihad'.[1] Exponents of this school include Mockler-Ferryman, Arnett, Daniel and Bovil, all of whom shared Mohammed Bello's views in various forms that the Habe rulers were practising a calculated syncretism in religion, which formed the basis for the Jihad leaders' charge of 'a return to paganism' preferred against these rulers.[2] However, this religious concept has equally and vehemently been assailed by at least two other schools of thought, the first of which sees the Jihad as an expression of Fulani nationalism, while the other looks at it as a class war between the Hausa-Fulani commoners – the *talakawa* – and their Habe rulers.

The advocates of the theory of 'ethnic nationalism' relied heavily on the accusations levied against the Jihad leaders by El-Kanemi, the *Mai* (*ruler*) of Bornu who, though he admitted the charges of 'paganism' or 'irreligion' brought against the Habe rulers, denied that such charges were grave enough to justify a Jihad.[3] In contrast, the 'Kanemites' see the Jihad as a national rising of the Fulani, both Muslims and pagans, against Hausa domination. In support of this thesis, J. S. Hogben, looking at the immediate causes of the war, believes that the Jihad was 'in reality . . . originally a national fight of the Fulani, both Muslims and pagans, against the forces of Yunfa, the king of Gobir who had decreed their extermination'.[4] Hogben went further to suggest that it was only after the Jihadists had been victorious, when the pagan Fulani who had borne more than their full share in order to achieve victory had retired to their flocks and herds, did the malams, who had been the leaders, exploit the opportunity under the cloak of religion to oust the native rulers and put themselves into their places. Moreover, while D. H. Jones, another 'Kanemite', spoke of the 'racial pride and tribal loyalty of the Fulani',

*Fig. 8.1   The Great Mosque at Zaria built as a result of the nineteenth-century
Jihads*

J. D. Fage, in the same vein, considered the spirit of racial pride as the single
factor or 'momentum which gave the Jihad its force'. For him the Fulani
were an able active people, unquestionably ambitious for political power,
and therefore saw the Jihad as a cover for 'Fulani imperialism'.

On the other hand, the 'class-war school' has its origin in the writings of the Russian scholar, D. A. Olderogge, and of Thomas Hodgkin, who were apparently under the influence of Marxist philosophy, and for whom the 'social theory' provided the easiest escape route from what appeared to be very complex issues involved in the Jihad movement. Olderogge had examined and rejected other views, and came to the conclusion that 'the rebellion' was neither a religious nor national rising but a clan war, a conflict between the Hausa nobility on the one hand, and the poor Fulani cattle rearers and the downtrodden Hausa commoners (the *talakawa*), on the other.[5] Olderogge further argued, perhaps rightly, that it was the Shehu's social teachings – his attack upon contemporary forms of oppression, exploitation and injustice – that caused the Jihad, in its initial stages, to appeal especially to the 'submerged classes' among the Hausa as well as among the Fulani. Basil Davidson summed up this Marxist position when he wrote that the origins of this Fulani invasion had lain in revolt against a gross social inequality.

Taken in isolation, each of these theories is capable of providing impressive and convincing arguments as to the causes of the Jihad. For instance, in view of the dominant role played by the Fulani in the Jihad movement, the charge of 'a racial conflict' seems very plausible. The Fulani – a mixture of Berber emigrants from the Sahara and of the Wolof and Serer stock – are known to have originated from the lower basin of the Senegal and Gambia, and by about the fifteenth century they were already settled in fairly large numbers in the Hausa states. Those of them who settled in the towns, the Town Fulani or Fulani Gidda, were fanatical Muslims and generally well educated. This level of education brought by them into Hausaland created a great intellectual gap that distinguished them from the Hausa. They quickly became favourites at Hausa courts and served the governments in various capacities – as *Qadis* (judges), Koranic teachers, civil servants, etc. – though often living as separate communities in the Hausa towns or in centres of learning. Therefore, the Jihad movement originating from these Fulani communities could, to that extent, be regarded as largely secular in concept with a religious admixture to smoke-screen that motive. Therefore, it could rightly be described not only as an expression of Fulani nationalism, but also, in the words of H. F. C. Smith, of 'a sense of common purpose which a group with ties of education, culture and ideology, as well as language and kinship is liable to generate'.[6]

However, even though almost all the 'flag bearers' who emerged as rulers (or Emirs) after the war were known Fulani supporters of the Shehu, the charge of Fulani imperialsim becomes very weak given the composition of the Jihad armies and the prevailing conditions under which the wars were fought. It is known, for instance, that the Shehu's later armies consisted of various elements – Hausa, Fulani and the Tuaregs – and that there were unspecified numbers of prominent Fulani who refused to join the Jihad army, including some of the learned men who, it has been alleged, openly denounced the Jihad.[7] Moreover, the Shehu's call for the Jihad was extended not only to the Fulani but also to all the Sultans of Hausaland, among whom only the Sultan of Zaria was known to have given a favourable reply. Apart from the Sultan, the part played by other prominent Hausa, particularly by Abdulsalam and Yakubu of Bauchi in the prosecution of the Jihad serves to further weaken the arguments of the 'Kanemites'. It is true that the Jihad army attacked Bornu, a known Muslim state, during the period. It must, however, be noted that the *mai* of Bornu was a nominal Muslim, known to have lived in seclusion, and was venerated by his subjects, thereby sharing divine attributes with God. Therefore El-Kanemi was attacked by the Jihadists not merely because he was at the head of a Hausa government, but because even though he openly professed the Muslim religion, he mixed it up with traditional or irreligious sanctions. Similarly, the social abuses in the Hausa political structure were condemned by the Muslim Fulani not so much because fellow Fulani groups – the cattle Fulani (Bororoje) as well as the Fulani Gidda (many of them cattle owners) – were directly affected, but because such abuses were direct violations of Muslim laws.

Similarly, the Marxist view, taken alone, can supply some of the basic answers to the problem of finding the causes of the Jihad. The presence of an oppressed and exploited group in Hausa society – the *Talakawa*, both Hausa and Fulani – is one of the most essential ingredients of a Marxist revolution. The fact that Usman dan Fodio picked upon the 'social abuses', particularly in so far as they affected the *Talakawa*, as one of his cardinal accusations against the Hausa rulers automatically, in the Marxist view, made him the 'champion of the oppressed' and leader of the revolution against an oppressive and exploitative political structure. Moreover, the fact that the *Talakawa* formed the core of the Shehu's later armies gave the Jihad the support of the masses and the picture of 'a coincidence of objective conditions and subjective readiness', thereby completing the evolution of a truly Marxist revolution. Thus by abstracting the social elements in the Shehu's teachings and correlating them with the political and social conditions of Hausaland, the Marxists seem to have conceptualised the Jihad movement in terms of a coherent ideology which sought to remove 'current forms of oppression, exploitation and injustice' in the Hausa societies.

In spite of its very tempting credibility, the Marxist position would appear to have over-simplified the complex issues involved in the Jihad movement. It does not, for instance, attempt to make any distinction between the original motives of the Jihad leaders and those of the various elements that later joined their armies. The Marxists have not given any adequate explanation as to why the leaders were so concerned with religious matters, as could be read in their numerous writings, or the fact that religion formed the pivot of the administrative machinery they later attempted to establish to replace the existing political organisation over the Hausa states. This is, however, not to deny the fact that 'objective conditions' did exist in the Hausa states and that many peasants joined the revolt in order to shake off the yoke of their oppressive rulers. Taxes were excessive and sometimes very arbitrary, properties were seized without compensation; there was the 'selling of justice to the highest bidder', bribery was rife, illegal market dues were collected and oppressive taxes (like the *jangali* or cattle tax), which were not provided for by the Koran, were imposed. Usman dan Fodio also accused the Habe rulers of 'appropriating any animals which strayed into their own herds, while theirs were allowed to stray and cause damage to cultivated lands with impunity'. He criticised them for 'delays in the payment of debts, the seizure of the property of those who died while passing through the country' and also accused them of not paying attention to the welfare of their subjects, but instead they were found shutting the door in the face of the needy.[8]

However, in spite of this catalogue of vices in the Hausa societies, a Marxist analysis cannot be a wholly valid explanation of the causes of the Jihad. In fact, according to H. A. S. Johnston, the oppression of the peasants was not a new phenomenon of the early nineteenth century in the Hausa states.[9] Even though Usman dan Fodio's teachings were then drawing serious attention to them, the Hausa rulers were not given to peasant revolts and were therefore not easily disturbed by such issues. It is true that most of those who joined the Jihad armies – peasants, cattle rearers, etc. – were economically dissatisfied with the existing socio-political structure of the Hausa states; to that extent, it could be legitimately argued that the Bororoje went to war merely in support of their kinsmen in the towns, the Fulani Gidda, against rulers who had on many occasions oppressed them. But the important issue to be determined is whether the motives of the followers should be allowed or given an overriding pre-eminence over those of the leaders themselves.

On the face of it, the idea of the Jihad as essentially a religious movement appears rather weak and of little credibility, faced with the overwhelming, if conflicting, ideological arguments of both the 'Kanemites' and the Marxists. Yet it would appear from the teachings and writings of the Shehu and those of his close associates that the Islamic religion in its 'undiluted form and content' would not make any serious distinction between the religious and socio-political aspects of contemporary Hausa societies. For the Jihad leaders, therefore, the causes of the 'abuses prevalent in the Hausa states' in the early nineteenth century could be traced to the rulers' violations of the 'essence of an ideal Muslim government'. It is from this viewpoint that one should understand why the Shehu criticised the socio-political vices of the Hausa rulers for precisely the same reasons as their self-indulgence and their clinging to pagan practices. It is for these same reasons that the Shehu went on to contrast these abuses with the conditions which should prevail under an ideal Muslim government. According to him, the purpose of such government should include 'setting to rights the affairs of the poor and the needy . . .'. The foundations of such government, he further pointed out, would include among other things, 'the abandonment of harshness of justice', and its ministers would include a *Wazir* (Prime Minister) who should be 'steadfast in compassion to the people and merciful towards them . . . and a chief of police who will not oppress the subjects'.[10] There is then no doubt that the Jihad leaders found a society which, as far as they were concerned, urgently needed reforms, and they were prepared to carry out such reforms in accordance with Islamic principles. To that extent therefore, the Jihad movement can be regarded as not just a struggle for Islamic purity, it was also an attempt at a comprehensive social revolution in the Hausa societies in tune with Islamic principles.

Hausa society before the Jihad

In order to appreciate fully the background to the Fulani Jihad, it is important to understand the foundations of the Shehu's accusation against the Hausa rulers. To achieve this, reference must necessarily be made not only to the events immediately preceding the outbreak of hostilities, but also to the more important aspects of the Islamic religion as it was introduced and developed in the Hausa states before the Jihad movement.

Islam in some form was already known in Hausaland as early as about the beginning of the twelfth century. It was introduced into this area through peaceful and commercial contacts with Bornu, whose rulers – particularly Mai Umeme Jilmi (1087–1097) – were known to have embraced Islam earlier. But the full impact of the religion was probably not felt in the country until the second half of the fourteenth century when the actual conversion of Hausaland was peacefully but intensively undertaken by the Wangarawa merchants, itinerant pilgrims and malams from the north. This was followed in the sixteenth century by the influential work of Al-Maghili, the well-known preacher of morals and religious austerity from Bornu, who had actually written a treatise on Islamic government for the ruler of Kano towards the end of the fifteenth century. In spite of these, however, the picture of Hausaland even at the end of the eighteenth century was that of a society whose rulers had accepted Islam very lightly or nominally, and they saw themselves quite free and prepared to mix it up with non-Islamic practices. As far as the masses were concerned, they were hardly expected, and did not pretend, to adopt the slightest form of Islam for a long time because, since it was the duty of the rulers to cater for them in this respect, 'the religion of the king was the religion of the people'. In other words, Islam was a class religion, adopted chiefly by the ruling group, and ran parallel to, but did not displace, their traditional religion.

On the other hand, and in contrast to the Hausa rulers, the Fulani Muslims who had long settled in the Hausa states held very orthodox views. The practice of their religion involved the strict adherence to the teachings and obligations – both social and ritual – of their faith. The arrival of these Fulani groups with their intellectual superiority, which enabled them to occupy high and influential positions at the courts of the rulers, did not at first disturb anyone. But as devout Muslims, the Fulani became very uneasy at the apparent admixture of Islam and 'paganism' among the Hausa rulers. Converts to Islam did not altogether abandon their pre-Islamic beliefs and social customs, and they were therefore accused of pronouncing 'a twofold confession of faith'. Since their orthodox views made it theoretically imperative for them to live under an Islamic government, ruled righteously according to the precepts of the Muslim laws (the Shari'a), the Fulani leaders therefore sought to purify the Islamic religion by appealing for 'a return to the pure and primitive faith of Islam purged of heresies and accretions'.[11] It was when this simple 'miracle' did not happen in the Hausa states that the Fulani Muslims decided to carry out one of their most important and fundamental obligations – to establish the political as well as the religious ascendancy of Islam and to defend this by force of arms when necessary.

The reformer who was very much concerned with the purity of the Islamic tradition, and who became the national hero of the Fulani Jihad, was Shehu Usman dan Fodio. He belonged to the Toronkawa clan of Gobir, one of the most prominent Hausa states, and from where the open confrontation erupted between the ruler and the Muslim community. The Toronkawa were a strongly Muslim group, and many of their members were teachers and preachers. In fact, they constituted something like a missionary clan. Usman dan Fodio had embarked upon his missionary work among the Hausa in the last two decades of the eighteenth century. His aim was to reform lapsed Muslim communities and also to make conversions among the non-Muslims. In the process, Fodio soon attracted a group of followers who were dedicated to the reforms he envisaged. Even though this group was growing rapidly in number, there was nothing at that stage to suggest that he intended to use this mass support to bring down any government in Hausaland. However, in his growing dissatisfaction with the rulers' indifference to Islam and their persistence in pagan practices, the Shehu's preachings found expressions in the criticisms of the governments as illustrations of the way in which Muslim laws were being violated. Consequently, the 'reform movement' of the Shehu gradually became a real threat to the political stability of the Hausa governments as far as the rulers were concerned. This situation was brought to a head by the emergence of a remarkable group of Fulani leaders led by the Shehu himself, in the Hausa state of Gobir.

Usman dan Fodio's connection with the court of Gobir started in about 1781 when Bawa, the ruler of Gobir, engaged him as a tutor to the royal family.[12] Bawa, like many of his predecessors and other Hausa rulers, was hospitable to Islam but as a nominal Muslim he did not himself enforce a Muslim form of government. Here then was a great opportunity for Usman dan Fodio to move closer to a Hausa ruler and possibly to influence him to institute the Shari'a as the basis of government. Indeed he was at first enccouraged by Bawa's cordial reception to hope that the king would not only accept, but also implement the desired reforms. But the Shehu was soon disappointed to realise that even though Bawa tolerated Islam – perhaps as the only surety against the disruption of his power over the kingdom in the circumstances that prevailed – he would not practise it, and was quite prepared to dispense with individuals or groups whose criticisms he considered too harsh or dangerous to the peace and stability of his government. However, the Shehu was far from being despondent and even while Bawa would not consider his call for the establishment of an ideal Muslim government over Gobir, open hostility or armed conflict was not ordinarily the inevitably result. In fact, while resisting his pressures and overtures, Bawa until his death remained on cordial relations with the Shehu who was himself anxious to avoid any clash with the king, and therefore continued to devote much time and attention to circulating and preaching among the generality of the people outside the court. The Shehu's ultimate open defiance and confrontation with the court started to develop after more than twenty years of the state of 'uneasy peace' which existed between his community and the subsequent rulers of Gobir (after Bawa), who not only proved unamenable to pressure, but also actually threatened the growth and even the very existence of a Muslim community anywhere in Hausaland.[13]

The long period of the Shehu's compromising involvement with the Gobir court came to an end during the reign of Nafata (c. 1795–99), his former student, who did not share the complacency of his father towards the new 'Islamic crusade'. Even though Bawa had never completely put Fodio's demand into practice, he had accepted his advice and was not unduly worried about his activities in Hausaland. But soon after his accession Nafata became so astonished by the existence and continued rapid growth in the number of Fodio's followers that he decided to check the growth and influence of the Muslim community in his domain. In pursuance of this, Nafata, perhaps in deference only to his former tutor, forbade anyone except the Shehu from preaching. He decreed that conversion of the people from their traditional religion to Islam should stop, and ordered that those already converted to Islam should return to the religion of their fathers. He also banned the wearing of turbans and veils, marks of identity and cohesion for Muslim men and women respectively. Nafata's hostility towards the Muslim community can be related to the anticipated threat to his continued authority over the affairs of his domain. For instance, by demanding the application of the Shari'a, Fodio was calling for a complete revolution which would necessarily involve the abandonment of the traditional system of government which had always upheld the supreme authority of the ruler. The situation had now reached a point at which the issue at stake was not only religious, but also political. For Nafata therefore, the battle line appeared more clearly drawn between himself, seeking to ensure the survival of his state, and the Muslim community led by Usman dan Fodio, which seemed determined to overwhelm it.

The 'Holy' wars

However, Nafata's penal measures did not deter the progress of the Muslim community. Even though the Shehu withdrew from the court, this was done apparently in order to avoid any open conflict with the king. In fact, the withdrawal gave the Shehu ample opportunity to speak out much more vehemently against the decadent Hausa government than he had done during the reign of Bawa. The Muslim community developed rapidly and began to attract those already discontented with the existing political order. For Nafata therefore, the Muslim community was not only a rival centre of power and authority, it had also, by the very nature of the Shehu's preachings, obviously threatened to undermine the allegiance of the masses to the secular authority. Nafata did not reign long enough to witness the full repercussions of his measures. He was succeeded on the throne by his son, Yunfa, a younger and more intransigent and tactless character than the previous rulers of Gobir. It was under him that the conflict broke out into open war.

Yunfa continued his father's policy of repression towards the Muslim community only to realise that such measures could not stop the growth of the community. Consequently he decided to take positive measures, including physical attack, which threatened the lives of many Muslims in Gobir. This drove a lot of Muslims out of Gobir, and thus gave to the Shehu groups of supporters scattered throughout Gobir, Zamfara and Kebbi, all of whom were willing to come to his aid at a time of trouble. It was this widespread allegiance to him and his ideals which was to be crucial when the final outbreak of hostilities occurred in 1804. Yunfa's attack on a group of Muslims led by Abd-al-Salam, a Hausa scholar and follower of the Shehu at Gimbana, was the first major military aggression against the Muslim community. Gimbana was taken by the forces of Yunfa in December 1803; many Muslims were killed and others who were not captured managed to escape into neighbouring villages. Yunfa's subsequent threat to destroy Degel, where the Shehu and his community lived and gave refuge to political prisoners fleeing from the wrath of Yunfa, was the final justification for the proclamation of the Jihad. By thus attacking the Muslims, Yunfa had answered the charge of an 'unbeliever' against whom a holy war was not only lawful, but also desirable.

In February 1804, the Shehu fled from his home in Degel and went to Dugu. The significance of the decision to perform the *hijra* was to underline the basic doctrine of Islam that it was undesirable for any Muslim willingly to live in the land of the 'unbeliever'. At Dugu, the Shehu's initial supporters were mainly his personal disciples, fellow clerics and other orthodox Muslims who shared his criticisms of Islam in Hausaland. But he was soon surrounded by large numbers of supporters, and he found himself at the head of a great body of warriors, all burning with religious enthusiasm and ready to lay down their lives in the service of the Shehu. The urgency of the situation transformed the Shehu from the position of spiritual leader of a religious reform movement to the 'commander of a holy war', and he was duly elected the 'commander of the faithful' (*Sarkin Musulumi*). After fleeing from his home in Degel in 1804, the Shehu issued an ultimatum to Yunfa and his fellow Hausa rulers either to reform or face the consequences of their intransigence. His appeal to all the Muslims in the 'abode of Islam' to wage the Jihad against those in the 'abode of war' (the unbelievers), was strengthened by the diverse nature of his grievances against the Hausa rulers. It is not surprising, therefore, that many people joined the Jihad army more because the Shehu expressed a religious justification for their general dissatisfaction with the existing Hausa governments than because of the desire to become converts.

With Yunfa's indifference to the Shehu's ultimatum, the uneasy peace which had existed between the Muslim community and the ruler of Gobir finally gave way to a widespread and open warfare. However, the first few months after the *hijra* were relatively calm: but this initial lull was broken on 21 June 1804 with the first major battle on the shores of

Tabkin Kwotto, twenty miles south-west of Dugu, in which the Jihad army defeated Yunfa's forces. It is significant to note that although the Gobir army was superior in numbers with about a hundred heavy cavalry, Shehu's forces emerged victorious because of their superior morale and determination – that of a group fighting a war of survival both for themselves as well as for their faith.

The effect of the first, though not decisive, victory on the later course of the Jihad was considerable. In the first place, by this victory, many Fulani groups from other states were attracted to the war in support of the Shehu, and hence the Jihad came to be more closely identified as a Fulani rising. Many of these newcomers were, no doubt, mercenaries who were more interested in securing war booty than in fighting actively for the ideals for which the holy war was being fought. Secondly, the defeat of Yunfa's army had caused such widespread alarm that the rulers of other Hausa states, particularly of Katsina, Kano, Zaria, Daura and Adar, decided to pre-empt the spread of the Jihad wars into their own states by attacking known followers of the Shehu in their domains. But this roused the Fulani against the rulers and the Jihad spread into all parts of Hausaland. Six months after the defeat of Yunfa at Tabkin Kwotto, the Gobir forces, with the help of the Tuareg at Tsuntsua, counter-attacked and defeated a Jihad army, killing at least 2 000 men. In spite of this heavy defeat, however, the Shehu's army was not totally dispersed. Early in 1805 the army was moved down into Zamfara, a more friendly environment, from where successful military expeditions were sent against Kebbi and Gobir. With the capture of Birmin Kebbi in April 1805 the Jihad forces moved to Gwandu, and by September Gwandu became a permanent base for the Jihad; and from there Muslim leaders established contacts with those in Katsina, Kano, Daura and Zamfara.

It is not necessary to go into the detailed events of the war. It is, however, important to note that, secured at the Gwandu base, the Jihad leaders continued the military campaigns against the Hausa states, and, one by one, these states were captured by the Jihadists. The most spectacular campaign culminated in the defeat, this time decisive, of the fortress city of Alkalawa, capital of Gobir, in 1808, when a major expedition – composed of the combined forces of Mohammed Bello's army from Gwandu and of other Fulani groups from Zamfara and Katsina – marched against it.[14] The fall of Alkalawa and the killing of the Sultan of Gobir in the process ended the initial phase of the Jihad in Hausaland as resistance to the Shehu's armies was swiftly undermined as news of the defeat spread. As for Bornu, even though local Fulani Muslim groups had already been engaged in conflict with the non-Muslims, particularly in Gombe and Bauchi, there had been no direct conflict between the Jihad leaders and the Bornu authorities until the rulers of Katsina, Kano and Daura appeal to the Mai of Bornu for help against the forces of the Shehu. In fact, conflict between the Mai and the Jihad leaders came into the open only after a protracted but inconclusive correspondence between the Bornu authorities and Mohammed Bello on the reasons for the Jihad.[15] Even though the 'mercenary army' sent from Bornu was defeated even before reaching the Hausa states, the Jihad leaders became increasingly involved in Bornu not only because of the 'pagan practices' reported among the so-called Muslims in that state, but also, and perhaps more importantly, because by aiding the 'pagan rulers' of the Hausa states, the *Mai* himself had answered to the charge of the 'unbeliever'. Though no definite conquest ever came about, the Jihad leaders could not feel secure so long as the power of Bornu remained unbroken, more so because the Hausa states of Kano, Katsina and Daura, all of which owed nominal allegiance to Bornu before 1804, continued to look up to the *Mai* for support. In the process of the armed struggle, however, Bornu's capital, Birmin N'Gazaragamu, was thrice captured by the Jihadists and also thrice recaptured by the forces of el-Kanemi. After 1810, the raids continued but no serious attempt was made to bring Bornu into direct military submission. But as a result of these conflicts, there developed in Bornu a legacy of hostility and jealousy towards the Sokoto Caliphate.

Inauguration of the Caliphate

The main purpose of the Jihad, as far as the Fulani Muslims were concerned, was to establish a new political order – commonly known in Islam as the Caliphate – based firmly on Islamic laws, to replace the decadent 'pagan' governments in Hausaland. As a political system, the Caliphate had developed since the time of Prophet Mohammed, who in addition to being the holy prophet, was also the leader of the Muslim community. It was this system that the *jamaa* in Gobir had in mind when they acknowledged Shehu Usman dan Fodio as the *amir-al-muninin* in 1804, shortly after his *hijra* from Degel to Dugu. In other words, the Caliphate as known in the nineteenth century was already inaugurated before the termination of the holy wars. From then, the Muslim community headed by the Shehu was transformed into the nucleus of an independent state. The acquisition and expansion of its territorial extent which followed almost immediately was undertaken with the 'holy wars', with the Shehu's supporters equipped with flags and invested with political authority as emirs over the various territories conquered by them. By 1810, the Fulani Jihad was practically over and the oldest emirates were already founded over states like Katsina, Daura, Kano, Zaria, Bauchi and Gombe, although for about half a century after the fall of Alkalawa (1808), capital of Gobir, the Fulani were still busy extending their conquests and consolidating the administration of the territories acquired.

During the early years of the Caliphate the authority of the Shehu as the Imam was limited to Gobir and the early administration was centralised. The Caliph had two *viziers*: his brother Abdullahi and his son, Mohammed Bello, who was more concerned with defence and security. Up to 1808, the Caliphal administration was *ad hoc* because the Gobirawa were not fully subdued and the community was still at war. With the fall of Alkalawa it became necessary for the community to organise a proper administration in order to restore peace and good government in areas already 'liberated' from Hausa misrule. Moreover, well content with the measure of his achievements, the Shehu soon turned his attention to the organisation and administration of the whole empire. In fact, he had himself never taken an active part in the military campaigns. As commander of the faithful his main role had been to advise his field commanders on how to prosecute the Jihad according to strict Islamic laws and on how to administer the conquered territories in the same way. In 1812 the Shehu divided the administration of the Caliphate into two parts between his brother Abdullahi and his son Mohammed Bello. With his capital at Sokoto, Mohammed Bello's territories included Zamfara, Katsina, Kano, Daura, Bauchi and Katagum, while Abdullahi's territories included the emirates of Nupe, Dendi, Borgu, Ilorin and Liptako, all of which he controlled first from Badinga, and later, after the death of the Shehu in 1817, from Gwandu.[16]

Like the causes of the Jihad itself, the political order of the Sokoto Caliphate meant different things to different people. In particular, members of the 'Lugardian school of thought', perhaps anxious to offer valid excuses for the conquest of Hausaland at the beginning of the twentieth century, have characterised the Fulani empire as constituting a 'Hobbesian state of nature'. According to one of them, J. S. Trimingham, the Caliphate represented an abortive attempt to found a theocracy but that the empire disintegrated into a large number of separate and often hostile states loosely acknowledging the titular suzerainty of the ruler of Sokoto.[17] He went on to suggest that the elements of anarchy were so predominant that within a few years his (Fodio's) empire had disintegrated into an assemblage of slave-raiding and tax-extorting fiefs in practice independent of the titular overlordship of Sokoto. Hogben, another member of the school who branded the leaders as devastating prophets, asserts that 'Justice was corrupted and bribery, nepotism, favouritism and extortionate taxation reigned supreme'.[18] Hence the overall picture was that of an empire whose rulers, especially in its later history, showed themselves to be guilty of evil ambition and rapacity and to be the oppressors and enslavers of the people over whom they ruled. It is therefore not surprising that they have concluded that when in full decline the emirates were given a new lease of life by the British and that no resistance was offered when British troops occupied Sokoto in 1904.

Even though later rulers of the Caliphate might have fallen short of Fodio's standards, and there was the possibility that he was unaware of the excesses of his own immediate followers, the picture of new Fulani emirs becoming 'old Hausa Saki writ large',[19] as painted by Hodgkin, is not only an exaggeration but also grossly misleading. It is true that there were wars and revolts throughout the nineteenth century, but these were mainly sporadic and of short duration. Far from reconciling themselves to their fate, the provinces of Yauri, Gwari, and Nupe as well as the former Hausa states of Gobir, Kebbi and Zamfara continued to struggle to regain their lost pride. In Nupe, the struggle between the Fulani and the former rulers continued intermittently until the Fulani won a decisive victory in the 1850s. About 1853, the Sultan was fighting against the forces of Gobir and Kebbi, who had revolted in the 1820s. Thus in the 1850s the Gwandu empire fell apart; but nearly all the rebels were conquered and formed into the Fulani emirate of Kontagora in 1860. The effects of these civil wars, which certainly must have caused some devastation and insecurity, were chiefly confined to the emirate of Gwandu and should therefore not be taken as a reflection on the state of the Fulani empire as a whole. They were neither raids for slaves nor the 'struggles carried on between paganism and Islamism'. In reality, they were nothing more than mere struggles for independence by the Hausa, the Gwari and the Nupe, struggles which continued until the British occupation.

It is easy to conclude from the foregoing discussion that the Jihad was an uncompleted revolution in terms of territorial consolidation in as much as there were states which, though Muslim, remained persistently hostile to the Caliphate throughout the nineteenth century. Yet there is no doubt that the Shehu's conquests gave Hausaland the first semblance of political unity. It led to a government by a new and permanently established Fulani aristocracy, operating a more or less standard Islamised form of old Hausa city administration extended to non-Hausa-speaking areas. The central authority and therefore the symbol of unity was the Caliph, whose authority was subject only to conformity with the Shari'a. He had effective control over the determination of the general administration of the emirates as well as their relations with one another. The empire was held together at the top by the loyalty and obedience of all the emirs to Sokoto. Tributes were annually paid to Sokoto (and Gwandu after 1812) and the emirs had to provide troops for the imperial army as required.[20]

However, after the division of the empire into two parts in 1812 the above picture was modified. Though the structure of government remained basically imperial, the emirates were largely autonomous and the authority of each ruler was centralised in his capital. In other words, the various emirates were administrative units under emirs who were responsible for the defence, security and other day-to-day problems of their areas of jurisdiction. The emirs were regarded as the lieutenants of the Caliph; the earlier emirs were learned Muslim scholars, some of whom were in fact former pupils of the Shehu. Each emir extended his emirate by capturing other surrounding towns and villages, which were administered by appointed 'intendants', called *Jakadu*. Hereditary chiefs were appointed to collect tributes from their own people to the coffers of the emirs who were charged with the day-to-day administration of their individual territories. In fact, as long as the tributes and other services were punctually rendered to the central government there was little or no interference from the Caliph in the affairs of the emirates. But as a 'theocratic empire' the administrative autonomy of each emirate was valid only when the emirs and their councils discharged their Islamic obligations to the people over whom they ruled, as well as to their overlord, the Caliph. Moreover, the Caliph was vested with the authority to approve the appointment of emirs and chiefs, even though he could not depose them. Sokoto was in charge of religion, which meant a close link with other emirates, including Gwandu, whose relationship with Sokoto had remained tenuous in terms of practical control, since 1812. On the other hand, the Caliph's obligations included a general supervision to ensure that equitable administration was maintained in all the emirates. In this connection, the emirs' duties included the maintenance of unity among the people; they were expected to repair the mosques and strictly observe the hours of prayers in them and to ensure that the Koran and Islamic sciences were taught and learnt. They were also enjoined to wage the Jihad against non-believers, as a duty imposed on all true Muslims. Their administrative duties included the abolition of all forms of oppression, the repairs of markets and the prohibition of all illegalities in them.

It is true that the history of the Jihad after the death of the Shehu is the history of individual emirates rather than that of Sokoto. Yet, in spite of the diversities in each emirate, the relationship between the Caliph and his emirs was largely determined by the bond of Islam. In this regard it is remarkable that up to the British conquest of the Caliphate the religious pre-eminence of the Sokoto Caliph was never questioned or seriously challenged. Their vassalage to the Caliph was expressed by the payment of tribute, and in addition, the emirates often paid *Khums*, the fifth part of war booty as fixed by the Shari'a, to the Caliph. Each emir was obliged to attend the *Manya Sara Kuna*, a form of 'annual parliament' of the Caliphate's eastern emirates. On such occasions, the emirs supplied military aid to Sokoto in its annual dry-season raids against its enemies. In spite of its shortcomings this system of administration held the Caliphate together throughout the nineteenth century, and its basic principles formed the guide-lines for the system of indirect rule established by the British colonial administration at the beginning of the twentieth century in Northern Nigeria.

Notes

1 See E. W. Bovil, *The Golden Trade of the Moors* (London, 1968), pp. 223–36; E. J. Arnet, *The Rise of the Sokoto Fulani* (Kano: 1972); F. de F. Daniel, 'Shehu dan Fodio', *African Affairs*, Vol. 25 (1925–26), pp. 278–83; M. al-Hajj, 'The Fulani concept of the Jihad', *odu*, Vol. 1, no. 1 (1964), pp. 45–58.

2 *Ibid*.

3 T. Hodgkin, *Nigerian Perspectives* (Oxford: 1960), pp. 198–200.

4 S. J. Hogben, *The Mohammedan Emirates of Nigeria* (Oxford: 1930), p. 73. See also J. S. Trimingham, *A History of Islam in West Africa* (Oxford: 1962), p. 162.

5 D. A. Olderogge, 'Feudalism in the Western Sudan from the sixteenth to the nineteenth centuries', *African Abstracts,* Vol. X, No. 1, January 1959, pp. 11–12. See also T. Hodgkin, 'Uthman dan Fodio', *Nigeria Magazine* (Independence Issue), 1960, p. 135.

6 H. F. C. Smith, 'A neglected theme of West African history: the Islamic revolution of the nineteenth century', *Journal of the Historical Society of Nigeria*, Vol. 4, December 1961, pp. 169–85.

7 W. R. Waldman, 'The Fulani Jihad: a re-assessment', *Journal of African History*, Vol. VI, No. 3 (1965), pp. 333–55.

8   Smith, 'A neglected theme of West African history'; M. Crowder, *The Story of Nigeria*, (London 1962), p. 80.

9   H. A. S. Johnston, *The Fulani Empire of Sokoto* (Oxford: 1967), *passim*.

10 *Ibid*. See also M. al-Hajj, 'The Fulani concept of the Jihad', p. 56.

11 J. S. Trimingham, *A History of Islam in West Africa*, pp. 199–200.

12 F. H. El-Masri, 'The life of Shehu Usman dan Fodio before the Jihad', *Journal of the Historical Society of Nigeria*, Vol. II, No. 4, 1963.

13 Waldman, 'The Fulani Jihad: a re-assessment', *JAH*, VI(3), pp. 333–55.

14 *Ibid*. pp. 341–43.

15 T. Hodgkin, *Nigerian Perspectives*, pp. 198–205.

16 J. S. Trimingham, *A History of Islam in West Africa*, pp. 202–05.

17 *Ibid*., pp. 205–06.

18 Hogben, *The Mohammedan Emirates of Nigeria*, *passim*.

19 *Ibid*., see also Hodgkin, *Nigerian Perspectives*, pp. 40–41.

20 R. A. Adeleye, 'The Sokoto Caliphate in the nineteenth century', in J. F. Ade Ajayi and M. Crowder (eds), *History of West Africa*, Vol. II (Longman, 1974), pp. 57–91.

9 The British penetration and conquest

Fola Soremekun

The period of more than a hundred years from the late eighteenth century to the early twentieth century was, for the British as well as for the peoples who lived in the area which was to become Nigeria, a period filled with momentous events. These events, weaving in and out of one another, were to shape the destinies of both peoples for a very long time. None of it was predetermined. From the late eighteenth century up to at least the 1850s there was no evidence to suggest that the area now called Nigeria would become a colony of Britain. This only began to appear likely in the 1880s with the era of the 'new imperialism'. These two major time spans, therefore, before and after the 1880s, constitute for us epochs into which our approach to this subject is divided. The themes of the first period include the British anti-slavery crusade, the coming of the explorers, the beginning of Christian missionary enterprise, the British shift in interest from trade in slaves from African coasts to their demand for 'legitimate' items such as palm oil, cotton, and other products, and the African reaction to all this. With regard to the second period, we shall take account of themes such as the rise and the demands of the European age of industrialisation; the drive to acquire colonies to support industrial capitalism; European nationalism; disorganisation and disunity among Africans and their inability to find adequate responses to the European challenges. In considering both periods it is important to note that all these themes are interrelated and cannot readily be so singled out for separate treatment. Nevertheless it will be seen how they all led to the penetration and eventual British conquest and occupation of Nigeria.

The antecedents: 1790s to 1880s

The eighteenth century was, for Europeans as well as for the British, the 'age of enlightenment'.[1] It could be viewed as the era when medieval Europe was finally passing away, yielding to the 'modern era'. All medieval ways of looking at human activities, be they political, social, and economic, came in for close scrutiny and thorough reform. For instance, the political ideas of the age, particularly those of the *philosophes* such as Rousseau, Voltaire and Montesquieu, helped bring about the French Revolution.[2] These ideas emphasised the significance of human freedom and the equality of all men before the law. Such ideas had also helped spark the American Revolution and made the existence of the slave trade and slavery unacceptable social and economic anomalies.[3]

The economic system of the pre-enlightenment period was called *mercantilism* in which trade was tightly controlled by governments and emphasis placed on bullion. The age of enlightenment demanded that if men should be free, trade should be free also. The prophet of this 'free enterprise' was Adam Smith. In 1776 he published a book entitled *An Inquiry into the Nature and Causes of the Wealth of Nations*. In it he showed Englishmen why government should not control trade or interfere with the economy. Government should allow such principles as those of self-interest of individuals and companies, and those of supply and demand, to regulate the economy. In his scheme of things slave labour was wrong for free enterprise. He said, in effect, that the work performed by free men came cheaper in the end than that performed by slaves. English slave owners should therefore emancipate their slaves, as such an action would be good for business. In a way, however, the whole question of producing sugar by slave labour was already becoming a thing of the past as England was already industrialising rapidly. The slave trade had to go. And industrialisation had to hurry it along. This was probably the main reason why the British ruling Whig oligarchy supported the slave trade abolition movement.[4]

A further factor in the abolition of the slave trade was the religious fervour of evangelicals like John and Charles Wesley of the Methodist Church, and a genuine belief on the part of many people in the idea of brotherhood of man under the fatherhood of God. The era spawned ideas of 'humanitarianism', intent on reforming morals in England, abolishing the slave trade, and the founding of foreign and local missionary societies. Humanitarians like Wilberforce and Buxton were also members of the British Parliament. When men of this calibre combined forces with politicians like William Pitt the passage of anti-slavery bills became possible.[5] In 1807 Parliament abolished the slave trade for English merchants. After the Napoleonic wars in 1815 at the Congress of Vienna the British tried to get European nations to abolish the trade as well. And in 1833 the trade was abolished in the British empire. Throughout this period there was thus a serious attempt to abolish the slave trade. Efforts were made to find solutions that would be just to all those who had a stake in the slave trade. English slave owners and traders were compensated and so too were foreign slave-trading nations.

Many pamphlets and books were written on the subject. Three major ideas emerged in these: that the slave trade should be stopped at its very source in the interior of Africa, that the British Government should help substitute another trade for it, and that Britain should take over certain parts of Africa to help Africans learn to produce items that would replace the obnoxious trade.[6] These three points immediately became attractive both for Christian missions who believed that the African soul should be saved, and for British merchants who saw themselves as being very important in fostering whatever trade might arise between their country and African peoples. And when it was postulated that the slave trade should be stopped at its very source in the interior of the continent, the next concern was how to get there. White men generally had always had a difficult time on the West Coast of Africa. Africans were reluctant to let Europeans encroach into the interior, and the climate of the West African coast, and its malaria, were a scourge to the European intruders.[7]

Moreover, Europeans were deeply ignorant of the African interior. In response to this, in June 1788 the African Association was formed by a group of men who hoped to combine the need to satisfy their thirst for knowledge (as befitted men of the age of enlightenment), with the suspicion that in the long run the knowledge acquired might be good for business. One of the founding members of this association was quoted as saying: 'Of all the advantages to which a better acquaintance with the inland regions of Africa may lead, the first in importance is the extension of the commerce and the encouragement of the manufactures of Great Britain.'[8] The African Association set out to solve certain specific geographical problems. The first of these was to find the source, the course and the exit of the river Niger and to report back. In 1795 Mungo Park was sponsored as an explorer. The following year he became the first white man to view the river at Segu. By 1797 he had explored a considerable portion of the river. He returned home and made another journey in 1805, during which he died in the Bussa rapids.

From the time of Mungo Park onward there were several other explorers who entered Nigeria from both the north and the south. Men like John and Richard Lander, Hugh Clapperton, Denham, Oudney, Dr Heinrich Barth, Dr Baikie, and Dr Overweg helped to increase European knowledge, mostly about the present northern area of Nigeria. The accounts written by these explorers are valuable sources of information on just about every aspect of lives of the peoples of the area.[9] For example, the explorer Hugh Clapperton befriended Sultan Bello and so was able to tell us about the political situation in Sokoto and in Bornu. Denham tells us about the struggle for power between Bigirmi, Wadai and Bornu. These accounts were in most cases very detailed indeed, with commentaries about political, social and economic matters. They were written in such a way that laymen, missionaries, businessmen and government officials could profit from the information given. In these respects they constituted remarkable intelligence reports, invaluable later in the era of imperialism. The best was Dr Heinrich Barth's monumental five-volume account; Dr Barth himself was sponsored by the British Government.

From the points of view of both the exploration of the Niger and of the anti-slave-trade campaigns, a major breakthrough was achieved in 1830 when John and Richard Lander were able to pursue the Niger right down to one of its major points of entry into the Atlantic. The significance of a strategic place like Lokoja thus became known to the anti-slavery activist Fowell Buxton, who began to plan setting up a Christian mission plantation so as to carry on useful pursuits to supplant the non-productive slave trade. He was of the opinion that Lokoja 'will . . . become the great internal citadel of Africa, and the great emporium of her commerce'.[10] Two years after the Lander discovery some Liverpool merchants, led by Macgregor Laird with the support of the British Government, tried to exploit this discovery so as to open up the interior to British trade through the south. The expedition went up the river for 500 miles, using the navigation charts which the Landers had made, but many lives were lost.

This period also coincided with the climax of the slave-trade abolition crusade, which saw the British trying another tack. They were now making treaties with the incredulous African coastal chiefs, urging them to stop the slave trade and at the same time trying to point out what could be gained by switching to such a trade as that of palm oil. Britain in the 1830s was already in the full swing of its Industrial Revolution and had discovered that palm oil was a necessary item to help keep British machines well-oiled. Later, this same oil was to be used for making soap and other detergents to enable Britons to take their bath regularly and to wash their cotton clothes – in other words, to help revolutionise hygiene in Britain. The area of highest production of this oil was the 'Oil Rivers'. In 1814, 450 tons of palm oil came out of this area but by 1832 the tonnage had reached 14 000.[11]

The 'slave-trade treaties'[12] which the British entered into on the West Coast of Africa was at first concentrated in the region of the 'Oil Rivers', but later expanded into other areas. As the coastal kingdoms were independent states in their own right, these treaties were to have the effect of creating unrest in almost every one of them. This was so because their original economic base, which had depended upon the slave trade, had to be shifted. This in turn was to have adverse effects upon the political stability of these states. And even when a new trade had been substituted misunderstandings between the British traders on the one side, and the African middlemen-heads of kingdoms on the other, were frequent occurrences. Such situations tended to lead English traders (and later consuls) to seek to intervene in the internal politics of these kingdoms to further their own interests – manipulating, for example, the *trust trade* system to their own advantage. British merchants made large profits out of this trade at the expense of the Africans. Africans on their own part would strike back wherever they could, always keeping a watchful eye for the presence of British naval gunboats. These gunboats, supposedly watching out for slave traders, did not always limit themselves to that activity alone and on occasions they tended to back their own people against the Africans in other respects. Hence the Oil Rivers in particular, and indeed the other coastal areas like Lagos and Dahomey (now the Benin Republic) were zones of perpetual conflict. The first slave trade treaty was signed with Bonny in 1839. Although the treaty promised some compensation for King Pepple for five years, the British did not fulfil their part of the bargain and some of the promised payments were missed. This sort of thing led Africans to distrust the white men. A further treaty had to be signed in 1848. In Old Calabar the treaty was also signed in 1840 but the people of Calabar had to be convinced of the difference between signing and ratification by the British Government.

British trading policy was essentially to build an empire based upon commerce, to monopolise that trade by pushing aside African middlemen whom they saw as obstacles to 'free trade'. The policy was to continue alongside their drive to open up the interior to trade, to stop the slave trade and to help the humanitarians spread Christianity. In 1841 a Niger expedition was sponsored by the humanitarians with the backing of the British Government, ostensibly with the aim of helping to stop the slave trade. It included two missionaries, one of whom was Rev. Ajayi Crowther, later to become Bishop of the Niger; a botanist; a mineralogist; a doctor; and a person to supervise an agricultural experimental station which it was intended to set up. Although the expedition was a failure, its determination to Christianise the interior was

Fig. 9.1   Atiba, Alafin of Oyo, receiving the Anglican missionaries, Townsend and Mann, at Oyo on 28 September 1853

there for all to see even if the British could not yet say they had mastered the Niger. Twelve years later, in 1853, Dr Baikie sailed into the Niger in the *Pleiad* and dispensed quinine to the members of his group: not a single man died. With the complete conquest of the Niger plus mastery over the health problems of 'the white man's grave' a landmark had been reached in British efforts to penetrate Nigeria's interior.

It must be emphasised that at that time this penetration had nothing to do with imperialism. Britain's main interest at this time was above all to trade, to build an empire of commerce, not to gain control of Africa's land. By the mid-nineteenth century that trade was increasing far beyond expectation. But the relationship of the British with the coastal peoples was haphazard, while at the same time an increasing complexity of issues faced both sides as the years went by. One of these issues which has not so far been mentioned was the beginning of British missionary enterprise into southern Nigeria.[13] The Methodist Church missionary Thomas Freeman founded the first Christian mission in Nigeria at Abeokuta in 1842. The CMS (Church Missionary Society) came into the same town in 1844, and were in Lagos in 1851 and Ibadan in 1853. The Church of Scotland mission was founded at Calabar in 1846. And during the Second Niger Expedition of 1857 plans had already reached an advanced stage for the opening of Christian mission stations in Onitsha and Gbebe and for inaugurating what was to become a Niger mission of the CMS. With these missionaries, at least in the Yoruba country, there came many recently freed slaves for whom the British felt responsible. Nonetheless, in the wake of these increasing complexities, the British Government decided to appoint a roving consul for the Bight of Benin and Biafra (now Bonny) in 1849.

The man chosen was John Beecroft, a man of considerable experience who was well known and respected by most local African leaders up and down the coast. At the time of Beecroft's appointment the British Foreign Minister was Lord Palmerston, who was bent on strengthening British trade on the coast and making life difficult for local African chiefs who were reluctant to give up trading in slaves completely, and one of John Beecroft's briefs was to try to induce the kings of Lagos and of Dahomey to stop the obnoxious trade. When the two African chiefs prevaricated over the issue, Lord Palmerston decided that pressure should be put on Lagos. In 1845 Oba Akitoye decided to abolish the slave trade in Lagos, and to carry on 'legitimate' trade. Lagos then split into pro- and anti-slave trade factions, and became locked in a civil war. The pro-slave trade faction succeeded in expelling Akitoye, and Kosoko took the throne for six years – 1845–1851 – during which the slave trade flourished. This was like throwing ashes into the face of the British who then resolved to take the initiative and reverse the trend. Beecroft brought Akitoye back from Badagry, where he had fled and was being harassed by pro-Kosoko groups.[14] Akitoye was reinstated. But peace did not really reign in Lagos until finally the island state was ceded to the British in 1861. Force and intimidation were used by the British to achieve that objective, and there were lessons in the sordid affair for both sides: for the British it gave a close insight into the functioning of an African society, while for the Lagosians it showed the technological superiority of the white man. At the time, though, the future significance of this for eventual British rule over a larger area now called Nigeria was far from apparent.

Another example of the divisions within an African society of which the British took advantage could be seen in the delta, an area of almost perpetual conflict. John Beecroft was also very active there in interfering in local politics. The Itsekiri–Ijo rivalry for the Urhobo palm oil was one of the main sources of this. Beecroft was also involved in trying to influence the choice of a new Olu of Itsekiri in the 1850s. When he failed in the attempt he helped create a new title and appointed a 'Governor of the River' in 1856. It was true, of course, that Beecroft's main motive was to protect the interests of British traders but this was usually done at the expense of the Itsekiri.[15] And in spite of all the efforts of Beecroft and those who came after him, the relationship between the two sides was never easy. There was always some problem over prices of palm oil and debts due through the trust trade. If no clear-cut British imperialist moves were evident before the 1880s, this was because the time was not yet ripe for it. Indeed it would seem that after 1865 the extent of British political activity on the coast of the Bight of Benin and Biafra declined considerably. In 1865 a parliamentary committee had suggested that Britain should wind up its political holdings in West Africa, re-emphasising that the West African coast was simply a source of trouble and expense. From then on some retrenchment was effected on the Niger, although by and large the *status quo* was maintained and every effort was made to encourage business.

To sum up, it could be said that the dispatch of explorers into the interior of Nigeria, the gradual solving of the Niger problem and the making of the river safe for navigation and the coast amenable to the white man through the use of quinine, the appointment of a consul for the Bight of Benin and Biafra, the colonisation of Lagos, the fight against the slave trade and the encouragement of palm oil in its place, the establishment of a trading station and consulate at Lokoja at the strategic confluence of the Niger and the Benue, the encouragement and protection of Christian missionaries – developments of this nature were all aspects of British penetration into Nigeria before the era of the 'new imperialism' commenced in the 1880s. They had taken place over a period of nearly a hundred years. No European nation could claim to have gathered as much knowledge of and to have been as closely involved with the area we now call Nigeria before the era of the 'new imperialism' as Britain.

The conquest and occupation of Nigeria 1880–1906

The 'new imperialism' and the 'scramble for Africa'

Before dealing with the conquest and occupation of Nigeria, it is pertinent to put those series of events within their proper historical context. It is generally agreed by most historians that the Franco-Prussian War of 1870 marked a turning point in the history of Europe as well as in that of Africa and Asia. The date marked the beginning of the era of the 'new imperialism' during which the 'scramble for Africa' took place. The 'new imperialism' began therefore as a consequence of the complex interplay of European internal political, social and econmic affairs.

When Prussia defeated France it became necessary for France to seek foreign adventure in Africa and elsewhere to alleviate the sting of its defeat. Bismarck, the Chancellor of the newly united Germany, encouraged France in these adventures. From then on, a chain of events was unleashed against a background of complex international diplomatic and economic developments in a period in which the interests of France clashed with those of Britain, while Bismarck sought to play the role of the master diplomat of Europe. With regard to African affairs, in Egypt, Britain and France were both seeking to control a country which was strategically important both for the Middle East and the Far East. From the time of Napoleon, the French had been heavily involved with Egypt and their involvement reached its height when Ferdinand de Lesseps helped build the Suez Canal (completed 1869). Unfortunately for the Egyptians, they could not meet the payment of the money borrowed from exploitative European financiers. This gave the British Government the opportunity to buy shares in the canal company. By 1878 both England and France, acting together, forced the Egyptian Khedive Tewfik to let them manage Egyptian finances so that the debtor country could pay its debts to overseas financiers. Naturally this event aroused the ire of Egyptian nationalists. Violent agitation resulted. The British response was to make a show of asking the French to join them in putting down the nationalist agitation. Britain then took unilateral action to bombard and take over Egypt in September 1882.

This annoyed the French who felt they had not been given enough time to consider the offer since they could take no action unless their national assembly first met to consider the issue. This unilateral takeover left a bitter taste in the mouth of the French. National pride demanded that they should retaliate elsewhere to recoup their lost pride. The situation was a godsend for Bismarck. Michael Crowder has indicated the significance of this Egyptian occupation in the context of wider African affairs:

> The occupation of Egypt by Britain supplied the climate in which the French government did not have much alternative to accepting the Makoko treaties in 1882 whereby the explorer de Brazza had acquired for France territory in the Congo. These treaties ... as much as anything else precipitated the scramble, though they did not cause it. They made the European powers face the realities of a situation that had been developing over the past three years.[16]

Within two years of the British occupation of Egypt in September 1882 it had become necessary for the European powers to get together to regulate the carving-up of Africa. The regulatory machinery was the Berlin West African Conference under the chairmanship of Otto von Bismarck. The conference lasted from November 1884 to February 1885. The key points in the resulting Berlin Act were that the European powers making territorial claims should inform other powers and, having done this, they should also effectively occupy the area. There was to be freedom of navigation on major rivers like the Niger and the Congo although no specific committee was set up to ensure that this was done. The overall effect of the Berlin Conference was essentially to confirm a process already going on. The bases of claims to African territories were the many paper 'treaties' being collected by rival European groups all over the continent from non-literate chiefs.

Side by side with the political aspects of the scramble there were also economic and social forces underpinning them. In the economic sphere, for example, the late nineteenth century found many European countries in a feverish pursuit of industrialisation. Some countries were producing goods which could not all be consumed at home and which now needed new markets.[17] And each nation, to protect its economy from incursions from other European nations, began to erect tariff barriers. Many felt it would be better to have exclusive markets where they could dump their products and from where they could also get very cheap raw materials. The struggle to get territories in Africa was therefore closely linked with the European economic situation at home. This competition for economic advantage was also tinged with the crudest form of nationalism in a Europe in which national pride could be said to be running riot from the late nineteenth century on, bringing them to the final disaster of 1914–18 world war.

As Europeans came into contact with Africans, their technological superiority vis-à-vis the black man evoked within them a mixture of contempt, hatred, condescension and a denial that Africans were human beings. Worse still, they had imbibed and twisted Charles Darwin's theory of evolution and interpreted the principle of 'survival of the fittest' to mean that white men had the right to occupy Africa and other 'backward' areas of the world. Nothing seemed to encapsulate the white man's attitude to the Africans whose lands were being seized and conquered better than Rudyard Kipling's oft-quoted stanza from his poem *White Man's Burden*:

> Take up the white man's burden
> Send forth the best ye breed,
> Go bind your sons to exile
> To serve your captives' need
> To wait in heavy harness
> On fluttered folk and wild,
> Your new-caught, sullen peoples
> Half-devil and half-child.[18]

Most of the late nineteenth-century missionaries, explorers, empire-builders, company directors, traders, soldiers, and many other Europeans who came into contact with Africans believed instinctively in the superiority of the white race, and many of their activities reflected this behaviour.

The occupation of Nigeria: the south

The period of the craze to acquire territories in the present area of Nigeria found the British in a favourable position. But they were not complacent and it soon became clear that they were ready to take whatever steps were necessary to defend their position. In their drive to acquire territories, the empire-builders on the spot not only marched to the tune of the home government, they also took initiatives of their own, and were aware of how best to justify their actions before their government leaders at home. They knew how to tell them what they liked to hear. They sought and found ample evidence to convict Africans in the high court of British morality: here it was anathema to trade in slaves, to perform 'human sacrifices', to obstruct the movement of 'free trade'. And when the men on the spot, with the backing of their home governments, struck at the African societies, they struck hard, carefully and with much cunning. Every military 'pacification' scheme was carefully and deliberately effected as it was realised that failure might spell disaster and diminish the white man's mystique. The objective of every pacification scheme was to 'decapitate' the society by destroying the power of the local chiefs. Such objectives tended to undermine the confidence of the people in their own culture, leaving them dazed and weary, turning their lives upside down. Unfortunately the Africans themselves, during this era of the scramble, unwittingly helped the imperialists by clinging to old rivalries and prejudices against one another, at a time when they should have come together to resist the British-led forces, often small in number, too often sent against them. The loss of their sovereignty might have been prevented, or at least delayed. Whether in the south or in the north the basic pattern prevailed, though with some variations. The incidents which are singled out for treatment here should be seen as the ideal examples, or types, as it is clearly impossible to deal with every aspect of the British occupation of Nigeria.

In the south, Lagos provides a convenient place to start as it was already a British colony by 1861. Since that date its history had rarely been peaceful. The turbulent internal politics of Lagos itself, together with an even more turbulent situation in the Yoruba country, led to a slump in trade, a very serious thing for the island colony, particularly in the 1880s. In 1886 a Lagos government delegation was sent into the interior to try to stop the Yoruba wars. It was only partially successful, and war did not end. By 1890 the British were becoming impatient. In what could only be interpreted as the beginning of the use of force to solve the problem of the Lagos interior, Captain Denton, the Acting Governor at Lagos, wrote home as follows, commenting on past efforts to bring peace: 'Looking to the frequent endeavours . . . which have been made in the past years, it will . . . be very difficult to bring the people to reason by negotiations.'[19] Elsewhere in his letter of lamentation he laid the blame for the slump in trade on the 'eccentric conduct of the middlemen' of the interior who made arbitrary demands and whimsically blocked the routes upon which the Lagos trade depended. At the same time the French were suspected to be trying to make some overtures to enable them to colonise the western part of the Yoruba country. In the following year efforts were made to prepare the way for the governor's tour of certain parts of the Yoruba country. On one of these visits Captain Denton, who had been sent to Ijebu-Ode, ran into difficulties with the people. Although he was not well received the people agreed to open the roads on condition the Awujale was paid £500 a year. In 1892 there were disagreements between the two sides about the meaning of this 'agreement'. An expedition was sent against the Ijebu and they were conquered. Already, the Yoruba country was being visited by the Carter expedition (1893–94) in which several 'treaties' were made, a major one being with the Alafin of Oyo. A British Resident was then placed at Ibadan in 1893. This done, most of the Yoruba country thus passed under the British except for Abeokuta where, due to early Christian missionary influence, the Egba United Board Government was formed and operated (1898–1914), and Ilorin, which had yet to be subdued. The declaration of a British protectorate in the Yoruba country, as well as in several other areas, was more a pronouncement for psychological effect than anything more concrete: it was only implemented later.

In 1885 the British proclaimed a protectorate over the area of the 'Oil Rivers', declaring the area to be a British sphere of influence. Having declared this the British then sought to justify their action by trying effectively to occupy the region. But they almost met their match in Opobo. The story of Jaja of Opobo and his struggles against the British to maintain the independence of his kingdom is widely known. Here is a typical assessment and observation of the man:

> Jaja, the most enterprising and accomplished of all the African merchant princes of the Niger Coast, had been a thorn in the flesh of every consul for the Bights of Benin and Biafra since he established his settlement over the mouth of the Opobo River in 1872. Handsome, efficient, rich, fluent in English, with manners that were almost polished, and a taste for good, dry champagne which was unanimously approved by his European guests ... Jaja had developed a nice sense of European logic and legal forms which he had employed with remarkable prescience to defend his commercial interests against future encroachments. In 1873 he had signed a treaty with Consul Livingstone which in exchange for the limitation of the export duties ... explicitly recognised his right to act as the sole middle man between the producers of the interior and the European trading firms; and though this treaty had been denounced by the Foreign Office on a technicality, he had reasserted his claim by refusing to sign the Protectorate Treaty form in use for the Oil Rivers District in 1884 until the clause providing for freedom of trade within his dominions had been deleted from it. At the same time he had further extracted a letter from Consul Hewett stating that 'with reference to the word Protectorate as used in the proposed treaty ... the Queen does not want to take your Country or your Markets but at the same time is anxious that no other nation should take them. She undertakes to extend her gracious favour and protection which will leave your country still under your government.' Jaja, as he thought, had made permanent a very comfortable source of income. Palm-oil and kernels to the annual value of £160 000 were exported through Opobo, upon which the European traders paid him 'comey' at the rate of four puncheons in every twenty, or £30 000 a year, in exchange for the questionable service of keeping the routes open and supplies flowing.[20]

The British found all this difficult to accept, and they broke their agreement with Jaja. In 1887 British merchants sent a petition to the Foreign Office saying that Jaja was obstructing trade. Shortly thereafter Sir Harry Johnston, who was then the current Acting Consul in place of Hewett, was ordered to proceed to Opobo to remove the obstacle to

British trade. The most significant factor to observe is that, in their drive to get colonies, the likes of Jaja could not be tolerated by the British. In addition to several wild allegations made against Jaja to tarnish his image in England, Johnston also accused him of scheming to invite France to take over his country. Jaja was then tricked into coming to Johnston on board a warship and he was then deported first to the Gold Coast and finally to the West Indies. A further significant aspect of all this was that in their struggle against Jaja the British authorities had carefully cultivated Jaja's enemies, such as King Pepple, and gave them support, taking advantage of the rivalries so common among the Africans at that time.

A somewhat similar tactic – the charge of obstructing trade, and of dividing local leaders – was used during the same period to destroy African opposition in Itsekiriland. Nana Olomu had put the Itsekiri under British 'protection' and had been given a staff of office in May 1885. He had been made the 'governor' of the Benin and Ethiope rivers. Soon, however, Nana ran into trouble as palm oil and kernels were not flowing through to the coast as the British had expected, although this was through no particular fault of his own. Part of the problem had been that the flow of trade from the interior to the coast simply followed the laws of supply and demand. If the Bini, for instance, wanted Itsekiri traders to pay a trade tax on oil the Itsekiri middlemen might decide to hold out for a while so that their profit margin might not be too narrow, given that they too had to cater to the demands of the trust trade. The British, on the other hand, tended to see matters differently, charging that Nana was holding up trade. Nana, in their eyes, had to be destroyed. And since Nana himself had made many enemies during his drive to be the foremost African trader in the area, he found no other local African allies to help him against the British when they organised the Ebrohimi expedition to topple him in 1895. Although Nana at first escaped, later he gave himself up to the Governor of Lagos, who handed him back to the authorities of the Niger Coast Protectorate. He was then exiled to Ghana.[21]

After the expedition against Nana came that against the Oba of Benin, Ovenramwen. Again, it was the demands of the age of the scramble that propelled the British to take action against him, but this impetus was reinforced and justified by British propaganda against Benin, presenting it as a city steeped in human sacrifices and dripping with blood.[22] A 'treaty' of protection with Benin had been in existence since 1892, but in 1897 Acting Consul-General Philips was determined to go to Benin at a most inauspicious time when the king was not supposed to see any foreigner. Philips' motives were sinister as he had recommended the use of force to depose the Benin king. Given the state of uncertainty and tension in the area it was natural that the Benin people would hate uninvited foreigners. It was scarcely surprising, therefore, that Captain Philips and his seven officials plus their carriers were waylaid and killed. The event immediately became known as the 'Benin massacre'. An expeditionary force was assembled in 1897 which led to the downfall and humiliation of the Oba, a god in the eyes of his people. He was exiled to Calabar where he died in 1914.

Across the Niger River on the eastern side of Igbo country, the

Fig. 9.2   The Benin expedition against the Oba

imposition of British control over this area was similar in some respects to the cases already described above.[23] Here also African traders and middlemen had to be broken to make way for British traders and British administration. Igbo traders were prevented from getting commissions from European traders from the 1890s onwards. The Colonial Office had ordered that these practices be stopped. At the same time the priority attached by the British to commercial matters led them onto a collision course with the Arochukwu Igbos. Of all the religio-political institutions in Igboland such as the Agbala (Anyanwu) of Oka, the Kamalu of Ozuzu, and the Igwe of Umunoha, the Aros of the Chukwu oracle were the most significant. The Aros were also middlemen traders who had skilfully combined the dictates of religion with the profitability of commercial activities, thereby wielding immense power among their countrymen. The Aros were peripatetic and ubiquitous, and they were the group that the British had to smash and make an example of as a means of controlling the Igbo as a whole. Steps toward achieving this objective were taken in 1892 when Consul Campbell embarked upon an intelligence-gathering tour of the periphery of Igbo country. He did not fail to note the immense commercial prospects for Britain, particularly with regard to the riches in palm oil. During the next four years the relationship between the Igbo and the British was relatively peaceful. Then Sir Ralph Moor appeared on the scene in 1896 as the Consul-General, determined to carry out the imperialistic policies of Joseph Chamberlain, the Colonial Secretary.

The Igbo had to be conquered by force of arms, and the target had been well chosen. The war to get rid of the Aros started on 1 December 1901 and lasted until 1902. The invading forces which toppled 'the Long Juju' was led by Lt.-Col. Montanaro of the British Royal Artillery. In this case, as in others similar to it, every care was taken by the invading group to make sure that they would succeed, as failure could well have shattered the charisma of British power. The crucial factor in the belief system of a people had been shattered, and the Christian missionaries who had given support to the invading forces were then able to capitalise on the dazed and shattered confidence of an African people. Once again there was no unified response on the part of the Africans to challenge the Europeans. And although it could be said in this case that the British were not going to find it easy governing the Igbo, the destruction of 'the Long Juju' had marked a turning point in the political, social and religious history of the people.

The occupation of the southern part of Nigeria represented perhaps only part of a wider process on the part of the British. There were many less dramatic incidents occurring in many places. In many instances the examples given above were enough to persuade other peoples into submission. The frequency of military patrols, for instance, was sufficient to drill the population into line and to accept the new British authority. Other less intimidating measures led people to believe that the white man had arrived to control their lives. Let us now turn our attention to the North.

The occupation and pacification of northern Nigeria

The period of the occupation and pacification of northern Nigeria lasted from 1877 to about 1903. Three major personalities played the most significant roles in this process: Sir George Goldie, Lord Lugard and Joseph Chamberlain, the Colonial Secretary in Lord Salisbury's ministry in the 1890s. Three considerations should be borne in mind in understanding how the occupation came about: firstly, the trading and empire-building ambitions of Sir George Goldie; secondly, British awareness that other European powers might wrest the control of the area from its agents if it did not act fast enough; and thirdly, the disunity among the Africans and their ability to respond successfully to the challenge of British designs upon their territories. All these factors intertwined in a rather long and very involved story which we can only tell briefly here.

As we have already seen, British explorers and humanitarians had been involved in northern Nigeria for quite some time. The names of Richard Lander, Magregor Laird, Dr Baikie and others can be tied to specific landmarks in the matter of solving the problem of the Niger, of navigating it and of making it possible to overcome malaria, the dreaded disease that had been killing white men in West Africa for so long. By the mid-nineteenth century the British had been able to establish a trading station and a 'Consulate' at Lokoja at the confluence of the rivers Niger and Benue. During the next thirty years trade developed significantly in the delta region (the Oil Rivers). Towards the end of that epoch (in 1877) George Goldie first appeared on the Niger and decided to be very active from the apex of the delta upwards. Goldie's visit in 1877 at the age of 30 was no more than an exploratory tour of appraisal of the trading situation in his area of choice. He was instantly aware that there was too much competition among English traders and was determined to amalgamate these traders into a monopoly trading organisation controlled by himself. In this way, he was able to create the United Africa Company (UAC) in 1879. Goldie, the monopoly capitalist, was also an intensely nationalistic man determined to ruin traders of other European nations that might come into his domain of operations. Also, Africans who did not do his bidding were to be ruined. In 1878, while Goldie was still trying to forge his United Africa Company, a French trader, the Comte de Semelle, had succeeded in obtaining a trade agreement with the Emir of Nupe. When Goldie got wind of this in 1880 after he returned to the Niger he immediately began to outbid the French trader, and to ingratiate himself with the Emir of Nupe by helping him against his enemies in 1881–1882. The Emir of Nupe emerged victorious. In the same period the ruthless method of trade which Goldie practised among Africans led to his company posts being destroyed at Akassa, Patani, Asaba, and Idah. Irate Africans were also in the habit of firing at this ships as they passed by their area for they hated Goldie's company so much. Then Goldie started a trade war with the Semelle French company, *Compagnie Française de l'Afrique Equatoriale*.

It was Goldie's belief that the coming of French companies was connected with French political activities throughout West Africa. He suspected political motives and held the belief that trade and politics were intimately connected. For him, without political power there could be no stable trade and no security. He therefore resolved to use his agents to gain control of the waterway from the delta to Lokoja and beyond, and envoys made a series of treaties. His aim was to govern the region, and to exclude competition by political means, either by getting a charter from the British Government or by getting concessions from African rulers. To achieve all these he decided to change the UAC into another company called the National Africa Company. He then made some cosmetic changes to make this 'new' company appear stronger than it actually was. And to give it class and respectability he appointed Lord Aberdare, a friend of Gladstone and a former cabinet minister under him, as the titular head of the company.

Goldie also manoeuvred the Foreign Office into appointing his chief agent, David MacIntosh, as Vice-Consul of the Niger. MacIntosh then went about making treaties, offering British protection in the name of the company. The British Government suspected this but could do nothing since MacIntosh was being paid by Goldie. It was also Goldie, not the Foreign Office, who in 1884 shouldered the expense of bringing the famous explorer, Joseph Thompson, to Nigeria in a successful bid to beat the French and Germans in obtaining an important treaty of 'protection' in Sokoto and in Gwandu. Also in 1884, Goldie finally, at great cost, successfully ruined the French company which was forced to amalgamate with his own. By 1885, Goldie's biographer tells us,

> Its [the National African Company] name was now . . . known in the department of state . . . and Goldie himself was now known personally to the Foreign Secretary and his officials. More important, the British Government was now obligated to the Company; it had placed its local staff at the disposal of the Consul, and it had earned the gratitude of imperially-minded Englishmen. It had secured by its own treaties . . . powers which were so extensive as to transcend the sphere of purely commercial activity. . . . Indeed, the Chiefs having 'ceded' the 'whole of their territories' it could be argued that the Company now possessed full sovereignty. At the same time the British Government's treaties secured British protection to the area, and therefore the Company, as a corporate British subject, was also entitled to protection. The basic relationships between a chartered company which governed its territories under concession from local rulers, and the protecting power of the Imperial Government, existed already, in theory, in every particular except the instrument of the Royal Charter itself.[24]

At the Berlin Conference, it was Goldie's acquisition of more than 200 treaties and his company's position on the Niger and Benue which the British Government used to ward off the attempts of the French and German governments to internationalise the navigation of the Niger. British flags were hoisted at the company's posts to give the impression that the British effectively occupied northern Nigeria, as the principle of effective occupation was considered to be of great significance at that conference. Nonetheless, the French and the Germans insisted that there should be no exclusive privileges of navigation by any one power on the river. Fortunately for the British and the National African Company, however, no international commission was set up. Years later the claims of Britain's rivals simply lapsed into nothing. Britain's claim to northern Nigeria was based upon treaty rights, and its occupation of the vast territory was non-existent except for the National Africa Company's posts, which functioned in a double capacity. Goldie's service to the British Government was rewarded, and the National Africa Company was chartered on 12 July 1886 under a new name, the Royal Niger Company. Two days later Goldie proclaimed a government for the area.

The main problem that was going to face this company was that which had faced many such companies at the time: for how long could it operate in this dual role – as both a commercial company and a government? The most immediate problem was the question of how much power it actually had to quell the violent protests of the delta peoples who were being made to pay custom duties and obtain trade licences. And how much control did the company have over the Benue, or indeed of the vast Sokoto empire centred in Sokoto and Gwandu? There were also difficulties with the French and Germans over trading rights and boundary matters. The company also had to carry on pacification

153

campaigns against Nupe and Ilorin. All these were the problems which faced the company in the 1890s and were to lead to the revocation of the Charter by 1899. The highlights of some of these events are now in order.

The situation along the Benue occupied Goldie's attention in the late 1880s. He increased the company's trading posts and the general presence of the company there, hoping to curb the Muslim elements' penchant towards the slave trade at the expense of the non-Muslim communities along the river. Shortly thereafter, in 1889, Goldie had to contend with the first of a number of international tests to the authority of the British on the Niger. In that year, one Jacob Hoenigsberg, a German trader, entered the Niger with a cargo of salt intended for Nupe. The authorities differed as to whether or not he was a German agent intent on stirring up trouble. The company deprived Hoenigsberg of his salt cargo but he was allowed to proceed to Nupe. Once there, he told the Etsu that the Goldie company said he had ceded his territory. The company was humiliated and had to try to pacify the Emir by raising his annual subsidy. The German was deported, much to the annoyance of the German Government which contended that international rights of free navigation on the Niger had been violated. An official inquiry was held by the British Government to satisfy Germany. Some malpractices were discovered in the company's operations but it survived on the technicality that Nupe was subject to Gwandu and that the Emir of Gwandu had granted to the company the banks of the Niger throughout Nupe.

About the same time, in 1889–90, the problem of boundaries between Nigeria and the Cameroons became an issue, which was settled as part of the Heligoland agreement in 1890. The final touches were put in 1893. Next the company felt threatened by the French Government. In 1889, the Lagos–Dahomey boundary line to 9° latitude was being negotiated. In the following year Lord Salisbury secured agreement, in negotiation, that the French Mediterranean area should not go southward beyond a line drawn from Say on the Niger to Barruwa on Lake Chad. This gave the company the opportunity to claim the emirate of Sokoto which up to that time it had not effectively occupied. Some French empire-builders were, however, determined to test whether or not the company actually controlled the fringes of the areas. Late in 1890 they sent three 'scientific' and 'commercial' expeditions to the northeast of the territory. The most troublesome of these expeditions involved one Lieutenant Mizon who claimed he had obtained a protectorate treaty over Yola. His whole scheme, however, collapsed in 1892 when on his return to the area he took part in a slave-raiding expedition, much to the embarrassment of his government, which ordered him out of the area.

The French decided next to test the company's authority in the northwest. The main problem here for the company was that the boundary agreements of 1889–90 had not quite delimited the Borgu area between the Niger and Dahomey. The company, prodded by the British Government, was able to get a treaty with the Borgu chief at Bussa who was erroneously thought to be the chief of all Borgu. The French rightly disputed this, saying that the area lacked effective occupation and was therefore up for acquisition. The true ruler of Borgu, they said, was at Nikki, and they were going to visit Nikki and take the whole of Borgu.

This precipitated the race toward Nikki by the two governments through their agents. The race was between Lugard for the British, and Captain Decoeur for the French. Although Lugard got to Nikki first he made his treaty not with the real Nikki chief, but with one of his deputies. The French Captain made much of this, and this Borgu issue was to remain a source of tension between the two countries until about 1898. Before then, however, both sides employed a policy of meeting occupation with occupation. It soon became clear that France and Britain would have to share Borgu. Thus the potential conflict, which might have led to war, petered out. A convention was signed to settle the matter in June 1898.

The stresses and strains over the Borgu issue were paralleled by the internal problems facing the Goldie company. At the very time that Lugard was marching to Nikki the people of Brass were revolting against the company. The main issue was the company's monopolistic practices, and a number of other trading regulations which eliminated these men as middlemen. On 28 December 1894 the company's factory at Akassa was sacked, causing the loss of many lives. The company retaliated by engineering a punitive expedition. Then came trouble in Ilorin, mainly due to the inability of the company to stop the slave trade there and to prevent Ilorin from being involved in wars with the other Yorubas. Nupe also was in turmoil, partly due to the consequences of the company's own practices. The company's main *casus belli* had to be to accuse the Nupe of trading in slaves. Late in 1894 Goldie had actually decided that both Ilorin and Nupe had to be subdued militarily, but with problems in Borgu and in Akassa at that time he decided to delay the military expeditions. Both areas (Ilorin and Nupe) were reduced in 1897. Both in Ilorin and in Nupe the superior military tactics of the company forces decided the outcome, although in Nupe the Niger River divided the Nupe militarily. There were also political jealousies and disunity among the ruling class. Among the people at large there was hatred for the Fulani rulers. These factors spelled the doom of Nupe. But the Royal Niger Company itself was doomed as a political agent for the British Government. After the 1898 convention with France over Borgu, the company found its resources overstretched over a vast territory and its charter had to be revoked with effect from 1 January 1900. British flags replaced the company flags over most of the territories, including those which had not really been effectively occupied.

It remained for Lugard, who was appointed High Commissioner for the Protectorate proclaimed over northern Nigeria, to bring to a successful conclusion the task of occupation and subjection of the rest of the territory. Slavery was suppressed in Kontagora; and in Nupe the Emir Abu Bekri had to be removed. In Yola, trade which had been cut off from the Royal Niger Company was restored. The reigning emir there was also replaced. By 1902 Bornu had been humiliated by Col. Morland who replaced the fleeing emir with his heir apparent. After these incidents Kano and Sokoto remained to be penetrated. Kano, the great metropolitan trade centre, and Sokoto, the spiritual centre of the Fulani empire, had to be dealt with with great care and firmness. Kano was walled and had a large army of horsemen who wore mailed armour, so it had to be engaged with care and caution lest it should defeat Lugard's

Fig. 9.3   The walls of Kano seen from the defenders' point of view

forces, thereby undermining the supposed authority of the colonising power. As for taking on the Sokoto authorities, Lugard was worried about how to avoid the eventuality of a Muslim authority declaring a jihad against a foreign foe. Attahiru, the Emir of Sokoto, was indeed to make such a declaration of a jihad as the British were closing in on this domain.

Isolated by British control of the surrounding areas, the defeat of the two cities was virtually ensured even before the final assaults on them were launched. By 1902 the Fulani overlords had lost all their southern emirates to the British. In January 1903 Col. Morland and Lt. General Kemball advanced on Kano. The Kano people made their initial resistance at Babeji, about eight miles from Kano itself. The skirmish ended when an artillery shell struck and killed the headman standing behind the gate. The message for the Kano authorities was plain enough. At Kano itself resistance to the British was brief but bloody. The leaders fled while the populace at large appeared unconcerned except perhaps to wreak their vengeance. Indeed, the people of Gobir caught the fleeing emir and handed him over to the British. A new emir, Wambai Abbas, was put on the throne. Once again the invading authority had taken advantage of the division within the society, in this case exploiting the resentment of the common people against their unpopular rulers. The declining Fulani rulers had lost all political and moral authority.

What was true for Kano was true also for Sokoto, the nerve centre of the Fulani empire: 'It was the misfortune of the Fulani . . . that at a time when they sorely needed another Bello to lead them out of their difficulties they were saddled instead with an incompetent and . . . senile tyrant'.[25] That tyrant was Sultan Abdu, who died in October 1902 to be succeeded by Muhamadu Attahiru. He could only watch the empire crumble. Perhaps a six-month emir could not have worked miracles. With Kano on its knees, Sokoto could not be far behind, and it fell to Lt. General Kemball in March 1903 with Attahiru soon in flight. The fugitive's galloping through the countryside gave the British the jitters. It was clear that further fighting had to take place. The British laid siege to Burmi where the emir was known to be. During the bloody battle, Attahiru, unarmed and flanked by his sons, was shot down by stray bullets. The hundred-year old Fulani empire thus came to an end. What remained for Lugard to do was to mop up and formally establish British authority in 1906; only nine years later, in 1914, the amalgamation of the North and South would create a new entity.

Notes

1 Introduction to Frank E. Manuel (ed.), *The Enlightement* (Englewood Cliffs, New Jersey: Prentice-Hall Inc., 1965).

2 P. H. Meyer, 'The French revolution and the legacy of the philosophes', *The French Review,* XXX, 1956–7, pp. 429–34.

3 See the American Declaration of Independence.

4 Eric Williams, *Capitalism and Slavery* (New York: Capricorn Books, 1960), p. 169.

5 *Ibid*, pp. 178–96.

6 James McQueen, *Geographical and Commercial View of Northern Central Africa*, 1822. Extensive quotations were made from this book by Christopher Lloyd, *The Search for the Niger* (London: Collins, 1973), p. 128.

7 K. Onwuka Dike, *Trade and Politics in the Niger Delta* (Oxford: Clarendon Press, 1956), pp. 1–9.

8 Stepen Gwyn, *Mungo Park and the Quest for the Niger* (London: John Lane/The Bodley Head Ltd., 1934), p. 19.

9 William Balfour Baikie, *Narrative of an Exploring Voyage Up the Rivers Kwora and Benue . . .1854* (London: John Murray, 1856); Hugh Clapperton, *Journal of a Second Expedition into the Interior of Africa* (London: Frank Cass, 1966); H. A. S. Johnston and D. J. M. Muffett, *Denham in Bornu* (Pittsburgh: Duquesne University Press, 1973); Heinrich Barth, *Travels in Nigeria: Extracts from the Journal of Heinrich Barth's Travels in Nigeria 1850–1855*, introduction by A. H. M. Kirk-Greene (London: O.U.P., 1962).

10 Sir Thomas Fowell Buxton, *The African Slave Trade and its Remedy* (1840). The quotation is from Lloyd, *The Search for the Niger*, p. 149.

11 Lloyd, *The Search for the Niger*, p. 149.

12 Dike, *Trade and Politics in the Niger Delta*, pp. 81–87, 90–96.

13 J. F. Ade Ajayi, *Christian Missions in Nigeria 1841–1891* (London: Longman, 1965), Chaps. I & II.

14 Papers relating to the Reduction of Lagos by Her Majesty's Forces on the West Coast of Africa (*British Sessional Papers*, 1852, Vol. XVI, *passim*) also Papers Relating to the Occupation of Lagos (*BSP*, 1862, Vol. LXI, *passim*).

15 Obaro Ikime, *Merchant Prince of the Niger Delta* (London: Heinemann, 1968), pp. 1–24.

16 Michael Crowder, *West Africa Under Colonial Rule* (London: Hutchinson, 1968), p. 61.

17 The general theses on which these are based are the Hobson–Lenin theories on imperialism, D. K. Fieldhouse, 'Imperialism: an historiographical revision', *The Economic History Review*, 2nd Series, XIV, No. 2 (1961), pp. 187–209.

18 Rudyard Kipling.

19 Lagos, 'Report on the Blue Book for 1890', *BSP*, Vol. LV., 1892, p. 476.

20 Roland Oliver, *Sir Harry Johnston and the Scramble for Africa* (London: Chatto and Windus, 1959), p. 108.

21 Ikime, *Merchant Prince of the Niger Delta*, Chapter III; Ikime, 'Nigeria – Ebrohimi', in M. Crowder (ed.), *West African Resistance* (London: Hutchinson, 1971), pp. 205–32.

22 Robert O. Collins, *Problems in African History* (New Jersey: Prentice-Hall Inc., 1968), pp. 365–71.

23 E. Isichei, *Missionary Enterprise and Rivalry in Igboland 1857–1914* (London: Frank Cass, 1971), Chapter VI.

24 John E. Flint, *Sir George Goldie and the Making of Nigeria* (London: Oxford University Press, 1960), pp. 60–61.

25 H. A. S. Johnston, *The Fulani Empire of Sokoto* (London: Oxford University Press, 1967), p. 240.

10 British colonial administration

Ibrahim A. Gambari

Introduction

The purpose of this chapter is neither to attack nor to apologise for British colonial administration in Nigeria but instead to attempt to evaluate its purpose and its impact on the peoples of that country. An attempt will also be made to identify the philosophy behind the British colonial administration in Nigeria and, briefly, to indicate how this differed from the principles of administration adopted by the French in their neighbouring West African territories.

British colonialism in Nigeria was not an isolated phenomenon. It was part of the wider European scramble for territorial acquisition and the economic and political subjugation of the African continent. The process was consummated at the international Conferences of Berlin (1884–85) and Brussels (1890) and in associated bilateral agreements whereby Africa was divided into territories or 'spheres of influence' controlled by European powers: Britain, France, Belgium, Spain, Portugal and Germany.

A great deal of attention has been paid by historians and other scholars to explanation of this phenomenon. The debate can only be briefly alluded to here; it does not fall strictly within the terms of reference of this chapter, but it provides background for an understanding of the topic.

It was the arrival of Belgium and Germany on the African scene in the early 1880s which precipitated the international negotiations which in turn led to the formalisation of the partition arrangements. But both Britain and France had been active on the coasts around the continent long before then, while the Portuguese interest has an even longer history. The debate about the partition involves examination of the origins and nature of European imperialism. This has been described (though hardly defined) by Joseph Schumpeter as 'an objectless disposition on the part of a state for unlimited forcible expansion', which neither advances the argument nor is acceptable to an historian. More seriously, in 1961 Robinson and Gallagher contended that British territorial acquisitions, if not imperialism itself, arose from 'an obsession with security, a fixation of safeguarding the routes to the East', which made the occupation of Egypt and later the Sudan necessary. Apart from the eccentricity of the language (since an 'obsession with security' is the first and most obvious concern of any government), this too seems inadequate, especially when the partition of West Africa is considered, although it does throw light on the persisting Franco-British rivalry which originated particular phases of the partition (including the pre-partition acquisition of Lagos, which became a British colony in 1861). There must then be taken into account the Marxist and quasi-Marxist explanations which emphasise the economic advantages which the imperialist powers hoped to gain; Lenin indeed claimed that the acquisition of wealth by means of the exploitation of subjugated peoples was the sole object of imperialism. This thesis has been subjected to such devastating criticism that it cannot be seriously advanced as a sole cause, but even the most severe critic of Lenin's analysis would not deny that economic gain played at least some part of the motivation, conscious or unconscious, of the imperialists.[1]

British colonial administration in Nigeria, to 1914

As appears above (and in the preceding chapter), British administration in what was to become Nigeria began in Lagos in 1861. The annexation of the small island kingdom and its dependencies was preceded by a decade of informal consular rule,[2] and the transformation of this into the status of a Crown Colony[3] ensured the continuation of important processes of change, mainly in a 'westernising' or modernising sense which were already underway: in particular, the expansion of Christian missions and of western-style education into the vast hinterland, the interdiction of the external slave trade and the more gradual elimination of the pervasive domestic slavery, and the growth of two-way trade with Europe. Equally important, however, were the changes which it brought about in the provision of a colonial administration, culminating in a Governor and a hierarchy of officials and in arrangements for both internal and external security.

In the years leading up to the scramble (as the accelerated phase of the partition is called), the Colony of Lagos gradually extended its authority over the surrounding Yoruba country (impinging in the west on the territory of the Egun people); this extension became known as the Lagos Protectorate, subject to looser control than the area of the Colony proper. Then, during the 1880s and 1890s, British expansion to the south-east, around the Niger and Oil Rivers and again based on the local British Consulate (founded in 1849 to cover the two Bights of Benin and Biafra, and divided between the eastern and western areas in 1853), culminated in the declaration of the Oil Rivers Protectorate, later called the Niger Coast Protectorate and, further inland, in the establishment of a chartered trading agency, the Royal Niger Company.[4]

Northern Nigeria, most of which fell within the territory of the emirates founded by the Fulani in Hausaland and its eastern neighbours early in the nineteenth century (comprising the federation sometimes known as the 'Sokoto empire' or even 'Caliphate') and of the Borno sultanate, felt the impact of British arms and administration later than the south. Only in 1900 was the Protectorate of Northern Nigeria set up, and only in 1903 was Sokoto itself conquered and absorbed into this Protectorate. After the revocation of the charter of the Royal Niger Company in 1899, its territories were divided between the Northern and Southern Protectorates. Finally, in 1906, the Colony and Protectorate of Lagos were amalgamated with the Protectorate of Southern Nigeria (as the Niger Coast Protectorate had been called since 1900) and in 1914 the two vast territories, North and South, were amalgamated as the Colony and Protectorate of Nigeria, with Lagos as its capital.

As has been described in the last chapter, British authority over the area eventually defined as 'Nigeria' was achieved partly by peaceful penetration and partly by force of arms. Although occupation of the entire territory took some years to accomplish (indeed, parts of Igboland were not brought fully under control until 1918), the two administrations which had emerged by 1906, that is, the Northern Provinces and the Southern Provinces with the Colony of Lagos respectively (and referred to below as 'the North' and 'the South' for brevity), imposed British rule with growing effectiveness. In both North and South was set up an orthodox colonial structure of Governor (or Lieutenant-Governor or High Commissioner) presiding over a civil service consisting of political officers (Residents, District Officers, etc.) established in the provinces, districts and other sub-divisions, a central secretariat, and a small but growing technical and professional staff. That basic similarity apart, however, the two constituent parts of a nominally unified Nigeria were administered in very different ways.

Whereas the South (both Colony and Protectorate) was subject to a conventional pattern of colonial government in which political responsibility was vested solely in the expatriate officials of the imperial power, in the North 'Indirect Rule' was practised whereby the indigenous rulers continued to exercise their authority over their peoples subject only to the supervision – often fairly remotely exercised – of the imperial agents. The result was that the South, on the one hand, was ever more open to the modernising influences of the expanding overseas trade, religion and education, all on western lines, developments which were unchecked by the introduction of a degree of indirect rule into the South (Yorubaland and Benin in particular) after 1914. The North, on the other hand, remained obedient to the Islamic pattern of government which had prevailed for a century before the coming of the colonialists – some of the local rulers, indeed, exercised greater power under the colonial regime than had their predecessors – and which largely prevented the spread of those outside influences which were rapidly changing the intellectual and physical face of the South.[5] Moreover, the British administration in North and South not only encouraged these differences but themselves remained strictly separate, largely isolated from each other, and in some senses rival services, transfers between them being in practice rare. There were, in fact, not one but two Nigerias.

British colonial administration, 1914–1960, and its impact

If reckoned from the annexation of Lagos in 1861, British colonial administration in Nigeria lasted for 99 years. It is more realistic, however, to reckon from 1900, the emergence of the Protectorate of North and South, a period of 60 years. Whichever of these figures is considered, the colonial era was a short one. Nevertheless, it was one of great importance and one which saw rapid and far-reaching change in Nigeria in the political, economic and social fields. Since it was in the last field, that of social change, especially with regard to educational advance, that so much in the other fields had their origin, this will be considered first, although necessarily in summary form. The other sub-sections of this part of the chapter will then deal respectively with economic development, the traditional authorities, and finally national integration and constitutional advances.

Social change

Although the slave trade had long been abolished, the status of domestic slave was allowed to die out only slowly, in order not to disturb unduly the social organisation of the country where, in every part, slaves had been employed both in households and on farms. By the end of the colonial period in Nigeria, however, even domestic slavery was everywhere only a somewhat distant memory. Meanwhile, religion, educational and general literacy made great strides in the South, much less so in the North. The Christian missions established themselves all over the South and also in the 'pagan', that is, non-Muslim, areas of the North, while Islam made many converts not only in those pagan areas but also among southerners, especially the Yoruba.

Education in the western form was, at first, the concern only of the Christian missionary societies, going hand in hand with the spread of the gospel. From the earliest mission days in the 1840s, primary education had been introduced, and this rapidly became an important part of the missionary programme. Secondary education was slower, although in 1859 the first Nigerian grammar school was opened by the Anglican Church Missionary Society in Lagos under the Rev. T. B. Macauley, a Yoruba born and educated in Sierra Leone and England.[6] Other secondary schools followed, first in Lagos, then Abeokuta, then further afield. The colonial government's reaction was to support these voluntary schools by grants-in-aid which go back to the 1870s, so that by 1913 there were no less than 80 mission schools benefiting from these grants. But the development was almost wholly confined to Southern Nigeria. In the North education for long continued to be virtually confined to the teaching of the Koran, a situation which was supported by the local rulers and which changed only slowly. By 1926, there were only 125 primary schools in the North and no secondary schools, compared with 3 828 and 18 respectively in the South.

Higher education came tardily, beginning only in 1934 with the opening of the Yaba Higher College near Lagos; this was intended to concentrate on professional and technical training, whereas the bias of education had previously been a literary one. Finally, in 1948 came the foundation of the Ibadan University College, the forerunner of today's numerous Nigerian universities.

The most important effect of these changes in Nigerian society was to create a small but growing and extremely articulate class of

Fig. 10.1 An infants' class at Aiyodi in Ondo Province in the early years of colonial rule

western-educated men – and eventually women – who, as will be seen later in this chapter, formed the vanguard of the nationalist movement. This élite (the word used to describe them) was predominantly, and at first wholly, of Southern origin, a factor which increased the division between North and South. It was an élite based not on birth (unlike the traditional aristocracy, and divergent too from the minute but significant class of Anglicised Yoruba descended from 'repatriates' from Sierra Leone) but on outlook, since it had absorbed so much of western ideas and ways of thought. Thus, as its members moved into the higher posts in the civil service (though here a restrictive policy came to be applied), education, and the expanding world of commerce, it soon became a class set apart by wealth, standard of life, and sophistication.

A second and associated effect of the increasing literacy of this class of Nigerians was the emergence of an active press. The first newspaper produced in the country was the *Iwe Irohin*, written in English and Yoruba and published by the CMS in Abeokuta from 1859 to 1867. Predictably it was in Lagos that the first commercial newspapers appeared; this was during the 1880s. Despite their ephemeral nature, these Lagos publications displayed great journalistic vigour and took full advantage of the almost complete freedom of comment and reporting which was allowed them by the colonial authorities.[7]

Economic development

British colonial economic policies were predicated on the assumption

Fig. 10.2   The railway at Baro in 1910

that the interests of the home country and the colonies were in harmony. Needless to say, this assumption was not always shared by the colonial peoples. Hence, the British introduced the cash crop economy in the colonies in order to produce taxable income there which could be used to defray administrative costs.[8] Furthermore, networks of railways and other infrastructures were built to facilitate the movement of the cash crops from the interior to the coastal area for export and of imported British manufactures from the coasts to the mainland. In Nigeria the railway began its long journey northward from Lagos in 1896; harbour works on a large scale began there eleven years later.

Naturally, the main goal of colonial 'development' policy was to serve metropolitan needs. It could be said that 'when the British economy sneezed, the colonies were forced to prevent or minimise the cold'. Nevertheless, such development, and in particular the opening up of transport links over vast distances, greatly fostered the country's unity.

In the case of Nigeria, the forerunner and agent of British administration outside Lagos was the Royal Niger Company, known earlier as the United African Company and founded by Sir George Goldie. The RNC was opposed to competition not only from other European companies but also from indigenous African traders. In 1879, Goldie's company had dismissed all the senior African managers and agents of the firms which he took over on behalf of the Royal Niger Company.[9]

The generally poor record of British colonial development policy, especially in the spheres of processing and marketing and in the creation of a sizeable indigenous middleman class, was responsible for the low level of industrialisation and secondary economic activities in Nigeria as in most African states at the time of independence. The colonial peoples often expressed their dissatisfaction with the general economic system, which included taxation and customs duties on imported articles in daily use at the time when the prices paid for cash crops were falling. The Aba Market Women's Riot of 1929, prompted by preparations to extend direct taxation, successfully carried out in Northern Nigeria, to the South, was a case in point.[10]

When colonial aid was given in the industrial and commercial spheres, the purpose seems primarily to have been to benefit ailing British industries. Through such aid, there was to be expansion to export production so that profits of British investors would be protected and the home country's labour force would be employed. Accordingly, the budgetary mechanisms in the colonies were designed to promote the favourable access of British goods and also to insure balanced budgets in the areas under British rule.[11]

Nonetheless, Nigeria's economic development, as defined by and largely in the interest of the British colonialists, was faster than that in the French colonies of West Africa. On the other hand, the rate of economic growth after the Second World War was faster in the Gold Coast (later Ghana) than in Nigeria.[12] Within Nigeria, the pace was quicker in the South than in the North. Ironically, the reverse had been the case before the advent of colonial rule in what later became the two segments of Nigeria. By 1950, however, the competitive position of the North with the South in cash crop export had improved so that, for example, its groundnuts alone accounted for one-tenth of all Nigeria's exports.[13] In all, the North produced about one-quarter of all Nigeria's exports in 1950, while in the South palm products and cocoa respectively accounted for one-third and one-quarter of the whole country's exports in the same year.[14] The other main items of the country's external trade were minerals such as tin, columbite and coal.

Generally, then, one can observe a pattern of colonial economic policies which brought about or exacerbated uneven development between and within the regions and different sectors of the economy. At all times, the needs of British industry for raw materials and minerals on the one hand and for guaranteed markets on the other were paramount. The political consequences of unbalanced growth between the North and South of Nigeria and between the industrial and agricultural sectors of the economy became of critical importance after the country's independence in 1960.

Traditional authorities

On the surface, the British appear to have recognised real value in African traditional socio-political institutions and hence strove to preserve, protect and supervise the indigenous systems in their colonies. By contrast, the French are credited with a principled disdain for African values which led them to strive to make Frenchmen out of their colonial peoples or, at least, out of a privileged minority of them. Thus, the British evolved their policy of 'indirect rule' while the French pursued an administrative policy of 'assimilation'.

In reality, indirect rule was introduced not for ideological reasons but empirically as an expedient for coping with the practical difficulties of administering vast territories under colonial rule with few administrators and meagre funds. Once put into practice the policy of indirect rule led to the entrenchment of the powers of indigenous rulers and their growth beyond the limits traditionally assigned to them. This was the system which was applied by Frederick Lugard in the Protectorate of Northern Nigeria of which he was the first Governor (1900–1906) and which Lugard attempted to extend to the rest of the country when in 1912 he was charged with the amalgamation of the two Protectorates under him as Governor-General.

Lugard, a theoretician as well as man of action, coined the classic phrase 'the dual mandate' to describe the task of the colonial administrator. According to him, the aim of British colonial administration was to promote the interest of the home country's industrial classes at the same time as advancing the interest of the 'native races' in their search for progress.[15] Lugard assumed that these two tasks were in harmony. Therefore, the key issue was to find the best instrument for fulfilling this colonial dual mandate. The policy of indirect rule was to provide that instrument, whereby the British ruled through the existing local rulers, preserving and supporting their authority 'so long as the fundamental laws of humanity and justice were observed' and with the British political officers confining their role so far as was possible to an advisory one.[16]

In pursuit of this policy, the British did not attempt to intervene in the composition of the traditional councils which gave advice, support and sanction to the local rulers.[17] Moreover, even in cases where traditional rulers acted against the public will and interest, the British administrators were reluctant to recommend prompt and radical changes, although, of course, instances of private rebuke and eventually even deposition by the colonial administrators did occur. Usually, the administrators would emphasise the need to preserve the 'spiritual significance of the chiefly office'[18] as well as the prestige and independence of the rulers. As a senior colonial administrator in Northern Nigeria admitted:

> It was not at all easy to bring about major reforms where a regime and a way of life had been established for centuries and where there was no popular demand for change.[19]

The British therefore fostered what they identified as the 'Sole Native Authorities', a system whereby the ruler administered his domain 'by leave of no one outside the British administration';[20] this system was much criticised, in particular by the emergent and politically minded elite of the South. The colonial administration later changed the system of 'Emir and Council' to that of 'Emir-in-Council', but the supervision of the ruler by his council and the colonial administration remained weak.

This colonial practice of strengthening the power of local rulers in

Nigeria was not limited to the North. Despite the different character of monarchical institutions in Yorubaland and Benin and their virtual absence in the south-east, the colonial government attempted to put their indirect rule policy into effect in the South as in the North. For example, the British backed the authority of the Alake of Abeokuta to the extent of using troops to put down rebellions in that town in 1901 and 1903.[21] The Alake was thus enabled to exploit the British predilection for a 'great chief' and thus to transform himself into an authoritarian (though not autocratic) ruler despite the fact that traditional Egba government was in a real sense republican in form.[22]

From its inception, however, there was a growing threat to the indirect rule system. Whereas the institutions of kingship and chieftaincy were almost always in the hands of the local aristocracies (one exception being the 'new men' thrown up by the Yoruba wars of the nineteenth century), the initially small but growing number of western-educated Nigerians were drawn from the lower strata of traditional society.[23] Hence, the British and their local instruments for the indirect rule system were pulling in one direction but the western-educated Nigerians were pushing in another. The ensuing conflict of attitudes by the British was much more pronounced in the South of Nigeria, due to the greater concentration of western-educated people there and the weaker base for indirect rule, than in the North. However, it is a mistake to assume that the conflict was totally absent in the North, at least potentially.

The challenge of change in the North was met to some extent by co-opting western-educated citizens into the traditional system in an attempt to shore it up.[24] Another aspect of the policy was that children of traditional rulers were sent to western-type schools, especially during the inter-war period, with the result that a 'substantial number of these Northerners who were so educated in the inter-war period were sons of titled families or of high ranking officials in the native administrations'.[25]

Whether in the North or South of Nigeria, however, indirect rule failed to satisfy the hopes and aspirations of the ruled. It was impossible for the Native Administrations to meet the 'rising expectations' of the emerging elite, while the capacity of the chiefs to support change and progress was often absent. While Lugard counselled the way of evolution rather than of revolution, it was precisely the opposite process which excited the budding nationalists and their leaders, who had no reason to be committed either to colonial rule or to the indirect rule system operated by the British.

National integration and constitutional development

Colonial administration inevitably destroyed independent African sovereignty. In practice, neither the French policy of 'assimilation' nor the British policy of indirect rule was designed or able to preserve African political sovereignties. The Lugardian concept of the 'dual mandate' was a contradiction in terms. Colonial administrations existed to promote the interest of the colonial powers as defined by successive governments in the home country. The colonised peoples had no voice in their government until the process of decolonisation began, hence their own interests and welfare remained incidental and secondary. As Gann puts it, graphically and accurately, 'by and large . . . the men from Europe came to hold the whip hand'.

As has been described earlier in this chapter, during the period 1900 to 1912 Northern and Southern Nigeria were ruled as two distinct entities. This reflected various factors: administrative choice and convenience, the inherently disparate nature of the peoples, the differences in their religion, mainly Islam in the North and mainly Christian in the South (with large though dwindling numbers practising indigenous religions in both), and the imposition on the North of the powerful personality of Lugard with his cherished policy of indirect rule.

The amalgamation of the two territories of Northern and Southern Nigeria under Lugard in 1912–14, necessitated by colonial administrative and financial convenience, was not total or complete. Despite the introduction into the South of a measure of indirect rule after 1914, the character of British rule in the two parts of the nominally united country was very different, and sharply separate bureaucracies were retained to run them. In general, the British were content to reflect, and indeed (though perhaps inadvertently) to increase the indigenous sources of division and disunity which they found in Nigeria rather than to reduce them. In H. O. Davies' words, 'if the British "created" Nigeria, British colonial policy largely contributed to its remaining a mere geographical expression'.[26]

From Lord Lugard to Sir Hugh Clifford, British governors of Nigeria could not conceal their distrust and sometimes even dislike for the educated Africans who were largely concentrated in the South of the country. Lugard believed that the 'Lagos group' were 'in no sense representative of the tribes of the interior'.[27] And Sir Hugh Clifford condemned, in very strong language,

> men born and bred in British administered towns situated on the seashore, who in the safety of British protection have peacefully pursued their studies under British schools, whose eyes are fixed not on African native history or tradition or policy nor upon their own tribal obligations and duties to their Natural Rulers which immemorable customs should impose upon them but upon the political theories evolved by Europeans.[28]

There were two major consequences of this colonial attitude to Nigerians who had acquired western education. First, they were from 1900 onwards very largely excluded from responsible positions in the administration. Lugard and his successors believed that Africans ought to be worked into the lower tiers of government rather than allowing them to participate in the higher levels of government. Therefore, it gradually became almost impossible for Africans in the colonial administration to rise to positions of any authority, despite the earlier evidence of ability shown by certain prominent exceptions.[29] Secondly, the British administration, convinced of the wisdom of indirect rule in the North and seeking to impose it on the South, invited western-educated Africans there to find political fulfilment of their aspirations within that system.

The Colonial Office accepted Lugard's report on the amalgamation scheme in which Southern Nigerians, except the Yoruba, were dismissed as 'of a low and degraded type'.[30] While conceding that the South had made 'astonishing' material progress, Lugard condemned almost all aspects of the Southern administration.[31] Sent out by the Colonial Office in 1912 to implement his own report, Lugard made sure that the 'only unifying administrative office was to be that of the Governor-General . . . otherwise the division of the country [was to] remain'.[32] The North and South had their own Lieutenant Governors and they prepared separate estimates for inclusion in the central budget submitted to the Colonial Office. In 1939 the Southern Provinces were divided into two parts, Eastern and Western. Since there were great social and cultural disparities between these two areas, the division had the effect of increasing the differences between the South and the 'monolithic' North – to use an adjective which came later to be much applied.

This situation facilitated the emergence among British officials of a 'dogmatic concept of Northern Indirect Rule and an assertive Northern patriotism'.[33] The colonial officials succeeded in alienating the western-educated Southerners and building a gap between them and their fellow countrymen in the North. British officials never seriously addressed themselves to the problems of harmonising conflicting policies in the two Nigerias or of 'how the rapidly growing individualism of the South with its cash crops, its rapidly expanding mission schools, its growing wage earning and clerical class, its African entrepreneurs and petty capitalists could be blended with Northern conservatism, Muslim law and self-sufficiency'.[34]

Nonetheless, colonialism and colonial administrations sow the seeds of their own destruction. The very assimilation of alien ideas and the creation of a group of western-educated Africans to service colonial economic and administrative needs constitute the main catalysts for the removal of alien rule and rulers. In Nigeria in the late 1940s the ranks of the nationalists began to swell with students who were returning home from studies in western Europe, usually Britain, or in the USA; ex-servicemen returning from war service in the Middle East, East Africa, Burma and India; and the local bourgeoisie and entrepreneurs who believed that self-government would improve their competitive position vis-à-vis foreign-owned businesses. The agitation for self-government assumed ever greater dimension and urgency.

The first all-Nigerian political party into which this nationalist impulse was channelled was the National Council of Nigeria and the Cameroons (NCNC), formed towards the end of the Second World War. Despite its ambitious name, its main strength was centred around Lagos, Eastern Nigeria and to a lesser extent, part of Western Nigeria. However, after 1951 and especially by 1957, the plural nature of Nigerian society had affected the growth and development of the nationalist movement. The result was the establishment of two new rival parties, the Action Group (AG) in the Yoruba West and the Northern Peoples' Congress (NPC) based on the Hausa cities. This process of decentralising national political development was recognised and encouraged by the colonial government. Hence, the three main political parties pursued the demand for self-government and independence with varying degrees of enthusiasm, urgency and commitment.

The British took advantage of this situation by emphasising the constitutional and other obstacles in the path of decolonisation rather than facilitating constitutional development towards early independence, the main obstacle on the Nigerian side being the Northern fear of Southern domination in an independent Nigeria and their consequent reluctance to be hurried into constitutional advance. Thus, whenever political concessions had to be made to the nationalists' demands, they came in bits and pieces. First, Nigerians were nominated into the Legislative Council. Then some, and later all, Nigerians who served as unofficial members of the Legislative Council were to be elected by African voters (between 1922 and 1925). Meanwhile in 1943 the policy had begun of appointing Nigerians into senior posts in the Civil Service. By 1945 unofficial members outnumbered official members in the Nigerian Legislative Council. The next step was to allow some unofficial members to be appointed into the Executive Council. Throughout the 1940s, however, the responsibility for the government of the colonies remained firmly in the hands of the British Governor and his colonial officials.

Thus, by the time that Governor Sir Arthur Richards introduced his constitutional proposals aimed at giving Nigerians a greater say in their affairs, the nationalists were no longer satisfied with such a goal; rather they demanded greater and more genuine 'participation' in the running of their country.[35] Although the Richards Constitution, which became law on 1 January 1947, brought the North and South together in a common legislative council for purposes of law making, and to this extent fostered unity, it also registered and entrenched regionalism in Nigeria's political affairs by its acceptance of the existing tri-regional structure.[36]

The process leading to the adoption of the successor constitution of 1951 (named after Governor Sir John Macpherson) involved a much wider segment of opinion in Nigeria. However, such enlightened opinion had, by that time, become regionalised between North, East and West, and also ethno-centred with Hausa, Igbo and Yoruba loyalties in the ascendency. Regional houses of assembly, houses of chiefs and executive councils were established. Part of the problem was that there was no country-wide party which commanded majority support in all the three regions of Nigeria. Furthermore, the most prominent political leaders in the country (the Sardauna, Azikiwe and Awolowo in the in the country (the Sardauna, Azikiwe and Awolowo in the North, East and West respectively) were not members of the Central House of Representatives.[37] This situation was responsible for the existence of three strong regions and a weak centre in the constitutional structure of the country at independence and throughout the First Republic. Meanwhile the dominance within each region of its regionally-based party was demonstrated decisively in Nigeria's first general election, held in 1951–52.

The Revised Constitution of 1954 (the Lyttelton Constitution) consolidated this regional focus of Nigeria's political development towards independence. Although a Central Council of Ministers was established, the three regions (with three seats each) were equally represented in it. The central legislature was no longer to give directives to the regional houses of assembly. The regional legislatures no longer needed to secure central government approval for their bills before enactment as was the case under the previous constitution.[38] The regions were to possess a reservoir of power in the sense that, except for definite subjects given to the federal government and certain concurrent (shared) subjects, all other matters were left to the regions for legislative purposes. At the executive level, regional premiers and ministers were appointed with the Governor of each region presiding over them.

Following the 1954 constitutional conference and the introduction of the revised constitution which had emerged, federal elections were held. These led to the formation of a coalition government between the NPC and the NCNC (the latter, having on this occasion won more seats than the AG in the West, were able to nominate six out of nine ministers, that is, three for each of the two southern regions). Although ministers were appointed with full departmental responsibilities, no provision was made for a Prime Minister although regional governments, on the other hand, were presided over by the Premiers. Then, after yet another constitutional conference in 1957, a national government was formed to prepare for independence; in this the three regionally-based parties, the NPC, NCNC and the AG, came together under Alhaji Abubakar Tafawa Balewa as Prime Minister with a representative cabinet. The 1957 conference also set up a Minorities Commission which made recommendations intended to allay the fears expressed by minority groups in the country.

The stage was now set for independence. Internal self-government was first assumed by the three regions in the period between 1957 and 1959. In the latter year further federal elections were held. As again no single party was returned with a large enough majority to form a government, the NPC and NCNC again entered into coalition, and once more Alhaji Abubakar became federal Prime Minister; the AG were in opposition at the centre, although the governing party in the West. At last, on 1 October 1960 the independent Federation of Nigeria was proclaimed, and was admitted to the United Nations and to the Commonwealth.

At almost all the constitutional conferences which preceded independence, the North–South divisions had been articulated and intensified. The representatives of the South (both East and West), muting for the time being their own profound differences of approach, tended to take Northerners for granted and clearly expected to replace the British at the centre after independence. Chief Anthony Enahoro's thoughts during the independence ceremonies of 1 October 1960 illustrate this expectation:

There was something missing from the central scene. Dr Azikiwe should have been there. Chief Awolowo should have been there. But they like *myself* [italics added] were spectators. Strange the way of providence.[39]

171

On the other hand, the Northern leaders looked on the Southerners all too often, though understandably, as a threat far greater than the British to their way of life and government.[40] Hence, with the encouragement of their British colonial officers, the Northern leadership tended to constitute the conservative force in Nigeria's political development as independence approached, counselling caution and a slower, more deliberate pace.[41]

Thus, influenced by the preferences of the colonial government, the size, homogeneity and separate cultural identities of the major ethnic groups in Nigeria, and the conditional responses of the early Nigerian nationalist leaders to the situation, the country's political development followed a regional and ethnic rather than a centralised path. This led to the tragic civil war in June 1967 to January 1970, occasioned by the attempted secession of 'Biafra', the former Eastern Region.[42]

Conclusion

Colonial administration in Nigeria (aided by the parochialism of some of the early nationalists) created a situation whereby, within a few years of the granting of independence in 1960, Nigeria experienced one political crisis after another until in 1966 military rule terminated the democratic experience.[43] To use Tonnies' sociological classification,[44] the socio-political and ethnic groups in Nigeria reflected a *Gesellschaft*-like rather than a *Gemeinschaft* relationship to one another – partnership merely rather than community – expecially at the centre. This inevitably affected inter-group behaviour and the ability to surmount crises. National unity and national tolerance of opposing views and interests suffered as a result.

It was not until after the civil war was over in 1970 that the embryo of a *Gemeinschaft*-like society at the centre – perhaps over-simplified in the slogan 'One Nigeria' – began to emerge. Even then this development conceals new antagonisms brought about by the polarisation of economic groups in Nigeria. Extremes of wealth and poverty in the country obstruct the process of national integration, domestic peace and economic development.

However, one thing is clear: the advent of colonial administration in Nigeria crippled the development of indigenous socio-economic and political sturctures. The purpose of European colonialism was to develop the metropolitan countries, and the contact between Europe and Africa has therefore led to the underdevelopment of the latter. The intellectual, industrial and technological areas of national life were the ones most seriously and deliberately underdeveloped by the colonialists. This situation is responsible for the continuing dependency relations between the decolonised nations and the West European nations. Self-reliance is clearly a way out of this dependent relationship between Africa and the former colonial powers.

Notes

1 The main sources of this paragraph are: J. Gallagher and R. Robinson, *Africa and the Victorians: the official mind of imperialism* (London: 1961), chapter 6; L. H. Gann and P. Duignan (eds), *Colonialism in Africa 1870–1960*, Volume 1 (London: 1969), especially pp. 107, 127, 224, 225, 238 (chapters by Gann and Flint); D. Pachala, *International Politics Today* (New York: 1971), pp. 97 (for the quotation from Schumpeter), 98, 107.

2 See R. S. Smith, *The Lagos Consulate, 1851–1861* (London, 1978), *passim*.

3 For the debate about the 'reduction' of Lagos in 1851 and its annexation in 1861, see Smith, *The Lagos Consulate;* also A. Hopkins, 'Property rights and empire building: Britain's annexation of Lagos, 1861', *Journal of Economic History*, XL, 4, 1980, and M. Lynn, 'Consul and kings: British policy, "the man on the spot", and the seizure of Lagos, 1861', *Journal of Imperial and Commonwealth History*, X, 2, 1982.

4 The Oil Rivers Protectorate was established in 1885, renamed the Niger Coast Protectorate in 1893, and the Protectorate of Southern Nigeria in 1900. The Royal Niger Company was an amalgamation of all the major British companies trading on the Niger; it received its charter in 1899.

5 For the colonial period, Sir A. Burn's *History of Nigeria* (first edition, London: 1929, many subsequent ones) is still useful. But see also M. Crowder, *The Story of Nigeria* (London: 1962, and subsequent editions); M. Crowder, *West Africa under Colonial Rule* (London: 1968); J. White, *Central Administration in Nigeria, 1914–1948* (Dublin and London: 1981).

6 J. F. A. Ajayi, 'The development of secondary grammar school education in Nigeria', *Journal of the Historical Society of Nigeria*, II, 4, 1963; J. H. Kopytoff, *A Preface to Modern Nigeria* (Wisconsin: 1965), p. 294; White, *Central Administration*, pp. 128–29; Crowder, *The Story of Nigeria*, pp. 165, 184, 239–40, 267–69, 294.

7 See F. I. A. Omu, *Press and Politics in Nigeria, 1880–1937* (London: 1978), 2*passim*.

8 For a detailed description of the colonial economic system, see E. A. Brett, *Colonialism and Underdevelopment in East Africa: 1919–1939* (New York: Nok, 1973).

9 J. E. Flint in Gann and Duignan (eds), *Colonialism in Africa,* p. 221.

10 See the account in Cartey and Kilson (eds), *The African Reader: Colonial Africa* (Random House: 1970), pp. 162–69, also E. A. Afigbo, 'The Native Revenue Ordinance' in *Studies in Southern Nigerian History*, edited by B. L. Obichere (London: 1982). The main object of this imposition was apparently not economic but to reinforce the authority of the chiefs, who were responsible for raising the tax.

11 Brett, *Colonialism and Underdevelopment*.

12 See J. Fage, *A History of West Africa* (Cambridge: 1969), pp. 192–95.

13 *Ibid*.

14 *Ibid*.

15 Cited and discussed by S. J. Hogben and A. H. M. Kirk-Greene, *The Emirates of Northern Nigeria* (London: Oxford University Press, 1966), pp. 132–33.

16 *Ibid.*

17 Cartey and Kilson, *The African Reader*, p. 97.

18 Sir Bryan Sharwood Smith, *But Always As Friends: Northern Nigeria and the Cameroons 1921–1957* (George Allen & Unwin: 1969), p. 241.

19 *Ibid*, p. 250.

20 *Ibid*, p. 240.

21 See chapter by J. E. Flint in Gann and Duignan (eds), *Colonialism in Africa*, p. 247.

22 *Ibid.*

23 James S. Coleman, *Nigeria, Background to Nationalism* (University of California Press: 1963), p. 116. For the 'new men', see J. F. A. Ajayi and R. S. Smith, *Yoruba Warfare in the Nineteenth Century* (Cambridge: 1971), p. 65.

24 See C. S. Whitaker, Jr., *The Politics of Tradition: continuity and change in Northern Nigeria, 1946–1966* (Princeton University Press: 1970).

25 Coleman, *Nigeria*, p. 355–56.

26 H. O. Davies, *Nigeria: prospects for democracy* (Weidenfeld & Nicolson, 1961). p. 91.

27 See Flint in Gann and Duignan (eds), *Colonialism in Africa*, p. 221.

28 Cited in Kalu Ezera, *Constitutional Developments in Nigeria* (Cambridge University Press: 1964), p. 24.

29 Flint in Gann and Duignan (eds), *Colonialism in Africa*, p. 221. See also G. O. Olusanya on 'The Nigerian Civil Service in the colonial era' in B. L. Obichere (ed.), *Studies in Southern Nigerian History*. Exceptions included Henry Carr, Commissioner and Director of Education, Joseph McEwan (a Sierra Leonean), Assistant Secretary, Judge Jibowu, and Sir Adeyemi Alakija, a member of the Executive Council.

30 *Ibid*, p. 256.

31 *Ibid.*

32 *Ibid.*

33 *Ibid*, p. 252.

34 *Ibid*, p. 255.

35 Ezera, *Constitutional Developments*, p. 77; White, *Central Administration*, pp. 280–91.

36 Ezera, *Constitutional Developments*, p. 81.

37 *Ibid*, pp. 153–54.

38 *Ibid*, p. 202.

39 Anthony Enahoro, *Fugitive Offender, Story of a Political Prisoner* (London: Cassell, 1965), p. 173.

40 See F. A. O. Schwarz, Jr, *Nigeria: the politics of independence* (M.I.T. Press, 1965), p. 71.

41 *Ibid.*

42 A. H. M. Kirk-Greene, *Crisis and Conflict in Nigeria, a documentary sourcebook, 1966–1970* (London: 1971).

43 For details of the political crises see I. A. Gambari, 'The domestic politics of major foreign policy issues in Nigeria', unpublished Ph.D. thesis, Columbia University, 1973, pp. 54–65.

44 Tonnies, *Gemeinschaft und Gesellschaft (Community and Society)*, edited and translated by Charles P. Loomis (East Lansing: Michigan University Press, 1955), p. 35.

11 The independence movement

Tekena N. Tamuno [*]

More than one independence movement?

It is pertinent to begin by considering whether Nigerians took part in more than one independence movement. All the Nigerians who have led agitations against colonialism since the middle of the nineteenth century had one clear and common objective: freedom to lead their own lives in their own way. The freedom they struggled for was a many-sided thing: freedom measured in political, economic and social terms first for their respective communities and, from 1914, for the newly-created Nigerian state as well. But the methods they used to attain this common goal of freedom were different. Equally different was the pace of political change demanded by the various advocates of freedom. If, therefore, we think of these differences in strategy, tactics and tempo we have some justification for talking of more than one independence movement in Nigeria before 1 October 1960. If, on the other hand, we consider the central theme of the struggle for freedom, we can correctly refer to one common independence movement in Nigeria during the same period.

Ideology

The struggle for freedom needed an ideology, and the colonial record since the late nineteenth century in Nigeria provided enough material for formulating one. The various acts of commission and omission attributed by Nigerians to British officials during colonialism played into the hands of the advocates of freedom.

Politically, African spokesmen urged equality and freedom in place of segregation, discrimination and subjection. They preferred responsible government to representative government. Eyo Ita put the case for Nigeria very clearly in 1949:

> If the Government is that of an alien ruler that is very reason why self-help and mutual support should become the very life principle of the people, for as the Efik proverb says, 'Enyene Idem ofiok oto nte Mfat edebede enye'. Only an organism knows best its own needs and can best serve them. Only we can know best our needs. Only we can satisfy our needs adequately.

*The author is grateful to the Historical Society of Nigeria and Longman Group Ltd, for permission to use portions in this chapter which first appeared in *Tarikh*, 4(1), 1971, pp. 1–14.

In economic terms, Nigerians wanted equal opportunity and greater participation in large-scale trading, banking and similar enterprises. They also wanted diversified economies, a free choice of world markets, industrialisation, and higher living standards. In *The Road to Freedom*, published in 1949, Mbonu Ojike outlined some of Nigeria's minimum economic objectives:

> The African must be independent of the West in his fundamental economic thought. He must appreciate and preserve his economic heritage, protect it and develop it in the light of contemporary economic trend. We should not be afraid if his economy is likened to any form of –ism. All he needs is GROWTH. Capitalism, socialism, or communisim, whichever answers his call most effectively, let him pursue it unafraid of name-calling propaganda. Let him follow any economic road that most quickly leads towards freedom to transact business in his own country and with the outer world.

Socially, Nigerians urged better welfare policies, free adult and primary education, health and sanitation projects, greater employment, freedom of association – particularly in trade unions seeking collective bargaining. The Talakawa Party – the political party of the working people of Nigeria – demanded independence in 1954 to establish a socialist state. That party believed:

> that only a free and independent Nigeria can establish a socialist system of production; and that only such an establishment of socialism can enable our people to plan the use of our material and productive resources in such a way as to guarantee to every Nigerian citizen real security, the right to work and leisure, a rising standard of living, liberty, and equal opportunity for a full and happy life.

As for religion, Nigerians realised that though Christianity brought education and prestige it dealt a severe blow to traditional religion and African customs generally. In the white man's churches, Africans saw segregation and other objectionable practices. They therefore included in their reforms the establishment of separatist churches. In his public lecture at the Glover Memorial Hall in Lagos on 10 April 1917, the Rev. S. A. Coker called upon Africans to organise and establish indigenous churches unattached to, and not controlled by, any foreign church organisation. Coker was then the President of the Congregational Union in West Africa and Superintendent of the Christ Army Church or the Niger Delta Native Church. In his conclusion Coker stated:

> I detest the growing hypocrisy which has been the outcome of forced or self-imposed spiritual slavery. The Church of England rehearses in our ears daily, 'whose service is perfect freedom'. I pray to see less – if not altogether abandoned – of believing in the earthly master and in the exotic Church's voice more than in Christ our one master and the Holy Writ. . . . The Church of England may be the best for the British nation as a national church. We shall and must be true to ourselves and

177

Christianity and loyal in a greater degree to our Gracious King and Emperor if we establish indigenous churches, the Holy Bible being the true foundation and in conformity to our social and national customs.

Those who demanded independence considered two other related questions: whether political freedom should precede economic prosperity, and whether independence should be granted only to those who considered themselves 'ripe' for it. In July 1949, Paul Birabi, during the Eastern Regional Conference on constitutional revision, compared Nigerian society to a forest in which no observer finds all the trees equally ripe at one and the same time. He therefore considered irrelevant any attempts to set a time-limit for assessing the ripeness of dependent people for independence. In *The Assurance of Freedom*, published in 1949, Eyo Ita dealt more exhaustively with the two related questions already posed:

All those who talk about ripeness and unripeness confuse the whole issue. They do not know the nature of freedom. They do not know that every human being comes into this world with freedom as his birthright. . . . Any talk of ripeness or readiness is entirely beside the point. . . . There are those who want to wait until everybody in Nigeria is educated. They are profoundly mistaken. They might as well wait until they grow teeth before they attempt to take any kind of food. Education may be a tool of freedom. . . . Education is not an essential condition of freedom.

Others want Nigeria to wait until it has economic prosperity before it seeks freedom. They do not know that economic and all other types of advancement are effects and not causes of freedom . . . . The best advice is 'Seek ye first the order of freedom and its righteousness, and all other good things will be added unto you'. It is freedom which is the prime condition of other values, including education, enterprise, art and science.

Leadership

For any such crusade to suceed, able leadership was essential. Several reasons explain the leading role of the educated élite in the struggle for independence in Nigeria in the early twentieth century. First, the earlier uncoordinated attempts made by the illiterate chiefs and masses in their bloody confrontations with representatives of the British Government in Nigeria till the end of the nineteenth century failed to obtain the freedom desired by the various communities in the country. Their failures dictated the need for a new, non-violent but more coordinated approach to the long and sustained drive to end colonialism. In place of pitched battles, the new tactics of the advocates of freedom stressed pamphleteering, criticisms in African-owned and -controlled newspapers, monster petitions, delegations to British officials, debates in the Legislative Council, and other activities through party political organisations. For these various activities, literate Nigerian leaders had clear advantages over the traditional élite.

Besides, since several chiefs had, through the operation of indirect administration in Nigeria, cooperated with colonial officials, they tended to be discredited as leaders of the agitation for freedom. At a time when most educated Nigerians were denied responsible posts in the public service and received little consideration in the apparatus of indirect administration, the new leaders of the struggle for independence understandably came from the ranks of educated Africans, wealthy traders, farmers and businessmen. Their common frustration under colonialism helped them to work together against a common foe.

There was not always a very wide gap between the old élite (mainly chiefs) and the new (educated) élite. Some of the new elite had close links with the old. For example, Ahmadu Bello, the late Sardauna of Sokoto and leader of the Northern People's Congress, and the former Action Group leader, Oba C. D. Akran, belonged to that class of Nigerians who established political and social bridges between the old and new élites in Nigeria before independence. Again, some chiefs tried to protect themselves by supporting, openly or secretly, the new political leaders in the last decade before independence. Some traditional leaders, particularly in the former Northern and Western Regions, came within that category. Moreover, some of the new leaders, though born commoners, later sought and received chieftaincy honours to establish their legitimacy, prestige or both. Thus Nigerians avoided open friction between the traditional and new élites during the delicate transition from colonial rule to independence.

Means: strategy and tactics

In Nigeria, the leaders adopted two methods in their struggle for independence – the inter-territorial and the territorial. Nigerian leaders did not feature prominently in the Pan-Africanist approach to independence between 1919 and 1945 when five Pan-African Congresses took place in the United Kingdom and Western Europe.

The inter-territorial approach was best exemplified by the National Congress of British West Africa (NCBWA) inaugurated in 1920 and led by educated Africans. The NCBWA urged many reforms, including elective representation. By 1930, however, the NCBWA was politically dead. The West African Students' Union (WASU) provided another example of the inter-territorial method of attaining freedom. During the 1940s, WASU, led by the late Chief Oladipo Solanke, tried to lobby West Africans and the traditional élite for the liberal constitutional reforms expected at the end of the Second World War.

The new leaders soon realised that they could expect better results from territorial organisation and effort. Such strategy and tactics, they believed, would effectively meet the challenge from separate British administrations in West Africa. Events proved them right.

The leaders of the agitation for freedom found certain advantages in channelling their attack through political parties. Since political parties were known to, and used by, the British Government, they did not evoke the same degree of suspicion and opposition as the African pre-colonial secret societies or cults would have done. Moreover, political parties were distinguished by their organisation and permanence – features which promised or assured success over a long period.

Other factors further helped the party political approach. The colonial officials did not suppress political parties in Nigeria except when necessary to maintain law and order; the banning of the Zikist Movement in 1951 was one rare example. Again, the improved means of transportation and communications made possible the activities of party organisers. The existence of associational activities – the cultural-political organisations of town dwellers, trade unions, Old Boys' Associations, and the like – spread party propaganda still further. A relatively free press, allowed by the British Government in Nigeria, again assisted the various activities of the political parties. And the use of English, made possible through Christian mission or state-aided education, helped to bring within the same party persons with several differences of dialect and culture. The political, economic, social and religious grievances of many Nigerians, under colonialism, provided a large following for the major political parties.

At first, Nigeria's political parties had their origins and main support in Lagos. That was the experience of the first Nigerian National Democratic Party founded in 1923 and led by Herbert Macaulay, C. C. Adeniyi-Jones, J. Egerton-Shyngle, E. O. Moore, Ibikunle Olorun-Nimbe, A. Adedoyin and others. Its supremacy in Lagos politics was seriously and successfully challenged in 1938 by a new party – the Nigerian Youth Movement (NYM), founded in 1934 and led by E. Ikoli, S. Akinsanya, Obafemi Awolowo, H. O. Davies, Samuel Akintola, F. R. A. Williams and others.

After 1944, these largely Lagos-based political parties were supplanted by new ones with wider support in several parts of Nigeria. These parties included the National Council of Nigeria and the Cameroons (NCNC), the Action Group (AG), and the Northern People's Congress (NPC). There were other smaller political parties such as the Northern Elements Progressive Union (NEPU), the United Middle Belt Congress (UMBC), and a few more in Southern Nigeria. These organisations dominated Nigeria's political scene during the 1950s.

Independent candidates as well as those representing political parties sought admission into the Lagos-based legislature so as to participate in the discussion and formulation of policies dealing with financial and other matters. Although from 1872 Nigerian unofficial members had been nominated by the government into the Legislative Council, it was in 1923 that four representatives elected by qualified Nigerians in Lagos and Calabar reached that house. The NNDP led by Herbert Macaulay and others repeatedly won the three elective seats for Lagos in the Legislative Council until 1938 when the NYM candidates triumphed in the same constituency. Between 1944 and 1947 the NNDP regained its supremacy. From 1923 to 1947, independent candidates in the Calabar constituency won the elections into the Legislative Council.

Nigerian representatives only reached the Executive Council based in Lagos with greater difficulty. In June 1906, for example, Herbert Macaulay, S. H. Pearse and other petitioners in Lagos had asked the British Government to appoint Nigerian unofficial members into the Executive Council. British officials were at first reluctant to admit Nigerians into the Executive Council – a very sensitive area of colonial administration because it was not only the Governor's principal advisory body but also the agency for discipline before public service commissions were established in the 1950s. Because of wartime considerations, the British Government made an important concession in September 1942 when for the first time two Nigerians – Mr (later Sir) Adeyemo Alakija and Mr S. Bankole Rhodes – had seats in the Executive Council as nominated unofficial members.

Tactics also had a lot to do with correct timing. Here the role of the two world wars must be considered. Neither war caused the movement for Nigeria's independence; the traditional élite had fought for their freedom from the late nineteenth century to about 1914. Since then, other Nigerians had continued the struggle till the Second World War began. There is, however, no doubt that the two world wars had some effect on the aspirations of Nigerians. During both wars, the Allied powers' propaganda paid lip-service to the ideals of freedom, liberty, equality and self-determination. For instance, the liberal ideals expressed in President Woodrow Wilson's Fourteen Points during the First World War and in the Atlantic Charter (1941) drawn up by President Franklin D. Roosevelt and Prime Minister Winston Churchill could and did inspire the new leaders in Nigeria and elsewhere.

The boost which Nigeria's participation in the Second World War gave the long-standing agitation for independence is best illustrated in a statement made in Lagos by E. A. Akerele, a former vice-president of the Lagos-based Nigerian Young Democrats, the allies of the NNDP. In his election manifesto of 30 October 1943 Akerele said:

The active part which we have played in this World War will justify our claims for a new and better world after its close. Nigeria must start and hasten her plants for post-war reconstruction. This matter is of vital importance to us .... The present Crown Colony system of government with official majority in the Legislative Council with virtually no representation in the Executive is obsolete and has no usefulness left in it .... A representative or possibly responsible form of government introduced immediately with African unofficial majority in the Legislative Council and adequate representation in the Executive. Africans must be consulted in matters affecting their destiny .... A far greater measure of political responsibility must be given to us. This should not wait till economic independence is attained. Our approach to political and economic independence should be simultaneous.

Moreover, the liberal constitutional progress made by such Asiatic countries as Ceylon till the early 1940s encouraged Nigerians to demand

Fig. 11.1   Dr Nnamdi Azikiwe

similar concessions. An editorial in the Nnamdi Azikiwe-controlled *West African Pilot* made a telling comparison on 18 November 1944. In an obvious reference to Ceylon's progress under the Donoughmore Constitution (1931), the *West African Pilot* then observed:

> We are not one whit backward, compared with Ceylon. We have the territory, the population, the agricultural and mineral resources, the commerce, and the revenue, and we see no reason why we should continue to live under an antiquated Constitution which stultifies our aspirations in the Commonwealth of the British Empire. It is time the Colonial Office sped up our move towards self-government. Otherwise the hands of the people of Nigeria may be forced to make embarrassing, but constitutional, requests. We are not prepared to take the back seat any longer.

The two world wars acted as catalysts to the demands for Nigerian independence. The British Government's willingness to grant independence to such Asiatic countries as India, Pakistan, Burma, and Ceylon between 1947 and 1948 showed Nigerians that such progress was no longer limited to people of Anglo-Saxon descent. The establishment in 1945 of the United Nations Organisation, and the coming to power in post-war Britain of the Labour Party, dedicated to ending colonialism, gave more favourable international circumstances to the Nigerian demand for independence.

The official response

British officials had the power to grant or refuse independence. Here, differences among Nigerians should be seen in proper focus. There was a major difference in the pace, although not the objectives, of post-Second World War political developments in Nigeria. Most Nigerian leaders, particularly those of the NCNC and AG, wanted the rate of Nigeria's political development towards independence to proceed as quickly as possible. The NPC leaders, on the other hand, asked for a moderate pace. By 1959, however, the NCNC, AG, and NPC agreed that Nigeria should become independent in 1960.

The official response to the Nigerian demands for responsible self-government and independence had two discernible periods: the period of troubles (1944–51) and the period of dyarchy or cooperation (1951–59). Events in both periods were to some extent affected by party developments in post-Second World War Britain. In July 1946 the newly elected Labour Government declared its policy, which favoured leading dependent territories to 'responsible government'. In November 1951, the new Conservative Government endorsed the same policy. But neither the Labour leaders nor their counterparts in the Conservative Party indicated the pace at which such dependent territories would be allowed to develop towards the publicly declared goal of ultimate 'responsible government'. There was, then, no official time-table for granting independence to dependent peoples asking for it.

In Nigeria, the period of troubles (1944–51) marked the rise of militant party politics – particularly of the NCNC, the Zikist National Vanguard, and the AG. This period includes the visit of the NCNC delegation in 1947 to London to urge, among other things, an early review of the Richards Constitution, the first in post-Second World War Nigeria. It was also a period of many economic and social problems in the aftermath of the war. Before these problems were solved, Nigerian workers went on strike in 1945 (the General Strike), in 1947 (the Burutu Strike) and in 1949 (the Enugu Colliery Strike). Units of the Nigeria Police Force clashed with striking workers, some of whom were shot and killed. Nigerian politicians used these disturbances as effective propaganda for attacking the colonial record on economic and social welfare. The politicians claimed that they would fare better if given power and responsibility in these and related matters.

The period of dyarchy – of accommodation and partnership – began from 1951 when Britain agreed to share power and responsibility with

Nigerian politicians. In place of the old constitutions, which till 1950 provided for only representative institutions, the new constitutions after 1951 allowed responsible government as well. In the same period, the government allowed regional and central (later federal) Executive Councils with a majority of Nigerian ministers.

There was a remarkable change of method in constitutional developments during the period of dyarchy. Until the Richards Constitution of 1947 Nigerians were allowed little say in constitution-making: they had constitutions imposed on them. But in the process of reviewing the Richards Constitution the British Government allowed Nigerians in their towns and villages to express views on the lines of future progress. The balance of popular opinion since the Ibadan General Conference of 1950 lay along the line of a Federal Constitution. The MacPherson Constitution (1951) marked a step in this direction. But it was under the Lyttelton Constitution (1954) that Nigeria formally became a Federation. Until independence, members of Nigeria's major and minor political parties attended a series of conferences in London and Lagos to discuss further constitutional reforms with British delegates. The post-1950 constitutions in Nigeria were negotiated by these Nigerians, who thereby shared the responsibility for the strong and weak points of the arrangements they made till independence.

The British Government further encouraged Nigerian participation in the political decision-making process by liberalising the franchise. Under the 1951 Constitution and its successors until the Independence Constitution (1960), Lagos and Calabar ceased to be the only municipal areas where the elective principle was allowed. The principle of universal adult suffrage, with the exception of women in the predominantly Muslim Northern Region, was allowed in the 1959 federal election, the last before Nigeria's independence. During the same 1959 federal election, all the regions including Northern Nigeria, the last to do so, abandoned the slow and cumbersome electoral college system in preference to direct and separate elections to the federal House of Representatives. The escalation of electoral violence since 1954 and other difficulties, which need no elaboration here, however, prevented qualified people from registering votes that were effective.

The gradual handing over of power and responsibility from British to Nigerian officials after 1951 went side by side with another important change: the 'Nigerianisation' of the public services. The government encouraged this process through more liberal scholarships and by accelerated promotion of promising Nigerians to posts hitherto reserved to expatriates. Nigerians were thereby gradually prepared to shoulder the problems of independence.

Problems of dyarchy

Nigerians did not experience the same difficulties as the Ghanaians (the people of the former Gold Coast) during the period of dyarchy which took place also in the 1950s. The educated élite, particularly the leaders of the Convention People's Party, had considered politics a dirty game not befitting the dignified status of chiefs. Therefore, Ghana, on independence, did not have a House of Chiefs. This was not so in Nigeria where there was relatively little friction since the chiefs were given friendly accommodation by the educated élite who led the various political parties.

The position outlined by the NCNC in its manifesto for the 1954 federal election was generally representative. In describing the place of natural rulers in a self-governing Nigeria, the NCNC then said:

> Our Emirs and Obas, Obongs and Etuboms, Obis and Amayonabos, are sovereigns in their own rights. This is the verdict of our history. Accordingly, our National Rulers must fit into the position of Constitutional monarchs.

There were, however, differences in detail in the extent to which political parties could tolerate the secret or open involvement of chiefs in politics. From the 1950s Nigerians increasingly accommodated their chiefs through the regional Houses of Chiefs. About the same time, they allowed such a leading chief as the Oni of Ife a ministerial portfolio in the federal cabinet and later as Governor of the former Western Region. There were more examples of chiefs being given ministerial responsibility in the former Northern Region. Generally, chiefs from the 1950s had more opportunities as instruments of local government in parts of Nigeria. Hence, the concept of indirect administration continued through the 1950s until independence.

Nigerians used dyarchy as an instrument for accelerated economic and social development. The leading politicians found it necessary to satisfy the needs of the masses – the workers, farmers, fishermen and others – who had supported the agitation for independence. Hence began the practice in Nigerian of using politics as a game of rewards and penalties. The leaders also sought to correct the neglect of economic and social development in pre-Second World War Nigeria – a defect largely attributable to the inadequacy of funds. The problem of limited budgets continued during the 1950s, and so more sustained economic development plans had to wait for the post-independence era when Nigerians were able to widen their sources of external aid.

Dyarchy in Nigeria intensified internal divisions. During this period, the former common enemy posed as a friend even before ultimate independence was won. Hence, there was a tendency to slacken the pace of concerted action against the former common enemy. Consequently, the leaders of the agitation for independence occasionally magnified the differences among themselves. It was not a united Nigeria which asked for and obtained its independence on 1 October 1960. The desire for independence was so intense that the nation struggling for freedom was taken for granted. The time for self-examination and self-awareness came after independence was won. That was the significance of Nigeria's bitter post-independence experience between January 1966 and January 1970.

Questions for further reflection

The discussion, so far, has shown how Nigerians, leaders and followers, as well as British officials, tackled various problems concerning the natural demand for independence from colonial rulers. There is no attempt, however, to suggest in this discussion that all problems relevant to the drive for independence were resolved before 1 October 1960. Different perspectives suggest different approaches to these problems. Mine has been dictated by a well-considered analysis of the facts at my disposal. Others are equally entitled to their own interpretation of these same events.

There are some Nigerian scholars, of a radical persuasion, who regard colonialism in Nigeria, as indeed elsewhere, as an act of 'armed robbery'. Dr Segun Osoba of the University of Ife suggested as much in a seminar paper delivered at the Faculty of the Social Sciences on 24 January 1980. Some Nigerian chiefs were also seen as collaborators.

Evidence of the early Nigerian capitulation to imperialist forces – north, south, east and west of the Niger–Benue estuaries – suggests considerable carelessness on the part of most Nigerians who failed, or were unable, to put up a common front against their new rulers. Property not carefully protected can be easily lost to people keen on having access to it. No single socio-political group provided either collaborators or resisters. The patterns of resistance to colonialism in Nigeria were extremely complicated and dictated largely by the variables of time, leadership and circumstances. The so-called educated élite and masses, as well as the traditional élite, were not neatly distributed among sinners and saints during the long drive for independence.

The struggle for independence also showed the gradual dislodgement of the traditional élite from the centre-stage in Nigerian government and politics. The token concessions made to them through Houses of Chiefs and other extra-constitutional means in the 1960s were revoked with the 1979 Constitution. For most of these chiefs, the attainment of independence was like paradise lost, not paradise regained. Nonetheless, what meaningful concessions could chiefs, as natural rulers representing the *monarchical* principle, expect and have under a patently *republican* constitution soon after the attainment of independence?

For tactical and other reasons, the political aspect of independence was won first before the struggle extended to its economic, industrial, social and other aspects. These aspects of the struggle for independence have posed different sets of challenges to the succession of regimes and governments since October 1960. There have been failures as well as successes in this regard which need no elaboration here.

The character of the independence movement in Nigeria was evolutionary rather than revolutionary. Some of the major problems which tended to slow down the pace of the movement were tackled through a series of constitutional conferences which lasted till the eve of independence. Yet, such issues as the correct basis of revenue allocation under a federal constitution discussed at those conferences and beyond have continued to bedevil the tone and substance of the perennial debates and controversies over fiscal matters.

Both the leaders and the led on one side as well as British officials on the other accepted the evolutionary approach to independence in Nigeria. Circumstances in Nigeria favoured this approach. In this respect, developments in Nigeria differed remarkably from those with large numbers of settler-communities and interests: South Africa, Algeria, Kenya, Zimbabwe, Mozambique, Angola, Namibia, Indo-China and Northern Ireland. Nigeria thus escaped the bloody aspects of the struggle for independence that occurred in areas with interests important to the colonial or other rulers.

The Nigerian case study also has peculiar features relating to the proper meaning and implications of a 'Protectorate' and 'Colony' in the same amalgamated territories with free movement of people, goods and services during the anti-colonialist phase of the country's development. British administrators, for several decades in Nigeria, did not find it easy to draw neat lines of demarcation between the people of the protectorate and those of the colony. Nigeria was neither a typical colony nor protectorate throughout the struggle for independence. These difficulties, with a tilt towards the protectorate status of the majority of Nigerians, also played some part in encouraging the *evolutionary* approach to the demand for independence.

Finally, both the leaders and the led in Nigeria saw the attainment of independence not as an *end* in itself but as a *means* to an end: the welfare of the people under their own rulers with complete freedom to protect all their vital interests. Seen thus, any threat to their welfare from internal and external sources was seen as a negation of their perennial desire to be truly independent. That aspect of the movement, which is reluctant to tolerate any obstacle at home and abroad, makes a study, such as this, one of continuing interest and relevance.

Further reading

O. ADEWOYE, *The Judicial System in Southern Nigeria, 1854–1954* (London: Longman, 1977).

O. ARIKPO, *The Development of Modern Nigeria*(Harmondsworth: Penguin, 1967).

J. A. ATANDA, *The New Oyo Empire* (London: Longman, 1973).

O. AWOLOWO, *awo: The Autobiography of Chief Obafemi Awolowo* (Cambridge Cambridge University Press, 1960).

———, *Path to Nigerian Freedom* (London: Faber and Faber, 1947).

———, *Thoughts on the Nigerian Constitution*(Ibadan: Oxford University Press, 1966).

E. A. AYANDELE, *The Educated Elite in Nigerian Society*(Ibadan: Ibadan University Press, 1974).

N. AZIKIWE, *My Odyssey* (London: C. Hurst and Co., 1970).

———,, *Zik: a selection from the speeches of Nnamdi Azikiwe* (Cambridge: Cambridge University Press, 1961).

AHMADU, BELLO, *My Life* (Cambridge: Cambridge University Press, 1962).

J. S. COLEMAN, *Nigeria: background to nationalism* (Los Angeles: University of California Press, 1958).

K. EZERA, *Constitutional Developments in Nigeria* (Cambridge: Cambridge University Press, 1964).

T. HODGKIN, *African Political Parties* (London: 1961).

O. IKIME, *The Fall of Nigeria* (London, 1977).

K. A. B. JONES-QUARTEY, *A Life of Azikiwe* (London: 1965).

J. P. MACKINTOSH, *Nigerian Government and Politics* (Evanston: Northwestern University Press, 1966).

S. O. OSOBA, 'Considerations on some conceptual and ideological aspects of Nigerian under-development in historical perspective', seminar paper given at the Department of Political Science, University of Ibadan, 24 January 1980.

A. TAFAWA BALEWA, *Nigerian Speaks: speeches of Alhaji Sir Abubakar Tafawa Balewa*, (Ikeja: Longman, 1964).

T. N. TAMUNO, *Nigeria and Elective Representation 1923–47* (London: Heinemann, 1966).

T. N. TAMUNO, *The Evolution of the Nigerian State: the southern phase, 1898–1914* (London: Longman, 1978).

T. N. TAMUNO, *The Police in Modern Nigeria, 1861–1965* (Ibadan: Ibadan University Press, 1970).

12 Politics since independence

Leo Dare

The purpose of this chapter is to trace the political evolution of Nigeria from independence through the various military regimes and the succeeding civilian administration. It will focus on how Nigeria, like other developing countries of Africa and Asia, has been preoccupied with the problem of national integration, and how the various ethnic groups can be made to feel they all have a stake in the system.

We shall see how the hopes and aspirations for peace and stability at the time of independence were dashed through fratricidal conflict and political deadlock which led to the bloody civil war. We shall also look at the efforts made by the military to see that disengagement would not lead to another period of deadlock; and finally, we shall examine the nature and operation of the 1979–83 executive presidential system.

The setting

When Nigeria attained political independence on 1 October 1960, a parliamentary system of government patterned after the Westminster system was adopted. In an effort to adapt this system to local conditions, it was set within a federal scheme consisting of three rather large but uneven units or regions: the Northern, the Eastern and Western Regions.

Numerous problems were inherited with the independence euphoria. Among these were the built-in winner-takes-all approach of the Westminster model, the imbalance in the size of the regions, the issues of minorities and their demand for separate states, and regional-based political parties which the colonial indirect rule policy had helped to nurture.

It is no oversimplification to state that a great deal of the post-independence problems of Nigeria originated in the party system. Owing to the indirect rule policy, the political parties which emerged on the eve of independence were regionally based. The major parties, the National Council of Nigerian Citizens (NCNC), formerly the National Council of Nigeria and the Cameroons, under Dr Azikiwe started off as a national party but gradually became identified with the Igbo. The Action Group (AG) which Chief Obafemi Awolowo launched in 1951 represented Yoruba consciousness. The Northern People's Congress (NPC), as the name clearly shows, was the Northerners' attempt to preserve Northern interests within the framework of Nigerian federalism. None of the parties, in the real sense of the term, could be said to qualify as a national political organisation. These three major parties grew primarily to champion the interests and particularisms of the major ethnic groups, and their struggle for power and the control of the Federal

Fig. 12.1   Chief Obafemi Awolowo

Government dominated the political scene until military takeover in 1966.

The road to independence

Federal elections were called in 1959 to form a government before independence. None of the parties won an absolute majority of seats even though the NPC was the leading party. An NPC government would have been a minority government with all the attendant uncertainties. To avoid these, the NPC invited the NCNC to form an alliance or a coalition government with it and the NCNC agreed. The Action Group party became the official opposition at the Federal level. The NPC was not particularly happy about the existence of an opposition party and employed various means to suppress the Action Group. In 1962, the NPC had a golden opportunity to interfere in the internal affairs of the Action Group.

Chief Awolowo, the national leader of the Action Group and leader of opposition at the Federal House, was having problems controlling his deputy who was Premier of the Western Region.[1] The disagreement blew open and Chief Awolowo unsuccessfully tried to remove Chief Akintola. In the ensuing fracas, the supporters of the two leaders in the Western House of Assembly resorted to open fist fights.

The NPC and the NCNC saw the disturbance as a good opportunity to destroy the Action Group and its leader, Chief Awolowo. The Federal alliance of the NPC/NCNC teamed up with dissident elements in the party. A state of emergency was declared over the Western Region and an Administrator was appointed by the Federal Government to oversee the affairs of the Region. Initially, all leaders of the Action Group were placed under house arrest, but within a week, Akintola's supporters were allowed free movement while Awolowo and his supporters were left in detention. Later, charges of treasonable felony were brought against Awolowo and his supporters.[2] They were convicted under circumstances which violated the rule of law and natural justice.

At the end of the state of emergency, rather than call a fresh election as is the convention in parliamentary systems, the Federal Government returned power to Akintola's unpopular cabinet. Furthermore, in this chain of hostility towards the Action Group, and in another effort to reduce the effectiveness of the party within the federation, the Federal Government engineered the creation of the Mid-West Region out of the Western Region. What this meant in fact was that the smallest of the three regions was subdivided while the giant North and the East were untouched. It should be noted that this was the only time during the civilian administration when a region was created despite the demands for such an exercise from the minority groups in both the Northern and Eastern Regions.

Though the Action Group was effectively broken, the Yoruba remained loyal to the spirit of the party and the goaled leaders. The continued persecution of the remaining members of the Action Group meant continued alienation of the Yoruba. The Federal Government lost its legitimacy in the Western Region.

Cracks in the alliance

After settling scores with the Action Group of the Western Region, the

Fig. 12.2   Sir Abubakar Tafawa Balewa

NPC-led government of Tafawa Balewa suddenly discovered that its greatest challenges were yet to come, and from its ally the NCNC, particularly its leaders based in the Eastern Region. This time, the conflict centred on politics and influence and related issues.

The census

There had been a national census in 1962. Many irregularities were alleged. After the count, it was discovered that the Northern Region had lost its numerical majority over the rest of the country combined. This result was unacceptable to the NPC leaders who then decided to cancel the results. The 1962 figures were never officially published. Another count was ordered for 1963. As in the previous one, allegations of double-counting and irregularities were made. The final figures showed the North improving upon its 1962 figures and once more having more people than the rest of the country. The Western Region also inflated its returns while the Eastern Region returned almost its 1962 figures.

The Eastern Regional government was unhappy with the figures. Dr Okpara, the Premier of the Eastern Region, gave a number of reasons why the figures were unacceptable, describing them as 'worse than useless'.[3] In support of Okpara, the NCNC Premier of the Mid-West Region, Chief Denis Osadebay, described the returns as 'the most stupendous joke of our age'. The Eastern Regional Government unsuccessfully challenged the figures in court. After this, to reduce political tensions, the political leaders throughout the Federation met and worked out 'agreement figures'. This in effect meant that the determination of the population was taken out of the control of the population commission and resolved by politicians. Those 'agreement figures' have remained in use for planning purposes since then, as other census exercises have ended in fiasco.

The second area of conflict within the NPC/NCNC alliance was the 1964 Federal elections. As the census issue had convinced the NPC that it could no longer count on the loyal support of the NCNC, the NPC – before the 1964 elections – began looking for a more reliable partner. After the NPC dropped the NCNC as its alliance partner, it linked up with the Nigerian National Democratic Party (NNDP, established in 1964 and led by a one-time Action Group Deputy Leader, Chief S. L. Akintola) and a few other splinter parties. This group called itself the Nigerian National Alliance (NNA). In response, the NCNC, the Action Group, the Northern Elements Progressive Union (NEPU), and the United Middle Belt Congress (UMBC) formed the United Progressive Grand Alliance (UPGA). The two grand alliances faced each other during the campaigns and the 1964 Federal elections.

The formation of these two grand alliances could be said to be an attempt to form parties that were national in scope and whose membership cut across ethnic groups and regions. It was a realignment of political forces or changes in marriage partners. The fundamental issues of the rules of the game were not changed.

As the election dates drew nearer, political violence reached an all-time high. UPGA members and candidates complained of intimidation and harassment, argued that the election could not be fair and free, and sought unsuccessfully for a postponement. Failing in this, the UPGA advised supporters to boycott voting on polling day. Unfortunately, the boycott was not total. In retrospect, to have ordered the boycott was a tactical error as NNA candidates won most of the seats where any balloting took place by default.

The president of the Federation, Dr Azikiwe, who had strong UPGA sympathies and had once been the leader of the NCNC, was not prepared to call on the Prime Minister and the NNA to form a new government on the basis of the election results. He had earlier warned the politicians against their excesses and had complained that the atmosphere for a free and fair election did not exist, but the NNA refused to accept any change in election dates. It was only to avoid a political showdown with possible loss of his post as president that Azikiwe finally agreed to call on Balewa's NNA to form a new government with the understanding that (a) the Prime Minister would build a broad-based cabinet, and (b) fresh elections would be held in constituencies where the boycott had been total.

The post-election government was essentially an NPC government, despite the attempt to make it seem otherwise. UPGA and southerners generally remained frustrated and despondent, and Balewa's adminis-tration, from 1964, commanded very little support in the south. The alliance partner in the south, the NNDP of the Western Region, was declining politically, and it had minimal support with the electorate. In fact, without NNA support Chief Akintola could not have retained his position as Premier of the Western Region.

The hostility felt towards Akintola was also expressed against the NNA in the West. For this reason, when it was time for the regional elections in 1965, UPGA supporters who had been disappointed in the 1964 Federal elections prepared for revenge at the polls. The ruling NNDP party foiled these hopes by massive election rigging, even going so far as to make it impossible for its opponents to stand for election. Having lost faith in the Federal Government and the prospects of seeking justice through the judiciary, UPGA supporters took the law into their own hands, burning the property of NNDP supporters. Appeals to the Prime Minister to intervene were ignored, but instead he called a Commonwealth Prime Ministers' conference to discuss the unilateral declaration of independence in Rhodesia. Nigeria literally burned while the Prime Minister fiddled. On the day after the Commonwealth conference, a military coup took place, killing the Prime Minister, his Minister of Finance, and the Premiers of both the Northern and Western Regions.

Military intervention

By the time the military intervened in January 1966 it had become obvious to all observers that the civilian regime had failed in its primary function of maintaining law and order. The masses became desperate in their quest for an effective government. It was mainly because of dissatisfaction with the civilian administration and because the military appeared to give them hope of a better government that the military coup of 15 January 1966 was hailed so widely. It was a popular operation.

Major Kaduna Nzeogwu, the coup leader, demonstrated this awareness of public despair when in his first broadcast he stated that the coup was designed to 'bring an end to gangsterism and disorder, corruption and despotism' and ended by saying, 'my compatriots, you will no longer need to be ashamed to be Nigerians'.

Within three days of the initial announcement of the coup it had become clear that the planners had not in fact attained office. The senior officers who had probably given no thought to a political programme manoeuvred themselves into office. It became clear that the victims of the coup were predominantly non-Igbo while the planners were Igbo. Due to this, a cloud of suspicion later hung over the coup and its successor regime. The explanation by Major Nzeogwu that the plan had miscarried and that those delegated to attack Igbo leaders and Igbo institutions had developed cold feet, did not remove the suspicion that the coup was sectionally motivated and executed. Even with the best of goodwill, Ironsi would have to prove that his regime had not come about to preserve Igbo interests.

Ironsi's administration

Ironsi's main preoccupation was with the problem of national unity and how to arrest the drift towards regionalism. One of Ironsi's first political acts was the appointment of four military governors for the regions. Each of the governors so appointed was an indigene of the state over which he was to preside. It was doubtful if, except for the fear of the military, Nigerians would have accepted a different arrangement. However, in retrospect, it appeared that a vital opportunity for breaking regional ties was lost. Ironsi did not seem to have a clear picture of how to proceed. His first solution revolved round bringing all the regions and their administrative and political machinery together into the Federal executive. He also appointed a sole commissioner to look into means of effecting a united bureaucratic machinery for all of Nigeria. To the same end, the four military governors were made members of the Federal Executive Council to underscore the unity of command at the centre.

From January to May 1966, Ironsi followed an informal, cooperative approach. However, on 24 May he made a bold departure from this pattern by promulgating Decrees 33 and 34, popularly referred to as the Unification Decrees. Decree 33 abolished all 81 political associations for a period of three years while Decree 34 abolished the Federal structure and introduced a unitary system. The Federal Military Government was renamed the 'National Military Government'.

Unfortunately for Ironsi, inter-ethnic suspicion had reached such a level that his actions were always considered in non-Igbo areas to be motivated in favour of the Igbo. For instance, Northerners had demanded the trial of the January conspirators. Ironsi did not and perhaps could not have tried them. Any action against the coup-makers who were regarded as national heroes in the South would have alienated the Southern intellectual and military élites. Generally speaking, while most Southerners favoured Ironsi's Unification Decrees, those from the North saw the efforts of Ironsi as moves towards the imposition of Southern, particularly Igbo, domination over the whole of Nigeria. Some Igbo residents in the North fed this suspicion through their behaviour and utterances.[4] It was mainly due to this that shortly after the promulgation of the decrees, protest demonstrations were organised by civil servants in Kaduna and Zaria.[5]

The culmination of this fractricidal conflict was that on 29 July 1966 Northern soldiers successfully rose against Ironsi's regime. They killed Ironsi, and gained control of government in all regions except the East, the home base of the Igbo. Northern officers and ranks freely participated in the murder of Igbo officers. The very foundations of Nigerian federalism were threatened. The army, which in January had presented itself as the only institution capable of checking ethnic rivalry, was, in July, being undermined by the very ill it came to cure. Northern officers and their civilian counterparts hounded down the Igbo officers and civilians they could find. The verbal warfare of the politicians had suddenly become armed confrontation and civil war under the soldiers. Nigerian officers were incapable of providing even the minimum conditions of political order.

The emergence of Gowon

As mentioned above, there were too many coincidences that linked the first coup with a grand Igbo plan for domination, and since the Unification Decrees of May 1966 Northerners had planned to ward off this Igbo menace. Northern military and civilian élites held talks on this subject. It remained unstated what the objectives of the Northern assault on the Igbo were, but the July 1966 coup rocked the foundations of Nigerian unity.[6]

After three days of confusion and secret talks, Lt.-Col. Yakubu Gowon, a Northern officer, emerged as the new head of state, Ironsi having being killed. Gowon had to piece together and reassert the sinking legitimacy of the Federal Government.

The options open to Gowon were limited in view of the fact that one of the original intentions of the coup-planners was to take the North out of the Federation, and since Gowon had been persuaded to abandon that course he only had to look for means to mend the wounds and seek a constitutional arrangement that would preserve unity. Gowon devoted his first broadcast to a discussion of this problem.[7]

During the announcement, Gowon made a number of promises, including undertakings to return to civilian rule as soon as it could be arranged, and to release political prisoners and call a conference to discuss future constitutional arrangements that would make for greater unity and peace.

Political prisoners, including Chief Obafemi Awolowo, the leader of the opposition in the Federal House of Representatives who was imprisoned in 1963, were immediately released. An *ad hoc* conference of delegates from all the regions was summoned to Lagos on 9 August 1966. Underscoring the depth of national division, the conference made three recommendations:

Fig. 12.3   Former Head of State, Major General Yakubu Gowon

1 That all military personnel should be made to return to their 'region of origin'.
2 That the garrisoning of Lagos was to be left to Gowon as the new Supreme Commander.
3 That an *ad hoc* constitutional conference of delegates from all the regions should be summoned to meet in Lagos to review the constitutional future of the Federation.[8]

After 9 August, Igbo soldiers and civilians outside the Eastern Region were repatriated to the East while remaining non-Easterners in the East went home. In effect, the remaining arteries of national unity were being severed, and Nigeria operated four virtually independent political units. This situation was aptly described by Dudley, who wrote:

> Though constitutionally, Nigeria remained a Federation of four regions, in practical terms these formed two units: One, the East, headed by Lieutenant-Colonel Ojukwu, and the other, the rest of the Federation, made up of the West, the North, Midwest and Lagos over which Gowon was in control. But this is perhaps a misdescription. In reality, Gowon's domain was an association of three 'kingdoms' – West, North and Midwest – each presided over by a Military Governor with Gowon as the *Primus inter pares* . . .[9]

The restoration of confidence became impossible as the civilian populations became involved in the massacre of people from other parts of Nigeria living among them. September and October 1966 were the months of mass exodus of 'stranger elements' or refugees throughout the Federation. Igbos suffered the most. It was therefore understandable why the Eastern Region leaders felt the political future of their region could best be safeguarded in an independent state. Thus, ironically, Igbo elements who had welcomed unification under Ironsi turned round to become supporters of secession and the breakup of the Federation.

From 12 to 30 September 1966 delegates from all the regions met in a very tense atmosphere. Soldiers had to be posted outside the conference hall to assure the delegates of personal safety. Gowon set the direction of discussions by ordering the delegates not to consider either a complete breakup of the Federation, nor a unitary constitution,[10] but asked them to discuss any of the following options:

1 a federal system with a strong central government,
2 a federal system with a weak central government,
3 a confederal form of government, or
4 an entirely new arrangement which would be peculiar to Nigeria and which had not yet found its way into any political dictionary.[11]

Nothing was achieved at this conference, nor at subsequent ones held in Benin and in Aburi in Ghana. The drift to civil war was irreversible. The demands of the Military Governor of the East could not be met without secession and complete autonomy for the Region. The discussions merely gave the Region more time within which to plan secession. This became obvious on 30 March 1967, when the Military Governor of the East unilaterally promulgated three edicts:

1 the Revenue Collection edict,
2 the Legal Education edict,
3 the Court of Appeal edict.

These edicts created an atmosphere where secession could not be subject to legal challenge within the Eastern Region. Furthermore, the Military Governor of the East sequestrated Federal institutions and property in the East so that the Eastern Region became both *de jure* and *de facto* an autonomous state.

Following on this gradual move towards secession, on 26 May the Joint Meeting of Chiefs and Elders and the Consultative Assembly of the Eastern Region gave the Military Governor the mandate to 'declare at the earliest practicable date, Eastern Nigeria a free, sovereign and independent state by the name and title of the "Republic of Biafra" '.[12]

This is not to suggest that the Federal authorities stood by while the leaders of the Eastern Region made their moves. It is, however, fair to say that the posture of Gowon and the Federal Government was that Eastern Nigeria had been wronged and the Federal authorities should not do anything to aggravate further an already tense situation. Gowon wanted to accommodate the East within Nigeria but would not tolerate secession. In a desperate response to the latest mandate allowing Ojukwu to declare the East free, Gowon's administration made a bold move on 27 May and subdivided Nigeria, including the Eastern Region, into twelve states, declared a state of emergency and assumed full military powers. It is necessary to state that this was the first time Gowon had shown any belligerent posture since assuming power. Even some members of his administration were already quarrelling with him for being too soft on Ojukwu. The creation of states was a courageous political move, and its political consequences have surpassed Ojukwu's rebellion.

Under this new twelve-state structure, the North was broken into six states. The Western region lost some parts of its territory to a newly created Lagos State, the Mid-West retained its 1963 size, the Eastern region was reconstituted into three states.

The breakup of the giant North was a demand which the West and the East had repeatedly made since colonial days. This act was therefore expected to remove the erstwhile charge of Northern domination. But the Igbo saw things differently. Among the Igbo, the creation of states was perceived as an attempt to reduce Igbo political strength. This perception was a result of the fact that non-Igbo areas of the former Eastern Region had been carved out of Igbo control and reconstituted into South Eastern and Rivers States. In addition, these areas contained the much valued oilfields which the East had anticipated would provide it funds for the impending war. Thus, as far as the Igbo were concerned, the twelve-state structure, rather than being a concession, was a punishment from the Federal Government.

Ojukwu publicly described the creation of states as an act which interfered with the territorial integrity of the Eastern Region and therefore invoked the mandate of 26 May to declare the East a free state. The last card had been played.

The story of the civil war has been retold a number of times. The highlights of the war must include foreign involvement on both sides, the recognition of Biafra by four African states, the misery and starvation caused to the masses who hardly understood the reasons for the war. The war raged for 30 months, ending in victory for the Federal forces. On 15 January 1970 the Biafran officers surrendered, Ojukwu having escaped from Nigeria days before the collapse of Biafra.

Three significant developments occurred during the war. Firstly, the Federal Government was forced to diversify its foreign sources of weapons following the refusal of the western powers to supply the much needed weapons to Nigeria. This in effect meant that Nigeria's foreign policy was freed from total dependence on the west. The Soviet Union, presenting itself as a friend in a time of need, secured a favoured position with the Federal Government. Secondly, when the civil war ended, Nigerians discovered that the minor centralisation and emergency measures taken during the war had strengthened the position of the Federal Government vis-à-vis the states. Thirdly, the creation of states had been generally taken seriously despite the disruptions caused by the war. As a consequence of the twelve-state structure, the power of the regional governments was effectively broken. Furthermore, when Gowon actually began asserting his personal authority, emphasising the military hierarchy, the state governors started playing subordinate roles to the Federal authorities. In addition, the cessation of hostilities made oil exploration possible, thus leading to the period which has been described

199

as 'Nigeria's Oil Boom'. The royalties paid the Federal Government enhanced its financial position and regulative capabilities over state projects and activities. In short, following the civil war, Nigerian federalism became a structure with a strong centre and twelve weak states. This development came about not through constitutional negotiation but through a combination of extra-constitutional causes such as the hierarchical nature of military rule, the exercise of war powers and the regulatory abilities of the purse.

Following the victory of the Federal forces, Gowon's degree of personal authority and legitimacy improved. He was therefore more able to assert himself and the authority of the Federal Government in his dealings with the state governments. In other words, the shaky Federal Government that went into the war emerged from it a supreme and self-confident government. The strong regional forces operative on the eve of the civil war were virtually destroyed. It was from this position of strength that the Federal Government embarked on reconstruction and repair of the damage caused by war.

The rapid reconstruction of the war-damaged areas and the degree of mutual tolerance among erstwhile foes confounded observers, particularly those of them who had earlier succumbed to the myth that the Federal authorities were engaged in genocide against the Igbo.

The post-war disengagement programme

Soon after the civil war ended and the guns became silent, military politics ebbed but a different form of politics that had been shelved, surfaced once more. For most of the war period the civilian population had not insisted on their right to participate in government and public affairs. Except for the farmers (Agbekoya) riots in the Western State, in 1968 and 1969, the civil war period saw few important political developments.

Once the war had ended the civilian politicians became restless and began demanding the effectuation of the plan of the officers for their disengagement from politics. In response to these pressures Gowon's administration sought to buy time by announcing, on 1 October 1970, a nine-point programme of military disengagement to be completed by 1976. The programme read:

1 The reorganisation of the armed forces;
2 Implementation of the Second National Development Plan;
3 Eradication of corruption in Nigeria's national life;
4 Creation of more states;
5 Preparation and adoption of a new constitution;
6 Introduction of a new revenue allocation formula;
7 Conduct of a national population census;
8 Organisation of genuinely national political parties;
9 Organisation of elections and the installation of popularly elected governments at state and federal levels.

The political history of Nigeria from October 1970 to July 1975 was characterised by one broken promise after another, and general governmental immobility, despite the fact that the resources and goodwill for success were readily available. After announcing the nine-point programme, Gowon did nothing about returning to barracks before he was removed in 1975. On the reorganisation of the armed forces, very little was attempted or accomplished. The disillusionment of the armed forces has been well put by Brigadier Jemibewon, who wrote:

> The sense of frustration and disappointment in the army was no less than that of the generality of the public.... Of the barrack programme that was launched by Hassan, not a single barrack project was completed by 1975. The much publicised staff college about which the hopes of the army had been raised never saw the light of day. Even the proposal to have an officers' mess befitting the Nigerian Army was never seriously pursued.[13]

It is impossible to evaluate the regime's success with the Second National Development Plan since nothing was done. Similarly, no action was taken on the creation of more states, a new constitution, a revenue formula, the organisation of political parties and installation of popularly elected governments. Two issues, however, received attention, namely, the national census of 1973 and corruption.

The population census

The 1973 census, in which Gowon took a personal interest, produced many surprises and nearly led to a North–South confrontation, reminiscent of the 1963 census. First, the total population of 79·76 million surpassed all expectations. Secondly, the distribution of the figures by state went contrary to demographic theories and illustrated North–South migration. Thirdly, the six Northern states widened their margin over the six Southern states, and this was at a time when aid was being sought for the migrants from the Northern states who were being forced to move southwards because of the drought.

The figures were as follows:

Comparative figures 1952/53, 1963 and 1973 Nigerian census (in millions)

SOUTHERN

	1952/53	1963	1973 (Provisional figures)
Lagos	.50	1.44	2.47
Western	4.36	9.49	8.92*
Mid-Western	1.49	2.54	3.24
Rivers	.75	1.54	2.23
East Central	4.57	7.23	8.06
South-Eastern	1.90	3.62	3.46*
Subtotal	13.57	25.86	28.38

*Population declined from the 1963 figures:

201

NORTHERN

Benue Plateau	2.30	4.01	5.17
Kwara	1.19	2.40	4.64
North Western	3.40	5.73	8.50
North Central	2.35	4.10	6.78
Kano	3.40	5.77	10.98
North Eastern	4.20	7.79	15.38
Subtotal	17.84	29.80	51.38
Grand total	31.41	55.66	79.76

It is therefore easy to see why Northerners would defend the accuracy of the figures and Southerners would be hostile to them. There were suggestions from Southern interests that the exercise should be cancelled and the National Census Board be dismissed. The census became a potentially explosive issue and Gowon never did publish the final figures. When Gowon was overthrown in 1975, his successor wisely cancelled the whole exercise, and planning and projections reverted to the 1963 agreement figures.

Corruption

Though largely unsubstantiated, there was a general belief that there was a great deal of corruption and misappropriation in the top reaches of Gowon's administration. There were calls for the promulgation of an anti-corruption decree, yet nothing was done. The dam broke in July 1974 when a private citizen (Godwin Darboh) went to court to swear to charges of wrongdoing against one of Gowon's Commissioners. This provided a golden opportunity for Gowon to act but he chose not to do anything. For his part, the Commissioner (Joseph Tarka) did not deny the charges, but merely sought a court injunction to stop the press from further publicity of the case and also dared anyone to attempt to probe him and risk his own revelations about them. The matter would have been swept under the carpet had it not been for persistent pressure from the Nigerian press, which finally forced Tarka to resign. No probe or enquiries followed. Gowon probably hoped Nigerians would forget. Here again, an opportunity to do something about corruption was lost.

Thus, of all the nine points in the programme, only three received any attention. Hence Brigadier Jemibewon justifiably stated with reference to Gowon's rule from 1970 to 1975:

> Gowon's administration became characterized by procrastination and indecision. Promises were made and broken, assurances were given and never fulfilled, and major issues of the day were swept under the carpet.[14]

The reversal of the disengagement plan

Whatever legitimacy Gowon's administration had left appeared to have evaporated with the announcement on 1 October 1974 that the regime had reconsidered its 1970 pledge to return to barracks. The announcement was long but unpersuasive. Part of it read:

Four years ago when I gave 1976 as the target date for returning the country to normal constitutional government, both myself and the military hierarchy honestly believed that by that date, especially after a bloody civil war for which there had been a great deal of human and material sacrifice and from which we had expected that every Nigerian would have learnt a lesson, there would have developed an atmosphere of sufficient stability. We had thought that a genuine demonstration of moderation and self-control in pursuing sectional ends in the overall interests of the country would become the second nature of all Nigerians.

Regrettably from all the information at our disposal, from the general attitude, utterances and manoeuvres of some individuals and groups and from some publications during the past few months, it is clear that those who aspire to lead the nation on the return to civilian rule have not learnt any lesson from our past experiences.

In spite of the existence of a state of emergency which has so far precluded political activity, there have already emerged such a high degree of sectional politicking, intemperate utterances and writings which were deliberately designed to whip up ill-feelings within the country to the benefit of the political aspirations of a few ....

A large number of well-meaning and responsible Nigerians from all walks of life and from all parts of this country, as well as well-wishers of Nigeria at home and abroad have called attention to the lack of wisdom and the dangers inherent in adhering to the target date previously announced. Our own assessment of the situation as of now is that it will be utterly irresponsible to leave the nation in the lurch by a precipitate withdrawal which will certainly throw the nation back into confusion. Therefore, the Supreme Military Council after careful deliberations and full consultation with the hierarchy of the Armed Forces and Police have decided that the target date of 1976 is in the circumstance unrealistic and that it would indeed amount to a betrayal of trust to adhere rigidly to that target date.[15]

From this point, opposition to the regime, which had been quiet since 1970 became vocal, coming mostly from university staff and students and aspiring politicians. The indecision of the regime and its inaction over the nine-point programme in retrospect appeared as a planned delay of disengagement.

As opposition increased, Gowon resorted to repression, arrest and detention of critics, and demonstration of military might, mock air raids and military parades in urban areas, the posting of soldiers to university campuses and so on. The more violence used, the stronger the opposition appeared to grow until on 29 July 1975, on the ninth anniversary of

Gowon's rise to power, there was a bloodless coup – while Gowon was away in Kampala, Uganda, to attend the Organisation of African Unity summit. Thus came the end of Gowon's long reign which, according to Jemibewon, was divisible into two parts:

> The first part, July 1966 to January 1970, appears to portray the story of a successful leader who by his very success had won the hearts of the people and had become the idol of the nation. The second part of the history of the regime, which can be said to date from the end of the civil war reveals the history of a weak and vacillating man, for ever procrastinating, and steadily but surely declining in popularity until he sank to the level where he earned nothing but the abuse and curses of the people who once adored him.[16]

The Murtala Muhammed/Obasanjo administration

In his maiden speech as the new Head of State, Brigadier Murtala Muhammed gave the reasons for the coup as misgovernment by Gowon's administration. He asserted:

> After the civil war, the affairs of state, hitherto a collective responsibility, became characterised by lack of consultation, indecision, indiscipline and even neglect. Indeed, the public at large became disillusioned and disappointed by these developments. This trend was clearly incompatible with the philosophy and image of a corrective regime. Unknown to the general public, the feeling of disillusion was also evident among members of the Armed Forces

Fig. 12.4 a & b   The late General Murtala Muhammed and his successor, General Olusegun Obasanjo

whose administration was neglected but who, out of sheer loyalty to the Nation, and in the hope that there would be a change, continued to suffer in silence.

Things got to a stage where the head of the administration became virtually inaccessible even to official advisers: and when advice was tendered, it was often ignored.

Responsible opinion, including advice by eminent Nigerians, traditional rulers, intellectuals, etc, was similarly discarded. The leadership, either by design or default, had become too insensitive to the true feelings and yearnings of the people. The nation was thus being plunged inexorably into chaos.[17]

The regime started by retiring from public service all eleven state governors and the Administrator of the East Central State, the Inspector and Deputy Inspector-General of Police and the Admiral and Rear Admiral of the Navy, and all military officers of the rank of Major-General and above.

Furthermore, the controversial 1973 census was cancelled because, according to General Muhammed, 'It is now clear that whatever results are announced will not command general acceptance throughout the country'. In a similar vein, the Festival of Black and African Arts was postponed and later held in January 1977.

Significant structural reorganisations intended to facilitate decision-making at the centre were introduced. The State Governors were excluded from the Supreme Military Council. For the effective co-ordination of the activities of State Governors, a National Council of States consisting of all State Governors, the chiefs of the Armed Forces, the Inspector-General of Police and the Attorney-General of the Federation, was set up. The Supreme Military Council remained the highest legislative body, and was able to act without the pressures which State Governors of Gowon's days brought to bear on that body through their membership.[18]

Muhammed's disengagement programme

In a very decisive fashion Brigadier Muhammed announced that his regime remained committed to total disengagement. Without mincing words, he promised to hand over to civilians on 1 October 1979 and planned for this in five stages with dates as follows:

Stage One: Settlement of the question of states.

The state review panel to report by December 1975.

The creation of states to be completed by April 1976.

A constitution drafting committee to submit a draft by September 1976.

Stage Two:	Local government reorganisation.
	Elections at the local level without party politics.
	Establishment of the Constituent Assembly, partly elected and partly nominated.
	Stage Two to be completed by October 1978.
Stage Three:	The lifting of the ban on politics and Abrogation of Emergency Decree.
	Formation of political parties.
Stage Four:	The elections to state and Federal legislatures.
Stage Five:	Complete handover on 1 October 1979[19].

All steps in the various stages were impressively accomplished. There was no doubt about the sincereity and integrity of the military as far as this programme was concerned. The decisiveness of the regime was demonstrated over a number of key issues such as the sub-division of Nigeria into nineteen states in 1976, the decision to relocate the Federal capital, the promulgation of a new constitution for Nigeria, the elections and actual surrender of power on 1 October 1979. In each of these cases, panels were set up and their reports were quickly considered. In the case of the new Constitution, a Constitution Drafting Committee of 49 men reported and the report was debated by a partly elected and partly nominated Constituent Assembly before the final report was presented for approval by the Supreme Military Council in 1978.

Following the assassination of General Murtala Muhammed on 13 February 1976, the Supreme Military Council met and nominated General Olusegun Obasanjo as the successor. Obasanjo pledged to continue the good work started by Muhammed. From all appearances, he followed the programme faithfully. For this reason the Muhammed and Obasanjo regimes have generally been regarded as one uninterrupted administration.

One of the highlights of the programme of the military administration was the new Constitution. The major premise of the new Constitution was that political problems can be solved through constitutional engineering. The military had concluded that the Westminster parliamentary system, a variant of which Nigeria operated between 1960 and 1966, had failed and must be changed. In its place was substituted the executive presidential system along the lines of the American system.

Similarly, the political parties of the pre-military era were said to have divided rather than united the nation. The new Constitution also addressed itself to how parties should function as national instead of as sectional organisations. Stringent conditions were set for the formation of political parties. For example, in order to qualify to be registered as a political party, sections 202 (b)(e) and (f) state of political associations:

(b) the membership of the association is open to every Nigerian irrespective of his place of origin, sex, religion or ethnic grouping;

(e) the name of the association, its emblem or motto does not contain any ethnic or religious connotation or give the appearance that the activities of the association are confined to a part only of the geographical area of Nigeria and,

(f) the headquarters of the association is situated in the capital of the Federation.

Section 203 goes further to require that the constitution and rules of a political party shall

(b) ensure that the members of the executive committee or other governing body of the party reflect the federal character of Nigeria (i.e. belong to different states not being less in number than two-thirds of all the states comprising the federation).

These sections have obviously been included as a solution to the sectional political parties of the pre-military era. These provisions forced all registered political parties to spread their membership drive to various parts of the country.

The Obasanjo administration also showed its desire to ensure success by creating the Federal Electoral Commission (FEDECO). FEDECO was responsible for all activities associated with the conduct of elections, and the screening of political parties to check whether they satisfied sections 202 and 203 of the constitution. Only five of the nineteen associations which applied for registration were actually registered by FEDECO in the 1979 elections.

With full backing from the military authorities who placed FEDECO above challenge in courts, FEDECO acted fearlessly. It is, however, doubtful if any civilian administration could have lived with the vast powers which FEDECO exercised under the military administration.

The elections were held in July and August 1979. There were some administrative lapses on the part of FEDECO, but generally the elections appeared the fairest and least violent in Nigerian history. Some alleged irregularities were challenged in court but all of these were normal charges that arose in any elections.

However, the presidential election generated a lot of controversy. This was due to the fact that section 126 (2a and b) of the Constitution requires that for a candidate to be declared elected as president, he must have secured the highest number of votes cast at the election; and he must have 'not less than one-quarter of the votes cast at the election in each of at least two-thirds of all the states in the Federation'.

FEDECO's announcement, read by F. L. O. Menkiti, the Chief Returning Officer, Presidential Election, said:

I certify that having carried out my duties and the formalities required by the Electoral Decree 1977, the result of the poll carried out in the federation on the 11th day of August 1979 is as follows in order of the number of votes each candidate received:

Candidate Alhaji Shehu Shagari (NPN): votes received, 5 688 857

Fig. 12.5   Abuja rock, the landmark of the site of the new federal capital of Nigeria

Candidate Chief Obafemi Awolowo (UPN): votes received, 4 916 651
Candidate Dr Nnamdi Azikiwe (NPP): votes received, 2 822 523
Candidate Alhaji Aminu Kano (PRP): votes received, 1 732 113
Candidate Alhaji Waziri Ibrahim (GNPP): votes received, 1 686 489

Alhaji Shehu Shagari has satisfied the provision of section 34A, sub-section (1)(c)(i) of Electoral Decree No. 73 of 1977, that is to say, he has the highest number of votes cast at the election.

From the details of the state-by-state results ... this candidate (President-elect Shagari) has also satisfied the provision of sub-section

(1)(c)(ii) of the same section as he has not less than one-quarter of the votes cast at the election in each of at least two-thirds of all states in the federation.

Soon afterwards, there was controversy over whether Alhaji Shehu Shagari satisfied section 126 and whether FEDECO's interpretation of what is two-thirds of nineteen 19 states could be defended in court.

Chief Obafemi Awolowo, the runner-up, challenged FEDECO's interpretation at the election tribunal. He lost there and later appealed to the Supreme Court where he once again lost. Following the Supreme Court decision, Alhaji Shehu Shagari was installed on 1 October 1979 as the first Executive President of Nigeria and the military returned to their barracks.

Political behaviour and the Second Republic

The Constitution of 1979 which the military left behind attempted to enforce certain practices. In addition to making elaborate prescriptions as to how political parties can form and operate, it also attempted to state how the national cake be shared so that all could benefit from the Federal Government.

For instance, sections 135(3) and 157(5) of the Constitution made it compulsory that the Federal cabinet must be representative of all the states in the Federation. In pursuit of this goal, the President 'shall appoint at least one Minister from each state who shall be an indigene of such state'. This provision was a clear departure from the winner-takes-all practice of the Westminster model. Consequently, in the 41-member cabinet of former President Shagari, every state had two representatives except for Plateau and Kwara states with one each. Bauchi, Anambra, Kaduna and Gongola each had three Ministers. Appointments into public corporations and the civil service were also geared towards representing all sections of the country, so that all could have a stake in the system.

Furthermore, in an effort to build a strong national government, President Shagari invited all political parties to join the NPN. Only the NPP accepted the invitation and went into an accord with the NPN and shared ministerial appointments with the latter. The accord eased the transition from military to civilian politics and made it easy for the President to have his way with the legislature in the first year. The accord, however, broke down in 1981 but before then procedures had been institutionalised and no major crisis followed the ending of the partnership.

Notes

1 R. Sklar, 'The ordeal of Obafemi Awolowo' in G. M. Carter (ed.), *Politics in Africa, 7 Cases* (New York: Harcourt Brace, 1966).

2 *Ibid*. It should be noted that a counsel for Chief Obafemi Awolowo, Mr Dingle Foot, was denied entry into Nigeria.

3 See Post and Vickers, *Structure and Conflict in Nigeria 1960–65* (Ibadan: Heinemann, 1973), p. 99.

4 N. J. Miners, *The Nigerian Army 1956–1966* (London: Methuen, 1971), p. 200.

5 S. K. Panter-Brick, *Nigerian Politics and Military Rule* (University of London, 1970), p. 24.

6 For detailed discussions see Dudley, *Instability and Political Order: politics and crisis in Nigeria* (Ibadan University Press, 1973), pp. 139–43.

7 Dudley, *Instability and Political Order*, p. 141.

8 *Ibid*., p. 142.

9 *Ibid*., p. 143.

10 *Ibid*., p. 141.

11 *Ibid*., p. 151–64, esp. p. 152.

12 Address by Lt. Col. Ojukwu to the Joint Meeting of the Advisory Committee of Chiefs and Elders and the Consultative Assembly, 26 May 1967.

13 Brigadier David Jemibewon, *A Combatant in Government* (Ibadan: Heinemann, 1978), pp. 32–33.

14 *Ibid*., p. 30.

15 Text of National Day Broadcast, 1 October 1974.

16 Jemibewon, *A Combatant in Government*, p. 25.

17 Brigadier Murtala Muhammed, text of 'Maiden Broadcast to the Nation', reproduced in *Daily Times*, 31 July 1973, p. 3.

18 For details see Jemibewon, *A Combatant in Government*, pp. 49–50.

19 Brigadier Murtala Muhammed, text of National Day Broadcast, 1 October 1975.

13 Nigeria's foreign policy

Olajide Aluko

Since Nigeria's independence in 1960 there has been a spate of works on its foreign policy. Some of these works have traced the historical evolution of the policy while others have considered different aspects of the policy from a variety of perspectives.[1]

We shall not try to outline all these perspectives here. What we shall try to do instead is examine Nigerian foreign policy from an angle that has hardly been applied to the study of Nigerian foreign policy. Towards this end we shall begin by asking some salient questions. First, what are the goals of Nigerian foreign policy? Secondly, by what means are these to be achieved? Thirdly, what are the major factors that have been shaping Nigerian foreign policy? These are not easy questions to tackle. Nonetheless, we shall try to provide answers to them.

Policy goals

While many Nigerian leaders have made, since independence, a number of wide-ranging pronouncements on the country's foreign policy it was not until the 1970s that some attempts were made to spell them out, following the Adedeji Report. However, this was soon abandoned in practice if not in form. But the 1979 Constitution has now spelt out the goals of Nigerian foreign policy as follows:

1 the state shall promote African unity;
2 it shall promote the total political, economic, social and cultural liberation of Africa;
3 it shall promote all other forms of international cooperation conducive to the consolidation of universal peace and mutual respect and friendship among all peoples and states; and
4 it shall combat racial discrimination in all its manifestations.[2]

The policy objectives listed above would seem to represent a summary of the views of the various Nigerian leaders since the late 1960s. Yet some of these ideas appear to be somewhat vague. For instance, what does promoting the total political, economic, social and cultural liberation of Africa mean, when the process of total decolonisation is still to be completed in Nigeria itself? Furthermore, what does combating racial discrimination in all its manifestations mean? Does it mean fighting against racial discrimination in the Soviet Union, Western Europe, North America, Latin America and the Arab world? Does this include the fight against apartheid which is not simply a question of racial discrimination, but a form of institutionalised racism unique in human history? We may never be able to offer satisfactory answers to these questions. Indeed, some of these professed objectives are hardly more than the surviving clichés of the anti-colonial crusade.

If unanswerable questions arise about the objectives of Nigerian foreign policy, there are many question marks in relation to the means to attain these ends. This is due to a number of reasons.

Capability

In any rational calculation, ends and means will naturally be related to each other. In the case of the ends of Nigerian foreign policy hardly any attempt has been made to identify and analyse these means, let alone relate them to the ends. While much has been written and spoken of the foreign policy objectives of Nigeria, little or nothing has been written about the means to attain such ends. Not only the various Nigerian governments but also the analysts – journalists and academics – have tended to concentrate on the goals of policy while ignoring the wherewithal for this achievement.

Against this background, then, some questions are bound to arise. First, how has Nigeria wanted to attain its foreign policies? Is it by the traditional means through which states achieve their external ends? Or is it through some means that are peculiarly Nigerian or African? It will not be easy to find answers to all these questions. What is certain is that the facts of international politics are too intractable to allow for any novel means of influencing them as effectively as the traditional means – military capability, political and economic leverage. Perhaps it is the lack of any of these factors in sufficient quantity and quality that led the practitioners and students of Nigerian affairs to avoid analysing them. If this is correct, then a great deal of damage must have been done to the standing of Nigeria in many world capitals. For when the foreign policy ends spelt out are totally unrelated to the means available to see them through, the up-shot is frustration, failure and even humiliation. Nothing can better serve the interests of Nigeria abroad than pursuing policies that are related to the resources available to the country.

Determinants of policy

We now come to the next section of this chapter by trying to deal with the question of what are the major variables that have determined Nigerian foreign policy. First, we must start with the obvious fact that Nigerian foreign policy, like that of any other foreign country, is largely a product of the external and internal environments. While scholars are not unanimous about what constitutes the environment of foreign policy,[3] we shall confine ourselves here to four major variables in the external environment, and four at the domestic level.[4]

The external environment

Here we shall consider pressures and constraints arising from the global situation, the regional, the sub-regional and the dominant situations. We shall examine each of these briefly.

In global terms, the pressures that impinge on Nigerian foreign policy arise at two levels: the level of super-power competition, and the leve of the UN. Given the competition between the two world powers – the USA and USSR – the only rational policy has been to adopt a policy of non-alignment towards them. This has meant maintaining political, economic, military and even cultural relationships with both of them, although in practice relations with the USA have continued to be greater for historical reasons. Nigeria's membership of the UN has meant that Nigeria has to accept the obligations arising from membership of the world body. This led to Nigeria's contribution of troops to the UN forces (ONUC) in the Congo (now Zaire) during the period 1960–64. And it is this that led recently to the Nigerian contribution of a battalion to the UN Interim Forces in Lebanon (UNIFIL).

At the regional level, the pressures are from two angles: membership of the OAU, and the continuing existence of apartheid in South Africa, as well as that country's continued illegal occupation of Namibia. Membership of the OAU has, among other things, meant some restrictions on freedom of action on the part of Nigeria, as well as the acceptance of obligations under the OAU Charter. For instance, it was partly because Nigeria was, and is still, a member of the OAU, and partly because Nigeria had the chairmanship of the Organisation during 1973/74 that made Nigeria agree to join and lead the other African, Caribbean and Pacific countries, in July 1973, in their negotiations with the EEC in what became known as the Lomé Convention in February 1975. The continuing existence of white supremacist regimes in some parts of Southern Africa has also meant that Nigeria, the most populous black country in the continent, has occupied a leading position in the active campaign against such regimes.

At the West African level, the fact that Nigeria is the single largest country with a population of about 55 per cent of the total population of West Africa has been of great significance. And as the only OPEC member state in West Africa, with the quadrupling of the oil prices late in 1973 and early 1974, it was not surprising that there were intense pressures from the other West African countries on Nigeria for oil at reduced rates. By late 1974 the Gowon government agreed to this, but with some conditions.[5] It was partly the pressures from this West African sub-region, and partly the determination of the Gowon government to reduce the dependence of the countries in the area on extra-African powers that led Nigeria to take the initiative in the formation of the West African Economic Community (ECOWAS) from 1970 until the treaty was signed in May 1975.

At the dominant bilateral level it can be said that the pressures on Nigeria have come from two sources, the United Kingdom and the USA. From independence until the early seventies Nigeria's relations with Britain were dominant. Throughout this period, the UK remained the largest single market for Nigerian exports and imports. Even though the USA has, since the late seventies, replaced the UK as the largest single market for Nigeria's exports, Britain has continued to remain the largest supplier of Nigerian imports: Nigeria bought goods worth over £2 billion from the UK in 1980, or about 20 per cent of its total import bill for that year. Furthermore, until the mid-seventies most of Nigeria's reserves were kept in sterling. Although this has since changed, a significant proportion of Nigeria's foreign reserves are still in sterling. Most of the Nigerian army and navy is equipped with British arms, and their officers largely trained in British military institutions. Cementing these commercial, financial and military relations were intangible but significant political, cultural and emotional ties between the leaders of Nigeria and the UK. Given these important intricacies of Anglo-Nigerian relations, then, one can understand why all Nigerian governments have tended to avoid any serious rupture with London.

Relations with the USA became similarly dominant in the late seventies, mainly because Washington was buying about 60 per cent of Nigerian crude oil which, by 1971, had become the largest single foreign exchange earner for Nigeria. This was supplemented with the purchase of substantial arms and ammunition and military transport aircraft, and the training of some officers in the USA. Cooperation between Lagos and Washington has, since 1979, been expanded to cover agriculture, technology, higher education, and technical education. Moreover, there has been a steady inflow of American businessmen into different sectors of the Nigerian economy, ranging from construction work through banking, pharmaceuticals to manufacturing industry and the oil industry. Against this growing web of relationships between Lagos and Washington it has become difficult for Lagos to take any tough action, or even posture, against the American administration either on Southern African or any other matter of concern.

The domestic environment

In the domestic environment four major variables will be examined: military capability, economic capability, political capability and the pressures of interest groups.

Nigeria's military capability is small in comparison with the great powers, but also in relation to some North African countries such as Algeria, Libya and Egypt. Indeed, until very recently the military was hardly considered to be a useful instrument of foreign policy by the Nigerian leaders. Thus during the period of the First Republic the size of the military was kept under 11 000 with outmoded military equipment. Although the size of the armed forces rose to some 250 000 at the end of the civil war in 1970, the increase was in response to the exigencies of the civil war rather than the need to use them to back up foreign policy interests.

It is even arguable whether the present Nigerian leaders see the armed forces as being important in the foreign policy objectives of the country. By 1980/81 the size of the armed forces had been reduced to

146 000,[6] and there are unofficial leaks about the move to reduce the number further to about 100 000 or less.[7] If the reduction in size has been compensated by the provision of modern equipment to make the military a mobile force this would have been proper. But very little effort is being made to modernise the armed forces despite the pronouncements to the contrary by the present Defence Minister, Alhaji Akanbi Oniyangi.[8] While the defence budget is still high, about 6 per cent of the GDP in 1979/80, much of the money went to meeting salaries and personal emoluments rather than the acquisition of modern sophisticated equipment. It is difficult to say anything about the level of military technology within the armed forces; this must be insignificant. The country is heavily dependent on the industrial powers for the bulk of its military requirements. Similarly, while one cannot say anything precisely about the level of training within the armed forces, there is no doubt that emphasis has continued to be put on training at different levels in the armed forces.

Within the African context, while Nigeria's economic capability is one of the strongest, in relation to the major industrial powers, its economic strength is slight and highly vulnerable. Although the country is rich in human and natural resources with an estimated population of about 80 million in 1981 and a variety of agricultural and mineral products such as cocoa, ground-nut, rubber, palm products, and minerals such as tin, columbite, iron, coal, tantalium, and crude oil and gas, the economy is under-developed. Manufacturing still accounts for less than 6 per cent of the GDP.

While the country has a variety of agricultural and mineral resources, the contribution of the former to the foreign export earnings has, since 1970, dwindled to less than 15 per cent, while crude oil alone has since the early seventies been contributing about 85 per cent of the total value of export. Not only has agriculture been depressed since the seventies, food production has fallen far below national requirements. Therefore, a great deal of money has to be spent on food imports. In 1980 this amounted to N1.3 billion or about 12 per cent of the total value of imports for that year. The heavy dependence on oil has made the economy vulnerable to sudden changes in the world oil market. This was the case during 1977/78; and has been so since the oil glut of March 1982.

The fluctuations in oil prices coupled with the gross mismanagement of the economy have created balance of payments problems for the country, which in turn have led to a sharp decline in the country's external assets from over ₦5 billion in 1979 to about ₦1 billion early in 1982.

Given all these developments the economic leverage available to Nigeria in pursuit of its foreign policy objectives is rather limited. However, it is proper to point out that during the early seventies Nigeria was able to use its economic leverage to influence some other countries in West Africa, especially by selling oil at reduced rates to them. The economic strength of Nigeria was important in bringing about the formation of ECOWAS. Despite the relative economic weakness of the country, Nigeria used the oil weapon against Britain in 1979 when it took over the assets of British Petroleum over the question of Zimbabwe's independence; it used it again against the Rawlings regime in Ghana in

June–September 1979; and yet again, against the second Rawlings regime since December 1981. But despite all these instances of toughness, the ability of Nigeria to employ economic leverage to back up its foreign policy options is very limited, and at present Nigeria is not in much of a position to use this against any of the great powers. And given the present slump in the world oil market, and the increase in the level of official corruption, the growing deterioration of public utilities as well as sheer inefficiency, the economic ability of the country to influence any external issue will be further reduced in the foreseeable future unless economic circumstances are to change for the better.

The political capability of Nigeria is not impressive. Structurally, the political system of the country was defective until 1967 when the country was split into twelve states. Political feuding as well as ethnic rivalries and hostility enfeebled the country during the First Republic.

By splitting the country into twelve states in 1967, the political gravity moved from the regions to the centre in Lagos. This position was further strengthened at the end of the civil war in January 1970, especially by the enormous financial and security resources available to the Federal Government, and by the military nature of the Nigerian government until September 1979. There can be no doubt that the Gowon administration skilfully exploited the political resources of the country to win support and friends for Nigeria. The successor Federal Military Government tried to build on this after finding out that in diplomacy bullying as well as the 'big brother' mentality did not work. Nonetheless, the Muhammed/ Obasanjo Government achieved some positive though limited results.

After the return of the country to civilian rule in October 1979 the political 'clout' of the country did not increase. There are a number of reasons for this. First, the Federal Government of Alhaji Shehu Shagari was a coalition of two strange bed-fellows, the National Party of Nigeria (NPN) and the Nigerian People's Party (NPP). Although the coalition broke down in 1981, this did not bring any political gain to the country. Secondly, there were five different political parties controlling different numbers of state governments in the country. Although foreign policy is an exclusive item of the Federal Government, consultation and cooperation with state governments is important if they are not to cause embarrassment for the Federal Government. Moreover, their cooperation is critical in implementing some obligations arising from the external commitments of the Federal Government. Thirdly, the 1979 Constitution placed a number of restrictions on the Federal Government in foreign policy matters. For example, the Federal Government could not send Nigerian troops on combat operation outside the country without the Senate's approval. Nor could the President declare war with any other country without a joint resolution to that effect in the National Assembly. Furthermore, the executive could not spend money from the Consolidated Revenue Fund without the approval of the National Assembly. Although it can be argued that the National Assembly did not succeed in stopping any foreign policy option of the Government, the fact remains that the power to do so was there. And some day a more imaginative National Assembly may learn to use these powers with consummate skill.

The virtual relapse of the country's politics into the ethnic rivalry and hostility typical of the First Republic has wreaked havoc on the political balance within the country. So great was the preoccupation with complex internal social and political issues that the Federal Government hardly found enough time and resources left for external matters.

This is a pity. But it can hardly be otherwise. For unless there is political stability at home, any attempt at playing a major role abroad is bound to fail. Both the external and domestic levels have to be properly related. Otherwise what is politically balanced abroad will not balance at home. What is clear from this is that unless Nigeria's leaders are able to sort out their domestic political problems in an orderly and civilised manner, their ability to influence any foreign policy matter will be very limited.

Interest groups can be grouped broadly into two: institutional and non-institutional. The institutional groups are the bureaucrats, the civil servants, the military officers, etc. This group of people provide a great deal of continuity for the country's foreign policy. Indeed, in a real sense, it is the Nigerian Foreign Service officers who have contributed to the modest, if not conservative, substance of Nigerian foreign policy since independence.

The non-institutional interest groups can be sub-divided into different categories such as the mass media, the commentators, religious associations, economic interest groups such as the Nigerian Chamber of Commerce, Industry, Mines and Agriculture, and anomic groups such as the sudden outburst of student demonstrations in the street. It has to be said that the pluralism of Nigerian politics as well as the high level of political sophistication among the people, especially the urban dwellers, has made the role of interest groups, even under the military, more important in Nigerian politics than those of other African countries. How these various pressure groups influenced Nigerian foreign policy has been examined elsewhere.[9]

However, we shall point to a few instances in which some of these interest groups tried to influence Nigerian foreign policy in important ways. It was largely pressure from various Islamic associations in Nigeria that led the Federal Government towards taking a tougher attitude against Israel since the Camp David agreement of 1977. Likewise, the close relationships between Nigeria and the Arab countries such as Saudi Arabia, Kuwait, Oman, etc., are, in the main, determined by Islam. The role of the Nigerian Chamber of Commerce, Industry, Mines and Agriculture was said to have been important in the decision of Nigeria to lead other African, Caribbean and Pacific countries in negotiating with the EEC late in 1973 in what became known as Lomé I, though this should not be exaggerated, for it was external circumstances that decisively changed the attitude of the Gowon Government to the European Common Market. It is important also to point out that the Nigerian Chamber of Commerce spearheaded the formation of the Federation of West African Chambers of Commerce in the early seventies when the Gowon Government was negotiating the formation of the ECOWAS.

217

Even during the First Republic, it was the newspapers, especially the *Daily Times*, the *Nigerian Tribune*, and the *West African Pilot*, to name a few, coupled with pressure from opposition leaders as well as student demonstrations, especially against the Anglo-Nigerian Defence Pact in November 1960, and against the role of the west in the Congo (now Zaire) following the murder of Patrice Lumumba early in 1961, that prodded the Balewa Government into taking a more balanced position between the west and the east rather than being closely tied to the apron-strings of the west.

These and similar examples can be multiplied. But the Nigerian government has not always followed public opinion in its foreign policy posture. This is hardly surprising. For not even in the older established democracies is public opinion always the guide to government foreign policy position. What is important in our case is that no Nigerian government has ever shut itself away from public opinion in foreign policy matters. Indeed, it is becoming increasingly clear in Lagos that without public acceptance there can be no sustainable foreign policy.

Conclusion

We have sought to examine both the goals of Nigerian foreign policy and the means of attaining them. We have also examined the major factors – external and internal – shaping Nigerian foreign policy. It is clear that the foreign policy objectives have not been realistically identified and analysed. Nor has any serious attention been given to the means of policy. While there is very little that Nigeria can do about its external environment, it can do much to improve its internal circumstances. Unless it takes swift action to re-order its priorities at home, and to reduce the burden placed on it by internal political, economic and military constraints, its ability to play an important role in Africa and the rest of the world will continue to be very limited in the immediate years ahead.

Notes

1 Among the notable books on Nigerian foreign policy are the following: Claude S. Phillips, Jr., *The Development of Nigerian Foreign Policy* (Evanston, Illinois: Northwestern University Press, 1964); Gordon J. Idang, *Nigeria: internal politics and foreign policy 1960–1966* (Ibadan: Ibadan University Press, 1973); Olajide Aluko, *Essays in Nigerian Foreign Policy* (London: George Allen and Unwin, 1981).

2 Federal Republic of Nigeria, *The Constitution of the Federal Republic of Nigeria* (Lagos: Department of Information, Printing Division, 1980), Section 19.

3 For example, Professor Joseph Frankel says that the environment of foreign policy decision is 'limitless' (see Joseph Frankel, *The Making of Foreign Policy: an analysis of decision-making* (London: Oxford University Press, 1963), p. 3; Professor Richard Synder says the task of identifying the variables of foreign

policy decision-making is 'unfinished' (see Richard C. Synder, H. W. Bruck and B. Sapin (eds), *Foreign Policy Decision-making: an approach to the study of international politics* (New York: Free Press, 1962), p. 5.

4 For further details about this, see Olajide Aluko, *Freedom and Necessity in Nigerian Foreign Policy, Text of An Inaugural Lecture delivered at the University of Ife on 17th March, 1981.*

5 For details, see Aluko, *Essays in Nigerian Foreign Policy*.

6 The Military Balance 1980/81 (London, IISS), p. 53.

7 Interview, April 1982.

8 *The Punch* (Lagos), 3 July 1982.

9 For further details see Aluko, *Essays in Nigerian Foreign Policy*.

14 Social change and stability in contemporary Nigeria

A. A. Akiwowo and Richard Olaniyan

This chapter deals with two inter-related themes: social change and stability in Nigeria since the end of the Nigerian civil war in 1970 until the early 1980s. We have chosen this period for study and analysis because it offers us the opportunity to examine the factors underpinning social change and the unfolding social processes and their effects. It is hoped that this chapter will help us to understand better the social policies which will be needed for further planned and unplanned changes. It is significant to note that the first decade of the period has been described by Professor Ojetunji Aboyade as one of the 'decades of unprecedented growth' but which, according to him, led to no 'significant social change'.[1]

From a sociological perspective, the period was, to be sure, full of significant social changes in Nigeria. And they may be explained as the aggregate consequences of social, fiscal, monetary and other developmental policies of the time. By this, we mean that the noticeable changes involved not only alterations in the patterns of living of people, but also the varied social problems brought about by the changes caused by the implementation of those major policies of government at Federal and state levels.

As can be observed, the implementation of policies, governmental ones principally, always brings both anticipated and unanticipated changes and social problems. This was especially true in Nigeria during the last decade and a half. And since we believe that the processes of change which brought in their train a number of vexing social problems are most likely to continue, we do not expect any fundamental alterations in the characteristic style of acting out intentions of the peoples of this country. Instead, we hold that some of the key events of the past may be repeated in the coming years, although the consensus of opinion about what should be regarded as the appropriate or prevailing *mores* of the time is most likely to change.

Having made these preliminary remarks, we may now ask as a guide to thought a leading question in the words of Karl Mannheim: 'How exactly does social change come about and spread through the different spheres of the society?' Or, as he restated it: 'What are the primary causes which make a society dynamic thus compelling both the groups and the individuals to remake their adjustment continually?'[2] Or, with specific reference to the objective of this chapter, what were some of the chief factors of change in Nigerian society during the period under review? Finally, in what ways did the dominant social attitudes subvert social order and stability in Nigeria? In other words, what was the degree of correlation between societal values and social stability?

As we mentally make the selection of the categories of change, we should bear in mind that the social realities of change and our hypotheses about them which they represent may not fit perfectly, like a hand in a glove. The following categories of social change are identified for our purpose: changes in interpersonal relationships; changes in the type of social groups formed in different parts of the country; changes in the composition of social groups; changes in the relationships between groups; changes in the relationship between individuals and their physical, social and educational environments; changes in the relationships between social groups and physical, social and educational environments; changes in the number and types of complex organisations in the society; and changes in the constitution of the country. These and other kinds of changes exemplify the factors of change which have affected both the Nigerian social order and the directions which new changes are probably taking.

Let us examine a few of the categories of change to see what factors contributed to them. As an example, take changes in interpersonal relationships. For many years, many Nigerians were exposed relentlessly to some of the shabbiest treatment at the hands of public servants who were supposed to serve them. The worst offenders among these public servants were women of different ages who were generally believed to be above question or disciplinary action from their immediate superior officers because, it was often alleged, these insubordinate officers had access to senior and very highly placed and influential public figures who could discipline their sectional heads if they applied negative sanctions against these women. The bases of legitimate authority at departmental level having been scandalously eroded, it did not take long before a general state of indiscipline emerged. These attitudes of discourtesy to members of the public by these female officials were soon to spread to young men who were alleged to have bribed people in the higher positions in the civil service hierarchy before getting their jobs; indeed, some of them were alleged not even to possess the necessary paper qualifications in the first instance. A bribe could either be financial or take the form of an offer of intimate friendship between a female relation of the young applicant and a highly placed person who was in a position to offer jobs. Eventually, acts of insolence, insubordination, and misappropriation of funds became so widespread in departments and divisions of ministries that the point was reached at which the traditional values of respect for one's elders, one's seniors or colleagues in one's age group by which the society was held together were no longer able to sustain anyone in his relationships in the office or at home. The corrupt informal pattern of relationships in the formal structure of the offices extended beyond the office walls into society at large and became the accepted norm of behaviour.

The much theorised impersonality and dehumanisation of the mass society had begun. It did not require massive industrialisation. The need to get a job by any means and the subsequent loss of both the particular sense of self-value and the general appreciation of human worth have emerged from the competitiveness of the urban way of life. The connecting tissues between urbanisation and social policy are not easily and immediately identifiable, however, except through what some experts once described as the activities concerned with 'the organization of employment services intended to adjust the supply of existing labour to the actual demand, and the long-term forecasting of manpower needs . . .'[3] But one thing is clear: 'social policy may be applied both to the existing situation and to the future. When applied to the former under the aspect of immediate or short-time action, it may be described as a "management policy". It becomes a planning policy when applied to the future for the purpose of defining the long-time social aims and means for attaining them.'[4] It is in this sense of management policy that the widespread change in the pattern of inter-personal relations and the weakened social sanctions among Nigerian rural as well as urban dwellers can be linked to social policy.[5]

An American economist, Charles Kindleberger, sees fiscal policy in developing countries as intended to facilitate 'the administrative convenience' of raising the requisite revenue, or 'Taxation to support government formation of Capital'.[6] This, however, is a narrow view of fiscal policy especially when applied to Nigeria. In addition to Kindleberger's functions, fiscal policy may be one of the government's measures for controlling the behaviour and direction of a national economy, and for checking the imbalances between the demand for consumer goods on one hand and the capacity of local manufacturers to satisfy the people's needs for consumer goods on the other. Furthermore, fiscal policy cannot be considered without reference to the concurrent monetary policy of a country which deals with government activities at managing the quantum of actual currencies and cash in circulation at any one time.[7]

Looked at together then, social policy, fiscal policy, monetary and population policies – all produce what economists call 'problems of domestic policy'. But from the point of view of this chapter, problems of domestic policies may be defined as possessing two sets of variables: purely economic and purely social. One cannot be understood without reference to the other as national problems, although economists, policy-makers and executors in Nigeria have always tended to see, define and manipulate these two sets of variables in economic terms.

Let us consider a few examples to illustrate this point. A consequence of monetary policy is the availability in the society of huge sums of money called liquid currency, for which there may not be sufficient quantities of manufacturer's or consumer's goods to buy. Such a situation often leads to inflation and its twin sister, hoarding. Hoarding goods is both an economic and a social problem. Another of the social consequences of inflation a few years ago was the phenomenal increase in the social practice called 'spraying', that is, the unbridled, conspicuous and lavish display of cash at social events and parties. 'Spraying', by any standards, was a significant contributory factor to armed robbery, which is yet another social problem.

When the military regime, however, resorted to its belt-tightening fiscal policy to curb inflation and to direct the economy into self-reliance and self-sufficiency, local manufacturers responded by raising the prices of their goods. Consumers, in their turn, reacted by developing a taste for foreign-produced goods. A social consequence was the sharp rise in the pursuit of foreign cultural values: music, skin-bleaching creams, hair-processing, and the wearing of expensive blue jeans and corduroy trousers by young men and women. These in turn led to the draining of the nation's foreign exchange. Another aspect of the hankering for alien goods and culture was the craze among Nigerians of going overseas to spend their long vacation. This social problem has produced its own moral and psychological problems, especially among young women and 'business men and women', some of whom engaged in anti-social acts of smuggling.

It is worth mentioning at this point, in passing, that the monetary and fiscal policies of the post-war rehabilitation period between 1970 and 1972 and the foreign and even domestic development policies of the military regime to 1979 helped to produce a widespread realisation of the need for a united, strong, and mutually respecting people as a necessity if the country was to continue to exist as an entity. It began in the varied efforts of the Nigerian Federal Government and peoples of Nigeria to welcome and integrate most of the leaders and all followers of the secessionist movement which had led to the civil war. It was also evidenced in the post-civil war economic and social rehabilitation programmes for the war-affected areas. It may be correct to say that the end of the civil war began the decline of the potency of tribalism in the public and private affairs of Nigerians and the normalisation of inter-ethnic relations. These attitudinal changes, one must concede, are at this time imperceptible, but even in their inchoate state, they facilitated the 'national character' of political parties in Nigeria between 1979 and 1983.

Another significant change with far-reaching effects to individual Nigerians occurred in the area of criminal justice. Men and women who were convicted of armed robbery referred to earlier, were executed by firing-squads in public places before large crowds of spectators. These public executions have gone a long way towards brutalising many citizens of this nation. Evidences of the brutalising effects are the growing insensitivity on the part of many Nigerians to victims of fatal car accidents on Nigerian highways, behaviour of utter disregard for driving codes of conduct, traffic regulations and possible fines in people's seemingly mad rush to reach their destinations. The overall consequence is the conversion of some roads in the country into death traps. Yet a very important purpose of the policies which led to the construction of many new wide roads in the country is to facilitate easier mobility of goods and people and the increase of physical, social and emotional contacts among citizens and residents in different sections of the country.

Furthermore, it is to encourage international contacts between Nigerians and the citizens of the neighbouring states of the Economic Community of West African States (ECOWAS) as well. These contacts have partly resulted in giving a better understanding and appreciation of other African countries who form the 'cornerstone' of Nigeria's foreign policy. Now, as a result of the signing of the protocols of the ECOWAS by nine West African states, Nigeria is to witness far-reaching changes, such as increases in population, higher rates of unemployment as well as increased pools of cheap labour, and cultural enrichment.

The implementation of fiscal, monetary and industrialisation policies made under the military regimes have brought about the greatest development of the physical fact in social change during the period. The changes in the physical environments in Nigeria resulted from the different programmes of development: from the continuous clearings of vast acres of land for industrial and residential estates, new towns, airports, roads, fish ponds and inland lakes, and oil refineries. The construction of the infrastructural facilities take time to complete, and the inconveniences experienced by vast numbers of Nigerian people who have to pass by the construction sites create acute feelings of frustration and delayed gratification with much arousal of herd behaviour. The protracted period of completing infrastructural constructions and the absence of maintenance services for existing facilities further aggravate and exacerbate feelings of frustration and herd behaviour. But once these projects are completed, Nigerians have proved that they can easily adjust and adapt their lives to higher standards of living.

There are, however, many obvious contradictions in the adjustment and adaptation to environmental changes. One notable example is the seeming readiness with which Nigerians live in the midst of widely reported filth and malodorous surroundings in both older and newer sections of our urban communities. Such unwholesomeness in surroundings, which many observers attest to, is caused partly by the inefficiency of various municipal governments, partly by the lack of equipment and vehicles with which to clear heaps of accumulated garbage, and partly also by the attitude of municipal workers. Lack of equipment and vehicles persist chronically because of non-budgetary support, poor city or town management, sheer mismanagement of funds, and poor supervision of municipal workers. Accumulating heaps of garbage can be explained in terms of poor enforcement of ordinances and regulations.

While we are thinking of poor law enforcement, we need to bear in mind the great move forward made in the evolution of laws in Nigeria and their relationship to social change. In a preface to a commemorative volume, Professor Taslim O. Elias observed the 'significant developments in the judicial and legal systems, the constitutional and administrative changes, as well as important aspects of our adjectival laws'. He highlighted an 'underlying concern for the rule of law and the observance of democratic principles and practices even under a military regime'.

Regarding the fundamental issues of human rights, Professor Elias notes:

> Given the peculiar circumstances of the recent three-year civil war and its aftermath of Federal Government policy of reconstruction, reconciliation and consolidation of national unity, this country has made commendable progress towards the achievement of the ideal of respect for human dignity and the promotion of larger freedom and well-being for the masses of this country.

He described the constitutional development of Nigeria as a sort of pulling together of 'the various strands in the legal, judicial and social developments in the direction of assuring a dynamic synthesis of cultures and values in a spirit of closer integration and national cohesion'.[8]

There may be many individuals who may disagree with Professor Elias as to the nature, scope and value of the nation's progress towards the achievement of the ideal of respect for human dignity, and so on. They may point to the heavy congestion in the courts of people who are awaiting trial and who have been locked up in prison without being convicted for several months, even years in some instances. They may point also to the differential sentencing of those who resort to armed robbery to acquire money from individuals and companies, and of those who defraud the nation of several millions or billions of naira. They will point, too, to many other forms of lack of respect for the rights and dignity of their fellow citizens.

These arguments do not, however, entirely destroy the achievement of 'commendable progress' which Professor Elias talks about; although they point to what A. O. Obilade, in his examination of the Nigerian legal system since independence, described as 'a growing need for harmonization of, at least, some of the sources of Nigerian Law' which included the received English law before independence, customary law, legislations which are locally called 'local legislations', and so on.[9] A. Ojo, among other legal practitioners, has, however, commended the military regimes for demonstrating that 'the traditional method of making laws' may be passed by 'swifter methods of promulgating decrees and edicts', and that it is possible for a government to respond decisively with legislations on purely legal issues.[10]

Examining the rule of law under the military regimes 1965–79, the late O. Ohonbamu, after setting forth the legal arguments by which a successful coup d'état can be said to have established a legalised regime and could be treated like other regimes, made these concluding remarks:

Like the scientific concept of socialism, the rule of law is a universal concept, but to survive it has had, like the chameleon, to adapt its colour to that of its immediate surroundings without, in the process, sacrificing its own personality. The rule, as defined above, is today a way of life and for the preservation of that way of life there are two basic needs – a free, informed and patriotic press and a fearless and independent judiciary. Where these two are lacking, the rule of law will be replaced by rule of force and fraud.[11]

These remarks by Ohonbamu point clearly to the relationship between constitutional change and social change, between government and the press, and to the potential roles each is likely to play in the control of social change and social problems.

It is therefore logical at this point to discuss one of the institutions which help to mould the opinion, attitude, and social action of many Nigerians, namely, the press. One of the notable changes in the Nigerian press, during this period, is the new sense of positive professional identity which journalists have of themselves as a social group, and of their profession as a calling. Following from all of these have been the efforts by journalists to institutionalise the training of their members, and to provide a trade-union basis of support for the individual practitioner who during the period suffered severe persecution from the hands of some military rulers. But perhaps 1975 was the golden year for the Nigerian press in its relentless role as social critic and the conscience of the people. It was the year of the July coup that toppled Gowon's regime. The press, most effectively using all kinds of techniques including humour, sarcasm, invective, touched upon all aspects of government and from time to time called for changes.

Journalists, too, as a body, have seen the need not only to create a set of codes of professional conduct, but also to create union chapels as administrative units of their professional body. It would therefore be correct to view the issue of press freedom as an interminable one. Government regimes come and go, but the press remains as a constant measure of their repressiveness, or of their liberality. When there comes a time that the objectives and practices of the press in Nigeria coincide with the best ideals of the society as promulgated by their government, then it can be fearlessly asserted that there is press freedom in the most liberal sense. Until then, the best that both the press and government can do is to accommodate each other, though not in their extremes, while being ready to act as the watchdog of each other's excesses.

Freedom of the press is one of the universally shared ideals of most countries of the world. It is, however, one of the cultural values of the Nigerian society that is in the process of being and becoming. No one has attempted a systematic study of the cultural configuration of the Nigerian cultures or cultural system. The works of Peter Enahoro on how to be a Nigerian and Mabel Imokhouede are satirical but most welcome efforts to draw attention to what may be emerging national *mores*.[12] There are several works now being undertaken in Nigerian universities which identify, explain and describe diverse configurations of ethnic cultures within the country, even though many of these may not get into the realm of public knowledge for some time. The sensitive observer of the daily happenings in the cultural aspects of our national lives can recognise that the Federal and state governments of the country are encouraging the understanding, appreciation and pursuit of the development of the people's culture. This is being done today by the establishment of cultural centres, the promotion of Nigerian songs, dances, dresses, plays, arts and crafts, and the compositions of oral expressions of knowledge at different levels of our educational institutions. Why is this all necessary? Part of the answer may be found in the need for national identity. As a country which emerged from colonialism, it is probably imperative to emphasise our cultural heritage as one sure means of self-definition amid of the welter of institutions and practices bequeathed to us by British colonialism. In spite of vociferous assertions of our cultural revival, however, neo-colonialist forces remain formidable as our fast-developing nation is called upon to make choices in an increasingly technology-oriented global environment. Conflict has been inevitable – that is to be expected; but since culture is a dynamic force, culture and modernity may not be mutually exclusive or antagonistic.

The reorganisation of the networks of television and radio services in the nation is intended to help bring to the conscious level of awareness of an ever-widening circle of viewers and listeners, the ways of life of the mosaic of ethnic groups found in each of the nineteen states of Nigeria. These cultural changes are taking place, although strong objections are voiced to the federalisation of the television by some state governments.

There is evidence, too, of the diffusion of cultural traits from one ethnic group to another in the country. Nigerian politicians and other leaders seize every opportunity nowadays to display their traditional costumes. These displays go a long way to enrich our national life, enlarge our cultural sensibility, as well as contribute to the emergence of a 'consciousness of kind' among the many nationalities of the nation state.

This leads us to the consideration of another realm of social change: change in the approach to national planning. Two years after Ojetunji Aboyade made a call for an African humanist philosophical approach to planning for the nation, H. M. A. Onitiri, another Nigerian economist, called for planning to begin from the local government level and remarked that 'it is at the local level that the task of development is most difficult'. He also expressed the conviction that at local government level, 'ideas generated at the rural areas will be passed up and will be examined and modified within the precincts of the national goals and objectives and eventually included in the national development plan'. He then added: 'However, if the goals [i.e. of national development] are to be taken seriously, the nation must be seen to be moving towards a certain set of broad national goals and objectives' in a steady and consistent manner. For this to happen, then the rural communities must be carried along the path of economic progress at much faster rate than has ever been the case.'[13]

In his own contribution to the 1978 workshop, Akinade O. Sanda, a sociologist at NISER, reviewed the development planning in Nigeria from 1960 to 1980 with a view to ascertaining 'the extent to which the planning framework has taken these two principles – public interests and results of development efforts – into account'. Sanda noted that in the 1962–80 period, planning involved 'mainly bureaucrats and intellectuals in formal and parastatal institutions' to the exclusion of 'youth associations, women associations, professional associations and traditional councils', and similar interest groups. He concluded: 'Development is about people and only the full involvement of the people in the process can bring desired results to the society at large.'[14]

Similar views have been expressed by other social scientists, for example Akiwowo and Pearce and O. Adamolekun, on the issues of developing social science policy. Such then are the manners of change that have been observed in the field of planning for development: the shift being openly advocated is from planning for the nation to 'planning with the people'.[15]

It is impossible to deal in this chapter with all the social factors which have contributed to change in the social life of Nigerians during the decade of the 1970s or to link them adequately with the relevant development policies. We can, however, list some more aspects of life affected by these factors so that our understanding of such changes can be fuller. We may mention the academic aspect, the general educational and health aspects, and the fashion aspects. If we were asked to characterise the constitutive ideas by which Nigerians of different ways of life saw themselves or organised their individual or group activities on a day-to-day basis, we would list the following, among others:

1 A general belief in the compelling need to acquire by any means a university education against all odds, to obtain certificates which are often referred to as 'meal tickets' – insurance policies and passports to gainful employment and all the good things of life.
2 The belief that if a successor to a post in a public institution wants to establish his own image, he must stigmatise or destroy people's faith in the integrity of his predecessor.
3 A widespread conviction that when it comes to the frustrations and relative deprivations that attend the supply of light, water, telephones, and other public services, there is nothing any government can do to end them, or improve for all time the poor conditions of existence in which the vast majority of people live.

Fast changes have brought gross inefficiency in the administration of these essential services. The population explosion during this period has also contributed to the inadequacy of these facilities which were planned for an earlier era. It is obvious that this is the frustration of change without progress. Nigeria has scored high marks for growth but dishearteningly low marks for real development. This is what Chief Awolowo meant when he observed that 'although the nation had achieved rapid economic growth, it had gained little economic development'.[16]

The direction and consequences of social change in Nigeria cannot be adequately comprehended if we fail to take into consideration our society's structures and social processes. In other words, the catalogue of social changes and the attendant social effects we have examined can only be properly understood within the framework of a critical analysis of the nature of Nigerian society, including its modes of production, social relations, belief and value systems, the psychology of the contending groups, and the social and economic imperatives of modern urban communities. For our purpose here, it will suffice to discuss the structure of Nigerian society, the obstacles to positive change and their relevance to social stability. Finally, we will discuss briefly what is to be done to channel our energies aright.

Looking at Nigerian society, we realise that it is a product of a colonial past struggling unsuccessfully to free itself from its history; that this life drama is taking place within a capitalist socio-political system with all its attendant implications; that the principal actors are products of western education and Euro-Christian cultural values. These facts about the society make it nigh impossible for Nigeria to escape certain consequences. Being a capitalist system – or a Third World variant of it – the fate and fortune of the economy would seem to be in part dependent on external economic forces and influences from the major capitalist countries and their trans-national corporations, whose chief motivation is profit. A dependent economy runs the risk of being manipulated to the advantage of the metropolitan power with neo-colonialist designs. The foreign interest may be promoted either by companies directly owned and operated by foreigners or, indeed, by favoured indigenous agents who know whose boots to lick in order to secure lucrative commissions. Such a relationship inevitably serves as a cushion for economic exploitation and inequality both at domestic and international levels.

In the Nigerian situation, the majority of the local participants in this neo-colonialist economic order, the rising middle class especially, have in themselves contributed to the economic exploitation of the country through all kinds of shady commercial deals. Such business transactions in their thousands and amounting to millions of naira have, in addition to the oil boom, created instant wealth for the few commission agents in a national population whose per capita income is still pathetically low.

The phenomenal rise of the affluent in the urban areas and their disproportionately increasing political influence have created a socio-economic situation in which the peasants in the rural areas and the urban working classes have become progressively impoverished and marginalised. Furthermore, the trend among the élite has been towards preoccupation with individual self-interest, and hence faith in our society's sense of justice, fair play and humanity is fast diminishing. To be sure, the attitude of the élite regarding acquisition and the ostentatious display of material wealth in a society that is plagued by inequality of opportunity, growing unemployment and grinding poverty, and where less fortunate citizens are embittered and made to feel left out, has created a natural breeding ground for general indiscipline, corruption, all kinds of anti-social behaviour, violence and crime pursued by the social drop-outs and some of the growing army of the unemployed or the marginally employed.

This was the situation which compelled Chief Obafemi Awolowo in 1973 to emphasise the need for a change to avert serious consequences. He said:

> A situation such as we now have under which [the] good things of life are assured to a small minority of Nigerians and almost totally denied to the vast majority of our countrymen is pregnant with unpredictable dangers for all of us, if allowed to continue for much longer.[17]

Four years later in 1977, the former Head of State, Lt. General Olusegun Obasanjo, had cause to observe that 'social turbulence in most human societies can be traced to the absence of justice and humanness in the distribution of returns from economic activity and the social esteem which flows therefrom'.[18]

The new morality brought about by the oil wealth, the sudden and unmerited affluence it has brought some people, the scandalous cases of corruption reported daily in the press, have gone a long way to create a credibility gap between the government and the masses. This has adversely affected people's sense of duty and undermined the belief that society could be improved. The growing cynicism seems to have given credence to the view now held by many Nigerians that 'honesty is the best way to poverty'. Since corruption and ethics are inseparable, it has been virtually impossible to expect the youth in the society to practise what the older people say rather than what they do. Increasing numbers of Nigerians have become insensitive to the impropriety of giving or receiving bribes; it is often a big surprise when they are refused.

If we take discipline, that is self-restraint, as the 'axial principle' on which a good society should rest, as Lt.-General Olusegun Obasanjo rightly maintains,[19] it is probably not unfair to indict the Nigerian élite for gross indiscipline, for not providing a value framework to the society, exposing people to honest values. The élite have in numerous ways and in diverse circumstances flouted the law, put themselves above the law, and in general by their indiscipline, subverted the Nigerian society and economy. This attitude caused Lt.-General Obasanjo to lament the embarrassing behaviour of 'government functionaries including officials entertaining their guests with champagne when the drink has been banned in the country'.[20] It was also a well-known fact that leaders in government, business and the professions continued to wear imported lace dresses when they had been proscribed. Virtually all the measures taken by government to indigenise business enterprises, or fight inflation, or conserve foreign exchange, or control house rents, or whatever, have been rendered ineffective by members of the self-same corrupt, grasping, get-rich-quick élite. The good intentions of the government have, in almost all cases of public policy, been frustrated.[21]

It is not uncommon to find our leaders, aped by our peoples, spending on scandalously expensive foreign products thereby draining the nation's foreign exchange reserves. It is obvious that our wants and demands have been completely at variance with the realities of our state of under-development.

Another area in which social change has had a tremendous impact is in the growth of individualism, emphasis on self first, causing the collapse of the communal ethos which had sustained our society for ages. Those old sterling practices like respect for authority, age and experience, isolating and stigmatising perpetrators of acts detrimental to societal interest and well-being, and giving of special recognition to positive contributions to the community instead of worshipping material wealth, have been denuded of much of their traditional respectability. It is now fashionable to admire unbridled egotism, affectations of foreign manners and customs, and ostentatious life style. Our western-educated élite have yet to abandon the colonially derived need to seek foreign models for development schemes and approval for initiatives that are geared towards coming to grips with the imperatives peculiar to our circumstances. As long as this continues, we will have development plans and policies which will make Nigeria a poor copy of foreign originals.

The various policies which we have examined were carefully thought-out guidelines for creation of social change in a most desirable direction. This implies normative considerations by planners in the planning for social change, namely: what should be the objectives of plans for social change and what should be the direction of change? However, in the review of the impact of the factors of change, a widespread feeling of disatisfaction with the 'new' social order thus created has been noted. This feeling led the Federal Military Government to set up in each of the nineteen states a Committee on Education for Citizenship to advise it in its efforts to tackle the problem areas of our national life.

What is to be done? How can our society free itself from the shackles of the social, economic, political and cultural encumbrances as a precondition for a leap forward into meaningful economic development and social change? Ideological sloganeering is hardly the correct recipe or the magic wand to cure the multi-faceted ills of our society and bail us out of our present state of under-development. What is needed is an urgent rational restructuring of our leadership style, general social attitudes, public policies and set of priorities.

By the very nature of Nigerian society and the imperatives of our situation, as Professor Aboyade correctly suggests,

> ... leaders and policy makers should bend their energies to a drastic reduction of the gap between the intellectuals and manual workers, between urban life and rural life and between industrial growth and agricultural development. At the level of social mobilisation, our national psyches must be fired to overcome a century of humiliation in the hands of foreign powers, and our resources harnessed to ensure military security, restore cultural dignity and assiduously promote economic independence.[22]

To be sure, our society urgently needs a revolution in mental outlook which will embolden our people to reject as unsatisfactory and therefore unacceptable many aspects of our socio-economic order. We also need to develop a new and enlightened consciousness which will make people refuse to believe that corruption is an inevitable, normal way of life. De-emphasising material possessions as a yardstick for defining social worth and importance in the community will reduce to a considerable extent one of the main causes of corruption. Furthermore, a free and fearless press, undistracted by possible gratifications or partisan political considerations, ready and willing to expose cases of corruption and other anti-social behaviour wherever found, would be a vital weapon in the battle to rid society of its ills. People should be made to realise that crimes will not pay in the end by establishing a strict system of accountability and enforcing some form of punishment which would serve as a deterrent against corruption, embezzlement and malpractices.

At this stage of our nation's development discipline is vitally important. It would be highly unusual to find a disciplined citizenry in a society where the leadership is openly identified with gross indiscipline, at times bordering on criminality. To be sure, without individual and collective discipline we will remain a nation in the rearguard, perpetually oscillating between advancing into more ordered and positive socio-political coherence and remaining bogged down in a quagmire of ineptitude, half measures, and progressive impoverishment.

Notes

1 O. Aboyade, *Issues in the Development of Tropical Africa* (Ibadan: Ibadan University Press, 1976), p. 34.

2 *Systematic Sociology: An introduction to the study of society* (New York: Grove Press, 1957), pp. 136, 137.

3 UN Research Institute for Social Development, *The Scope and Method of Social Planning: administrative aspects of social planning*, 1968, p. 3.

4 *Ibid.*, p. 2.

5 *Ibid.*, p. 7.

6 Charles P. Kindleberger, *Economic Development* (New York: McGraw-Hill, 1965), p. 240.

7 Nigerian economists, I. J. Ebong, Q. B. Anthonio, Victor P. Diejomaoh, and Adedotun Phillips have not only identified what are Nigeria's social objectives but have detailed out the role that governments' fiscal policies have played in the implementation of these objectives in the villages and towns in the rural areas. See Adedotun O. Phillips, 'Fiscal policy and rural development in Nigeria', in *Rural Development in Nigeria* (Proceedings of the 1972 Annual Conference of the Nigerian Economic Society, University of Ibadan, 1973); I. J. Ebong, 'Nigerian social objectives and the rural sector', *ibid.*, pp. 17–22; Q. B. Anthonio, *ibid.*, pp. 23–40.

8 T. O. Elias (ed.), *Law and Social Change in Nigeria* (University of Lagos and Evans Brothers, 1973), p. vii.

9 A. O. Obilade, 'The legal system since independence', *ibid.*, p. 46.

10 A. Ojo, 'Constitutional developments in Nigeria since independence', *ibid.*, p. 20.

11 O. Ohonbamu, 'The rule of law in Nigeria', *ibid.*, p. 227.

12 Peter Enahoro, *How to be a Nigerian* (Ibadan: The Caxton Press, 1970).

13 See 'Proceedings of the National Workshop on Planning Strategy for the 1980s' (NISER, 8–15 January 1978).

14 *Ibid.*

15 *Ibid.*

16 Address by the Chancellor, 9th Convocation, University of Ife, 1973.

17 *Africa Contemporary Record*, 1973–74, p. B723.

18 Lt.-General Olusegun Obasanjo, *Speech at the formal opening of the Command and Staff College, Jaji, September 12, 1977* (Lagos: Govt. Printer, 1977), p. 10.

19 *Ibid.*, p. 5.

20 *Ibid.*

21 S. O. Osoba, 'Discipline and indiscipline: a definition', Paper presented at the seminar of the Oyo State Committee on Education for Citizenship, University of Ife, Ile-Ife, 22 January 1979.

22 O. Aboyade, 'Scholarship and underdevelopment' (An address by the Vice-Chancellor to the Convocation of the University of Ife, 16 December 1978), p. 11.

15 Religions in Nigeria

J. O. Kayode and E. Dada Adelowo

Nigeria can be said to be a melting pot of religions. It is a country where three religions – Nigerian traditional religion (traditional religious sects considered as one religion), Islam and Christianity – are each striving hard to gain more adherents. While Nigerian traditional religion has deep historical roots in Nigeria and is based on oral traditions, the others, Islam and Christianity, are entirely new faiths and were introduced into Nigeria much more recently. Of these two foreign faiths in Nigeria, Christianity is the more recent: indeed, Islam had become well entrenched, particularly in the Hausa–Fulani areas of the north and in a good number of areas in the south, before Christianity was introduced into Nigeria. In this chapter, we shall examine the history and nature of these religions, as well as their place among the peoples of Nigeria. Finally, it is important to appreciate the fact that an understanding of the history of the penetration of a religious culture into an area is essential if we are to understand its present-day manifestations.

Traditional religion

All the various ethnic groups of Nigeria are religious in the sense that they claim to be votaries of one religion or the other. Religion permeates all facets of their lives, and constitutes the foundation and the all-governing principle of life for them. They firmly believe that the full responsibility for all the affairs of this life and the one beyond belongs to the Supreme Being (God); their own part in the matter is to do as they are ordered through the priests and diviners whom they believe to be the interpreters of the will of the Supreme Being. Through all the circumstances of life, through all its changing scenes, its joys and troubles, it is the Supreme Being that is in control. Before a child is born, the oracle is consulted and the proper rites are observed; when the child is born, the oracle issues directions about it; at every passage of life – puberty, betrothal, marriage, choosing a career, building a house, going on a journey, the thousand and one things which constitute the human sojourn here on earth – man is in the hands of the Supreme Being whose dictate is law, and who is waiting on the other side of this life to render to man as he deserves. Religion expresses itself in multifarious ways among Nigerians. It forms the themes of songs, provides topics for minstrels, finds vehicles in myths, folk-tales, proverbs and sayings, and is the basis of their philosophy.

Adherents of traditional religion believe that God is transcendent, that is high up in the sky (heaven). He is independent of the world and because of this, they worship him. They often see signs of his presence or rather his immanence in extraordinary events and in the extraordinary powers which are at work in the natural world. These, however, are not the only ways in which they see signs of his presence.

Furthermore, they hold the thesis that God is closely related to the natural world, and they believe that he controls it. So they feel dependent upon God, the Determiner of destiny, the Controller and Sustainer of the world of living men and women. They seek his help and protection and they fear his wrath. In most religions people believe that there are evil powers or forces at work in the wicked world which cause harm and illness. They seek God's help against the machinations of the wicked world. This is also the case among the peoples of Nigeria.

People feel that they owe a duty to worship God. They do this by means of praise and gifts offered in religious ceremonies. In their day-to-day lives they try to behave in ways which they believe will please God, and this helps them to decide what is right and what is wrong. This is about moral values. They also link the more important events of human life with the worship of God, including those having to do with birth, marriage, and death, or the planting and harvesting of crops. When men fail to behave according to their accepted ideas of right and wrong, they often feel that they have angered God, that is, that they have committed a sin. They employ various means, particularly sacrifice, in order to restore a good relationship.

People also believe that it is possible to gain the favour of God through prayer which they, more often than not, accompany with sacrifice. The prayer of petition is, in some ways, the simplest and yet the most important of all religious acts. By praying, people express their dependence on God, and make their needs known to him. Moreover, they think of God in personal terms.

Most religions teach that human beings can have a personal relationship with God. Many religious thinkers, however, teach that God transcends human life in this matter as well as in others. He is a personal Being, but He is truly personal in a way in which human beings can never be because of their imperfections, their finitude.

Furthermore, the adherents of traditional religion see the universe as a whole as related to the will of God. In the light of the relationship seen between God and the natural universe, they work out for themselves a description or picture of how things fit together. With this picture, they are able to think of the different creatures and things which make up their world as related to each other according to the will of God. Such a picture is often called a 'world-view' or 'cosmology'.

As there are no written records of the ancient past of the peoples of Nigeria, all that has been preserved of their myths, philosophy, liturgies, songs and sayings has come down to us by word of mouth from generation to generation – that is to say, in the form of oral tradition. Oral traditions enable us to see that questions fundamental to religion have been asked and answered in the past, and that it is in consequence of those questions and answers that the body of oral traditions now available to us has come into being. The oral traditions are, in fact, the source or what we may call the scripture of Nigerian traditional religion wherein is contained the history of their religious awareness.

The structure of Nigerian traditional religion

Like other African religion Nigerian traditional religion has no written scriptures, at least in the sense we regard the scripture of Islam, the Koran, and the scripture of the Christian faith, the Bible. The main elements of the fundamental beliefs in the religion of the people of Nigeria are as follows:

1 belief in the Supreme Being (God);
2 belief in the deities or lesser gods;
3 belief in spirits including ancestral spirits and others;
4 belief in the power of magic and medicine.

We shall now examine each of these items one by one and in greater depth.

Belief in the Supreme Being (God)

In Nigeria, each ethnic group has a local name for the Supreme Being. Invariably there are other names apart from the principal name. The principal name of the Supreme Being may be the generic name for deity in general, in which case there is a qualifying suffix or qualifying word to distinguish between the Supreme Being or the deities; and the generic name plus the suffix or qualifying word belong uniquely to the Supreme Being. There are cases where the name for the Supreme Being is uniquely his, and no part of it is shared by any other being. It should also be noted that where the deities share the basic generic name with the Supreme Being, it only serves to emphasise the fact that the deities, according to Idowu, derive their being and nature from him.[1]

The names by which the Supreme Being is known in Nigeria are descriptive of his character and emphasise the fact that he has a true reality and is not an abstract entity. The names denote that, as Westermann observes, 'he is a reality to the Africans' and convey 'the purest expression of their religious thinking' and of their religious experience.[2]

The Yoruba name, *Olódùmarè*, is an illustration of a name which is unique to the Supreme Being which adds a suffix to the generic name for deity in general; it is made up of *Chi*, and *-ukwu*: *Chi* meaning source, being or spirit, and *ukwu*, meaning great, immense, undimensional; while the Efik name *Abasi Ibom* (*Abasi* = God + *Ibom* = above) illustrates the name of the Supreme Being which is made up of the generic name for deity in general plus a qualifying word to distinguish the Supreme Being from the deities.

It should be emphasised here that in Nigeria the various names given to the Supreme Being are not mere labels, but are descriptive of his nature, the experience of the people about him and their belief in him. The theophorous proper names that people bear all over Nigeria constitute further evidence of how real the Supreme Being is to the people. *Oghenedjakpokohwo* – 'God directs the person' (Urhobo); *Ebere Chukwu* – 'God's mercy' (Igbo); *Olutooyin* – 'The Lord deserves to be praised' (Yoruba); these are a few such names which signify what God means to the people of Nigeria in their various circumstances.

Apart from the names, Nigeria is very rich in attributes of God which show unmistakably that people consider the Supreme Being as the living one, the ever-present, ever-active, and ever-acting reality in the world. Thus the people of Nigeria pray to him anywhere and in fact everywhere, at any time and every time; they approach him not only in time of distress but also when they are joyful. They are sure to secure God's favour anywhere and everywhere for he is believed, according to the Yoruba, to be *Atérerek'áyé*, 'one who occupies the whole extent of the world'. No wonder they do not have images to represent him and no temples are erected to localise his worship.

To the people of Nigeria, God is unique and incomparable. In Edo mythology, there is a story that Olokun (the arch-divinity), the beloved son of Osanobwa (the Supreme Being) vested with all the attributes and glory due to his position, once challenged his father to a display of splendour and majesty. In tune with African practice he chose an open market place for the display. When the appointed day came, the father sent his messenger, the chameleon, to tell Olokun that he was ready and that Olokun should meet him at once at the appointed venue. Olokun dressed himself in what he regarded as excellent regalia and came out of his room. Imagine his chagrin when he discovered that his father's messenger was dressed identically! 'This will not do,' he thought. He therefore went back into the room and changed his garment. When he came out again, he discovered that the messenger was also wearing an identical dress. He tried this seven times but each time he was frustrated because his father's messenger dressed as he. In the end, he capitulated, admitting that it was impossible for him to go out and compete with his father since he could not beat even his messenger in such a display.

This is a way of saying that the Supreme Being is unique, incomparable. The uniqueness of the Supreme Being is one reason why there are no images of him. There are many symbols, but no images, no likeness. He is the *only* Supreme Being: he is not of the rank and file of the deities; he is not a person in the sense that human beings are. God is the absolute Controller of the universe.

The absolute control of the universe and of all beings is due basically to the fact that all other beings exist in consequence of him; because they derive from him. God is the ultimate fountain-head of all power and authority, of all sanctions for orderly relations between men, the Creator of all things from nothing, since nothing existed before him.

This idea is contained in a Yoruba myth that 1 700 deities conspired against Olódùmarè, and resolved that he must abdicate power and authority. They went before him and demanded that he should hand over power to them, at least for an experimental period of sixteen years. Olódùmarè suggested to them that it might be wise for them to experiment for sixteen days to start with. This suggestion they joyfully accepted. Olódùmarè then told them that the world was theirs to run according to their discretion for that period. They immediately set about their task. But after only eight days they discovered that things had fallen apart for them and the centre could no longer hold – that the machinery of the universe was at a stalemate.

Nigerians are explicit about the divine rulership and absolute control of the universe. The Edo name for God, Osanobwa, means 'the source-being who carries and sustains the universe'. The same theme is expressed in the Nupe song:

A being which Soko did not create,
neither did the world create it . . .
Should you do anything that is beautiful,
Soko has caused it to be beautiful
Should you do anything evil,
Soko has caused it to be evil.

This is to say that *Soko* (Nupe name for God) is behind every act of man.

Belief in the deities
Let us start by highlighting the relationship between the Supreme Being and the deities or divinities.

1 From the point of view of the theology of Nigerian religion it will be erroneous to maintain that the deities were created the way human beings were created or brought to life. It will be correct to say that they were brought into life, or that they came into being in the nature of things concerning the divine ordering of the world. Òrìsà-ńlá (arch-divinity in the Yoruba pantheon of gods) is definitely a derivation reflecting the very nature and metaphysical attributes of Olódùmarè. Hence he is often known as the son of Olódùmarè, or his deputy, vested with the power and authority of a royal son. Olokun is in a similar position in the Edo pantheon, hence he is known as the son of Osanobwa.

2 The lesser gods are derivatives from the Supreme Being. All that we have said about the unitary control of the universe by the Supreme Being applies here. Since the deities derive from the Supreme Being, their powers and authorities are meaningless apart from him.

3 Each deity has his own local name among the various ethnic groups which is descriptive either of his allotted function or the natural phenomenon which is believed to be a manifestation or emblem of his being. Examples are Jàkúta ('one who hurls or fights with stones') in Yorubaland; and Sokogba (*Soko egba* – 'God's axe') in Nupeland. In each case the phenomenological reference is to the thunderbolt which is believed to be the instrument of execution. Among the Igbo of Nigeria the arch-divinity is known as Ala (or Ana, Ani); this is the same word used for 'earth' or 'ground' – *Ala* is the earth-goddess.

4 The deities were brought into being as functionaries in the theocratic government of the world.

5 The deities are ministers each with its own definite portfolio in the theocratic monarchic government. Each is an administrative head of department in his own sphere. They are also intermediaries, the liaison

officers between the Supreme Being and man, with particular reference to their particular functions. They constitute only a half-way house which is not meant to be the permanent place of repose for the human soul.

6 The deities under their various generic names constitute the pantheon in each locality. Thus we can talk of the Yoruba pantheon, the Igbo pantheon, the Nupe pantheon and the Edo pantheon.

7 We need to supply an answer to the question whether the deities are real or not. We may get round the question by saying that to those who believe in them and believe that they derive succour from their ministration or afflictions from their machinations, they are real; and to those who have outgrown them or to whom they have never had significance, they have no real objective existence. For our part, the following points are important.

a) There are some deities that may be described as the 'divinities of heaven'. That is, they are the principal deities who are a part of the original order of things.

b) Some of them, as discussed below, are conceptualisations of certain prominent attributes of the Supreme Being, particularly as discerned through natural phenomena.

c) There are a good number of the deities that are no more than ancestors and heroes who have become deified after their death. Sango (the deity of thunder and lightning in Yoruba religion) is a good example here.

In all, the number and the variety differ from one community to another; it is difficult to say how many there are in Nigeria as a whole.

Belief in spirits

Let us begin with those apparitional entities which form a separate category of beings from those described as deities, although we should note that deities and ancestors come under the general nomenclature of spirits. Hence we shall treat the apparitional entities and the ancestral spirits under the same heading, starting with the former.

Spirits, or what we describe as apparitional entities, may be anthropomorphically conceived, but they are more often than not regarded as powers that are almost abstract – as shades or vapours which take on a human figure; they are immaterial and incorporeal beings. They are so constituted that they can assume various dimensions wherever they wish to be 'seen' – they may be either abnormally small, fat or thin. It is believed that when they appear beside the natural object which is their domicile, they may appear in the form or shape or dimension of the object.

Spirits, according to Nigerian belief, are ubiquitous; there is no part of the world, no object or creature, which does not have a spirit of its own or which cannot be inhabited by the apparitional entity known as a spirit. Thus there are spirits of trees, that is, spirits which reside in trees. There are special trees in Nigeria which are considered sacred and these are held to be special abodes of spirits. The Yoruba *akòko*, or Igbo *ogilisi* or *ogirisi* (*mewboldialaevis*) is a sacred tree which is an emblem to a good number of deities; it is also reputed to be a home for certain nondescript spirits which throng and chatter like birds among its leaves in the heart of the night.

Such trees as spirits inhabit become their emblem. At the foot of it, sacrifices and libations are made to them, and people make ejaculatory prayers as they pass by. Similarly, there are spirits which reside in rocks, mountains and hills, forests and bushes, rivers and water-courses, whose natural objects are accepted as their emblems and media by which they are approached.

Then we have the spirits of the born-to-die children. These are called *Àbíkú* among the Yoruba and *Ogbanje* among the Igbo. The belief here is that these spirits are wandering spirits that specialise in the sadistic mischief of finding the way into the womb to be born in order to die. The traditional explanation is that there is a company of spirits whose members are under an agreement to undertake, in turns, this errand of mischief; before those who are thus assigned leave the company temporarily, they enter into a pact that they will return, that is, die, at certain named dates and times.

One important spirit which Nigerians have had to reckon with, often very painfully, is the spirit of witches. Witches are known by different names in different communities. In Yorubaland, for example, they are known as *àjé* (witches), *eleye* (one who possesses a bird, usually a night-jar); *àwon alayé* (those who control the world); *awon iyàmi* (my mothers); *àwon òsòròngà ajapájorí* (the *òsòròngà* that eat both hands and heads). In short, witches and sorcerers are known for their anti-social activities. Witches and sorcerers embody the workings of evil without having any physical contact with their victims. The Hausa refer to a witch as *māye*, and they say *māye yā kama kuriransa*, 'the witch seized his soul'; and if death ensues they use the expression *māye yā chi shi*, 'the witch has eaten him'. The Nupe call a witch *eshechi*; and when one dies, they say *esechi fifinge*. In Hausaland there is *sarikin mayin* whose function is that of detection. His counterpart among the Yoruba were the *Atinga* or *Semio* who operated in Yorubaland, especially in Oyo and Egbado in the early part of the present century. The *Semio* were a group of witch-doctors who detected and punished a lot of witches.

The common belief is that the spirits of the living human beings can be sent out of the body on errands to wreak havoc with other persons in the body, mind or estate; that witches have guilds or operate singly; and that the spirits sent out of the human body in this way can act either invisibly or through a lower creature – an animal or a bird, usually a night-jar.

Next is the category known as ancestral spirits. The ancestors, like the deities, could be described as domesticated spirits – the ancestors have always been a part of the human family, and the deities are a tutelary part of the personal or community establishments.

In Nigeria, there is a general belief that communion and communication are possible between those who are alive and the deceased, and that the latter have the power to influence or molest the former.

It is to be noted here that the ancestors have ceased to be in the ordinary world. They are spirits and are approached accordingly, even though they are spirits with a difference in consequence of their family connections with their earthly folk.

Among the Yoruba and the Edo, festivals in honour of ancestors have in certain cases become definitely religious festivals. The cults of *Orò* and *Egúngún* and what in Benin is known as *Agwe* are illustrations of this fact. *Orò* or *Egúngún* represents either the fact of the spirit – ancestors in general or particular ancestors. *Agwe* prefixes either an ancestral festival or the festival of Osanobwa, the Supreme Being.

Belief in the power of magic and medicine

Magic by definition is an attempt on the part of man to tap and control the supernatural resources of the universe for his own purposes. Magic serves man's egocentricity and is for him a short cut to spiritual bliss. The same word is often used for both magic and medicine in most areas in Nigeria. In Yorubaland for example, the word *òògùn* can be used for both magic and medicine, though *idán* may be used specifically for magic. Among the Hausa, the word *magani* is used; the Nupe use the word *chigbe*.

Here, it is to be noted that magic is not the same as medicine. Magic is normally employed to ward off evil in the family, in the society as a whole, or in the village or town. However, when a certain medicine cannot achieve the desired end without some element of magic, then we say we employ magical medicine.

Medicine is basically for healing purposes. It usually involves the preparation of herbs or making herbs into a concoction. The herbalist does not start trying to heal his patient without first diagnosing the type of ailment, particularly the chronic ones, and this is done through divination: this tells him the cause of the illness and the means to cure it. Diagnosing ailments therefore acts like a torch-light in the dark, and as X-raying is important in scientific western medicine, so also is divination in African traditional healing methods. The cause of the ailment may be ascribed to contravening taboos, the wrath of a person's ancestor, witchcraft or sorcery.

The traditional herbalists make use of plants, roots, and animal species in the preparation of medicine for healing, and such materials have, by oral tradition, been studied and believed to be efficacious.

Symbolism is taken into serious consideration in the collection, preparation and application of the prepared medicine. The herbalist would know the best time to collect leaves or plants, or bark of stems and may have to recite some incantations before or after collecting them. Mircea Eliade calls such enactments 'symbolism of mythical precedents'.[3] E. G. Parrinder rightly observes that 'it is not easy to find out why certain remedies are used – they may have some fancied resemblance to the symptoms of the disease'.[4] Having prepared the medicine, the elements are applied either by drinking the concoction or eating the paste, or soup. It could then be used for rubbing or making the prescribed number of incision marks on the affected body.

240

It is important to note here that religion, magic and medicine cannot be divorced from one another. With regard to the practice of medicine, religion is considered necessary since the popular belief is that only the Maker can remake, only the Creator can recreate, repairing the damage to mind and body, and affecting wholeness in man's being.

Islam in Nigeria

Islam gained access to Nigeria from two directions: from the north into Kanem–Bornu, the area which forms the present Bornu state of Nigeria; and from the west into Hausa country, parts of the present Sokoto, Kaduna and Kano states of Nigeria., In both directions, Islam followed the caravan trade routes that came from North Africa through the Sahara into the western and central Sudan.

As the merchants passed along the trade routes, settlements were formed in which some of the foreign traders and craftsmen remained with their indigenous customers, inter-married with them and formed separate communities. They practised their religion in the open and soon made an impact on their hosts through their religious devotion, supernatural healing power, ability to make both women and cultivated lands productive, and in averting the dangers of witchery and sorcery which were, more often than not, dreaded by the traditional societies among whom they settled. From among such settlers would emerge teachers and preachers of Islam who, through their strict Islamic practices coupled with their mystical powers, were regarded as holy men. They were often believed by the community in which they lived to possess the attribute of *baraka*, a kind of power by which they could bring blessings upon the ruler and his subjects. They soon became mediators in both temporal and religious issues, and finally endeared themselves to the rulers who eventually led their subjects into embracing Islam.

With the introduction of the camel into North Africa towards the end of the period of Roman control of that area, travelling southwards into the hinterland of the continent became much easier than hitherto. This facilitated the movement of the North African merchants across the Sahara into the western and central Sudan. They travelled along three main routes:

1 from Morocco through Mauritania into the Senegal basin and also through Taghaza and Taodeni into the Niger bend;
2 from the area between Tunis and Tripoli through Ghadames into Katsina and Kano and also through Fezzan into the Chad area;
3 from Egypt and Cyrenaica through Fezzan into Kanem and the Chad area; and also from Egypt through Darfur and Waday into the Kanem–Bornu area.

After the thirteenth century, a steady decline set in to the Kanem kingdom. The dynasty was re-established in Bornu by the Safawa and by the time of Mai Idris Alooma (1570–1602) the kingdom had again

241

become powerful, having its diplomatic nexus with North Africa and the Ottoman Sultanate. The influence of Bornu in this period extended westwards into Hausaland and southwards into the Benue basin as far as Kwararafa. The application of the divine law, *Shari'a*, and the administration based on it were intensified and the common people increasingly submitted to Islamic conversion. As a matter of fact, Islam became the state religion in Bornu during the reignof Mai Idris Alooma, and some neighbouring states accepted it.

In the second year of the seventeenth century, the power of Bornu began to wane as a result of the attack from the Tuaregs in the north and the Jukun in the south. Though this decline continued into the eighteenth century, Bornu still retained its importance as a centre of Islamic culture during this period. In this period also the Fulani emigrants from the west started to increase in number and expand within the state of Bornu. Their intermittent attacks on small ethnic groups within the state increased the already prevalent political insecurity which the inhabitants had experienced. At the beginning of the nineteenth century, a new threat to the stability of the state emerged in the rapidly growing power of the Fulani in Hausa country, under Shehu Usman dan Fodio.

Moreover, Islam's access to Nigeria through the Senegal basin continued to spread peacefully, aided by the efforts of the Soninke of ancient Ghana and the Dyula clan (Wangarawa or Mandingo) traders who, in addition to trading in kolanuts, preached and taught Islam. Consequently, the ruler of Jenne embraced Islam in about AD 1200, followed by all his subjects, with the result that Jenne became the greatest Muslim metropolis in the western Sudan. Traders from Jenne gradually moved into Timbuktu which, from the thirteenth century, also grew eventually into both a commercial and the great religious centre, later supplying both the western and central Sudan with learned men who left the imprint of their Islamic heritage.

In the fourteenth century, the Dyula traders brought Islam into Hausaland. It reached Kano during the reign of Ali Yaji (1349–85). By the fifteenth century Islam was being taken very seriously. The ruler who actually gave Islam a strong footing in Hausa country was Muhammad Rimfa (Rimfa), king of Kano (1463–99). Katsina itself could not be said to have accepted Islam seriously until the reign of Ibrahim Maje (1492–1520). Some other parts of Hausa country were not exposed to the influence of the Muslim traders and preachers until later. People in some other places followed the Hausa religion. Examples of such places were Zaria, Zamfara, Gobir, and Yauri.

After the Wangarawa traders had introduced Islam into Hausa country, it was left to the Fulbe to extend the Islamisation of the area. Though their activities, the Muslims of Hausa country became acquainted with the Koran, the *Hadith* and the Islamic law books. Later, Fulani missionaries added books on *tauhid* and Arabic grammar (*sarf*). During the reign of Muhammad Rimfa more Fulani poured into Hausa country and settled down to preach and teach Islam. His regime also witnessed a number of Muslim dignitaries visiting Kano and Katsina. For example, the Kano Chronicle informs us of *Sharifs* from Saudi Arabia who visited Kano during this time. Ahmad Ibn Umar b'Muhammad Aqit of Timbuktu, the grandfather of Ahmad Baba, also visited Kano and other towns of the Sudan.

From this time onward, both Kano and Katsina were increasingly becoming not only important commercial centres but also great seats of Islamic scholarship.

From the eleventh century, in the case of Kanem, and the fourteenth century in the case of Hausaland, Islam made steady progress in Northern Nigeria, particularly among rulers and town dwellers, after passing through the initial struggles with the traditional religion. This period was one of transition. The abuses against Islam during the period were not confined to the rulers alone – the common people as well as some of the *Ulama*, and Muslim learned men or theologians, were equally guilty. The common people were accused of introducing innovation (*bid'a*) into their practice of Islam, thereby altering and adulterating the basic principles of Islam, and their venal *malams* proclaimed such illegal innovations to be legitimate. From the confused and corrupt situation Usman dan Fodio was able, through his preaching and teaching, to collect a group of Muslims to form a community, a *jama'a*, out of the wider Muslim community that existed in Hausa country during the second half of the eighteenth century. This *jama'a* contained not only the Fulani who were of the same ethnic group with Usman dan Fodio but also the Hausa and Tuareg.

By the beginning of the nineteenth century, the situation had reached a stage at which the knowledge of Islam was widespread enough to make Islamic reform welcome. When, therefore, Usman dan Fodio appeared as the Islamic reformer and eventually launched a Jihad in Hausa country he was able to secure enough support to assure him of victory, and he helped to lay the foundation for the stabilisation and further spread of Islam within Nigeria.

Whatever motives anyone may ascribe to the Jihad, the obvious fact is that it welded together the Hausa states, which had previously been antagonistic to one another, into one solid unit under the divine law, *Shari'a*: it represented a formal attempt to convert Islam from the level of personal beliefs to that of communal law, an attempt to shake off the remnants of the traditional customs and to create a theocratic Islamic empire.

The Jihad did not stop with the Hausa states but continued eastward into the Bornu kingdom. It also pushed southward and incorporated Nupeland as well as northern Yorubaland. The Yoruba successfully resisted the Jihad but they could not halt the spread of Islam.

Islam in Hausaland

In Hausa country, Islam is said to have been first introduced in the second half of the fourteenth century by Wangarawa traders, though it appears that through external contacts something of Islam had been known before this.

The Kano Chronicle, an anonymous nineteenth-century compilation based largely on oral traditions, claims that Islam was introduced into

Kano in the reign of 'Ali Yaji (1349–85) as mentioned earlier. According to this work:

> In Yaji's time the Wangarawa came, bringing Islam and numbering up to forty in all. When they came, they advised the *Sarki* to observe ritual prayer (*al-salat*), which he did. They appointed an Imam and a muezzin (*muadhdhin*) and a man to slaughter beasts according to Islamic law (*sharia*); they also appointed a *qadi* (*alkali* in the Hausa language). The *Sarki* gave orders that every town in Kano country should observe ritual prayer and they did so. He also built a rectangular mosque and the five prayers were celebrated there.[5]

This minor wave of Islamic influence was apparently rather transient. Yaji's successor, Kanajeje (1390–1410), was a follower of the traditional religion. During the tenure of office of Ya'qub (1452–63) there was an influx of the Fulani who brought with them books on Islamic law and theology and Arabic grammar. His successor, Muhammad Rimfa, started to pursue more active Islamic policies including the erection of mosques and the observance of the two festival prayers *Id al-Fitr*, which marks the end of the fast in the month of *Ramadan*; and *Id al-Adha* which celebrates the pilgrimage to Mecca. Muhammad Rimfa also began to look to the Muslim scholars for advice on how to rule his state, and when Al-Maghili, a Muslim scholar who had travelled far and wide, visited Kano towards the end of his regime, he asked him to write a treatise on Islamic administration for him. It was during his reign that the sacred tree of Kano (*ardeb*) was cut down – an act traditionally associated with Al-Maghili – marking a clear and official break with the non-Islamic past. A further step towards marking the break with the traditional beliefs and practices was the construction of a mosque on the site of the old sacred tree. Scholars from Timbuctu also began to pay visits to Kano to teach and preach from the last quarter of the fifteenth century and it was at this time that the *Mukhtasar* of Khalil, now the standard work of Islamic law used in West Africa, was first introduced to Kano by a visiting Egyptian scholar.

Katsina, too, has a tradition of Islam going back to the mid-fourteenth century, but Islam did not gain much ground there until the end of the fifteenth century when scholars from Timbuctu also began to visit the city, often on their way back from pilgrimage; the famous and ubiquitous Al-Maghili also stayed there.

The Gobir area, immediately to the north of Hausa country, however, was reported by Leo Africanus in the early sixteenth century to be still persisting with the old religion. By the seventeenth century Katsina itself had established a tradition of Islamic scholarship and produced indigenous scholars such as Dan Marina (d. 1655) and Dan Masanih (d. 1667), some of whose works have been handed down to us.

In Zaria, Islam appears to have made only a meagre impact until after the early nineteenth-century Jihad of Usman dan Fodio. Islam among the Hausa (or Habe) was probably mainly confined to the urban areas, but in some areas the immigrant Muslim Fulani, especially of the Toronkawa, may have converted some of the Hausa cultivators. The expansion of Islam in the era of Usman dan Fodio's Jihad is the subject of another chapter in this book and we need not go into it here.

Nigerian Muslims, like Muslims all over the world, regardless of differences of sects or brotherhoods, are united in the belief in the oneness of God, Allah. This is expressed in their confession of faith: 'There is no God but Allah and Muhammad is his Prophet.' Furthermore, they are obliged to pray at five specified times every day, fast for thirty days in the month of Ramadan, offer alms to the needy, and perform the holy pilgrimage to Mecca and Medina at least once in their lifetime, if they have the means. Islam means simply 'submission', that is, submission to the will of Allah. The Koran is Islam's holy writ which contains all a believer ought to know in order to be in good relations with his Creator. Since Islam is both a religion as well as a culture, the Arab culture with which it has been associated from its inception has left indelible marks on some aspects of Nigerian culture, such as language, dress and writing. Similarly, Islam too has accommodated and acquired Nigerian cultural traits which are observable among Muslims in the various Nigerian communities.

It is noteworthy that the cause of Islam has been greatly enhanced by the fact that each believer is enjoined to spread the faith. Unlike the European Christians who presented trade and religion as two separate tasks championed by two separate sets of agents and motivated by two different sets of objectives, Islam had, among its agents of expansion, preachers who were traders and traders who were preachers. The activities of Muslim sects and societies like the Ahmadiyya, Ansar-Ud-Deen, and others, and formal Islamic education and training provided in colleges and institutions of higher education, have also aided the process of Islamisation in Nigeria.

Christianity in Nigeria

Beginnings and expansion

The beginnings and spread of Christianity in Nigeria were a product, by and large, of the nineteenth and the twentieth centuries respectively. We should mention, though, the problems that delayed the advent of Christianity into Nigeria before the nineteenth century and say something of the attempts, futile as they were, made by various Christian groups to plant Christianity in Nigeria before 1800. The first point to mention here is the erroneous idea of the Europeans about Africa as 'the dark continent'. The conception, born of ignorance, lingered on for a considerable length of time and delayed European contact with Africa.

Coupled with this problem was the problem of communication and transportation which were at that time not well developed. Another problem was that of climate. Christian missionaries from the temperate regions of the world feared coming to Nigeria since it is situated within the hot tropics. The problems constituted by the forest zones of Nigeria cannot be over-emphasised in this regard. The tropical forest with its epidemic of insects or fungal pests like the anopheles mosquito which

Fig. 15.1 a & b   Islamic and Christian buildings. Iragbiji Baptist Church (above) and the New Mosque at Kano (below)

causes malaria, and the tsetse-fly which causes sleeping sickness, contributed in no small measure to the delay. Furthermore, most of the rivers in Nigeria were not navigable; inter-communal conflicts and the wars of the nineteenth century made travelling perilous; and the language barrier impeded communication for a while before interpreters could be produced.

It must also be pointed out that convincing the adherents of the older traditional religions and winning them to Christ presented a major challenge. To them the heritage of their forebears was of paramount importance. Thus there were reports of how older people remained adamant and unpersuaded by Christian missionaries. The existence of age-old religions, loyalty to the ancestors, the conception that the white man was a stranger and an intruder, all contributed to the slow pace of Christian influence in Nigeria before 1800. And in northern Nigeria, Islam had become so well entrenched that it was not easy for missionaries to gain even a toehold there.

Now let us trace the spasmodic growth of Christian influence in Nigeria before 1800, starting from north to south. The amount of historical information concerning the early history of Christianity in northern Nigeria varies from place to place. Less is known of those parts in which there are now many Christians than of those in which there are a few. This is because Christians are mainly found in the formerly traditional areas where there were no written records. In the Muslim areas of the far north there was literacy in the Arabic script among the educated, and records were kept. There appear to be some traces of the Christian faith in the religion of the Bachama of the Numan division, in Gongola state, in the Nzeanzo cult, and in the religion of the Kilba of Adamawa with their belief in hell and in the use of the cross. The use of the cross was also noticed in Jukunland. It was suggested by Sultan Bello of Sokoto that the Gobir people of Sokoto province were originally a group of Coptic Christians who had emigrated from Egypt. Frobenius also made a number of suggestions as to early contact with Christians in the Nile valley. If, as he suggests, the founder of Daura was a Persian Christian named Ali-el-Baghadi, this legendary snake-killer would be the Nigerian equivalent of that legendary middle eastern Christian, St George, and the killing of the snake represents the replacement of the traditional religion by the Christian faith. These traces of Christianity are discussed by Richard Gray, but he is inclined to leave the question open. There was an abortive attempt to introduce Christianity from the north. This was the mission of Father Carlo de Genove who in 1710 and 1711, travelled overland from Tripoli with the aim of beginning a station in Bornu. Unfortunately he died in Katsina.[6]

Now let us switch our attention to the south. Except for the futile attempts by the Portuguese to bring Christianity to the people of Benin and Warri, European contact with the Bight of Benin, dating back to the fifteenth century, was primarily commercial until about the middle of the nineteenth century.

The introduction of missionary propaganda through the opposite ends of the Nigerian coastline, Badagry and Old Calabar in 1842 and 1847 respectively, altered the above situation and marked an important turning-point in the political and social structure of southern Nigeria. So formidable did Christianity become that by the end of the nineteenth century, it threatened to overthrow the Islamic revolution which had occurred between 1804 and 1831 in northern Nigeria.

Any historical discussion of Christianity in Nigeria must begin with Sierra Leone. Not only was the colony of Sierra Leone the first field of modern missionary endeavour in West Africa but it also produced numerous black missionaries who fostered the growth of the faith in all the coastal cities. Moreover, because it happened to be the first to receive the gospel, Sierra Leone led West Africa in church organisation, and then in supplanting the European-controlled mission and in creating an African-controlled church.

The colony of Sierra Leone was founded by a philanthropic company as a home for repatriated slaves. In 1789 the first freed slaves arrived from England. In 1792 over one thousand black loyalists arrived from Nova Scotia, and in 1800 further New World repatriates, the Maroons, came from Jamaica. By 1808 the colony had proved too great a financial undertaking to the Sierra Leone Company and it became a crown colony. After the Act of Abolition in 1807, the British Government worked hard to put an end to the slave trade.

The Church Missionary Society (CMS) was founded in 1799 by men who had been active in the Sierra Leone Company. It was not surprising that Sierra Leone should be one of the first areas of interest.

Before the slave trade was completely abolished many ex-slaves of Freetown in the 1840s began, for various reasons, to migrate to cities all along the coast of West Africa, from the Gambia to Calabar. Some returned to their areas of origin; others searched for their relations, and some settled in other cities for the sake of the economic opportunities available there. By 1860, there existed small communities of Christian ex-slaves – Sierra Leonians, or 'Saro' as they were called in Lagos – in all the cities along the coast and several towns in the interior. The missionaries in Sierra Leone were called to start Christian work in these towns.

The largest migration of these freed men flowed back to Lagos and its hinterland, the Yoruba country, and especially to Abeokuta, the headquarters of the Yoruba Egba kingdom. Both Anglican and Methodist missionaries responded to the call of the Christian Egba and began missionary activities in Abeokuta in 1846. In 1851 the British government forced the closing of the slave markets in Lagos and placed a consul there to prevent illicit smuggling of slaves. The missionaries came to Lagos immediately. Because of its location, for commercial and political reasons Lagos attracted a large number of the repatriates. The Christian church developed rapidly. The history of Sierra Leone was repeated. The city was divided into parishes, each with its own church – St Paul's (Breadfruit), St John's (Aroloya), Holy Trinity (Ebute Ero), St Peter's (Faji) and St Jude's (Ebute Metta). Christ Church, where Europeans and most of the westernised Africans worshipped, was without a parish. Educational institutions similar to those of Freetown were developed early in Lagos. Again like Freetown, Lagos was organised, as soon as the churches were self-supporting, into a 'native' pastorate. This organisation began in 1876 and was completed in 1887 after a decade of European missionary opposition.

In Lagos, when the independent pastorate was established, Europeans were no longer in ministerial positions except in Christ Church, which remained outside the pastorate. A few remained employed in educational work. The European missionaries concentrated upon the interior cities of Abeokuta, Ibadan and Oyo. It is noteworthy that in Lagos and Freetown the organisation stopped short of appointing an African bishop, both being under the English bishop of Sierra Leone. It was only later that Samuel Ajayi Crowther was made the first African bishop.

It is also important to point out that the coastal areas of Nigeria – Lagos and Badagry, for example – could be regarded as melting-pots of various Christian denominations and that they served, and to some extent are still serving, as centres from which Christianity reached out into the hinterland of Nigeria.

The emergence of African churches

Christianity has been both cause and catalyst of social change in Nigeria. One of the most prominent features of modern Africa has been the emergence of independent churches, founded by Africans in protest against some features of the Christianity of the missionary societies sponsored from abroad. Here we will highlight the reason for the phenomenon in the history of the Christian church in Nigeria.[7]

During the formative era (1891–1921) the African church movement developed into five major denominations which claimed the adherence of one-third of the Christian Yoruba, and one-fifth of the total Christian population of Southern Nigeria. All the Protestant mission societies – the CMS, Wesleyan Methodists, and Southern Baptists – experienced a revolt within their membership which resulted in the establishment of African churches essentially similar to their parent societies.

The African churches in Nigeria constituted a revolt against changing mission practice in the twentieth century, but lightly veiled under proclamations of adherence to policy laid down in the nineteenth century. Broad and liberal theories aiming to establish churches culturally identified with Africa were replaced by policies of stifling conformity which sought to produce in Africa an exact replica of the parent denomination.

Policies of conformity pursued after 1891 were not entirely new. They originated in the controversy over English missionary bishops (1853–62), which the CMS opposed because they made an indigenous episcopate 'forever unattainable'. Once foreign control was established, it would not be easily given up. The CMS made an attempt to circumvent the obvious goal of English control by the appointment of Samuel Ajayi Crowther as a missionary bishop to inaugurate the African episcopate. On the question of polygyny or plurality of wives, it was the CMS that became the conformists in Venn's Memorandum of 1857, which was labelled intolerant by high church opinion.

By 1891 the policy of conformity had triumphed in dogma and the episcopate. The Lambeth ruling against polygyny in 1888, a pronouncement against the entire social set-up of Africa, placed the authority of the church behind Venn's Memorandum. When a European succeeded Bishop Ajayi Crowther, the CMS rejected African leadership, realising the advantages of an English episcopate to ensure the society's control. Control became an issue of paramount importance.

No compromise with the new policy was possible. The choice was either to submit or revolt. The African churches which decided in favour of rebellion became not merely rebels, but outlaws. They remained on the defensive against the overwhelming tide of foreign money, foreign personnel, foreign government, foreign education, and foreign thought and idiosyncracies which swept the mission societies along to statistical success.

Africans became impatient with societies which put so many hurdles in the way of 'heathen neophytes'. As late as 1900, Christianity was almost exclusively confined to a small coterie of western-educated Africans, living in separate quarters of 'pagan' cities which were slowly turning to Islam. The popularity of Islam was due to the same reasons which sustained the growth of the African churches – adaptation to the African milieu. It was in consequence of this adaptation that some Christian missionaries in the nineteenth century were forced to describe Islam as an 'African religion'.

Missionary teaching and other alien influences were creating a people who were losing faith in their 'pagan' deities. They were denied membership in the missions until they possessed an intellectual grasp of Christianity and had divested themselves of wives and children. African churchmen held the belief that this denied the workings of a divine power. The last votaries of the traditional religion were left in a 'spiritual vacuum'. Intellectual attainment left a rather cold impression upon men seeking a new faith.

Yoruba society, for example, sought within Islam a bulwark against the moral laxity introduced by Christians. A good number held the belief that the traditional morals of the Yoruba were superior to those offered by Christianity. The church's duty lay in reinforcing this code. The Yoruba convert was not only expected to accept a new faith but develop a new set of values, or rather, a different conscience. It was the time it took to develop this different conscience which caused the delay in acceptance into the mission. Into this 'spiritual vacuum' Islam stepped, ready to uphold the known moral code and offering a spiritual exercise – the daily prayers (*al-salat*) – in contrast to the mission catechumen classes. Upon these arrangements the African church based its evangelistic method of preach, baptise, and teach, thus reversing the mission's strategy of preach, teach, and baptise.

Polygyny was only one of the issues which ought to have been widely debated in the Christian community. Chieftaincy and societies such as the *Ogboni* fraternity were as easily disposed of as polygyny as a snap pronouncement of an uninformed bishop without public debate.

Neither the missions nor the African churches, as organisations, took an active part in politics. It was not difficult to discover where their loyalties lay, and they usually took opposing positions. The missions applauded the extension of British sovereignty. They hesitated to challenge the abuses of imperial rule or to acknowledge the justice of protest movements. They actively opposed the early nationalist movements. African churchmen were engaged in all the early protest movements of Lagos – the land tenure issue, the seditious ordinance bill, the extension of the franchise, and the beginnings of the National

Congress of British West Africa.

The first of the African churches of Lagos came into existence in 1888 out of the mission organisation of the Southern Baptist Convention, which had its headquarters in Richmond, Virginia. The Native Baptist organisation which came into being did not claim to be an African church, but Native Baptist as its name implied. The aim of the schismatics was to create a truly Baptist organisation governed by the congregation as in the United States of America. After a schism in 1903 over the issue of Baptist versus African, one wing of the Native Baptists – Araromi – aligned itself with the African churches, and its pastor became a leading exponent of the aims of the movement.

It is noteworthy that today the 'native' pastorate, or Ethiopianism, is a phenomenon to be reckoned with in most of the Nigerian churches. The struggle for hegemony on the part of the black Christians has been crowned with enviable success and a new dimension has been added in the form of the rise of pentecostal, spiritual or Aladura churches[8] now operating all over Nigeria, mostly in tune with the local milieu in which they find themselves. In addition to this wide variety of religious experiences and practices now available, Christianity brought to Nigeria western education and value systems.

Conclusion

People opt for one religion or another for different reasons. What is clearly evident in Nigeria today is a period of religious efflorescence in the Muslim and the Christian faiths. The prophetic, pentecostal or prayer sects (Aladura) are perhaps the greatest beneficiaries of this religious flowering. Attempts have been made to assess the numbers of adherents to each religion, but most of the figures are unreliable. It is safe to say that while the number of true believers in the Nigerian traditional religion may be declining, Islam and Christianity continue to gain more adherents. However, it is also true that while many Nigerians hold to either Islam or Christianity it is not unusual that at the same time a significant number still patronise some aspects of the traditional religion. A pastor or an *al-hajj* can be found observing some traditional rites which are alien to his Christian or Islamic faith, and he may in fact be using the services of the traditional healers and medicine-men.

What we have attempted in this chapter is a survey of general features, broad patterns of development; we have not delved into the purely canonical ramifications and controversies. We have touched upon how man relates to God in the variety of religious groups. We must stress that religion makes available to every man the means of making contact with the spiritual power of his choice, deriving strength from the ultimate realities which man believes determine his destiny.

The place of religion in Nigerian culture cannot be overemphasised: it provides a system of values relevant to the fundamental requirements of individuals and society. At every crisis, personal or collective, religion is called upon to provide solutions, prevent disintegration, and strengthen the bond of human cohesion and sanctity of life and conduct.

Notes

1 E. B. Idowu, *African Traditional Religion: a definition* (London: SCM Press, 1973), p. 149; H. Sawyer, *God: ancestor or creator* (London: Longman, 1970).

2 Other names include, in Igbo: *Chineke* – one who creates, or the creator; Yoruba: *Olórun* – the owner of the sky-heaven; *Olúwa* – the owner of being or existence. See E. B. Idowu, *Olódùmarè: God in Yoruba belief* (Longman, 1966).

3 Eliade Mircea, *The Sacred and the Profane* (New York: Harper & Row, 1961), p. 99.

4 E. G. Parrinder, *African Traditional Religion* (London: Sheldon Press, 1974), p. 105.

5 The *muadhdhin* is the announcer of the hours of prayer; a *qadi* or an *alkali* is a judge. See J. F. Ade Ajayi and I. Espie (eds) *A Thousand Years of West African History* (Ibadan: Ibadan University Press, 1972), p. 125; Thomas Hodgkin, *Nigerian Perspectives: an historical anthology* (London: Oxford University Press, 1960), pp. 75–76; 'Penetration of Islam into Nigeria', *Nigerian Journal of Islam* (1), 1970; J. S. Trimingham, *A History of Islam in West Africa* (Oxford: Clarendon Press, 1976).

6 See Leo Frobenius, *The Voice of Africa* (2 vols.), (London, 1913), pp. 370–71; A. B. Mathews, 'The Kisra legend', *African Studies*, IX (1950), pp. 144–47; Richard Gray, 'Christian traces and a Franciscan mission in the Central Sudan 1700–1711', *Journal of African History*, I (1967), pp. 383–93. See also Ogbu Kalu (ed.), *Christianity in West Africa: the Nigerian story* (Ibadan: Daystar Press, 1978).

7 See J. B. Webster, *The African Churches Among the Yoruba* (Oxford: Clarendon Press, 1964).

8 J. D. Y. Peel, *Aladura: a religious movement among the Yoruba* (London: Oxford University Press). The list of Aladura churches in Nigeria includes: Christ Apostolic Church, Cherubim and Seraphim; the Church of the Lord; Gospel Faith; Celestial Church of Christ; Church of the Lord; Holy Flock of Christ; etc.

16   The visual arts of Nigeria

Sue Picton

When discussing the visual arts of Nigeria, we must remember two important basic points. Firstly, our knowlege of their history and development is still far from complete. Secondly, we should disregard the European category of 'fine art' as opposed to 'craft'. Their separation came about with the devaluation of labour during the Industrial Revolution in Europe, but the words for 'artist' (concerned with producing 'fine art') and 'artisan' (that is labourer or craftsman) are from the same Latin root. John Ojo has discussed the problem of defining the word 'art' in relation to African culture at length.[1] We need to remember that the art forms and styles existing in Africa today cannot be understood from a purely aesthetic viewpoint but must be seen in their particular historical, social and economic contexts. As Dennis Williams says, 'the existence of a work of art implies processes outside itself linking it to the life from which it has emerged and whose product it is'.[2]

The most widespread art medium of Nigeria is undoubtedly the spoken and sung word. This is dealt with in other chapters in this book. The visual arts of Nigeria comprise an amazing diversity of traditional forms and motifs in every conceivable material. We consider not only the three-dimensional forms, notably the sculptural traditions in stone, ivory, brass and other metals, pottery and wood, but the two-dimensional also: the painting on rocks and walls; textiles, weaving, dyeing and embroidery; other fabrics such as bark-cloth; beadwork, raffia, calabash decoration and so on. Going beyond these two essentially static media we must also remember masquerade and the arts of the body, the most universal of all visual arts, and architecture. Moreover of all the countries in sub-Saharan Africa, Nigeria has the most evidence of ancient sculptural traditions.

The three-dimensional arts

Stone

A great deal of stone carving is found in Nigeria, very little of it executed within living memory and some of considerable antiquity. The rocks used have included granite, quartz – a very difficult medium to work – and steatite or soapstone. The latter has been the most widely used as it is a soft though durable stone that can be easily worked with metal tools. The two main groups of stone carvings are those of Yoruba country, scattered in an area within a radius of sixty miles of Ife, and those in the Cross River valley.

In Ife a number of figures, monoliths, stools and small soapstone carvings have been found in the sacred groves around the town. We do not know when they were made but many of them have been given a date between the tenth and fifteenth centuries AD – that is, the so-called classical age of Ife, when the famous brasses and terracottas were made. Ife is assumed to have been a powerful city-state at this time. Although some of these carvings are still used in ritual today we cannot know their original significance. The largest of these, carved in granite and about 18 feet in height, is called *Opa Oranmiyan*, the staff of Oranmiyan. He was the son of both Oduduwa, the mythical founder of Ife and Ogun, the God of iron and a son of Oduduwa, by a captive woman. He is said to have used it in fighting the enemies of Ife. The use of the remarkable quartz stools however, is illustrated by a small brass casting and a partially reconstructed pottery figure that were discovered during archaeological excavations. They are the seat and footstool of an important person, probably an Oni, king.[3]

At Eshure in western Ekiti a number of stone figures have been found that seem to resemble those at Ife. Another, quite different from those at Ife, is the Eshu figure in the market of Igbajo. Eshu is the Yoruba god of chance and uncertainty, the trickster of Yoruba mythology, and every marketplace in Yorubaland has a shrine to him where offerings are made to prevent trouble and strife breaking out. This is usually a pillar of laterite but Igbajo is exceptional in having a representational carving. Why this should be we cannot know and no information has yet emerged from the oral traditions of the area.

The largest group of stone carvings in Yorubaland are those in the town of Esie, in Kwara state, where about 800 male and female figures carved in soapstone have been found. Some have elaborate headdresses or hairstyles and the majority are seated on stools. Although every year a ritual hunting ceremony takes place around the carvings it seems that this was not their original purpose. One popular oral tradition relates that they represent the former inhabitants of the area turned to stone by the intervention of gods.[4]

Three hundred miles to the east of Ife in an area of the Cross River valley now inhabited by northern Ekoi peoples are the carved stone figures known as Akwanshi or Atol. They occur in small groups, mainly in existing or abandoned village sites, and vary in size from about one foot to six feet in height. They are all carved in low relief with human features and most have a protuberent navel. It is thought that they were memorials to dead chiefs but the date of the carvings is uncertain. The present-day use of Akwanshi during annual ceremonies does not necessarily reflect older practices.[5] There is little if any stone carving practised today in Nigeria.

Ivory

Wherever there is a tradition of sculpture it is likely to include carving in ivory. This is a very hard, durable material that requires great skill to carve. There are a large number of ivory carvings that have survived for hundreds of years, mostly from Benin. Portuguese travellers of the early sixteenth century collected ivory objects of such great skill as to suggest that the tradition of ivory carving was already of great antiquity in Benin. These first European visitors found a highly developed kingdom there, with organised craft guilds working for the king, Oba, and chiefs. Regalia for the king and his chiefs, carved tusks (one tusk from every elephant killed in the kingdom had to be given to the Oba) for the ancestral altars, kolanut boxes and leopards sacred to the Oba and a metaphor of kingship, have all been carved in ivory. With the advent of the Portuguese, traders and craftsmen turned to making objects for export such as spoons with carved animal or bird handles for the ordinary sailor, and elaborate salt cellars and hunting horns for the wealthy. The Portuguese are themselves represented on many works of art from Benin together with traditional motifs.[6]

The Yoruba also have a long tradition of ivory carving and the Portuguese collected objects from this area as well. Today in Yorubaland small human figures and batons in ivory used by an Ifa priest can be found. Ifa is the divination method used by the Yoruba to solve problems, cure afflictions and make decisions. The batons, *iroke*, are used to strike the tray that the diviner uses to record the answers given him by his apparatus, and 'to make the oracle speak'. The most common representations carved on these *iroke* are the warrior-hero on horseback, and the kneeling woman bearing a bowl. In Yorubaland elders and visitors command great respect and women traditionally kneel to present gifts, especially to present kolanuts placed in a bowl. In Owo ivory regalia is carved in Benin style for chiefs (see the section on pottery for the relationship between Owo and Benin).

In the past elephants and therefore supplies of ivory were much more plentiful than today, but in Benin and in parts of Yorubaland ivory carving is still practised, serving both traditional and, more recently, tourist demands and thus maintaining the pattern of the sixteenth century.

Metalwork

The most important metals used in Nigerian art are iron and copper, and they have very different uses because of their different chemical properties. Iron is the harder metal and is used mainly for tools and weapons, although it does have some ceremonial or decorative uses. It is worked by hammering at red-heat. Traditionally iron was made by smelting local iron-ore, but today there is so much scrap iron available (e.g. from motor cars) that smelting is rarely done. Copper is used mainly for decorative and ceremonial purposes. It is a much softer metal and it is worked either by hammering it cold (unlike iron) or by casting the metal in molten form, usually by the lost-wax process (it is only possible to cast iron with modern industrial machinery). Copper is often alloyed with other metals, in particular, tin which gives bronze or zinc which gives brass. Both these alloys usually have some lead added as this makes them easier to cast. These metals were obtained by trade, originally across the Sahara but later by trade with the Europeans.

The earliest evidence for iron working in sub-Saharan Africa is provided by the Nok culture, named after the village in Plateau state where the first discoveries were made. At Taruga the earliest iron smelting furnaces were discovered during archaeological investigations, together with some of the famous Nok pottery sculptures (see the section on pottery), iron objects and other materials.

The earliest uses of copper and its alloys in West Africa has been found in the Ibo village of Igbo-Ukwu, about 25 miles southeast of Onitsha. Objects were first discovered by accident, and later archaeological investigations showed the site to be a store-house for elaborately-decorated objects, including ceremonial bowls and cups, often copies of calabash shapes, staff heads, pendant ornaments and other ceremonial apparel. Nearby a burial chamber was excavated in which an obviously important person had been buried with the various regalia of his office including a crown, pectoral, fan, flywhisk, beaded metal armlets and a huge quantity of beads. The bronze objects had been cast with great skill sometimes in several stages, by the *cire perdue*, lost wax, process while the copper objects had been worked by smithing, hammering and chasing. The date of the site has been given as the ninth to tenth century AD. These objects with their elaborate and detailed decoration bear no relation in style to the later castings of Ife or Benin, but may relate to other finds of brass or bronze objects in Cross River state and elsewhere in southeastern Nigeria whose age is unknown. There is no record of casting in this area, but the concentration of wealth and social authority implied in the Igbo-Ukwu finds has some parallel with parts of Ibo society today where the Eze Nri, a priest king, has considerable religious importance.[7]

In Ife a number of brass heads were found, as well as the stone carvings mentioned earlier and the pottery sculptures to be described later. Leo Frobenius, a German anthropologist, arrived at Ife in 1910 and was the first European to spread the news of its now famous artistic traditions. He saw one brass head wearing a crown and several pottery sculptures and was so amazed by their quality that he was convinced they belonged to some remnant of ancient Greek civilisation!

The brass heads have not been satisfactorily dated, but are closely related in style to the pottery sculptures, which have been dated to between the tenth and fifteenth centuries AD. The Ife sculptors cast the heads and figures using the *cire perdue* method in both brass and pure copper, the latter metal requiring great technological skill for successful casting. As there is no continuing artistic tradition of metal or pottery sculpture in Ife, and as many of the sculptures that are in ritual use today seem to be so as a result of accidental discovery, we cannot be certain about the original use of these pieces. Some of them may be portraits of kings and chiefs reflecting the political structure of Ife as a city-state in that period of its history.[8]

Another important group of cast metal figures is the so-called Tsoede bronzes that were kept in Nupe villages on the south bank of the river Niger. Oral tradition states that Tsoede, the founder of the Nupe kingdom, on his escape from Idah brought these bronzes with him. One piece, a seated figure cast in pure copper, bears a close resemblance to the Ife heads, while the others appear more closely related in style and iconography to Benin.[9]

The city of Benin, capital of the Edo kingdom, is the home of probably the best known and certainly the most numerous brass and ivory sculptures in the whole of black Africa. Benin art forms are often referred to as 'court art' due to the fact that at least since the fifteenth century the specialist guilds of craftsmen were maintained by the king and provided for all his ceremonial needs. The early Benin castings that have been analysed have proved to be bronze but the objects cast from the sixteenth century onwards are of brass.

Benin is of special interst for the historian because there are so many sources of information about its past. There are oral traditions, the results of archaeological excavations, and European records of the past as well as present-day living evidence of ritual and political organisation and the works of art themselves. Although there are gaps we can at least be fairly sure of the broad development over a period of several hundred years and at least something of the significance of the continuing tradition of Benin art.

Objects cast in brass in Benin include memorial heads of royal ancestors, and the earlier trophy heads of captive rulers, figures of noblemen and warriors, animals, rectangular plaques illustrating court ceremonial and military exploits, regalia for the king and his chiefs, and ritual apparatus and furniture. Benin brass casting appears to have been at its height during the sixteenth century. The presence of the Portuguese at this time seems to have influenced the brass casters as well as the ivory carvers. The Portuguese imported large quantities of brass bracelets (manillas) for their trading activities which seem to have increased the quantity of metal available to the casters. Moreover, the visual impact of these strange-looking visitors and their goods gathered from both Europe and the Orient seems to have stimulated the Benin artists to create new forms and introduce new motifs.[10]

There are extensive but little known brass casting industries among the peoples of the northern Benue valley, stretching up to the Mandara mountains on the border with the Cameroons. All kinds of decorative, ritual and other objects are made but as yet little documented.

In Yoruba culture, the use of brass was restricted to certain cult groups. The most important of these groups is the Ogboni society. A small number of large cast brass figures are known, which were probably used inside the cult house, and some of them may date back to around AD 1800. These large figures are sometimes referred to as '*Onilè*', owner of the earth. Ogboni is a society in which, in the past, all senior men in a community would belong. Details of what went on at its meetings were kept secret from non-members but the term 'secret society' is highly misleading. Ogboni is a public institution, the members and officers of which are well known and it had considerable political judicial and ritual functions that varied from one place to another. The gesture of membership of the society, the left fist with thumb concealed over the right fist, is portrayed on these large brass castings. The commonest form

Fig. 16.1   Female Ogboni brass figure called onilè, *Yoruba*

Fig. 16.2   Terracotta head from the Nok culture

of casting found in Yorubaland, which is still being made today, is the *edan*, a pair of figures, one male and one female, usually joined by a chain. These are used in Ogboni ritual and every member of the Ogboni society has a pair of these figures, made for his initiation into the society. The making of these figures is not secret, but they became secret once adopted into ritual use. The Yoruba brass industry was traditionally based at Ijebu from where it spread to Abeokuta, but other centres of brass casting include Obo Ile and Obo Aiyegunle in Kwara state. Armlets, two face masks and stools have been found, but today it is the Ogboni society and to a much lesser extent the cult of Ogun, the god of iron and patron of all blacksmiths and warriors, that keep it going. The cult of Ogun in some areas requires title staffs in iron that end with brass figures, and ceremonial cutlasses with cast brass handles. Another cult using brass is that of Oshun, the river goddess. One of the few surviving Yoruba brass casters, Yemi Bisiri, has acquired an international reputation by producing figures, based on traditional forms, on commission from expatriates.[11]

The hammered brass industries of northern Nigeria, particularly of Bida, produced luxury vessels for use by the rich and important or as gifts by the emir or chiefs. They now survive largely by serving the tourist industry. The Nupe traditionally had a class-stratified society, but were conquered by the Fulani in 1851. The new Fulani emirs encouraged the organisation of craft workers into guilds and this, together with the regular gift-giving of the emir and others, did much to stimulate the hammered brass industries of Bida.[12]

It is interesting to note that a hammered brass-working industry also developed in Calabar in the late nineteenth century. Imported brass ware was decorated using traditional pokerwork designs as on the fans, calabashes and mirror cases used by girls in the fattening room. The designs and use of these decorated trays and bowls have become more varied and they now often form prestigious gifts to important people, frequently recording the highlights of their career with inscriptions in Efik and English.[13]

In Ikot-Ekpene Keith Nicklin reports a new brass industry using old brass manillas, bangles and shell cases, melting them down and recycling them to make church furniture, candle stands, swordsticks and bells. The goods are commissioned by local churches and sold to tourists in craft shops. This recycling of scrap metal is an important aspect of present-day crafts.[14]

All over Nigeria blacksmiths are still to be found working with iron and scrap metal of all kinds. In some areas these blacksmiths have produced fine decorative staffs and bells for ritual use and decorative oil lamps as well as the full range of agricultural implements and weapons.

In Akoko Edo, northern Bendel state, elaborate wrought-iron oil lamps were made in the past by the Uneme blacksmiths who still live in the area and up to the present day serve the northern Edo, Igbirra and the Yoruba of the Kabba area with all manner of iron and other metal tools, implements and weapons. The advent of paraffin lamps and electricity has reduced the need for traditional oil lamps, but a few examples of their fine work remain.

Among the Yoruba, wrought-iron staffs are used in a number of cults, with particular motifs associated with particular cults. For example, the iron staffs for Osanyin, the god Orisha, associated with traditional medicine, have sixteen birds in a circle around a central bird. The sixteen birds represent the sixteen basic signs of the Ifa oracle (see the section on wood and ivory) which provide a system of classification for all medicinal ingredients. In Benin the blacksmiths also made ceremonial decorative wrought-iron staffs for use in the medicine cult, Osun.

Among the Ibo the most famous blacksmiths came from the Awka,

Nkwerre and Abiriba areas. Blacksmiths from Awka have traditionally travelled all over southeastern Nigeria, providing a large number of peoples with blacksmithing services. The Ibo themselves use long, pointed, ceremonial wrought-iron staffs in the Ozo title-taking association.

Today, although lamps are rarely made, ceremonial staffs continue to be produced and in many areas blacksmiths have developed their activities to cater for modern requirements, using the huge variety of scrap metal available. Decorated tin trunks used for storage are popular in all areas and parts for machines and vehicles are often manufactured by the local blacksmith. In some places fancy metalwork has developed as a commercial art form to advertise the products of the blacksmith; Keith Nicklin reports that weather vanes in the form of aeroplanes are popular in Oron and Calabar. He also reports the work of Edet Anamukot of Obong Itam who has built up a thriving business selling soldered and welded scrap metal sheets in the form of masquerades, animals, humans and a range of modern images to the tourist trade.[15]

Finally, the work of Asiru Olatunde must be mentioned. A Yoruba artist from Oshogbo, he comes from a family of blacksmiths and has developed his own techniques for hammering and incising patterns on to sheets of aluminium and copper. His decorative panels illustrate scenes from traditional and modern life. Although a Muslim he often works on commission to Christian churches; for example, a pair of his aluminium panels illustrating scenes from the Bible decorate the doors to the Catholic chapel at the University of Ibadan.

His work is nearly always exhibited in a modern context, and he is one of the new generation of artists in Nigeria that is using a new medium, style, technique and patronage but draws on the traditions that have existed for hundreds of years. His panels are popular with both Nigerians and expatriates and have been exhibited in Europe, America, China and in several cities in Nigeria.[16]

Pottery

Not only was the earliest evidence of iron-working in sub-Saharan Africa found in the Nok culture, but also the earliest known sculpture. Pottery heads, figures and fragments have been collected over a large area, initially during open-cast mining activities and later during archaeological investigations. These finds have been made in an area of three hundred miles by a hundred miles taking in Abuja, Jos and the Benue valley. The Nok culture has been dated to between 500 BC and AD 200. Moreover, a pottery tradition still flourishes in many parts of Nigeria for both domestic and ritual use. With certain exceptions, pottery is the work of women and survives despite the influx during the last fifty years of manufactured bowls, buckets and so on in plastic and enamel. The basic materials are available free of charge and no expensive tools are required for pottery-making – only personal skill and time. Usually the same people make domestic pottery who also create pottery sculptures. Many writers have used the word 'terra-cotta' to describe pottery sculpture, but this is confusing. The same kind of clay is used for both domestic pottery and pottery sculpture.

Nok sculpture was probably baked in an open wood fire, as traditionally-made pottery is today, and displays a sophisticated technology. Some of the human heads found were originally part of full-length figures that have not survived so completely; most are stylised but others are naturalistic. There are also small figurines which are often complete, and these together with the heads provide many details of dress, hairstyle and personal adornment. Animals found include monkeys, elephants and snakes. However, apart from these visual details very little can be known of the people who lived at that time nor can archaeology tell us the use and significance of the sculpture. There are no surviving oral traditions relating to these people, but agricultural implements found with the sculptures in both stone and iron do indicate that they practised some form of settled agriculture.[17] It is interesting to note that research on the pottery in the village of Ushafa, northeast of Abuja and well within the classical Nok culture area, has shown a tradition of pottery sculpture used to decorate house roofs and graves. Domestic pottery of a very high standard continues to be made by women and is the main source of income for the village. Pottery sculptures are, however, no longer made but they can be found at former settlement sites. Unfortunately, no further details of their use or significance are available.[18] Other early settlement sites that have revealed pottery sculpture, unrelated stylistically to Nok or each other, are the excavated mounds at Daima in Borno state and at Yelwa in Sokoto state.

The Ife brasses already discussed were discovered or excavated amongst a much larger collection of pottery sculpture displaying a much greater variation in style and subject matter. Many heads, some freestanding, figures, animals and vessels have been found, a few complete but others in fragments. The pottery heads show more detail of hairstyle and headdress than the brasses and some are also striated with vertical fine lines down the face. The figures indicate a wealth of beaded decoration. Much of this pottery sculpture comes from the sacred groves in the forest around Ife while other examples were excavated in what were possibly former shrines. One of the most remarkable of the sculptures is a fragmentary and only partially reconstructed group showing a seated figure with attendants on each side. Of the animals found, the ram could represent those used in sacrifice. Potsherd pavements have also been discovered indicating the interiors of substantial buildings, but these have not survived.

No more can be said about the use and significance of Ife pottery sculpture than has been said about Ife stone-carving and brass-casting in the previous sections, but much archaeological investigation remains to be done.[19]

Owo, a city-state in the southeast of Yorubaland and founded, according to tradition, by the youngest son of the founder of Ife, has been subjected to strong Edo influences. Owo itself is less than a hundred miles from Benin city and the extent and power of the Edo kingdom in the fifteenth and sixteenth centuries clearly affected Owo. Benin architectural styles have been adopted for chiefs' houses, Benin chiefly titles have been introduced, and the regalia of the Olowo closely relates to that of the Oba of Benin. It is thus not surprising to find that sculptural styles in pottery, wood and brass today reflect the influence of Benin whereas the excavated pottery sculptures of the early fifteenth century show the influence of both Ife and Benin as well as a native Owo style. As ever, much archaeological excavation remains to be done.

From Benin there are pottery heads in the style of the brass heads, some of which date back to the sixteenth century or earlier. These heads are used today by the chiefs of the guild of brass-casters for their own ancestral altars in the same way as the Oba uses the brass heads. These heads are used to day by the chiefs of the guild of brass-casters, who are men, who continue to make these pottery heads; other pots for both domestic and ritual use are made by various groups of women potters in and around the city. Some of the pots in ritual use for Olokun, the lord of great waters and provider of health, wealth and fertility (mud sculpture also features in Olokun worship and will be dealt with later), are decorated with relief figures. These represent, for example, female devotees who have received the most important gift of Olokun: children.

Olokun is identified specifically with the Ethiope River, the tributaries of which flow through the Benin kingdom, and the river bank is the point of contact between the divine world of Olokun and the earthly worshipper. The pot is made of clay from the river bank and is filled each day with fresh river water as an appropriate representation of the life-giving qualities of Olokun. Not only the mud for the pots but the mudfish that are considered the most efficacious sacrifice, and the python believed to be the messenger of Olokun, are found at the bank of the river.

The Yoruba continue to manufacture domestic pottery in various centres but the more elaborately decorated ritual pots and relief sculptures traditionally associated with their various gods have almost ceased to be made. These pots still exist in many shrines dedicated to the different Yoruba deities, *orisha*, but particularly on altars dedicated to Shango, the god of thunder and to Erinle, a river god. The relief decoration on these pots often depicts the implements of the cult such as the double-headed axe and gourd rattle of Shango. The axes are thought to represent the thunderbolt believed to have been hurled from the sky by Shango and unearthed by his worshippers wherever lightning has struck, but which are in fact Stone Age axes, relics of earlier inhabitants of the area.[20] In the past the motifs and symbols on ritual pots were usually those relating to the particular *orisha* they were intended to serve, but in recent times researchers have found the same pot used for any of a number of *orisha*.[21]

The Waja and Longuda, neighbouring people north of the Upper Benue valley, have a pottery tradition that includes the making of clay figures that are used as charms in curing illness. As yet there has been little research in the area, so little else is known.

The Dakakari people of the Zuru area southwest of Sokoto have a tradition of pottery-making that includes the making of grave monuments to decorate a family burial mound. Any women in the community can make domestic pottery, but the exclusive rights to the manufacture of grave sculpture were held by the women of particular families, usually one family per village. The ordinary man in a village will simply have common domestic pottery that is purchased in the market to decorate his burial mound, while important or wealthy men will commission grave sculptures and/or 'pots of the grave'. The sculptures can take the form of animals, human or equestrian figures all with their mouths open as a sign of mourning, and the 'pots of the grave' are specially decorated honey pots with their lids sealed. The village head is entitled to have all these kinds of grave ornament and they are placed at level ground, not on a mound, inside a thatched hut. Moreover, he is buried alone, unlike other men who warrant different combinations of sculpture and/or 'pots of the grave', who have their wives and unmarried daughters buried with them. Thus a man's status in the community is indicated after his death by the various combinations of grave sculpture and/or household pottery found on his burial mound and/or the type of burial place accorded to him.[22]

All over southeastern Nigeria the pottery tradition includes the making of large ceremonial palm-wine pots, that are usually decorated in a variety of ways; some with relief decorations in the form of knobs, handles or animal motifs. These pots serve an important purpose in the community, as the ceremonial communal drinking of palm-wine is a central feature of all ritual and social activities. Moreover, as Keith Nicklin says, 'the communal drinking of palm-wine is an overt act of fellowship and expresses a stranger's good intent. There is a belief that any evil person who partakes of wine from a ceremonial pot will die.'[23] Thus the pot itself is an agent of social control.

Domestic pottery-making is a continuing tradition in most parts of Nigeria still fulfilling a social and economic need. In some areas the manufacture is centralised in particular places to serve a wide area, while in other areas most villages contain potters serving their own community.

The shapes, techniques of manufacture and patterns and methods of decoration vary from region to region but the general principles are the same. No wheel is used, and the pottery is always open-fired at a much lower temperature than that obtained in the European-type kiln. The porous nature of these pots, given the structure of the clay and firing methods, makes them ideally suited to water storage, where evaporation keeps the water cool in a way no manufactured vessel can, and for cooking on a wood fire. They are still cheap compared with aluminium, enamel, glass and plastic goods, and where refrigerators and modern cookers are not available, more suitable for the required purpose.

It is the tradition of the more elaborate ritual pot-making that has suffered most in the last fifty years or so. There is a falling away from traditional cult practice; most children are attending school and are therefore not able to spend the time with their mothers learning the more complicated techniques required, they are also acquiring new value systems. However, the tourist market, both expatriate and Nigerian, has provided a new stimulus in some areas. In one Akoko-Edo village, Oja, the women potters in the last ten years have built up a thriving business serving the tourists, who are mainly Nigerians. They use their traditional methods to produce new forms based on, for example, flower vases and jugs, but decorated with the traditional relief sculpture used on ritual pots. New motifs such as hedgehogs have also been incorporated into the decoration and others have been acquired from the changing world they live in. Alongside this new activity, however, the traditional forms for both domestic and ritual use continue to be made and find a market.

Attention must be given here to the late Michael Cardew's work in setting up the pottery training centre at Abuja. Given the rich and widespread pottery tradition in Nigeria, the colonial government asked Michael Cardew, a well-known English potter, to come and develop it using the potter's wheel, the technique of glazing, and high temperature firing that are found in Europe and elsewhere.

Michael Cardew was so impressed by the traditional Gwari pottery being made in the area around Abuja that with the consent and support of the Emir he decided to base his centre in Abuja. He brought in local women and Hausa male potters and taught them the new techniques. He encouraged them to adapt traditional shapes and decoration for the new products, as well as introducing the imported cup, tea and coffe'e set and so on. At first these new pots were too expensive and not as suitable as traditional pottery for the Nigerian market but they built up a large expatriate and export demand. In recent years, however, the pottery made at Abuja and that from other potteries set up by former students of the centre has become popular among middle-class Nigerians, as their lifestyles have changed and the demand within Nigeria is now increasing.[24]

Mud sculpture and moulded decoration on the walls of buildings should be mentioned here. Mud sculpture, despite its name, is made from the same materials as pottery sculpture but is unfired. It is used to decorate shrines, cult houses and dwellings in many areas. The Mbari houses of the Ibo, the shrines to various deities of the Edo, palaces of the Yoruba and the urban buildings of the Hausa are probably the best known. The Mbari houses have been described by John Ojo as 'perhaps the best example of the association of art with social life'.[25] These houses include the arts of painting, mud relief and sculpture in an elaborate architectural setting. Mbari are built for a number of reasons including the propitiation of a particular god in order to avoid or repair some disaster such as famine, drought, epidemic or warfare. A group of people including men, women and children are selected from the community and set apart to do this work, and the whole range of social, religious and economic life is represented in the sculpture. Sacrifices are made, songs and dances are performed, all as part of the building process, and the changing environment of the community as well as taboo subjects are displayed. For example, the white man in various roles, new technology, masquerades normally not seen close to by women and children, and perverted forms of sexual intercourse have all been represented.

The mud sculpture of the Edo has traditionally served the needs of various cults. In some Olokun shrines there are sculptured figures of Olokun dressed as a king in full ceremonial regalia alongside figures of Ogun, the god of those who use iron tools, recognised by the tools and weapons hanging around his neck. Other shrines include figures of soldiers, titled chiefs and court musicians.

The tradition of mud sculpture is not now practised so widely for much the same reasons as the making of ritual pottery, but in Benin some priestesses of urban cults are introducing mud sculpture to their shrines because 'the gods have demanded them'.[26]

In Benin and all over Nigeria a new medium, cement, has been used to develop the tradition of mud sculpture and relief decoration. It is widely available and, although not cheap, it is easily worked and very durable. It has become popular to decorate the entrance to government buildings, such as schools, that have achieved positions of great importance in modern Nigerian society, or houses of the wealthy and powerful. Grave ornaments are fashionable with Christians, particularly among the Ibibio and Annang of southeastern Nigeria, those adhering to traditional religions and in some cases with Muslims. In all these uses of cement we find that traditional motifs and images are used alongside modern symbols of power and authority, such as policemen or soldiers, symbols of technological advance like the bicycle or car, Christian imagery that includes angels and crosses, and Islamic geometric designs. In western Nigeria there is an older tradition of mud sculpture or relief decoration now executed in cement, that uses floral and other motifs brought back from Brazil with the freed slaves.

Thus we can see that although the traditions of domestic pottery, pottery sculpture and mud sculpture have been affected by the changes that have taken place in Nigerian society over the last fifty years or so, they have not died out altogether, and pottery of a high quality continues to be made today. Cement is a new factor in the economic life of the community and has thus given rise to a new but related art form that is responding to changing religious and social values. We may suppose that without the tradition of pottery and mud sculpture or relief decoration, cement would have remained simply a building material.

Wood

Wood has been the most widespread medium used for carving or sculpture during the present century as it probably was in the past. Where there has been a tradition of stone, ivory, pottery or metal sculpture we can assume there was probably one of working in wood. However, wood is far less durable, given a tropical climate, and it is vulnerable to fire and to infestation by insects such as termites, so less can be known of its past history. The oldest known wood carvings in Nigeria are the hardwood figures, Ekpu, from Oron opposite Calabar at the estuary of the Cross River that were carved to portray a dead man and then kept with others in a special shrine. The oldest of these is said to date from the late eighteenth century. However there is a Yoruba divination tray in a German museum that is believed to be from the seventeenth century.

Wood has been carved in a remarkable diversity of forms serving a wide variety of purposes. These range from the roughly cut branch of a tree used as a·post for part of a house or roofing timbers and simple domestic utensils, to the elaborately carved and decorated verandah posts and doors of the Yoruba and Nupe, and cult objects of many other areas of Nigeria. There are food and gift bowls, mortars, mirror frames, combs, spoons, loom pulleys and swords, stools, drums, canoe paddles, staffs, human and animal figures and, of course, masks, which will be discussed later.

Wood carving is a male activity and in some areas, such as among the Nupe, Yoruba and in Benin, professional groups of carvers exist with a formal apprenticeship system. In other areas, such as among the Kalabari Ijo, Ebira, northern Edo and Tiv, carving is a part-time activity and learnt informally. These days, however, even where professional groups exist it is rarely the sole source of income. Moreover, the professional carvers do not usually concern themselves with simple undecorated domestic objects. These are sometimes made by their apprentices or else by others who could better be described as carpenters, as amongst the Yoruba where a distinction is made between the sculptor and the mere woodcarver. Among the Nupe even the simple wooden stools that traditionally every woman possesses to sit on in the market or to perform her household duties in the home are decorated. As Phillips Stevens comments, 'Nearly all of the more common domestic articles bear geometric designs.'[27]

The Nupe are unusual in Nigeria today in that although the demand for ritual and ceremonial objects no longer exists and has increasingly diminished this century, the skill and production of the carvers is almost unaffected. This carving tradition, unlike that in so many other areas, does not depend on the ceremonial or ritual use of the artifacts, although there are some masks still in use. These days Nupe carving is almost entirely 'art for art's sake'. Again, Phillips Stevens, writing in the mid 1960s, reports that nearly every town had at least one master carver, carved door panels and house posts remain popular, and sturdy stools and pestles and mortars are a requisite of every household.[28] Although much of the decoration of houseposts, mortars, stools and so on is geometric, some of the motifs are representational. Familiar objects, animals and the human figure are portrayed in a stylised form. The sturdy and attractive stools, and pestles and mortars are finding an increasing market in modern Nigeria, as western imports cannot compete with them.

The Yoruba, on the other hand, who have been perhaps the best-known and most prolific woodcarvers in Nigeria in the last couple of centuries, carve mainly for ceremonial and ritual use. They have been known to, and still do in some cases, carve objects such as mirror frames, combs, food bowls and pulleys for weaving that are 'art for art's sake'; but these are a very small part of the much wider field of ceremonial and cult objects. Some of the verandah posts and doors of the Yoruba are among the largest and most complex carvings of the whole of Africa, adorning both religious and secular buildings.

It was usually only the houses of kings or chiefs that were ornamented in this way, and this carving therefore delineated social status in the community. These doors and posts portray Yoruba ritual and village life, styles of dress and the changing environment, for example the invasion of slave traders and the white man in his various roles and different means of transport. Where these doors or posts belong to a shrine, various emblems and scenes of worship of the particular god are common. However, as building styles and methods have changed these large architectural sculptures are now rarely commissioned. In any case the Yoruba sculptor was always far more dependent on traditional religious work than his Nupe counterpart.

For use in traditional religion, Yoruba sculptors made human and animal figures, ornamented bowls, drums, stools, spears, masks and so on. The god for whom the object is made can be identified by the symbols or emblems and motifs used. Shango, the god of thunder and lightning, priest of the rainmakers of Yorubaland and identified as one of the earliest kings of the Oyo kingdom, has been mentioned in connection with ritual pottery, but his shrines also contain many wood carvings. They are veritable art galleries containing a great variety of wooden dance staffs, *ose Shango*, decorated with the double-headed axe emblem and human figures, inverted mortars, *odo Shango*, decorated with devotees and the emblems of the god, and carved figures holding a bowl, *arugba*, the last two storing the 'thunderbolts' referred to in the previous section. Ifa, the god of divination, mentioned in relation to ivory carving, also requires a carved wooden tray, *operi Ifa*, to mark the signs discovered by the diviner, and bowls, *agere Ifa*, to hold the palm nuts used in the divination process. The bowls are often supported by one or more human or animal figures, showing almost every aspect of Yoruba life, usually including a kneeling woman or priest, and the trays are decorated with geometric designs and human heads or figures. The tapper, *iroke*, that is sometimes carved in wood as well as ivory, is often portrayed in the priest's hand when he is represented on the carving.

The Yoruba hold the world record for twin births, and visits to a diviner and special rites are necessary when twins are born. Wooden figures, *ere ibeji*, are carved as substitutes for the twins if one or both of them should die, to ensure the continued fertility of the mother and the health of any surviving twin. Twins, *ibeji*, are believed to bring good fortune if ritual attendance on them is careful but misfortune or even death if it is not. The *ere ibeji* are ritually washed, dressed, decorated and fed, and the mother will keep the carving at home on the family twin altar, in her sleeping room where the carving is often wrapped for sleep, or in a container. If a diviner finds that the twins require the mother to dance in the market for alms, she will continue to do so with the carved figure or figures tucked in her wrapper as a substitute after the death of one or both twins. In the past *ere ibeji* were the commonest carvings in Yorubaland, but many have been sold to traders and the number of carvers capable of making them has rapidly declined. However, despite a growing population of Muslims and Christians, the rituals associated with twins continues to be important even for some who belong to the new religions; plastic dolls and photographs, both products of modern Nigerian society, and other types of carving such as the traditional Yoruba doll are recorded as being in use.[29]

Among the Kalabari Ijo the casual visitor would usually see no visible evidence for a tradition of wood carving. There are no carved doors, house posts, elaborate stools or decorated utensils; most of the carved figures are sacred objects and kept inside shrines. Sculpture acts as a means of localising and confining the power of the three major categories of free spirits that influence Kalabari life: the dead, the water spirits and the village heroes. According to Robin Horton, there 'is a serious feeling that any spirit without a sculpture to represent it is dangerous because it cannot be adequately controlled'.[30] A typical ritual sequence involving these spirits begins with the priest and others summoning the spirit and asking for benefits by invocation and sacrifice. By this ritual the spirit is confined in its sculpture. When this part of the ritual is over the spirit is liberated and it possesses or guides the priest who goes on to 'give a dramatic representation of the god'.[31] The priest is dressed in clothes symbolic of the spirit, often including an item that has been in close contact with the carving, which in the case of the water spirits is a carved headpiece worn in a masquerade performance. The various motifs used to decorate the carvings indicate whether the spirit is of human/social origin or not, and whether the spirit is concerned with human/social affairs or matters outside the village. Thus the ancestors are sharply distinguished from the water spirits while the heroes are in some respects similar to the water spirits and in others to the ancestors. Horton sums this up by saying that sculptural motifs are a shorthand for some of the salient features of the Kalabari belief system. Moreover, like the Ikenga of the Ibo, discussed by John Ojo,[32] Kalabari sculpture is only carved on commission by a group of worshippers, and the carving process requires sacrifice to the spirit of the tree felled for use. In some cases the carver is then free to get on with the carving without further rites and the sculpture is not associated with the spirit until ritually installed in the cult house. In other cases the carver has to follow ritual rules and prohibitions in order not to offend the spirit with whom he is considered in close contact.

In many areas of Nigeria, kings and chiefs require title-taking ceremonies, and carved stools and/or carved staffs as part of the regalia necessary for their ceremonies. These traditions are maintained to this day, and although many are slowly dying out nevertheless with new means available to achieve status in a community by virtue of education and professional standing, ceremonial stools and staffs continue to be made.

In Benin the ancestral altars of chiefs require carved wooden commemorative heads and special carved circular stools, while rectangular carved stools are used as chiefly status symbols. There are two distinct groups of sculptors in Benin. One is the professional guild who make sacred objects for shrines, and who carve in ivory for royal regalia. The other are the court pages who may take up carving simply to fill in time between their other duties. They carve decorative objects such as stools and door panels. Both groups in Benin continue to practise to meet traditional demands but at the same time are adapting traditional forms for the increasing tourist market.

Ikot Ekpene should be mentioned here as an important traditional centre for Annang wood carving, producing masks and figures for ritual use. However these days Ikot Ekpene has built up a large and flourishing commercial trade, and carvings from Ikot Ekpene are found all over Nigeria. The masks, human and animal figures now produced are often gaily painted and serve both the tourists and a more traditional market. It is interesting to note that here women are now involved in decorating the carvings. Ikot Ekpene masks are now found in ritual use in many parts of Nigeria where in the past only locally made ones would have been used.

Finally we must mention the work of Father Kevin Carroll and his attempts since the late 1940s to revitalise and adapt the tradition of Yoruba wood sculpture, amongst other activities, to the Christian context.[33] As has been said, with traditional religious practice increasingly being replaced by Christianity or Islam, the traditional sculptor has had a diminishing market for his products. However, as a result of Father Carroll's initial experiment with a small group of Yoruba sculptors in Ekiti, a number of both traditionally trained and modern art-school-trained sculptors have successfully applied their talents to the new context. Some of these sculptors are now employed in university fine arts departments, and Lamidi Fakeye, now at the University of Ife has established an international reputation. Traditional styles and techniques have been used to create new and traditional forms required in Christian worship. Traditional motifs have been used alongside Christian ones to portray scenes of Christian life and beliefs to decorate the carvings. Moreover, government and private patronage are also giving wood sculptors the opportunity to adapt to the requirements of modern Nigeria as well as tourism, examples of which are the carved doors found on several public and private buildings.

Two-dimensional art forms

Rock painting

Very few ancient rock paintings have been found in Nigeria, compared with the wealth of paintings and engravings to be seen in the Sahara. Paintings of humpless cattle, both longhorn and shorthorn, have been found in a rock shelter at Birnin Kudu near Kano. The longhorn humpless variety are no longer found in Nigeria but the shorthorn humpless are similar to the dwarf cattle now only found in southern Nigeria. These paintings are probably a thousand years old as they appear to pre-date the introduction of humped cattle that predominate in the north today, while paintings found at Geji, between Jos and Bauchi, probably date from about the fifteenth century. The Geji paintings show humans, antelopes, cows, monkeys and a horse. The latter animal is important because its date of introduction to Nigeria sets the earliest possible date for the paintings. The original purpose of the paintings is not known but, like the Ife bronzes and other ancient sculptures, the modern inhabitants of these areas have incorporated them into their belief system and ritual practice. All we know about the original inhabitants is that they kept cattle.

Wall painting

Wall paintings are found in all areas of Nigeria, but as yet they have been little documented nor have they been the subject of systematic research. In Yorubaland you can expect to find paintings in all traditional palaces, shrines or chief's houses. Both representational and geometric patterns were executed and among the Yoruba it was always the work of women. In other areas it was men's work but sometimes both sexes could be involved, for example in the painting of the walls of an Ibo Mbari house (see the section on pottery). In northern Nigeria there is often lavish painting on houses, palaces and mosques, and the mud relief decoration, discussed before, is often painted. In many cases the paintings are

Fig. 16.3 A small mosque in Hunkuyi village decorated by Musa Yola with a design based on the modern mosque in Kano

Fig. 16.4 'Nwomo', or shrine cloth, at Nto Nsek, Ikot Ekpene, Cross River state

geometric designs typical of Hausa art, but representations of birds, animals and common artifacts are also seen. In the past wall paintings were generally in the naturally occurring colours of black, white, red and yellow, but with the introduction of washing blue earlier this century and, more recently, manufactured paints the range of colours used has increased.

In modern Nigeria the painting tradition has been developed by the painting of walls of educational and governmental establishments, bars and hotels, the colourful signboards that advertise every kind of goods or services and the painting of lorries. The thousands of wooden-bodied freight and passenger lorries (Japanese mini-buses are rapidly replacing the 'mammy-wagon' for passenger transport and are not normally painted) that travel to all parts of Nigeria have become a powerful new medium. Images from the popular foreign films are common, often portraying scenes of violence (perhaps a statement of the all too frequent violence, death and danger met on Nigerian roads), power symbols, such as lions or guns, Islamic and Christian images can all be found alongside traditional motifs. Mottoes expressing moral sentiments or the dangers of modern life and pleas for divine intervention serve to inform and educate the public. The changing world and belief systems of modern Nigeria are an integral part of these new developments.[34]

The further education establishments that offer art as a subject for study and the Mbari Club, based in Ibadan and Oshogbo, have made and continue to make an important contribution to painting in modern Nigeria. So often these artists, sometimes but not always trained in western techniques, draw on their traditional background for the content of their paintings as well as their contemporary experience. There is now a new tradition of painting, more closely aligned to the 'fine art' of Europe and elsewhere, but firmly rooted in Nigeria, that flourishes in modern Nigerian society and serves its own, new and different requirements.

Textiles

The word 'textile' means *woven* cloth (rather than, for example, bark-cloth, which is made by a different process) and there is a long tradition of weaving in Nigeria. Pieces of cloth were found during the excavations at Igbo Ukwu (see the section on metalwork), and early Arab traders in the Sahara and European visitors to the coast record the existence of this industry. Textile manufacture includes the preparation of the raw materials, weaving, and the subsequent embellishment of the fabric by dyeing, embroidery, appliqué, painting and so on. Unfortunately space does not permit a full account here of the richness and diversity of traditional textile manufacture, its development and adjustment to modern demands, but some aspects can be mentioned.

Some form of weaving was traditionally found in most areas of Nigeria, and it was, and still is, the work of both men and women. While men may be full-time weavers, for a women it is a part-time activity, just one of her many expected household duties. With some exceptions, for example in southeastern Nigeria where men use a vertical loom to weave raffia cloth, men use the horizontal narrow strip loom and women the vertical loom.

The fibres that have been traditionally woven in Nigeria include cotton, silk and raffia. The hand spinning of cotton and the local wild silk was the work of women, as was dyeing, except among the Hausa. However, whereas you can find both men and women weaving (though never on the same type of loom) in the same place, such as among both Yoruba and Hausa, you do not find both sexes dyeing. For the Hausa dyeing is a male activity, while among the Yoruba it is usually left to the women. These days of course there is an abundance of machine-spun and ready-dyed cotton and synthetic yarns available to the weavers, and hand-spinning is rapidly disappearing. Dyeing has also disappeared in many areas, though elsewhere it survives for a number of reasons: it can be used to decorate the already manufactured fabric, whether of hand or machine-spun yarn, and factory-made cloth can also be dyed in the same · way. The host of new artificial dyes now available has further increased the dyers' decorative range.

Embroidery is predominantly found in the context of Islam, and tends to be men's work. In the past embroidery was done by hand with hand-spun cotton or silk, but these days machine-embroidery is common and machine-spun yarns are available. Nupe and Hausa traditions of embroidery have spread to many parts of Nigeria and now women often practice it, by hand and machine. The designs used on Hausa and Yoruba gowns are based on a relatively small number of geometric elements, but the petticoats, blouses, pillowcases and modern gowns embroidered for, and often by women, show a greater range of geometric and figurative designs.

When we look at the cultural context of textiles in Nigeria, their most obvious use is clothing. Clothes, however, do not merely serve as protection against the elements or covering for the body when that is socially required, but as a marker of wealth or status. Particular colours, various decorations or shapes of a garment may have political, ritual or social significance. Clothing also includes the covering of the dead, and manifestations of the dead, spirit world or the gods in masquerade form (for masquerade see the final section). Certain kinds of textiles have been produced to decorate houses for some important event or shrines. Nor must the economic significance of textiles be forgotten. Cloth has been used for trade purposes within and beyond Nigeria as well as local consumption, in the past and up to the present day. In some places one range of cloth was, and still is, woven for trading purposes, while others are woven for local use.

The importance of particular colours is demonstrated by the wearing of red cloth by the chiefs of Benin. Here red is associated with anger, blood, war and fire; it is threatening. The red cloths and beads that are part of ceremonial dress are worn as a threat to the enemies of the kingdom and to one's own enemies, whether witches, sorcerers or political rivals. Elsewhere in Nigeria red is associated with success and achievement, as among the Ebira.

Particular decoration of a garment for ritual use is seen in the cloth appliqué skirt worn by the leader of an age-set during the ritual performances that mark the passing from one grade to another in Oja, in northern Bendel state. Appliqué is a way of decorating cloth by sewing on pieces of different colours to make a pattern. The masqueraders who perform during the ceremonies also wear appliqué cloth aprons in the same style as the leader's skirt. Although there is a tradition of weaving in Oja, the making of appliqué decorated skirts and aprons is reserved for the age-grade rituals. Another example of appliqué is found amongst the Jukun people, who use appliqué to decorate the garments worn by a chief during rain-making ceremonies in this way.

Among the Yoruba cloth has been traditionally used to indicate wealth or rank in the community, and membership of a society or religious group. In the past the best of locally produced and imported cloths (cloth has been imported into Nigeria since at least the early fifteenth century) were reserved for the kings, and only with their permission could they be used by men of rank in the community. Membership of the Ogboni society (see the section on metal working) required a special cloth that was worn in a particular way over the right shoulder. The large embroidered *agbada*, so popular and prestigious today, is probably a fairly recent adaptation of northern dress, the Hausa *riga*, apparently introduced after the Oyo wars of the early nineteenth century. Before that the woven strips from the men's horizontal loom would be sewn to form a length of cloth that was wrapped around the waist or over the left shoulder.

Ebira women have traditionally woven a variety of cloths from hand-spun and indigo-dyed cotton. One particular set of striped patterns has been used to wrap corpses and the same cloth is used to drape around the doorway of a house while the body of a man lies in the house awaiting burial. Masqueraders also wear this cloth to remind the living of the links between the masquerade and the world of the dead. Yet another set of striped patterns was woven for sale to traders who would sell the cloth elsewhere in Nigeria for use on deck-chairs or for work clothes. An example of the use of a textile as a shrine cloth can be found among the Annang-Ibibio. There, large patchwork and appliqué decorated cloths were made, and still are to a lesser extent – the more durable cement is now popular for commemorative sculpture instead of the cloths – for the commemorative shrines erected during the ceremonial burial of important chiefs. The patchwork and appliqué formed a bold geometric patterned surround to a central figurative panel, and the cloths were hung in the shrine building to be clearly visible.

Today traditional weaving has disappeared in many areas as imported and factory-produced cloth has proved too competitive in terms of price and function, but it survives and flourishes in others. Today hand-woven traditional cloth is staging a comeback against the imported laces and damasks. With the increasing awareness of the value of Nigeria's traditions in this modern world, it has become fashionable again.

Although Yoruba women's weaving has largely died out, the men's weaving thrives and their cloth retains its traditional prestige value. It is in demand for both men's and women's dress. Today, in Yorubaland and other areas, any important social or religious event, traditional, Christian, Islamic or modern requires proper clothing. A family or club involved will often wear identical expensive and fashionable cloth as an expression of its wealth, pride and position. Okene, the Ebira capital, is probably the most important weaving centre in Nigeria today, but Akwete, Kano and Bida are among the other places where weaving flourishes. They still in part serve local needs but in general their success depends on exporting the cloth, both to other parts of Nigeria and beyond. The weavers have adapted their traditional techniques to the new materials available (lurex thread is the most recent innovation), and to new demands – for example, curtains or other modern furnishing requirements. New patterns are woven into the cloths, such as 'skyscrapers', that reflect the changing world. In other places a few weavers survive by the making of cloths that are ritually or ceremonially important.

Finally we must return to the tradition of dyeing, and its use on a cloth subsequent to its manufacture. Kano has long been famous for its indigo dyeing, but there, unlike in Yorubaland, the dyers specialised in dyeing plain white cloth with no pattern added. Among other things, the dyers of Kano specialise in a very shiny blue-black cloth. The finish is obtained by beating the cloth after overloading it with indigo. This cloth has been, and still is, popular and prestigious for use as turbans and it is exported all over northern Nigeria and throughout the southern fringes of the Sahara.

Resist dyeing, by tying or stitching a cloth tightly, or by the application of a starchy substance, was practised in many areas of Nigeria. However, the Yoruba *adire* cloth is probably the most famous. This is the name given by the Yoruba to indigo resist-dyed cloth. Its production has been centred on Abeokuta, Oshogbo and Ibadan. In the past these cloths were worn by women and there was a large range of traditional patterns. Special patterns were created for special occasions, for example, the coronation of an Oba. Some patterns were made for specific religious ceremonies. Moreover *adire* was a device for making use an an old cloth and giving it a new lease of life. Traditionally hand-spun and locally woven cloth was used but the advent of cheap plain manufactured cloth and more recently of cheap coloured printed or woven fabrics has given the dyers a greater variety of materials. Machines are now often used to stitch the patterns and new artificial dyes have been introduced. Both the Yoruba and Hausa have developed their tradition to serve modern Nigeria. A range of patterns, old and new, has been produced using modern dyes but traditional resist-dye techniques, and the cloth is sewn into skirts, gowns, mens' shirts and childrens' dresses, and decorated with machine embroidery.

Bark-cloth, matting and basketry

Bark-cloth is a non-textile fabric made by beating moistened strips of bark from a tree. In the forested area of southeastern Nigeria it was traditionally used for domestic and ceremonial clothing. It was also used for wrapping precious objects such as special masks. Its production almost ceased as soon as cheap machine-manufactured cloth became available. However the production of barkcloth survives in a few areas for traditional ceremonial or religious occasions, such as the installation of a new chief.

Mat making was practised by many people in Nigeria in the past and served many different functions. Without a modern bed and mattress a mat to sleep on is a necessity. Special mats were made for kings or chiefs to sit on, or sometimes to wrap corpses. Mats were also used to fence compounds and screen off areas. Mats have been made out of various types of palm leaf including raffia, grasses and other suitable vegetable materials. The fibres were often dyed in various colours and plaited into elaborate patterns and an increased range is possible today given the artificial dyes available. The tradition continues although not so widely, and in some places mats are sold for the tourist industry, for example amongst the Nupe and in Ososo, Bendel state.

In all areas of Nigeria baskets, hats and caps have been made out of similar materials to mats and used for a variety of domestic and ritual purposes. Caps are sometimes part of a chief's regalia, and in the north wide-brimmed hats are common as a shield from the sun. Simple domestic basketry is rapidly being replaced by plastics and other machine-made containers, but others, particularly Hausa baskets, are important items in the tourist trade. In some cases the traditional basketry has developed to produce modern furniture, which is finding an increasing market these days in Nigeria.

Beadwork, leatherwork and calabash decoration

Intricate coral and cornelian crowns have been an indispensable part of the regalia of the Oba of Benin, and the recently installed Oba continues the tradition. Fabric embroidered with beads features in the paraphernalia of the kings in Yorubaland and is also associated with a number of religious groups. The tall conical crown with its fringes of strings of beads is particularly well known. One modern artist working with beads is Jimoh Buraimoh, a product of the Mbari Club Oshogbo. He has evolved a technique of laying small mosaics with strings of local beads. He has drawn on his Yoruba traditional upbringing to develop this new medium and has gone on to create much larger mosaics using a variety of beads, stones and potsherds. He is very much part of the new tradition of Nigerian artists mentioned earlier.[35]

The Hausa and Oyo Yoruba have a tradition of leatherwork, decorated with appliqué in geometric designs. Bags, cushions, harnesses, hats, shoes and ornamental daggers are among the items made. Traditionally these items were made for domestic, ritual and ceremonial use, but now the production is largely maintained by the tourist industry.

Calabashes grow all over Nigeria in various shapes and sizes and have been prepared and often decorated in a variety of ways. Calabash decoration is still the most widespread of graphic arts and every part of Nigeria has its distinctive style. Their uses include fishing-net floats, masks, musical instruments, food bowls, trays, and storage containers.

Although imported manufactured vessels are readily available and are gradually replacing calabashes, the production and use of calabashes survives. Most markets in northern Nigeria still have groups of Fulani women selling their milk products from decorated calabashes and in Oyo there is a successful cooperative set up to exploit the tourist market.

Masquerade, arts of the body and architecture

Masquerade

Masquerades, masks and headdresses have already been mentioned in several sections of this chapter, but a fuller discussion of them has purposely been left to the end.

In the past much emphasis has been placed by European art historians on the mask or headdress, but the mask is only one part of a much greater whole. Masquerade is one of the performing arts and must be seen in the context of the arts not dealt with in this chapter, the spoken or sung word, music and dance. Moreover each masquerade must be seen in its own particular cultural context. The mask, worn on the face, and headdress, worn on the head, has to be seen as part of the total costume. Indeed, in some cases the mask or headdress is an *integral* part of the costume and not distinguishable from it. Sometimes the mask or headdress is carved in wood and occasionally cast in metal but it may also be made from textiles, basketry, the knitting, knotting and dyeing of various fibres into elaborate forms, beadwork, feathers, or a host of other materials. The costume itself may include most of these materials, though not metal or wood carving, except in small elements stitched to the costume, for example the metal ankle rattles often worn by performers.

The immediate purpose of the mask or headdress and costume is to disguise or transform the wearer, so that he can more effectively play the part expected of his masquerade. Nigeria boasts an enormous diversity of masquerade forms and characters, and the purpose of these masquerades are equally diverse: entertaining, judgment and healing, among other things. Moreover, even when a mask, headdress or costume leaves its sculptor or maker it is not always 'finished'. The mask, headdress or costume may be decorated and re-decorated with beads, seeds, pieces of mirror or cloth, paint and so forth. This may happen so often and so consistently that the point at which the 'work of art', in the European sense, is finished may only be when it is finally discarded.

Thus we can see that masquerade involves most of the two- and three-dimensional art forms already discussed and several more. Given the host of masquerading traditions and art forms they generate that have traditionally existed in Nigeria, only a few can be discussed here. Many traditions have declined under the influence of Christianity, Islam and the general climate of socio-economic change, but many have been revitalised by adapting to and evolving out of these new conditions. An example of the latter point is the annual festivals of the arts now popular, and the appropriation of new materials such as imported cloth and

Fig. 16.5 Wooden helmet mask with superstructure used in age-grade ceremonies, Ogbe, Akoko Edo, Bendel state

printed plastic bags.

In some areas of Nigeria men are organised into age-sets and the ritual passing of these sets from one grade to another every five to seven years often involves masquerades at one or more stage in the process. The masquerades may take different forms and may represent different things for different peoples. Jean Borgatti has worked in Otuo, a northern Edo village where enormous carved wooden and painted helmet masks, single or janu-faced, with figurative superstructures are used during the festival that marks the entry of an age-set into the grade of community leaders. She states that the masks and their images refer to the notions of power and leadership that underline the festival and to which those passing through the grades ultimately succeed.[36] The huge variety of images displayed include leopards, colonial officers, angels and aeroplanes. Associated with these masks are elaborate fibre costumes. At the festival only a few of these huge carved helmet masks may appear but there are many more masquerades whose costumes are made of the same fibres, with the masks and headdresses an integral part of the whole and made from the same materials. Music, song and dance are also involved.

Prestige is attached to the man in the set who provides (that is, pays for) the greatest number of these masquerades, which are made by specialists in the grades senior to the set who commission them. Moreover, Borgatti states 'by providing this magnificent display for the community, the men of this age company establish themselves as men of substance who are capable of undertaking leadership tasks. On an individual basis, each man's performance probably affects his later political success in the ruling grades.'[37] The northern Edo live in villages or village clusters that are traditionally governed by councils of elders. There was no overriding political authority such as existed in the Benin, Yoruba, or Ishan kingdoms; they were linked by ritual and kinship. Central authority needed to rely on consensus rather than coercion for support and the age-grade system was an important social principle in the functioning of these societies.

The same type of woven fibre costumes and headdresses but with variations in style occur in many other northern Edo groups, associated with age-grades and title societies. They have been documented in Ogbe, Oja, Ikpeshi, Dagbala, Ugboshi, the Uneme villages, eight Okpella villages and in the Yoruba-speaking town of Imeri by either myself or Jean Borgatti.

Masquerading among the Afikpo-Ibo of southeastern Nigeria is generally carried out in the context of the men's society that exists in every village. Often called secret societies, like the Ogboni society of Yorubaland, these groups are only secret in so far as much initiation ritual and a few other events are exclusive to members. The masquerade performances are usually held in public although there are always secret aspects associated with them.

Decorated calabash, painted carved wooden and net mask forms are used with a variety of cloth and raffia costumes. Putting on the mask and costume transforms a person into a spirit, *mma*, and allows the masqueraders to act in an unusual way towards each other and their public. The masquerade performances take place at village level, and according to Simon Ottenberg they reflect some of the structural oppositions that exist in Afikpo society; age difference and authority, the maintenance of distinct social roles, and the question of individual enterprise versus the ideal of the cooperative group.[38] The masquerades appear during the period September to February that begins with the celebration of the new yam festival when the new yams are harvested and eaten and ends at the beginning of the new farming season, when the land is cleared and planted. Ottenberg believes that this ceremonial season is one of social adjustment and realignment in which the masquerades play their part alongside the other activities such as initiation into the men's society and the taking of titles. The most popular Afikpo masked play is Okumkpa, which is composed of a series of acts, in which amongst other things, elders are made fun of if they have misbehaved!

Masquerades found among the Yoruba are many and varied and no general comments are possible. The Yoruba are a heterogeneous group of peoples linked together by a group of related dialects and a general cultural pattern, but within this broad framework there is an enormous amount of autonomy in all aspects of community life. The common language of today, known as Standard Yoruba, has come about largely as a result of the combination of the translation of the Bible and the spread of education.

An example of a Yoruba masquerade tradition is that associated with the Gelede cult of southwestern Yorubaland. The cult is concerned to propitiate the mystical powers of women in their dual role as witches and mothers. A witch, *aje* in Yoruba, does not simply have the power to perpetrate evil. Although a witch's ill-will must be warded off, her good-will must be cultivated because it is essential for the continuation of life and society. Many important Gelede titles are held by women, but membership of the cult is open to both sexes and the masquerades are performed by men. The head of the Gelede society wields great religious and political power in the community and Gelede festivals generally occur every year and at funerals of members of the group.

Two main types of carved wooden masks, often painted, are used by the Gelede masquerade together with a cloth costume. The most important type is called *Efe* and it is usually large and elaborate. It is the main placator of witches, and the masquerades come out at night, one by one, to sing. The second type is the *Gelede* mask which is usually smaller, and these masquerades appear in the afternoon in pairs to dance.

All the masks are worn on the top of the head and both types often involve superstructures. These may represent animals, important members of the cult, or contemporary subjects such as motor bikes, cars, sunglasses and sometimes other masks used in different cult groups. Indeed, the carver can represent anything providing he has the permission of the officers of the Gelede society, and his representations are often intended to be humorous.

John Ojo discusses some of the other masquerade traditions that survive in Nigeria but there are many, many more.[39] Some have been well researched and documented and others have not. Sadly, today, so many of the sculpted masks or headdresses, in wood and other materials, have become separated from their traditional setting. It is my hope that this section will demonstrate to students and others who are interested in Nigeria's artistic traditions, that these objects alone cannot be appreciated or understood without a study of the many other art forms involved in the masquerade and its cultural context.

Arts of the body

Face and body painting and cicatrisation, changes to the shape of teeth, lips and ear, hairdressing, jewellery, clothing and other regalia have been used in various combinations all over the world to transform and adorn the human body. It is the most universal of all art forms and in Nigeria has been practised throughout its known history. Moreover, the arts of the body are always motivated by and directed towards political, economic, religious and particularly social ends.

The early stone, ivory and pottery sculpture and metal castings discussed earlier in this chapter show elaborate hairstyles, scarification, jewellery and clothing. Today in Nigeria, although some of the older practices have died or are dying out, new ones are being adopted to adorn and transform the bodies of men, women and children. Hairdressing is perhaps the most obvious example of an art form that is continually changing and developing.

There is no space here for a detailed discussion, and of all Nigerian arts these are still the least well researched. In view of the time, energy and wealth still expended on these arts they remain a valid and urgent subject for study.

Architecture

This subject has also often been neglected in any study of Nigeria's artistic heritage, and there is no room here to rectify the situation. However, in the last ten years or so increasing attention has been paid to the wealth of traditional architectural forms still found in Nigeria: this is particularly important given the speed with which so much traditional building is being destroyed in the development process and with the adoption of new materials.

The size, shape and resilience of buildings in Nigeria have always been determined by cultural and environmental factors, and even though society is changing rapidly, modern architects and builders can learn much from the traditions of their past. Properly used, earth is very far from being a 'primitive' building material. Indeed, in many respects, it is actually superior to the now popular concrete, for example in its heat resistance. An indication of the importance of architecture in Nigeria's cultural heritage is the Museum of Traditional Architecture now being set up within the compound of Jos Museum.

Conclusion

The richness of Nigeria's visual arts, which is probably unsurpassed in Africa, cannot be fully documented in the space of a book, let alone a single chapter. However, in this chapter I hope students have begun to understand something of the historical, social, religious, political and economic importance of Nigeria's traditional visual arts. Moreover, while 'art for art's sake' certainly does exist and has existed in Nigeria, much more 'art' exists for other reasons. The National Commission of Museums and Monuments has done much to restore and preserve architectural monuments and to conserve and display many other items of Nigeria's cultural heritage, and its all-important documentation and research work goes on. Students interested in Nigeria's visual arts can still find much research to be done in the traditional fields, but the new vigorous Nigerian art that has been touched upon here must not be ignored. It is neither divorced from nor dependent on traditional forms, and although closer in many respects to the European notion of 'fine art', it is still a product of Nigerian society.

Notes

1 See the first section of the chapter by John Ojo, 'Art in Traditional African Culture' in Richard Olaniyan (ed.), *African History and Culture*, (Longman Nigeria, 1982) pp. 200–23.

2 Dennis Williams, *Icon and Image* (Allen Lane: 1974) p. 4. See also his chapters on iron and bronze working in Nigeria.

3 For more information on Ife stone sculpture, see Frank Willett, *Ife in the History of West African Sculpture* (Thames and Hudson: 1967), pp. 70–84; also Philip Allison, *African Stone Sculpture* (Lund Humphries, London: 1968), pp. 11–24.

4 Phillips Stevens, Jnr., *The Stone Images of Esie, Nigeria* (Ibadan University Press and Nigerian Federal Department of Antiquities, 1978).

5 Allison, *African Stone Sculpture*, pp. 25–35.

6 Paula Ben Amos, *The Art of Benin* (Thames and Hudson: 1980), p. 27.

7 Thurstan Shaw, *Unearthing Igbo-Ukwu* (Oxford University Press: 1977); also Thurstan Shaw, *Nigeria: its archaeology and early history* (Thames and Hudson: 1978), pp. 99–122.

8 Willett, *Ife*, pp. 18–52; also Ekpo Eyo, *Two Thousand Years Nigerian Art* (Federal Department of Antiquities, 1977), pp. 96–122. This book should be used as a general reference to Nigeria's sculptural traditions.

9 Eyo, *ibid.*, p. 150.

10 Ben Amos, *The Art of Benin*.

11 Ulli Beier, *Contemporary Art in Africa* (Pall Mall Press: 1968), pp. 15–19. This is a useful but now dated survey of 'modern' Nigerian visual art.

12 Judith Perani, 'Patronage and Nupe craft industries', *African Arts*, XIII (3), 1980.

13 Keith Nicklin, *Guide to the National Museum, Oron*.

14 *Ibid.*

15 Keith Nicklin, 'Ibibio metalwork', *African Arts*, X (1), 1976.

16 Beier, *Contemporary Art in Africa*, pp. 154–64; Maude Wahlman, *Contemporary African Arts* (Field Museum of Natural History, Chicago, 1974).

17 For more information on the Nok culture, see: Shaw, *Nigeria*; Eyo, *Two Thousand Years Nigerian Art*; Willett, *Ife*.

18 Carl Liedholm, 'The pottery of Ushafa', *African Arts*, X (3), 1982.

19 Willett, *Ife*, pp. 57–78; Eyo, *Two Thousand Years Nigerian Art*; Shaw, *Nigeria*.

20 Eyo, *ibid.*

21 Maude Wahlman, 'Yoruba pottery-making techniques', *Baessler-Archiv*, N.F. Band XX, 1972.

22 Alan Bassing, 'Grave monuments of the Dakakari', *African Arts*, VI (4), 1973.

23 Nicklin, *Guide to the National Museum, Oron*. Amongst the Ibo, and

introduced by them to the Ibibio, there is a tradition of musical pot manufacture. See Keith Nicklin, 'The Ibibio musical pot', *African Arts*, VII (1), 1973.

24 Danlami Aliyu, 'Nigerian pottery tradition and new techniques', *Pottery Quarterly*, 52.

25 Ojo chapter in *African History and Culture*, p. 212.

26 Ben Amos, *The Art of Benin*.

27 Phillips Stevens, 'Nupe Woodcarving', *Nigeria Magazine*, No. 88.

28 *Ibid*.

29 Marilyn Hammersley Houlberg, 'Ibeji images of the Yoruba', *African Arts*, VII (1), 1973.

30 Robin Horton, *Kalabari Sculpture* (Department of Antiquities, Federal Republic of Nigeria, 1965), p. 8.

31 *Ibid*., p. 11.

32 Ojo chapter in *African History and Culture*.

33 Kevin Carroll, *Yoruba Religious Carving* (Geoffrey Chapman; 1967).

34 Jack Pritchard, 'Nigerian Truck Art', *African Arts*, XII (2), 1979.

35 Beier, *Contemporary Art in Africa*, p. 128.

36 Jean Borgatti, 'Age grades, masquerades and leadership amongst the Northern Edo', *African Arts*, XVI (1), 1982, p. 51.

37 *Ibid*., p. 44.

38 Simon Ottenberg, *Masked Rituals of the Afikpo* (University of Washington Press, 1975).

39 See chapter by Ojo in *African History and Culture*.

Further reading

HERBERT COLE, *African Arts of Transformation* (Santa Barbara: University of California, 1970).

FRANK WILLETT, *African Art* (Thames and Hudson: 1970).

ROBERT BRAIN, *Art and Society in Africa* (Longman: 1980).

SYLVIA LEITH-ROSS, *Nigerian Pottery* (Ibadan University Press: 1970).

For further information on Nigerian textiles see:

JOHN PICTON and JOHN MACK, *African Textiles* (British Museum Publications: 1979).

VENICE LAMB and JUDY HOLMES, *Nigerian Weaving* (Shell Petroleum Development Company of Nigeria Ltd., 1980).

JANE BARBOUR and DOIG SIMMONDS, *Adire Cloth in Nigeria* (Institute of African Studies, University of Ibadan, 1971).

For further information on calabash decoration see:

T. J. H. CHAPPEL, *Decorated Gourds in North-eastern Nigeria* (Ethnographica, The Nigerian Museum, 1977).

Nigeria Magazine provides much useful information on Nigeria's visual arts, but in particular try and find No. 74 Crafts Issue and their special publications:
1 *Everyman's Guide to Nigerian Art*
2 *Nigerian Body Adornment*
3 *History of Modern Nigerian Art*
4 *Festac issue of Nigeria Magazine*

17 Aspects of language in Nigeria

S. H. Olu Tomori

The words *language* and *tongue* are synonymous in meaning in many of the languages of the world. This is because the organ in a person's mouth known as the tongue plays a very important role in producing the sounds of language. The primary role of language is that of effective communication in the day-to-day activities of mankind. Language is one of the important factors that distinguish man from inarticulate animals. Language is also one of the most conspicuous factors among traits that mark the whole world into different racial groups. If any person in a strange community hears a person speaking his or her own language – that is, the language of his or her distant home or nation – the person becomes interested in the other person at once. This attraction is due to their sharing the common language or a common tongue. A national language, therefore, is a very important factor in unifying a nation: in giving a nation a distinctive identity.

Before going into further detail in this chapter we should attempt a definition of language. In the everyday sense of the word, a language is a system of arbitrary vocal symbols used by human beings to communicate with one another. One of the most important characteristics of a language is that it is *a system*: that is, a language operates in accordance with certain recognised and accepted rules. If there were no accepted and understood rules and patterns, it would be impossible to understand anything said by another person. The next point in the definition is that language is *vocal*: that is, it is conveyed by sounds emanating from the mouth of the speaker. Language is therefore primarily oral; it is spoken. All other forms referred to as language are various reflections of the real oral event.

The word *symbol* is also used in the definition of language; a symbol is something that stands for something else: that is, a symbol is a sign or an indication of something else. The word *table*, for instance, is a vocal symbol which stands for the concrete object recognised as a table by people who understand the particular language. The word and the object it represents have nothing in common. The name is just an arbitrary symbol. The word *arbitrary* means, in this context, 'just chosen without an apparent reason'. What is called a *table* might just as well be called a *cow*; if the word *cow* was accepted for the object now known as a *table*, then the word *cow* would apply to that wooden piece of furniture.

In most cases, in all the languages of the world, the sound that represents a concrete object or an idea is just an arbitrary one that has no natural connection with the thing represented. In the three major Nigerian languages what is referred to as *water* in English is represented by the following words: *ruwa* (Hausa); *mili* (Ibo); *omi* (Yoruba). This same liquid substance that we drink to quench our thirst is given three different names – three different sets of sounds – in the three major

Nigerian languages. The same thing can be said of the many other languages in Nigeria. It can thus be seen that the three names are arbitrary symbols to represent the same thing.

A language is usually the communication tool used by a speech community. We have already referred to the three major Nigerian languages, Hausa, Ibo and Yoruba, each of which is spoken by more than 15 million Nigerians. Each speech community speaking what is referred to as the same language does not speak it in the same way. There are *dialects* of the same language. A dialect is a variety of a language that is spoken by a distinctive geographical or social group within the main speech community. Everybody knows that when they travel from their own town to the next town or village, their language is spoken slightly differently from the way it is spoken in their own town or village. A variety of a language that can usually be understood by other speakers is a *dialect* of that language.

There are some dialects of the same language that are not mutually intelligible. That is, one person in one geographical area of the language cannot understand what is said by another person in a distant geographical area of the same language. The greatest problem in understanding dialects is in the area of *phonology*: that is, in the area of the types of sounds used in speaking that dialect. If an unfamiliar dialect is spoken very slowly and very clearly, most of it may be understood by other speakers of the same language. The next area of difficulty in understanding dialects is that of the items in its vocabulary. Various words are used for the same things or the same ideas in various dialect areas. A dialect, therefore, is characterised by the differences it exhibits in its sound system and in its vocabulary items. There are other areas of differences that we shall refer to later; but the major problems in mutual intelligibility of dialects are in the areas of phonology and vocabulary.

A third term used in describing certain aspects of language is *idiolect*. An idiolect is the particular brand of the speech of an individual. A *language* is spoken by a large speech community: a *dialect* is spoken by a sub-group of that speech community: an *idiolect* is spoken by an individual in that sub-group of the main speech community. No two persons in the world speak any one language in exactly the same way. There are slight differences that are particularly noticeable in the quality of the voice and the manner of delivery. This is one of the reasons why members of the same family can easily recognise each other through the voice only, without seeing the person speaking. The particular characteristics of the speaker's voice are already known by the intimate members of the family or his friends. In a household of forty people, it is easy for members of that household to recognise who of the thirty-nine others is speaking just by hearing the voice. This shows that the other thirty-nine people speak the language differently from the person identifying them, and also differently from one another. This particular brand of a dialect spoken by an individual is known as an *idiolect*.

We have defined language as a system of arbitrary vocal symbols used by human beings to communicate with one another. We have examined the key words of that definition. We now go on to examine briefly what are known as the linguistic characteristics of a language.

A language is a *system*. There is order in the way any language of the world is spoken. All those who know the language keep, within reasonable limits, to the basic ordering of the elements of the language. If they depart too violently from the elements of the language, whatever they say cannot be understood by anybody else. Order or system in any of the languages of the world is exhibited in the following elements of language:

1 The sound system, which is studied in an academic discipline known as *phonology*;
2 The grammatical system, which is studied academically as *morphology* and *syntax*;
3 The vocabulary system, which is studied as *lexis* or *lexicology*.

These three major systems of a language also have sub-systems within them.

The sound system of a language comprises various sounds that are known as *vowels* and *consonants*. We are all familiar with the traditional five vowels and the twenty-one consonants of written English; the vowels of spoken English are much more than five. The vocal blending of the vowels and consonants of a language gives us the sounds of words and sentences. Various languages of the world use various vowels and consonants. It is known, for instance, that many Nigerians find some English words difficult to pronounce because those words contain vowels and consonants that are not present in their own language. Some areas of difficulty are the sound 'th' as in 'the'; the sound 'z' as in 'zoo'; and the sound 'v' as in 'very'. These sounds are wrongly pronounced by various linguistic groups in the country because one sound or the other is not in their own language, and they have not learnt how to pronounce the strange English sounds properly.

The phonological system of a language also includes various tone patterns that are used to convey meaning. In English, the various tone patterns are known as pitch and intonation patterns. It is known that certain questions are asked in English by raising the level of the voice at the end of the question. Without using a question order the following three words can be understood either as a statement or as a question: *John is here*, depending on the tones used. With a falling tone on the word 'here', the hearer understands the sentence as a statement. If the tone of the voice is raised at the end, it is understood as a question as in: *John is here*? The word order is exactly the same; it is the tone that marks out what is a statement and what is a question in the above example.

There are many other things that are studied in the phonological system of every language of the world that we shall not go into in detail in this section. We shall merely conclude by saying that there are some languages of the world that are known as tone languages. These are languages like Yoruba, Ibo and Hausa which change the *meanings* of words by using different tones for the same vowel and consonant combinations. Different tones in a tone language change the *basic meaning* of the word. We shall cite examples from one of the three major languages of Nigeria. In Yoruba, for instance, *Odo* (with middle and high tones on the vowels) means a mortar; *Odo* (with middle and low tones) means a river. Every language, therefore, has its own system of combining vowels, consonants, tones and intonation patterns to convey meaning. An innate knowledge of how these are combined is the speaker's competence in the area of the sound system of the particular language.

The second important system of the elements of a language is that of *grammar*. Grammar has been referred to as being made up of *morphology* and *syntax*. Morphology is the study of the formation of words. We know that in English, for instance, *achievement* is formed from *achieve*, and *promotion* is formed from *promote*, to cite only two examples. Each of these words uses different rules for the formation of words. An error occurs if the rules for forming one word are used for forming another that belongs to a different group.

Syntax is the level of language at which the placing together of two or more words to form a larger unit is studied. For instance, the three words *a*, *good*, and *boy* are put together in English in that order – 'a good boy'. That is the rule for putting such words together in English. In some other languages, the rule for putting together the equivalent words for *a good boy* is different. In Yoruba, for instance, the order is *boy*, *good*, *a*. This is exactly the opposite of the English order of words. Each language has its own rules of syntax, or the placing together of words, which must be known by anybody who claims to know the language.

The last level of language study that we shall discuss is that of *lexis* or *semantics*. It is at the level of lexis, sometimes called semantics in other grammars, that the characteristics of individual words and how they convey meaning are studied. It is also at the level of lexis that words that can, or cannot, occur together are studied. For instance, the rule of English syntax allows putting the adjective *cold* and another noun together: for instance, *cold winds*. This example, cold winds, is also allowed by the rules of lexis. But even though the rules of syntax allow putting together *cold* and *fires*, this is nonsensical in normal usage according to the rules of lexis – the rules governing words that can occur together.

The multi-lingual situation

We shall now examine some of the facts about the language situation in Nigeria before going on to more general facts about languages in general. We have mentioned that there are three major languages in Nigeria that are spoken by more than 15 million people each. These are Hausa, Ibo and Yoruba. After the creation of the twelve states of the Federation, the Nigerian Broadcasting Corporation started broadcasting its news in the following nine major Nigerian languages: Edo, Efik, Fulfulde, Hausa, Igbo, Izon, Kanuri, Tiv and Yoruba. The nine Nigerian languages were chosen because they are the major Nigerian languages covering all the twelve states of the Federation at the time.

The matter of a language being referred to as a major language in a nation is decided by the relative numbers of people speaking that language. No one language is linguistically superior to another, or more important than another one. With the creation of more states in the country, and with the reorganisation of the Nigerian Broadcasting Corporation into the Federal Radio Corporation of Nigeria more local languages, in addition to English, are now used in broadcasting news at the different zonal levels:

Enugu Zone:	Efik, Igbo, Izon and Tiv.
Ibadan Zone:	Edo, Igala, Urhobo and Yoruba.
Kaduna Zone:	Hausa, Kanuri, Fulfulde and Nupe.
Lagos Zone:	Enjoined by law to broadcast to the nation in English only.

Of course, local radio stations also use the local languages of their area to broadcast news items and some other programmes. Not all the languages of Nigeria are used at present in broadcasting programmes. Specialists in linguistics and Nigerian languages inform us that there are more than 400 different languages in Nigeria at present. The figure refers to the number of *different languages*, and not different dialects. There are definitely more dialects than five times the number of languages in Nigeria. That is, the 400 languages of Nigeria have more than 2 000 variants known as dialects.

Some of the languages of Nigeria have been written; hundreds have not been written at all. The unwritten languages have no written literature. Some of the languages of Nigeria were reduced to writing more than 100 years ago. The three major Nigerian languages were studied very early by the Christian missionaries and there are documents written in them that are older than 100 years. In fact, the Hausa language was written in Arabic script, known as Ajami script, before the Christian missionaries came to Nigeria. More and more Nigerian languages are still being reduced to writing today.

The problems of converting an oral language to one that has a written form is a specialist and difficult task. We have mentioned that the various languages of the world have different consonant and vowel combinations. A language that has never been written before must be carefully studied by a linguist, who is specially trained to do the job, before he or she can decide on the consonants and vowels used, and also on how to represent them in writing. It is not all the languages of the world that can be written with the well-known letters of the English alphabet only. In some cases, some special characters are invented by the trained linguist to represent the sounds of a language. Forming a script, or letters of the alphabet, for an unwritten language is a specialist task for which specially trained linguists are required. Anyone interested in forming letters of the alphabet for an unwritten Nigerian language can apply to the appropriate departments of linguistics and Nigerian languages in our universities for advice and guidance about how to do the difficult job of providing an *orthography*.

The language of education

This now brings us to the language of education in Nigeria. It is obvious that for the formal, western type of education, only a language with an alphabet – that is, only a language that has an *orthography* – can be used in schools. This is because books have to be written and printed for the educational programme. As mentioned earlier, some of the languages of Nigeria already have an alphabet. Books are already published in them. School primers are already written in them: pupils in such areas where books have been written can learn to read and write in their own language. Work on designing orthographies for various languages, and also on writing primers in thoses languages, is still going on in many parts of the Federation at the present time.

The ideal language for the education of any child is his mother tongue. A mother tongue is usually the first language learnt by a child. It is usually the language of his or her environment. But in some cases a child's first language may not be literally his or her mother tongue. The first language of the environment is easily learnt by any normal child. This is the best language for introducing him to formal education. The language of the environment is intricately woven into the culture of that environment. It is the ideal tool for describing the various aspects of culture and social life of that environment. Any language that does this for a child is naturally the best language for introducing him or her to formal education.

We know that the ideal of using a child's mother tongue for introducing him or her to education has not been achieved in Nigeria. This is because of the multi-lingual situation of the country – the situation in which there is no single national language. There are very many languages as already mentioned. Because some of these languages are spoken by just a few thousand people, the major language of a state is used in some cases for introducing the child in that state to formal primary education. The major language of the state is the language spoken by the majority of the people in that state. But it may not be, and in fact it is not, the first language of many pupils. Such pupils are forced to learn at school in a language that is not their mother tongue. While this is not the ideal, it is the next best thing if the child understands the language. There are even greater problems in some urban areas where as many as ten different languages may be represented in primary class one – the first year of education. The teacher may not even speak any of the languages spoken by his or her pupils.

In a situation where the teacher and the pupils have no common language, English is often used as the language of introducing the pupils to education. This has its problems because it is a language not understood by many of the pupils.

It is usually imperfectly mastered by the average primary school teacher. The good primary school teacher, who is above the average, knows enough good English. But most primary school teachers in Nigeria are below the average; their English is very poor. It is a big problem, then, for the badly equipped teacher, the unqualified teacher, to introduce pupils to formal education in the English language that he or she does not

289

know well. In most cases the pupils are introduced to formal education through pidgin English. While this is not ideal, if there is no other common language, pidgin English can be used as a stepping-stone for going on as early as possible to acceptable, good English. In any case, it is not advisable to use pidgin English for more than just a short part of the first year of education in primary class one. As soon as the pupils know enough good English, pidgin should be dropped completely.

The policy of the Federal Government on language education, as published in the *National Policy on Education* in 1977, is that a child should be introduced to education through his mother tongue. That is, primary education should start in the mother tongue. The *National Policy on Education* further states that pupils should be introduced to the English language at a later level in their primary education, and that English should be used as the medium of instruction throughout their secondary school life. It is also part of the language policy of the Federal Government that another foreign language, especially French, could also be introduced at the appropriate level of education. The two tiers of language in education in Nigeria are therefore the mother tongue and the English language.

The English language is the main language of education in Nigerian universities. Some local languages are also studied at the university level; even these are taught mainly through the English language. Until recently all answer scripts in the local languages studied in universities were written in the English language. The following local languages are now available for study at the university level: Yoruba, Hausa, Ibo, Edo, Efik and Fulfulde. More and more Nigerian languages are being added to the list every year. Those who study one Nigerian language or another in universities have a chance of getting good jobs as teachers of those languages in the educational system of the country.

Some other modern European languages are also studied in the country at the university level. These include German and Russian. Arrangements are being made by some universities to introduce the teaching of non-European languages such as Chinese. All these foreign languages are directly useful to the country in its foreign relations with other nations of the world.

The issue of a national language

One of the problems of national identity in Nigeria is the absence of a national language. It has been mentioned above that a national language is one of the distinctive characteristics of a nation. The language is the custodian of a nation's culture; it is also the mirror that reflects its culture. It is the distinctive mark of comradeship and togetherness. While it is true that no single individual in the world ever succeeds in conveying all his thoughts clearly and precisely, a common national language makes it easy for one to communicate more clearly in one's speech community. Something is always lost when one language is translated into another one. Some of the misunderstandings that exist in Nigeria are due to different cultural backgrounds and different connotations of words in the different languages of the country.

Nigeria is not the only multi-lingual nation in the world. The United Kingdom, for instance, had a number of tribal languages before the ascendancy of English. Even today there are still a few minority languages in Britain. For more than 700 years now, the major language of the United Kingdom has been English. During the reign of Edward III (in the Middle Ages) French was still the language of the court and the language of education generally. At that time, however, the peasants of the United Kingdom spoke English which was then considered the language of illiterates. It was King Edward III who ruled in 1362 that the English tongue should be the official language of the British Isles, for use in all official transactions. It was easy for the king to give this order at that time because the majority of the people of the island spoke the language.

Even today, there are countries in Europe that are multi-lingual. The Soviet Union is one such nation. Russian happens to be one of the languages of the USSR. Russian is the official language of the Soviet Union. But there are isolated villages and towns where the national language is a second or even a third language for school children. The national language, Russian, is the language of higher education in the Soviet Union. The very small nation Switzerland has two national languages, French and German. Canada also has two national languages, English and French.

The United States was formerly inhabited by Red Indians before the English got there. The official language of New York was at one time Dutch, and later English. Probably all the languages of the world are represented now in the United States. But English remains the official language of the country. All immigrants must speak the language well before they can be given rights of citizenship and permanent settlement. This is a policy of linguistic absorption for presenting a united national front. Brazil in South America now has the Portuguese language as its national language, another example of a tongue from a land far away.

During the Middle Ages Latin was the language of culture and the language of education in western Europe. With the fall of the Roman empire, the various Roman colonies in Europe continued to speak some vernacular (local) Latin. These local variations soon developed into distinct languages. That, in a simplified manner, is the origin of the following languages known as the Romance languages: Italian, French, Roumanian, Spanish, and Portuguese. None of these languages is now known as Latin. In fact, no one who knows only classical Latin can understand these languages when spoken today, though a knowledge of classical Latin still helps one to understand a bit of the written languages, with great difficulty. This shows how much the languages have diverged from the original Latin language.

We have said that there are more than 400 languages in Nigeria now. The various languages spoken in Nigeria belong to various language families of the world. This is due to the influence of migrations from different parts of the world at different times. Yoruba and Ibo belong to the Kwa group; Fulani is in the West Atlantic Northern Niger–Congo group. Hausa is in the Chadic group, an Afro-Asiatic family. The Arabic language is also spoken in the northern parts of the country as a result of contact with Islam. The various languages spoken in Nigeria, therefore, belong to different families. This accounts for major differences in their systems of phonology, morphology, syntax and lexis.

With the various backgrounds of the languages spoken in Nigeria it is not easy to effect a harmonisation for producing a national language, as some people have suggested in newspapers. The natural way in which a national language can evolve is through rapid increases in the numbers of speakers of any of the present-day Nigerian languages. If this happens, in about 25 to 50 years' time, the majority of the people in the country may understand, and may be speaking, a common language which will have the advantage of becoming the national language.

With the rapid expansion of educational programmes, English will continue to be taught more and more as the language of international communication. Very few people in Nigeria are able to communicate intelligibly in English at international level. Very few people ever need to go outside Nigeria to attend international conferences. Therefore, the immediate goal of the teaching of English in Nigeria is to make communication easy within the country among the various ethnic groups. Only a tiny minority need be educated to the highest standards demanded by international intelligibility. It will be wasteful of the nation's resources to expect to train everybody who goes to school to the level of international acceptability in the use of the English language. This is not to say that standards should be lowered. It is a matter of getting the nation's priorities right at various levels of education. At the highest level of education, especially for those specialising in the English language, only the best acceptable international standard is good enough for the country. But such people will always be very few in the community.

If it is true that the immediate goal of the teaching of English is the ability to communicate with other ethnic groups within the country, then, over the years, the type of English taught and spoken will deviate from the type of English spoken in any other community in the world. A time may come, after hundreds of years, as in the case of the Romance languages, when a sort of language based on English will become the national language. The language will no longer be English; just as French is no longer Latin. It will have a distinctive name of its own and the language will then become an indigenous language of the country just as French is now the national language of France where Latin used to be spoken about 1 000 years ago.

There is nothing unpatriotic about suggesting that a foreign language may become the basis of the national language of Nigeria. It is mentioned only as a linguistic possibility, looking at the linguistic history of some other nations of the world. The culture of the world is not static. The culture of any nation of the world is not static, except in the case of the smallest, most isolated peoples cut away from the rest of the civilised world by mountains and other physical barriers. All the nations of the world are now influenced by the culture of other nations. It is one of the unavoidable results of social intercourse. If we take examples from only two areas of the culture of African nations, we see quite clearly that the music and the fine arts of the western world have been influenced by

African music and African art forms. If developed nations of the world, like the United States and the United Kingdom, can be influenced by African culture, there is no reason why one should think it is unpatriotic to say that various aspects of their own culture too can, and do, influence African culture.

In concluding this section on the matter of a national language, one could say that the most patriotic thing would be the emergence of a national language from one or more of our local languages. However, it is difficult to define what an indigenous language is. It can be said that Arabic is clearly not indigenous in Nigeria. Fulani and Hausa are Nigerian languages; but they are also the languages of some other African states. I wonder if one can say that these are not indigenous languages. The verdict of history is that anything becomes indigenous when it has stayed long enough in a particular place and it has taken root. All the main mother tongues spoken by Nigerians now have taken root in the country irrespective of their previous history.

We have said above that the best language for introducing any child to education is his mother tongue or the language of his home. Every child in Nigeria, wherever possible, should be introduced to education through the language of his immediate environment. But each child in a Nigerian primary school should also learn one of the three major languages of the country – Hausa, Ibo and Yoruba – as his second Nigerian language. The learning load on all Nigerian children will virtually be the same because children already speaking one of the major Nigerian languages will also have to learn a second one. The advantage such children will have is that they will understand two of the major Nigerian languages while those from minority languages will understand their own local language and only one major Nigerian language. As time goes on, the English language, as explained above, or one or more of the three major Nigerian languages, will become the national language (or languages) of the country. This process of linguistic evolution will produce fluent second- and third-generation speakers of the various second Nigerian languages in about 50 to 100 years. Educational policy-makers should begin to arrange for teaching the three major languages from now on. Preliminary arrangements for teaching the languages effectively may be completed within five to seven years. Nationwide and effective teaching of all three languages would therefore be possible by the beginning of the school year in 1988 or 1990.

Factors that influence language learning

We have defined language as a system by which human being communicate with one another. The first language is learned effortlessly. Further languages are learned with varying degrees of difficulty. We now come to the major factors which affect language learning. The first and most important factor is motivation.

Motivation is the urge that one has for doing or not doing something. It is a driving force which impels one to the desired goal. The stronger the force, the more easily the person achieves the goal if he or she has basic ability and the requisite favourable circumstances. We shall now examine some aspects of biological and psychological motivations.

Biological motivations are the urges that one has for satisfying a felt physical need. Basic among these needs is the alleviation of hunger: when one is hungry one is impelled to look for something that will remove the pangs of hunger. There are other biological needs that one has to satisfy. In the area of psychological need, an important one is the need to be loved. Every normal human being feels the need to be loved, to be appreciated, to be praised. To satisfy this need, many people are ready to sacrifice immediate comfort and safety. What drives one on to satisfy such a need is referred to as motivation.

In the field of language learning both biological and psychological motivations are at work. When one gets to a foreign country, one of the first things one learns is how to ask for shelter, food and water. There is a strong motivation for wanting to communicate with people so that one's personal needs may be satisfied. In the area of psychological needs, someone in a foreign country needs companionship and affection. He or she is therefore strongly motivated to learn the language of the community so as to be able to communicate his needs to others. We have said that all normal human beings have the basic ability for learning any of the languages of the world in its natural environment or in a devised setting. With this basic ability, therefore, any normal human being who is strongly motivated to learn a language of any environment always does so fairly effortlessly and successfully.

It is known that women usually pick up the language of their immediate environment in a foreign setting more easily than men. There is no physiological evidence to show that women are better endowed to learn languages more easily than men. There is no conclusive, incontrovertible evidence. What is quite clear is that motivation is strongly at work. In a new environment, the average Nigerian woman has to mix with market women and other people to buy things needed for the family. The husband in the new environment may be someone who works in an office where the spoken language is English. Because of the strong motivation to communicate with market women and others, the wife picks up the language more readily than the husband who goes to work, speaks English all day at work, and returns home to the family till the following morning. It is motivation, more than anything else, that explains why most Nigerian wives pick up the language of a new environment more readily than their office-based husbands. Petty-trader husbands and wives do equally well in a new environment.

It is also motivation, or rather lack of it, that explains why many foreigners, particularly Europeans, live in Nigeria for more than twenty years without being able to speak any local language. Most Nigerians aspire to learn and speak the language of the European, particularly if it is English. The European on the other hand does not have any pressing need for learning the local language. Europeans who learn the local language usually have other strong reasons for doing so, quite apart from the need to communicate with the ordinary person in that environment.

Children, too, learn a second language in a new environment almost as effortlessly as their first language. Such children mix freely with the other children of the new location and are strongly motivated to play with them, to communicate with them, and so to learn their language informally. It is not unusual, therefore, to find the wife and the younger children of a family speaking the language of a new environment within a few months, whereas the father of the family does not speak the language even after a residence of very many years, if he is office-based. It is motivation, or lack of motivation, to learn that explains success or failure in acquiring a second language in a new setting.

The ideal in learning any language is that the learner should be able to speak it as a native speaker. This makes for full integration of the learner into the new environment. Nothing biological stands in the way of this accomplishment. It is erroneously said that Africans cannot speak English well because they are not biologically endowed to speak the white man's language. This is false. Some people say that it is the thickness of the lips of the African that prevents him from speaking the English language well. This is a mistake. All human beings are biologically endowed to learn and speak any language in the world faultlessly.

After the age of about 12 years it is difficult to pick up a second language and speak it as a native speaker because the sounds and structures of the first language continually interfere with those of the second language. That is why many Nigerians pronounce the sound 'the' as 'di' or 'z' and 's' because the sound is not in their language; they produce what is nearest to it in their language. This phenomenon is known as *linguistic interference*. It is not natural endowment or lack of it that prevents learning a second language flawlessly like a native speaker; it is the first language and the ways of speaking it that interfere with perfection in the second language. In the environment of the second language it is possible for some people to overcome the handicap of initial linguistic interference and learn the second or even the third language as perfectly as a native speaker. Motivation is also strongly at work in deciding the level of perfection in learning a second language.

Intelligence is another very important factor in learning a language. A minimum of intelligence is needed for learning any of the languages of the world. It does not follow that the more intelligent a person is the more easily he learns a language. But a certain amount of intelligence is needed. Intelligence is a natural endowment; it is the quality of the brain of a person. This is reflected in the person's ability to see complicated relationships quickly and to solve new problems in the light of previous experience and a new insight. This ability to see new relationships quickly is what is meant when a person is referred to as being clever or being brilliant. It means that he can solve certain new problems more quickly than some others because he can see complicated relationships more easily and arrive at a good solution. While it is difficult to say what intelligence is, it is fairly easy to observe it in operation as defined above.

In educational psychology, intelligence is usually measured in units that are referred to as IQ, meaning 'Intelligence Quotient'. The IQ of any average person is 100. People who have below 100 units are referred to as having below average intelligence; while those who have above 100 are referred to as being above average in their intelligence. A university undergraduate needs an IQ that is above average: of at least 120.

People who have an intelligence quotient as low as 70 have been known to learn the language of their environment. This means that an intelligence quotient as low as 70 is sufficient for language learning. It is also known that people who have an IQ as low as 30 can hardly learn any language of the world. Even at the age of 10 or 15 years they cannot speak any language. The critical IQ for learning a language is not known. The fact is that practically everybody in the world can learn the language of his or her environment. It is a very small percentage of the population anywhere in the world that has an IQ that is so low that the person cannot learn a language of the environment.

Intelligence as we know it, and as we have attempted to define it above, is stimulated by language growth. That is, the more one learns a language while one is young the more quickly one's intelligence develops. This means that intelligence helps language learning and language learning further helps the development of intelligence. Studies have been made about identical twins who, having developed from a single egg, have identical natural endowments including intelligence. One twin was reared in an environment that stimulated the normal development of language. The other was reared in a depressing environment where there was very little opportunity for normal language learning. Intelligence, as observed overtly, was found to be better developed in the twin who lived in a normal environment where language could be learned. The intelligence of the other twin did not develop as rapidly. The study was concluded by putting the other twin in a normal and stimulating environment. This other twin quickly developed in intelligence too – before any permanent damage was done in the depressing environment.

While talking about environment we have mentioned the third factor that influences language learning. It is the *speech community*: the environment in which one lives. In any normal human environment in the world, normal social intercourse takes place: any child born in that environment develops normally. Language learning is one of the most difficult things ever learned by any human being. It is at the same time one of those things learned most effortlessly in life. Some of the reasons for this will be explained now.

In a normal social environment there are usually more teachers than pupils in the language learning situation. By 'teachers' we do not mean professional teachers. We mean every adult who speaks that language to the hearing of the child. The adults do not set out to teach the child the language in a formal way as is done in a school. Everybody just goes about their business speaking their language. The child learns from anything that is said to his hearing, from any response that is said or acted under his observation. This is what we mean by saying that there are usually more teachers than pupils in the normal language learning environment.

In a conventional school, while there may be one teacher to thirty pupils, in a natural language learning environment there may be thirty 'teachers', that is, ordinary adults speaking the language, to one 'pupil', that is, the child learning the language.

The adults, here referred to as teachers of the young learner, are patient and humorous whenever the child makes a language learning mistake. These adults succeed very well in their work because they are not conventional teachers as such. It is ironical, therefore, to say that it is those who are not teachers who succeed best at teaching the language. Strictly speaking, their 'teaching' is not economical and is not very efficient. If one reckons by numbers of hours, one sees that there are very many wasted man-hours. On the other hand, the man-hours are not wasted because the adults are not 'teaching' language directly; they are using language for their everyday purposes: the child just happens to be learning incidentally from them.

The main lesson we are drawing from the way non-teachers pass on the knowledge of language is that school-teachers should be sympathetic in their approach to the correction of mistakes. Just as no informal teacher ever stresses a mistake by frequent repetition, the professional teachers should stress the positive and not repeat mistakes. It should be a matter of saying that the correct thing is 'He wants to go', for instance. It is the correct version that should be repeated to the hearing of the pupils and not any errors that may be contained in this, and similar sentences.

The next lesson that the formal teacher has to learn from the non-formal is good humour; the child who makes a mistake is normally not ridiculed, not humiliated. He is greeted with a sympathetic, understanding smile; the adults in the community then say the correct linguistic form that the child should have used. We teachers of language should learn these important lessons.

The fourth important factor influencing language learning is the state of *maturation* of the learner. We all know that a young child of about three months of age does not normally speak any language. In addition to the factors that we have already referred to, an important factor is that of readiness to use the various organs connected with speech production. When a child develops normally, his coordination of muscular movements also develops along the right lines. The ability to grasp things, to gesticulate properly, to use the various organs of speech, come with proper maturation of all the muscles and organs needed for performing such a task. In certain cases of malfunction a child may be blind, deaf and dumb. In such a case the various organs needed for language learning have not developed in the normal and useful way. A deaf and dumb child cannot learn language normally. There are some malfunctions that can be corrected by doctors. In any cases of suspected malfunction, a child should be taken to a doctor at once for examination. Some abnormalities of the tongue, lips, teeth, and so on, can easily be corrected in hospitals to put the child in a normal state of maturation for language learning.

The use of models in language learning

We now come to the different models that are available for learning and teaching a language. We have talked about variants known as dialects. One of the dialects usually becomes what is known as the *standard language*. The main advantage of the standard language is that it is understood by every person literate in that language; it is also usually understood by people who have travelled widely within the community speaking the language. The standard form of any language therefore has wide acceptability and intelligibility. No language is scientifically and linguistically superior or inferior to another one. Notions of inferiority or superiority, as applied to languages, are socio-cultural judgements that are not scientific or linguistic. To take just one example: if a society is highly industrialised and is prosperous, the language of that society is usually believed to be superior to the other dialects or languages. This is a value judgement based on socio-cultural notions.

The best model for imitation in teaching a foreign language is that which is widely accepted and widely intelligible. With particular reference to the English language, used as a second language in Nigeria, the form usually known as *Received Pronunciation* is widely intelligible and widely accepted in most parts of the world. Received Pronunciation is a social dialect of Britain. It is not spoken by any distinctive geographical group in the British Isles as such. It is the language of the group of people educated in the élitist public schools of Britain. With renewed interest in local dialects, the importance of Received Pronunciation is now being overshadowed even in Britain itself. Each local variant of the language, and quite rightly, is being promoted as an acceptable form of the language. In fact, many younger generation phoneticians in Britain today deride what is known as Received Pronunciation.

In spite of what anyone may say against the form of spoken English known as Received Pronunciation, it is still the ideal form of the language to be learnt by foreigners. It is not that a value judgement is attached to the dialect as such; the fact is that most of the books written in the British Isles on the sounds of spoken English describe the Received Pronunciation. By and large, the BBC news readers still use a form of pronunciation that is very close to Received Pronunciation. As I have mentioned above, with renewed regionalism in Britain, all other dialects are also being promoted, particularly by the younger generation of British phoneticians. There is nothing wrong with this in the British Isles. What we are saying is that for the use of foreign learners of the language, a widely acceptable, widely intelligible, and well documented variant of the English language is better taught in the form of English as a second or foreign language. That variant is Received Pronunciation.

The foreign learner of English still has access to the Received Pronunciation dialect over the BBC network, particularly in the reading of news items. Various other dialects of English are spoken on the BBC by various regional speakers who, rightly, pride themselves on their local dialects that have little world intelligibility and acceptability. In fact sub-standard English is sometimes broadcast on the BBC when some semi-literate, non-native speakers of English, of some political or other importance, are invited to broadcast their views on the BBC. It is not recommended that their illiterate or semi-literate speech should be copied by any foreign learner of the English language. We repeat, once again, that the elocution of the BBC news readers is still generally acceptable for use as a worthy model.

Many foreign learners of the English language have sociological and psychological problems about learning to speak the language well. Their semi-literate countrymen, who have no training and no opportunities for speaking the language well, deride anyone who attempts to speak the English language beautifully. They refer to him as 'black European', and as someone suffering from 'colonial mentality'. The truth is that most of the people who speak English as a foreign or second language in any country have not had the best facilities for learning the language. The very few who have had the best opportunities of learning it well are in the minority in any nation that has learnt English as a second or foreign language. The effort of the illiterate or semi-literate society is to force the good speakers to descend to their own level of illiteracy in speaking the language.

Funnily enough, the same people who deride those who attempt to speak the English language well also make fun of people who do not speak their own language well. That is why there are terms like *kobokobo* (a babbler) used by a group of Nigerians about another group of people speaking their own language badly. Most Nigerians accept as intimate brothers and sisters people who speak their own language flawlessly. The question of 'colonial mentality' does not arise when a learner of a Nigerian language speaks it flawlessly. It is clear, therefore, that there is something basically wrong with the attitude of the people who feel that it is bad to learn to speak the English language well. It is quite clearly a psychological case of trying to cover up, and explain away, their own inadequacy in the use of the language. No one quarrels with, or blames, anyone who has not had the best facilities for learning the English language or any other language. The ideal language learning situation is that the model should be copied as efficiently as possible, and used as efficiently as possible, in spite of what semi-literates may say about anyone attempting to speak the English language flawlessly.

It is always very difficult to surpass a model except when one has been exposed to better models. The highest model available for imitation in any language may not be available at all levels of learning. This does not mean that the language should not be learnt. What is being advocated is that the best model available at every level should be taught and imitated. At the level of the small, isolated village school, for instance, the best model available may be that of the semi-literate teacher of English. His qualification may be below the Teachers' Grade II Certificate. He may even be untrained. This is not to say that no untrained teachers speak the English language tolerably well – those who do are the exceptions, not the rule. That untrained village teacher just has to teach English if he is the best speaker available at that village school. He or she, being the highest model, though not a good one, has to be imitated.

As soon as pupils move away to a better school, they will have to unlearn many of the things formerly learnt from the unqualified speaker who was their teacher of English. People have to begin somewhere. If they have to wait until conditions are ideal before anything can be done, they may have to wait for ever. At the secondary grammar school level, the teachers of English should be qualified teachers of the language who also speak it very well. There is a bad trend in the country now in which speakers of other languages have been imported into the country to teach

English. Some of us have met many of them at conferences of teachers of English; it was very difficult to understand their brand of English. Such teachers, recently recruited, are doing more harm than good in the field of English language teaching in the country. If foreigners have to be recruited to teach English, they should be people who speak it very well. There is no sound educational reason behind recruiting people to teach the semi-intelligible English of certain sub-continents of the world.

At the university level, the English language should be taught by people who know it very well. Only the highest standards of writing and speaking are advocated for the teaching of English in our universities. Teachers of English in universities, and students in the departments of English in our universities, should not be deflected from the right course by semi-literates who may deride them as 'black Europeans' or people suffering from 'colonial mentality'. There is nothing 'colonial' in learning to speak the English language well. In conclusion we repeat that the best model available at every level should be taught and learnt with particular reference to the English language as the language of education in Nigeria. Only the best is good enough as a model.

We now come to efforts that have been made to make the learning of languages easy. We shall start with *pidgin*. The pidgin form of any language is a type of it usually used by traders and local people. One of the main characteristics of 'pidgin' is that it has a simplified structure. This means that the grammatical and other complicated rules of the parent language are simplified. Pidgin is usually used in Nigeria to refer to what is known as *pidgin English*. It happens that the variety of the language is a pidgin form of English. As already hinted, there are pidgin forms of other European languages.

Pidgin English is a variety of simplified English used by early European traders with the local people. It is the most widespread form of English in Nigeria. It is usually referred to as the English of the illiterate. There is some justification in this description of the users of the language because most of its speakers are not literate. They speak the language but they cannot write it. It is extensively used in the eastern parts of the Federation of Nigeria and elsewhere. It is a sort of *lingua franca*. As mentioned above one, of the main characteristics of pidgin is the simplification of the parent language.

Pidgin English is a simplification of the English language. It also has added to it many local words. Its grammar is simplified in many ways. For instance, it is not necessary to use plural formations of nouns or past tense forms of verbs in speaking pidgin English. It is quite correct in pidgin to say: *I see am yesterday. See* is used in connection with a past event that happened yesterday where normal English would require *saw*. This is one of the ways in which pidgin English is simplified; it is one of the characteristics that make it simple to use by the illiterate and semi-literate. Another example of simplification of grammatical rules is the non-use of plural forms. It is correct in pidgin English to say *I see the two man wey come here yesterday*. The parent language requires the inflected form *men*.

Simplification of English to form pidgin English takes place at all the various levels of linguistic analysis. In the area of phonology, for instance, a lot of simplification has taken place. Because the 'th' sound is not used in many Nigerian languages, as earlier mentioned, 'di' or 't' is substituted for the sound as in *di tin wey you say*. We see here a substitution of 'di' for 'the' and a substitution of 't' for 'th' in 'thing', which is pronounced as 'tin'. In the area of lexis we find that very many local words, and some older English words, are used in pidgin English. The word pronounced as *yas* is the older English form *arse* meaning *buttocks*. The word *kiakia* in the following pidgin sentence is a local one: *Make you go kiakia. Kiakia* is a Yoruba word which means *quickly*. Very many such local words are integrated into pidgin English in various parts of the Federation.

The core of pidgin English is understood by very many ethnic groups within Nigeria. But because of the incorporation of local words, it may be difficult to understand certain statements made in different parts of the country. One needs a knowledge of the local language to understand some of the incorporated vocabulary items. But by and large, pidgin English is a widely acceptable form of communication in Nigeria. We have earlier suggested that, in the absence of any other common language, a teacher may use pidgin English briefly to explain a situation in class and then move on to normal English as soon as possible – to explain, not to translate. Using pidgin English in teaching is not the best form of education; but where the class teacher shares no language with the majority of his pupils, he or she has no other choice if they all understand pidgin English.

Creole is another form of language which has deviated from a parent language. Usually, the first stage of deviation is the *pidginisation* of the parent language. When the language is used in a simplified form along with the local languages it is called a pidgin. But when the pidgin form completely replaces the local language or languages it is called *creole*. In Sierra Leone, English has acquired the status of creole. It has become the native language of a group of Sierra Leoneans. Creole is different from the parent language at many points. It has moved further away, in some cases, than the pidgin derived from the original language. In a country like Sierra Leone where English has become creole, the educational system still has provisions for learning standard British English. It follows, therefore, that while creole is a native language, a variety of standard English exists side by wide with the language. The same situation where creole and the English language exist side by side can be found in Jamaica. In Nigeria, English has reached the status of pidgin – but not that of creole.

Artificial languages

Many attempts have been made by linguistic inventors to introduce artificial languages into the world. Many of the attempts have failed to gain root. But the most successful attempt is the one known as *Esperanto*. It is named after the inventor of the language who, in 1887, wrote an article in Russian purported to have been written by one Dr Esperanto.

The pen name Esperanto is from the Latin word *spero* (I hope) which suggests that the inventor of the language hoped that it would become a world language some day. The actual name of the physician and linguist who invented Esperanto is Dr Ludwig Lazarus Zamenhof (1859–1917). His main reason for inventing the language was to remove national and racial hatreds by the elimination of language barriers. We have said once that one of the characteristics of togetherness and brotherliness in a nation is a common national language. Prejudices, misunderstandings and hatreds are bound to arise where various languages are imperfectly understood, or not understood at all, by groups of people living close together. Dr Zamenhof attempted to remove this sort of barrier.

In spite of the initial prejudice against an artificial language, Esperanto got on fairly well. It was estimated that by 1974 there were more than 100 000 speakers of Esperanto. All the speakers, however, understood one or more other languages and only used Esperanto as a language of international communication. There are also more than 30 000 books written in Esperanto in the British Isles. There is an Esperanto Office in London in the United Kingdom set up in order to disseminate information about the artificial language Esperanto.

The basic principles of the language are the following:

1 grammatical regularity;
2 formation of root words from major European languages;
3 derivation of a large vocabulary by affixation.

Affixation means the use of *affixes*, that is, parts of a word before or after a root word; for instance, in English, *disqualify* is formed by using *dis*, which is an affix, before *qualify*. *Achievement* is formed by using *ment* after *achieve*. In English *dis* and *ment* are two of the very many affixes used.

Esperanto is therefore a simplified, artificial language meant for use as an international language. In spite of its being the most successful of all artificial languages, it has not caught on very widely in the world. In almost a hundred years it is still unknown in many parts of the world. It is not recognised as one of the major languages used by the United Nations. It is not known that any significant group in Nigeria writes or speaks Esperanto.

The problem with an artificial language is that it is not bound to any living culture. There are no native speakers who have a bond of affection for the language. It has no soil on which to germinate. This brings us once more to the problems of concocting a national language for Nigeria. If the history of artificial languages is anything to go by, such an effort will be a wasted one. No one will have any native affection for such an artificial language; there will also be very many unsolved problems of grammar and lexis.

Principles for the evolution of a national language

Having discussed some of the principles of artificial languages we now come to the main principles of a national language policy. We consider the following principles vital in formulating a national language policy:

1 Demographic factors;
2 Equality of opportunities;
3 Cohesiveness;
4 Mobility;
5 Cultural integration;
6 International links;
7 Attitudinal change;
8 Written literature.

We shall now discuss the principles in detail one by one.

Demographic factors

The number of people who already speak a language should, naturally, be taken into consideration when taking a policy decision on what should be the national language. As we have already said, no language is linguistically better or more important than another. The demographic factor is important in that there are advantages in choosing as a national language one that is spoken by a large number of any nation's peoples. Large numbers of existing speakers predispose such a language to easy spread.

Equality of opportunities

Any language that will be considered for choice as a national language must not rob speakers of other languages of the chance of equal and even development in the nation. Efforts must be made to give non-speakers of the language every facility to acquire the new language to the level of competence needed for, say, obtaining jobs with the national language.

Cohesiveness

A national language brings cohesiveness to any nation; a language that meets the requirements of the other principles will promote the spirit of togetherness in any nation.

Mobility

Physical mobility by road, sea, or air should be made possible in any nation that has to decide on a national language. Commerce is one of the most potent motives for moving from one place to another. Movement and ownership of property should be unrestricted within the nation.

Cultural integration

The language to be chosen should, ideally, be one that is already integrated into the culture of the country or a large part of it. The language should be native, or be already indigenised through generations of native speakers who speak it as their first language.

International links

It is very useful if the language can be fairly easily used in communicating with other nations, particularly neighbouring countries. Such a situation helps to break down international barriers.

Attitudinal change

The non-speakers of the language must be carefully prepared to have a positive attitude to the language or languages. They must be assured of preservation of their identity.

Written literature

An existing orthography and an abundance of written literature are big advantages in choosing a language as a national language. Teaching it and using it as a medium of education will have been based on a sound literary foundation if there is abundant literature.

As we have mentioned already, the best way of allowing a national language to evolve is to teach the three major Nigerian languages. Arrangements to teach them effectively in schools should start now so that the languages can be taught as previously suggested, from about 1988 in all Nigerian schools. This will cater for the population of children who are at school. We also need to make provisions for adults who are not attending school. The medium of teaching the masses should also start now for teaching the three major languages over the air.

Techniques of teaching second or foreign languages will have to be used because the three major languages will be taught to non-speakers of the languages. The National Language Centre should take the lead in consulting with relevant departments of Nigerian universities for making adequate preparations to teach the three Nigerian languages by radio and by television. It will not be an easy task teaching the three languages through the electronic media. There must be directors of the project who will organise script-writing for teaching the languages by wireless. This is a gigantic task involving very many disciplines. The universities of the

Federation, collectively, have the manpower requirements for developing the necessary teaching programme.

Needless to say, in organising such a language teaching programme for the whole nation, the universities will have to cooperate with the broadcasting authorities and many other professionals. It is wise to invest part of the nation's resources in this way. The effort will be a massive investment for the future; it will be a fruitful national assignment for uniting our nation. The smaller Nigerian languages will still be spoken, as Welsh is still spoken in Britain; but every Nigerian will understand one or more of the three major languages. Nigerians will be able to communicate in and outside the country in a common tongue.

Further reading

A. AFOLAYAN, 'Problems, Principles and Prospects of English Studies in an African University', Inaugural Lecture, 38, University of Ife, 1979

A. BANJO, 'On the state of English studies in Nigeria', *Journal of the Nigeria English Studies Association*, 6 (1), May 1974.

ENCYCLOPAEDIA BRITANNICA. Article on Esperanto.

FEDERAL MINISTRY OF EDUCATION, *National Policy of Education* (Lagos: 1977).

J. A. FISHMANN, *et al, Language Problems of Developing Nations* (New York: J. Wiley, 1968).

J.SPENCER (ed.), *Language in Africa* (London: Cambridge University Press, 1963).

———, *The English Language in West Africa* (London: Longman, 1971).

R. QUIRK, 'The study of the mother tongue', in P. D. Strevens (ed.), *Five Inaugural Lectures* (London: Oxford University Press, 1966).

S. H. O. TOMORI, 'The role of the vernacular in education', *West African Journal of Education*, June 1965.

———, 'The role of language in education', Inaugural Lecture, University of Ibadan, 1973.

E. UBAHAKWE, (ed.), *Varieties and Functions of English in Nigeria* (Ibadan: African University Press, 1979).

18 Oral and written literature in Nigeria

Bade Ajuwon

The carriers of oral tradition in Nigeria

Pre-literate Nigeria once enjoyed a verbal art civilisation which, at its high point, was warmly patronised by traditional rulers and the general public. At a period when writing was unknown, the oral medium served the people as a bank for the preservation of their ancient experiences and beliefs. Much of the evidence, therefore, that relates to the past of Nigerians could be found in oral traditions.

The various carriers of oral traditions in Nigeria include court historians, freelance oral artists, professional guild artists as well as leaders and devotees of traditional religion. The continued performances of these verbal artists provide a means whereby the present generation has a glimpse into the past of their ancestors, and this explains why Nigerians hold their oral traditions in high esteem. We observe with interest that to these people, oral tradition is the final court of appeal in any disputed matter. And commenting on the continent-wide value attached to oral traditions in general, Kwame Daaku once declared:

> Oral traditions have been the main method of teaching the history of many African peoples, and it is by studying them that the Africans' view of themselves and their relations with their neighbours may be understood and appreciated.[1]

A deeper knowledge of the carriers of oral traditions in Nigeria, either in terms of their activities, or in respect of their geographical distribution, and their various patrons will serve a useful purpose. While it is true that nearly all adults in traditional communities in Nigeria may be familiar with their lineage histories, and are capable of relating them, it is not everyone who possesses the stamina to narrate or chant them for a long period of time. What distinguishes Nigerian oral artists from their fellow men is their ability to chant oral literature over a lengthy period of time, and even entertain their audience dramatically. And as keepers of the people's ancient wisdom and beliefs, some oral artists were appointed, as in the case of the Yoruba, as councillors, sitting in judgment with traditional rulers.

In the north, there are the Maroka verbal artists who are usually versed in Hausa folklore and cultural history. Not only do they chant, entertain and praise the emirs, they also relate histories, and make appraisals of the life of their masters. In this regard, they function in a way similar to the Akunyungbas of Yorubaland who carefully refer to the merits and weaknesses of Yoruba Obas in their performances. It is observed that the Marokas also share some identical characteristics with the griots of the Wolof of Senegal in their usual attachment of certain families to sing their praise, or mock and criticise them. But in order to have a deeper knowledge about the nature, functions, and movements of the Marokas, let us examine Mungo Park's nineteenth-century description of these popular poets:

> They consist of two classes; the most numerous are the 'singing men' called *jilli kea* . . .

> One or more of these may be found in every town. They sing extempore songs, in honour of these chief men, or any other persons who are willing to give 'solid pudding for empty praise'. A noble part of their office is to recite historical events of their country. The other class are the devotees of the Mohammedan faith, who travel about the country, singing devout hymns and performing religious ceremonies, to conciliate the favour of the Almighty, either in averting calamity, or insuring success to any enterprise. Both descriptions of these itinerant bands are much employed and respected by the people, and very liberal contributions are made for them.[2]

The Marokas were shown as making their livelihood through the gifts received from their masters. This being so, it meant they would stay with a master as long as the gifts continued to flow, but change masters as soon as they dwindled. But in order to win these rewards, the Marokas tried to bring aesthetics into their oral performances.

In Yorubaland are found in abundance skilful narrators of folktales, who are not necessarily professionals, but who relate tales to meet the cultural needs of the people. The Yoruba are predominantly farmers who normally return to their villages tired and worn-out after a hard day's work on the farm. As a means of relaxation, farmers gather their children and sit under the moon for tale-telling. In a community where succession is patrilineal rather than matrilineal, where legacies are determined by the *idi igi*[3] system, and where contracts are executed purely on faith, the telling of stories is used by narrators to instruct the young and teach them to respect the dictates of their custom: as a result a large body of moral instruction, of societal values and norms are preserved for posterity by the Yoruba. What is also of interest is that the Yoruba folktale narrative technique was later adopted by Yoruba novelists as a creative device. It is often assumed that the content of narrative praise-poems in most Nigerian communities is mainly praise. This is far from the truth. In fact the content of narrative praise-poems in Nigeria often consists of an appraisal of the failure and successes of the patrons of an artist. What one may claim is that it is usual for many praise singers in Nigeria to deal at length with the attributes of their patrons and carefully gloss over their weaknesses, thus having a mixture of praise and reprimand. In a Kanuri praise-song, for example, an artist saluted an individual because 'his eye-lashes are as arrows'.[4] And this praise-poem chanted by a Yoruba poet is also a mixture of praise and condemnation:

307

O ṣe é tó ò ń bá mi í pòṛéè mi.[5]
Torí ẹníkìí là á kí.
Bánigbóṛò la lè fòṛò lò

Omọ gbì ńlè.
Ọmọ gbì lókè òde.
Ọmọ kàarà, mọ kòorò léhín ílèkùn.
Bí ò bá ṣe bí olè lóbà,
A ṣe bí ajínifé.

(Thank you for helping me pay salute to my friend.
Salute is due to whoever salutes one.
Matters are better discussed with those who will listen.

Offspring of one who jumps inside the house.
Offspring of one who jumps outside.
Offspring of one who worked behind the door.
If he is not a thief at Ọ̀bà,
He will be a jilter.)

The first three lines of the above praise-poem give us a feeling that the poet is out to praise his patron. An impression of close affinity between them is also sensed. What follows from the fifth line is a revelation of the unethical ways of the poet's subject who has a tendency to steal or jilt a lover like his ancestors. All this is said by the poet without any fear of slander because he is operating within the poetic liberties granted him by his culture.

Our aim so far has been to show that oral artists, whether narrators of folktales or carriers of narrative folk poetry, are found in many culture areas in Nigeria. It should be noted, moreover, that it is from the repertoire carried by the oral artists in Nigeria that indigenous writers find much of their literary creativity.

Nationalism and the emergence of non-realistic novels in Nigeria

With introduction of western education in Nigeria in the nineteenth century came the birth of what we may term as non-realistic literature in many parts of the country. The eighth century AD saw the importation of Arabic ideas and culture into Africa. As early as the middle of the fourteenth century, the Arabic language was widespread and written in the northern part of Nigeria, and it was also the language of government. During the seventeenth century, Hausa literature in Arabic came into existence when, in 1665, Dan Marina of Katsina wrote an ode to celebrate the victory of Mai Ali, a ruler of Bornu, over the Jukuns.[6]

The introduction of western education in the north, however, was met with strong protest in poetic form, having been condemned by poets as essentially Christian in character and content. Fear was expressed by poets that Arabic culture and tradition would be replaced with that of the West, and that the whites would take over and disrupt the administrative set-up which they had laboured over the years to build. Above all, it was believed that the tenets and practices of the Islamic religion would be falsified by the visiting whites, and Moslems converted to Christianity. One of the most articulate poets was Aliyu dan Sidi, Emir of Zaria, who used materials from oral traditions for poetic protests. The positions of these protesting poets was strengthened by the activities of such Muslim leaders as Usman dan Fodio, who was the greatest exponent of the tenets of Islamic religion. His poems demonstrated the religious devotion and humility which were to characterise this verse:

> I am pleased to thank Allah,
> For giving me the opportunity to praise His generosity.
> I am introducing myself to our Prophet.
> You should know that I know many of his qualities;
> I will surely mention them in thanking Allah,
> For Muslims to know them in the East and West.[7]

As in the other parts of the country, Hausa novels of a non-realistic character appeared in the 1930s. Most of the Hausa novels at this period were based on fantasy, akin to the folktale tradition. In 1934, Muhammadu Bello wrote a novel titled *Gandoki*, the plot of which was built around 'mysterious' characters who perform wonders. The characters transform themselves into other things, and dialogues take place between humans and fairies. One is led to say that the book is a reduction of Hausa oral traditions to written literature.

While there appeared poets and writers in the north protesting against western education and religion, the concern of the early writers of Yoruba novels was partly to attempt to advance the cause of the missionaries, and partly to teach humility and accept western ideas. This is understandable because the early missionaries to Nigeria first settled in Yorubaland. Traditional rulers were bribed by the missionaries and converts made easily. There were many Yoruba novelists who sought to teach the Christian religion, two in particular are worthy of mention – D. O. Fagunwa and Isaac Delano.

Fagunwa is often seen in his books engaged in saying Christain prayers; his characters also indulge in similar action. In *Ìrìnkèrindò Nínú Igbó Elégbèje*, Fagunwa begins:

> Mo ké pe Olódùmarè pé kí o jòwó se alatilehin wa bí a ti ńlo mo ra owó sí ojú òrun mo sì wí fún Olódùmarè pé sìgìdì ko lágbára níwájú Olórun . . ..[8]

> (I call on God Almighty to please support us as we journey along: I rob my hands towards heaven and tell God that before Him, Sigidi is powerless. . .)

And at the end of the same book he declares:

Ng o pari iwe ti eleyi nisisiyi, ki Ọlọrun dá ẹmi sí, a o tún máá gburo ara wa ni ọjọ miran.[9]

(I will end this book now: may God spare our lives so we shall meet each other some day.)

We see Fagunwa as a preacher, drawing morals and putting across religious instruction in his books. And although Delano does not sermonise with *Aiye D'aiye Oyinbo*, he attempts to persuade people to appreciate the values of western ideas and institutions.

Fagunwa's pre-eminent place among the Yoruba novelists, however, makes it necessary for us to examine his works further. He wrote his first book, *Ogbójú Ọdẹ Nínú Igbó Irúnmalè* in 1938. The style of the book is fantasy. His hero sets out on a quest into the thick forest. He engages demons in battles and conquers them with the aid of magic or the assistance of his deceased mother; he transforms himself into things to avert danger, and even grows feathers and flies away from trouble spots. A textual reference is useful:

Ibiti nwọn ti npa èrò bi awọn yio ṣe ré mi lulè, ni mo ti ranti ogun mi kan bayìí, egbé ni; mo ba sà á wéré mo si ba ara mi ni iyàrá mi ni ilé, egbé ti gbe mi de ibè.

(As they were planning to drop me down, I remembered a charm of mine; it is egbe[10]: I applied it and soon found myself in a room in my house. Egbe had flown me there.)

Fagunwa was very prolific and his other books include *Igbó Olódùmarè* (1949); *Irèke Oníbùdó* (1949); and *Àdìtú Olúdùmarè* (1961), to mention only the most important of them.

A feature common to all his novels is a heavy dependence on ethnic folklore for creative writing. His works show an extensive use of proverbs, riddles, traditional jokes and other lore central to Yoruba belief. By his publications, Fagunwa has contributed immensely to the development of Yoruba written literature.

Amos Tutuola is another Yoruba writer who deserves our attention. Amos Tutuola was perhaps the first Yoruba to experiment in writing a novel in English. His main emphasis is upon a revival of his cultural heritage, and he feels, like Cesaire, that the cultural past should be detected, magnified, and be given back its value in a world of false values. In 1953, he published *The Palmwine Drinkard*, the hero of which is in quest for his tapster in Dead's Town. Tutuola has little education and this accounts for his poor grasp of the English language. Thus he wrote in a personal style which western critics have given various names. His dependence on ethnic folklore for writing the book attracted the attention of Kofi Awonoor, who wrote:

Tutuola's works, therefore, because of their clear antecedents, cannot be discussed as novels, but rather as romances which base themselves on Yoruba folktale. Cast in the world of what Northrop Frye calls the 'native quest romance', the stories follow the pattern of the folk story in which the man or animal hero or heroine departs in order to acquire knowledge, wealth, food, and the wherewithal for survival in an uncertain world.[11]

Apart from *The Palmwine Drinkard*, Tutuola also wrote a number of other books in the same personal style. They include *My Life in the Bush of Ghosts*; *Simbi and the Satyre of the Dark Jungle*; and *The Brave African Huntress* and *Ajayi and his Inherited Poverty*. The foregoing list of Tutuola's publications demonstrates to us the impact he has made on the growth of Nigerian literature.

Let us turn our attention now to literary activity in Igboland, especially between the 1930s and 1950s. As far back as 1841, the Church Missionary Society sent out a mission to sign an agreement with Obi Ossai of Aboh that the Igbo people over whom he reigned were prepared to embrace Christianity.[12] The Igbos of Onitsha also accepted Christianity, which later spread fast to other Igbo communities. And commenting on the spread of Christianity in Igboland, Ilogu says:

> . . . the establishment of the evangelical wing of the Anglican church which in course of time spread northwards to Enugu and southwards to Owerri covering groups of villages along its route like Nnewi, Ihiala, Nkwerre and basing its southwards headquarters at Egbu, very near Owerri. The spread of the gospel westwards from Onistsha across the Niger led to the establishment of the Anglican Church in Asaba and Agbor areas of Iboland.[13]

Other Christian missions like the Catholics in 1885, the Methodist Society in 1892, and the Baptists also found ready converts in Igboland and soon spread their tentacles to several villages and hamlets. What the missionaries then did, with the reduction of Yoruba and Igbo languages to writing towards the end of the last century, was to translate the English Bible and Bunyan's *Pilgrim's Progress* into local languages, thus making available a large body of literature in the two languages.

A time soon came when educated Igbo people developed a critical view of Christianity and its influence on the people's life style. Since the virtues of traditional life where preferred to those of the west, the Igbo intellectuals started to make demands for the churches to indigenise, by taking in greater features of Igbo culture-like the title of Ozo, polygamy, and so forth. And with the growth of Igbo novelists in the early 1930s, the disgust of the Igbo people towards the Christian missionaries was well articulated – particularly by Pita Nwana, whose prize-winning book *Omenuko*, was published in 1935, six years after a standard orthography for the Igbo language had been developed. While the style of the book is based on fantasy, as in the case of the Yoruba examples cited above, Nwana has a didactic intention which he does not hide. He declares:

> I have set on record some of the events and incidents in the life of Maze Omenukoso that readers may learn something from such a life.[14]

The success of the book lies in Nwana's use of materials drawn from traditional lore for cultural revolution.

In 1950, Achara came to the fore with the publication of *Ala Bingo*, a book having a riddle as its framework. A deceased king is survived by two sons who seek nomination to the vacant stool. A riddle is placed before them and whoever supplies the better solution succeeds their father. Each of the two sons attempts to provide an answer, but the better one comes from the elder son who consequently succeeds their father. The intended lesson is to let people see why eldest sons normally ascend the throne of their fathers. While we may admit that the book lacks the essential attributes of a novel, it demonstrates how Igbo writers use the literary medium to highlight traditional values and beliefs – at an age when western ideas were fast spreading in Igboland. With *Ala Bingo*, Achara succeeds to some extent, however, in shifting the attention of the Igbos towards a re-examination of the western ideas and institutions which they had warmly embraced.

The emergence of realistic literatures in Nigeria

The founding of the University College of Ibadan in 1948 was a great blessing to many Nigerians trained in western literary art. A major factor, however, which led to the shift in the literary style from the fantasy tradition to realism, was the persistent calls from scholars for a change. Demands were made, for example, at learned conferences, in journals, and in the local newspapers by Nigerians who had benefited from a university education. But perhaps the most articulate calls came from Yorubaland, the nature and form of which we now try to show below:

One author, Delano, once reacted thus in *L'ójó Ojó Un* (1963);

A ko ohun ti ó ṣe pataki tí ó jé ótító ṣugbon a gbé é ka orí ìtàn àròṣo.

(We wrote important things that are true, using the form of the novel.)

Akin Isola remarks in his unpublished dissertation that Jeboda, in the Foreword to *Olowolaiyemo*, says that when the Ministry of Education, Western Region of Nigeria, organised a novel-writing competition in 1963, competitors were warned:

... pé irú ítàn ti àwọn ń fé ni ìtàn tí ó n sọ nípa irú àwọn ohun tí a lè fi ojú rí ni ilè Nigeria ni òde òní.

(... that the kind of story they wanted was the story that dealt with the kind of things we could see with our eyes in Nigeria today.)[15]

The immediate effect of the calls for the new literary direction was a sudden change by writers from the existing literary style of fantasy to that of realism. Thus Faleti declares his compliance to the calls by stating in *Omo Olókùn Esin* (1969): 'láàrin àwọn ará ìlú sí ara wọn ti kìì ṣe láàrin àwọn iwin . . .' (that his book is characterised by humans and not based on events amongst fairies). Thus a new literary tradition was being adopted by many Yoruba novelists; they dealt with such universal themes as religion, labour, corruption, and justice; they employ human characters and concrete symbols. The list of Yoruba writers of realistic novels by this time will be long, but it suffices to mention only the following: Oladejo Okediji, Akin Isola, T. A. Ladele and Lawuyi Oguniran.

There was a corresponding growth in the number of Yoruba writers in English in the same period, the most prolific of whom is Wole Soyinka, author of *The Interpreters* (1965). Indeed it is through this book that Soyinka gained his initial reputation as a novelist. And commenting on the book, Emile Snyder declares:

> . . . although a magnificent novel in its own right, it is also a pivotal novel in terms of new literary directions. It innovates at every level: breaking further with the tight form of the Victorian novel, breaking with the purely historical and societal concerns of the past Nigerian novels, breaking with the conception of plots and characters in a novel.[16]

Wole Soyinka uses *The Interpreters* to interpret his society, looking at it from various angles. His characters are seen discussing a society of which they, too, form a part. Today, Wole Soyinka is better known as a dramatist and poet than a novelist.

The period immediately after the Second World War saw a sudden rise in the growth of Igbo written literature in the market town of Onitsha. E. Obiechina has this to say:

> The first pamphlets appeared in 1947, the work of the new literates. School teachers, low-level clerks, artisans, provincial correspondents of daily newspapers . . . and even secondary school students now dealt with the problems and experiences of ordinary men and women and their efforts to cope with such matters as love and marriage, life in the town and especially how to earn and save money. . . . For the first time, written literature became a medium for clarifying the issues of everyday life and experience, for seeking and proffering answers to social problems and for celebrating the realities of the changes sweeping over the land.[17]

In recent times, the governments of the Igbo-speaking states have given full encouragement to the development of Igbo literature. Dathorne's remarks are appropriate:

> In recent years official attempts have been made to encourage Ibo literature. In 1960, the African Language Bureau in Eastern Nigeria awarded prizes for three winning short stories and more recently the society for promoting Ibo Language and Culture has published prize-winning short stories.[18]

As in the case of Yoruba writers of the post-1950s, Igbo novelists

Fig. 18.1a   Wọle Soyinka

Fig. 19.1b   Chinua Achebe

abandoned the fantasy tradition of novel-writing and turned to realism. Let us now look at a few examples.

Chinua Achebe's maiden novel, *Things Fall Apart*, was published in 1958. Although the book contains a large amount of Igbo folklore and culture, it possesses the essential attributes of a novel. The book shows the tragic falling apart of the Igbo clans with the arrival of the Europeans. In it we also see the bitter cultural struggle between the Africans and the Europeans. Achebe's use of Igbo proverbs in *Things Fall Apart* has attracted the attention of many literary men. Kofi Awonoor, for example, comments:

> These proverbs are intricately woven into the fabric of his style, completely absorbed to the extent that they constitute one of the most significant features of his totally African-derived English style;[19]

And Bernth Lindfors refers to the use of proverbs in Achebe's novels, calling them 'the palmwine with which Achebe's words are eaten'.[20] Let us have a short passage from the text for consideration:

> Near the barn was a small house, the 'medicine house' or shrine where Okonkwo kept the symbols of his personal god and of his ancestral spirits. He worshipped them with sacrifices of kolanuts, food and palmwine, and offered prayers to them on behalf of himself. his three wives and eight children.[21]

The actions of Okonkwo, the protagonist of the book, gives us a deeper insight into some other vital aspects of the ritual and religious practices of the Igbo people. He warns the children never to whistle at night for fear of evil spirits. According to Okonkwo, 'Dangerous animals became more

314

sinister and uncanny in the dark. A snake was never called by his name at night, because it would hear.'[22] The effective use of folklore as a literary device is, indeed, part of the special attributes of Achebe. After the publication of *Things Fall Apart*, he remained prolific; his other publications include *No Longer At Ease* (1960); *Arrow of God* (1964); and *A Man of the People* (1966).

The literary focus continued to be directed towards societal life in Igboland after the 1950s. Cyprian Ekwensi, for instance, published *People of the City* in 1954, and *Jagua Nana* in 1961. The heroine of *Jagua Nana* is a celebrated prostitute, who stands as a representative example of women resident in cosmopolitan cities in Nigeria: she sleeps with whoever can afford her price, shuttles back and forth from one night club to another, rides in long Mercedes cars belonging to her patrons, and smokes marijuana at will. And with *Jagua Nana*, Ekwensi makes a sharp departure from fantasy novels to realism. His characters are humans rather than fairies, and the scenes of action are those of everyday human life, and not in the spirit world.

Any discussion of Igbo writers since the 1950s must take account of Christopher Okigbo. Okigbo's success as a poet, like that of Wole Soyinka and John Pepper Clark, could be traced to his knowledge of the oral traditions of his people. As a leading Igbo poet, he gained the attention of the literary world with the publication of such poems as 'Lament of the Silent Sisters', 'Heaven's gate', 'Limits', 'Path of Thunder', and 'Hurrah for Thunder', to mention only a few. A common criticism of his poems is that they are difficult to comprehend; this is due to his use of many traditional symbols and peculiar Igbo folklore traits with which non-Igbos are not familiar. Let us look at one of the poems.

AND TO US they came . . .
   (Malisons, malisons, mair than ten)
And climbed the bombax
   and killed the sunbird.
And they scanned the forest of oilbean,
   its approach,
Surveyed its high branches . . .

And morndew beckoned, beckoned afar,
   from the oilbean trees,
From the branches of the gods of IRKALIA.
Within it . . .
   within me . . .
Not a stir,
   not a dead leaf whispered,

Not the still breath of the gods of IRKALIA.

Apart from the fact that Okigbo's choice of words in the above poem is difficult, one also requires some familiarity with the cultural significance of the gods of Irkalia in order to appreciate the poem in full. Our interest, however, falls on Okigbo's reliance on materials drawn from oral tradition for poetic composition, a style that earned him a high reputation.

As literary activity gained momentum in the south, there was also a marked increase in it in the north. Contemporary Hausa poets emerged and published poems dealing with a broad range of subject matter. A prominent Hausa poet whose poems circulate far and wide in the country is Mu'azu Hadeja. His poetic themes include morality, education, religion and a variety of everyday events. His famous poem, *Wakar Karuwa*, is a bitter satire of a celebrated prostitute, similar in manner to *Jagua Nana*.

But as far back as 1952, Abubukar Imam wrote *Tafiya Mabudin Ilmi*, a novel whose style is visibly different from the fantasy tradition. Like Achebe's *Things Fall Apart*, the book deals with the rejection of western ideas and values. Also in the 1950s the first Prime Minister of Nigeria, Sir Abubakar Tafawa Balewa, published a novel titled *Shaihu Umar*, which was published by the Gaskiya Corporation in Zaria. The novel deals with African life and cultural values before the arrival of the Europeans. To date however, we observe that the literary tradition in the north, although realistic, has continued, in gentler form, to cast aspersions on western values and ideas.

Our attempt so far has been to show how Nigerian literatures were fertilised by oral traditions. The works of writers like Fagunwa, Achebe, and Mu'azu Hadeja permit us to make this conclusion. We also observe how writers from the different parts of the country have succeeded in articulating communal feelings from time to time. With the continued use of oral traditions to inspire literary creativity, however knowledgeable Nigerian writers may be in the western literary traditions, their works will remain easily recognisable by the traditional cultural motifs they use.

Notes

1 Kwame Daaku, 'History in the oral traditions of the Akans', in A. Dorson (ed.), *Folklore and Traditional History* (The Hague: Mouton, 1973), p. 43.

2 Scharfe and Aliyu, 'Hausa Poetry', in U. Beier (ed.), *Introduction to African Literature* (London: Longman, 1967), p. 34.

3 *Idi igi*: this is the Yoruba traditional reference to each one of the wives a deceased man possessed when his legacy is to be shared. Under the system, no wife is superior to another and this principle is used to determine legacy sharing.

4 J. R. Patterson, *Kanuri Songs* (Kaduna: 1925), p. 17.

5 Oludare Olajubu, *Akojopo Iwi Egungun* (Ibadan: Longman, 1972), p. 44.

6 O. Dathorne, *Black Mind* (Minnesota: University of Minnesota Press, 1974), p. 96.

7 *Ibid.*, p. 98.

8 D. O. Fagunwa, *Irinkerindo Ninu Igbo Elegbeje* (London: Nelson, 1952), p. 24.

9 *Ibid.*, p. 117.

10 A charm believed capable of flying someone away from trouble spots to save him from harm.

11 Kofi Awonoor, *The Breast of the Earth*, p. 227.

12 Edmound Ilogu, *Christianity and Ibo Culture* (New York: Nok, 1977), p. 56.

13 *Ibid.*, p. 57.

14 P. Nwana, *Omenuko* (London: Atlas Press, 1953), p. 1.

15 A. Isola, 'The writer's art in the modern Yoruba novel', unpublished Ph.D. dissertation, Ibadan University, 1978, p. 311.

16 Emile Snyder, *New Directions in African Writing* (Bloomington: Indiana, 1972), p. 2.

17 O. Dathorne, *Black Mind*, p. 102.

18 Kofi Awonoor, *The Breast of the Earth*, p. 25.

19 B. Lindfors in *African Literature Today*, Vol. 1, 1968, p. 3.

20 Chinua Achebe, *Things Fall Apart* (Greenwich, Connecticut: Fawcett. 1959), p. 18.

21 *Ibid.*, p. 13.

22 Christopher Okigbo, *Limits* (Ibadan: Caxton Press, 1962), p. 16.

19 The performing arts in Nigerian culture[1]

Yemi Ogunbiyi

Any meaningful discussion of art in the context of a neo-colonialist situation such as Nigeria's implies an examination of the crucial question of the role played by that art in the people's cultural education and their ordinary daily interaction and contact with other people. This position assumes from the outset that art, particularly the performing arts, at the collective level, is a product of man's intellectual and imaginative activity, embodying his images, songs, words, mime. It is also a product of the conflicts and contradictions at the very centre of a community's being and the process of becoming. An an expression of the relationship between man, society and nature, drama and the performing arts arose out of fundamental human needs in the dawn of human civilisation and have continued to express those needs ever since. The performing arts in Nigeria can therefore be said to have originated with the Nigerian himself, embodying his first pre-occupations, his achievements, failures, conflicts, set-backs, triumphs and all.

The nature of the origin and development of elaborate performing arts traditions from man's struggle with nature is amply documented.[2] Suffice it to state here that the origins of the performing arts traditions in Nigeria lie in the numerous traditional religious and functional rituals to be found in practically every Nigerian community. What remains, however, to be more carefully examined is the more intractable question of classification. What constitutes drama in the African context? What is ritual? And what is the difference between dramatic ritual and plain ritual? At what point is ritual no longer ritual but drama – that is, assuming, as we stated above, that the origins of the performing arts lie in traditional rituals?

In response to these questions posed by the classification problem, some people have argued – Dr Ossie Enekwe, for instance – that the question is relative.[3] Starting from the premise that the origins of drama in Africa and ritual are inextricably linked, members of the so-called relativist school argue that what is ritual in a particular context may be drama in another. Outside its original context, or 'when the belief that sustains it has lost its potency',[4] ritual is transformed into entertainment. Professor M. J. C. Echeruo and Kalu Uka, among others, disagree. 'What is usually called traditional drama ... is not yet drama', Kalu Uka has written.[5] 'What some usually and glibly call traditional drama is properly and essentially elements of drama.' Others, like Professor Ola Rotimi, have pointed out other problems to be encountered in an attempt to classify any or all ritual as drama. For Rotimi, any ritual display which contains what he calls 'mimetic-impulse' ought to be classified as drama and not ritual. Conversely, any ritual without 'mimetic-impulse' cannot be classified as drama.[6]

These problems of classification are further compounded by the absence of generally accepted conventions of performance in the Nigerian context – conventions which could also aid us with classification. Just as one cannot speak of a single Nigerian culture, one cannot speak of conventions of performing arts as if there were a single set of conventions. There are, admittedly, conventions of, for instance, *Igbo* performing arts or *Ibibio* performing arts. But even here, too, one has to be careful, since within one ethnic grouping there may be as many conventions of performance as there are performances.

But there is yet another reason why the effort to distinguish drama from ritual can be frustrating and self-defeating in Nigeria. Even if we were to accept the evolutionist theory and argue that drama evolved from rituals, the problem would not have been solved. Drama is also known in Nigeria to have developed not necessarily from ritual but *alongside* ritual, without cutting itself off from its origin. In his important study of traditional Yoruba theatre, Professor J. A. Adedeji argues that as masque theatre, that is, as a courtly form of entertainment characterised by song, dance, lavish costume and extraordinary spectacle, *Alarinjo* theatre (the first professional travelling theatre among the Yoruba) did not supplant the ritual ceremonies of the *egungun* (masquerade) society from which it initially evolved. Rather, the *Alarinjo* performers developed an almost independent entertainment-oriented style, different in emphasis from the essentialist art of the original *egungun* performance, even as they remained adjoined to it. So that while it remained sacred in tone (since it remained adjoined to the *egungun* cult) it was, by virtue of being geared towards plain entertainment, essentially secular in character. Here, theatre has developed not necessarily *from* ritual but *alongside* ritual.

Obviously, the situation is a complex one, requiring that we approach the problem with caution. One very clear fact to emerge from this is that the situation calls for more research and work on our different rituals and traditional ceremonies. A festival or ritual may be dramatic in itself without being drama. The Fulani *Soro* dance, for instance, which is a manhood endurance test, may be spectacular as an event in itself, but it is not drama. Conversely, the flogging sequence that precedes most Yoruba masquerade festivals is drama when considered as a part of the larger masquerade festival to which it belongs. There are even traditional festivals (e.g. the Obatala festival as celebrated in Ede) in which the dramatic enactment of a story is central to the event. Our task, therefore, is to distinguish between spectacle and drama. But more than that, we should take each ceremony and festival on its own merit and examine it against the background, not only of its content but also of its context. And as we saw with the *Alarinjo*, the often-accepted dichotomy drawn between entertainment and religion is hardly useful since an event can be adjoined to religion and remain secular in character. Lastly, of course, it should be stated that no classification can be totally all-inclusive, all-comprehensive – at least not as more ongoing research yields newer insights into traditional performing arts techniques and approaches.

It would therefore seem from the foregoing views that the popularly accepted classification by J. P. Clark is in need of reconsideration.[7]

319

Clark's broad classifications of Nigerian drama into two broad divisions of traditional and literary forms of performance is appropriate. But beyond that point, his classification runs into trouble. Faced with a myriad of varied traditional forms, he further breaks the group (i.e. traditional forms) into the religious and secular, a division which, as we saw with the *Alarinjo*, is wholly inappropriate.

Still taking our cue from Clark's classification, two broad divisions are proposed, traditional and non-traditional forms of performance. More specifically, the traditional group can be further broken into three sub-groups – dramatic ritual, the popular tradition and Yoruba travelling theatre. The first of these sub-groups, dramatic ritual, will include traditional festivals, whether they be held in celebration of cult or ancestral heroes; ritual ceremonies where dramatic performance is patently discernible; serious masquerade plays (as distinct from much lighter ones). The term *popular* applied to the second category of traditional performances is used in the positively correct sense – that is, as art intended to be eminently popular, art that is commonly approved and widely liked by the 'common' people. The term is also used in the finest tradition of a genuinely popular theatre where all that a living popular performer needs is not necessarily a text or an elaborate stage but a place, a time, an audience and himself. In this category one must include all those plays in which amusement and entertainment are cited as the foremost functions. Among these are the *Annang* drama of the Ibibio, Yoruba *Alarinjo* theatre, Kwagh hir and Bornu puppet shows, and even the Hausa comical art of *Yankamanci*.

The third sub-division under traditional drama is contemporary Yoruba travelling theatre – the performances of Hubert Ogunde, Duro Ladipo, Kola Ogunmola, Moses Olaiya Adejumo (alias Baba Sala), and the hundred or more such groups that now exist in the entire Yoruba-speaking sub-region of West Africa. The justification for classifying contemporary Yoruba travelling theatre under the traditional mode of performance is self-evident. For one thing, the plays are not scripted. But more importantly, in form, tempo, presentation style and overall meaning, they are traditional. A full appreciation of Duro Ladipo's theatre, for instance, would be impossible without some familiarity with the conventions of traditional Yoruba theatre. And in spite of Ogunde's flirtations with the European forms of the variety theatre, he remains largely a traditional artist. 'The Nigerian theatre practitioner is not a product of any Drama school', he asserted at the University of Ife, in March 1981.[8] He continued: 'He is a self-made man who found himself in the environment in which he was born – the ritual ceremony, the ritual priest and communal life.' And yet, he remains a modern artist – that is, in his contemporaneousness, his immediate relevance and his modernity of vision. If we must provide a label for contemporary Yoruba travelling theatre it would have to be 'modern traditional'.

Finally, the second major classification of the performing arts in Nigeria, the non-traditional form, refers to the literary tradition. Although this is generally taken to mean the literary works that have appeared since Ene Henshaw's *This is our Chance* (1956), it ought to

Fig. 19.1   Performing at a Durbar held in Kaduna

include works if any, written before that period. Again, three sub-divisions are discernible under the broad classification of non-traditional performances, namely Onitsha market plays, Nigerian national language plays and the sophisticated standard English plays of some of our most enduring playwrights to date. The national language plays include the growing tradition of works in Yoruba, Igbo, Idoma and Hausa, for instance.

With a classification such as this, it becomes easier to examine the more crucial question of the dominant characteristics of the performing arts in Nigeria. It seems that the incipient focal point of most forms of traditional performance in Nigeria is the masquerade. Although it is slightly less so with Hausa performances, examples abound among the other ethnic groups of the inextricable link between the masquerade and ritual performance. There seems to be a dominance of the masquerade in traditional performances. The occasion for the presentation of these performances varies from ethnic group to ethnic group, indeed from a particular performance to another. Generally, however, they are held during festivals, usually seasonal or annual festivals of cult groups, societies, or even professional groups. The rituals dramatised at these festivals may involve the representation of spirit, ancestral or mythic heroes, either in symbolic and therefore non-mimetic representation of the powers of these ancestral figures, or in a more dramatic impersonation. And as always, these dramatic presentations are

321

overwhelmingly interwoven with songs, drumming, extensive improvisations and dance. The setting for these performances is generally an unidentified area, usually the village square.

The nature of the preparation and execution of these festivals varies a great deal. Among the Igbo, for instance, Dr Meki Nzewi has identified four kinds of preparation, namely, religious, material, artistic and political, with each representing different stages of the activities that occur prior to the festival.[9] However, J. C. Messenger's study of Ibibio drama suggests that *Ekong* drama undergoes a period of meticulous, detailed preparation, far surpassing that of most examples that have been recorded or experienced. The relevant extract from his study deserves to be quoted in full because it also reveals the splendour and beauty of one of the most elaborate and complex examples of traditional performances in Nigeria. After a carver is hired to produce all the needed materials for the six-year cycle, rehearsals begin:

> Rehearsals take place in the square for several hours during the afternoon on a specific day of each eight-day week for forty-six weeks of every year or six years, and performances are given publicly during the dry season of the seventh. . . . During the six years of rehearsals a complete seven-hour routine was worked out and mastered to perfection by the *Ikot-Obong* players. The routine included music played by an eleven-man percussion orchestra; dances performed by a chorus of eighteen men; songs sung by the musicians, dancers, and marked soloist – plays enacted by puppets or a group of fourteen men, some wearing masks; dances on stilts by two costumed performers; and the mystifying movements of a life-size carving of the principal female fertility spirit, *ekanem*, enwrapped by the coils of a python.[10]

These elaborate forms of Ibibio performance stand as refutations of the claim that in non-literate, traditional African societies, 'drama is not a developed form'. When the advocates of this view suggest that traditional African drama hardly exists, they mean that it does not exist in the form of European drama, as if this is the only yard-stick for determining what drama is. Writing, though not specifically about Ibibio drama in particular but about African drama in general, Ruth Finnegan wrote:

> . . . though these performances possess certain of the elements *we* associate with drama, the emphasis is very different from that of modern drama. . . . Though they may be no 'plays' *in quite the Western sense*, their indigenous artistic forms nevertheless possess some of the elements *we* associate with drama.[11] (my emphasis)

And yet, the truth is that in its intensity, contained not just in its elaborate preparation, but also in its amplitude and profundity, its brilliantly executed farcical skits, its penchant for spontaneity, vigour and extemporisation, Ibibio drama surpasses the fluffy smoothness of much of what passes for modern European drama.

Two other forms of traditional performances deserving of mention are the Kwagh hir puppet and story-telling theatre of the Tiv people, and the Bornu puppet show, both of them being forms about which little is known. The problem of the Bornu puppet theatre is compounded by the fact that it may have virtually become defunct. Perhaps the only known extant account of a Bornu puppet show was written in 1935, with photographs, by an English colonial officer, R. T. E. Ellison.[12] Kwagh hir, on the other hand, is still very much practised and is the topic of a recently completed doctoral thesis at the Ahmadu Bello University.[13]

Although the origin of puppetry in the northern parts of Nigeria are not readily known, it is quite probable that they may have been originally imported by Arab traders. An important feature of Arab theatre is the shadow play, which was first mentioned in travellers' narratives and Muslim literature in the fourteenth century. These were popular puppet shows distinguishable from marionette performances since the figures were manipulated behind illuminated curtains, so that the audience saw only the shadows moving on the curtain. Under the Turks, shadow plays became extremely popular throughout Turkey, Syria, Palestine, Egypt and much of Muslim North Africa. Considering Bornu's pre-eminence as 'the undisputed mistress of the eastern section of central Sudan',[14] during the early part of the nineteenth century, and El-Kanemi's extensive foreign connections with Medina and Egypt, it is not surprising that puppetry was introduced in Bornu in the nineteenth century. Although the example which Ellison observed in 1935 is different from the Arab prototypes, it does come across as equally dramatic, complete with scenes lasting two or three minutes, supported with background music.

The modern tradition

By 1863, Britain had secured a foothold in Nigeria, through its annexation of Lagos. Before 1863, the twin face of British colonialism, the Church Missionary Society, had, under a broad policy of the so-called three 'C's – Christianity, Commerce and Civilisation – pursued a systematic policy of producing an élite class of Nigerians who would be leaders in church, commerce, and politics. As early as 1839, the first batch of immigrants, freed slaves and their children, who had acquired some form of western education, had started to arrive and readily provided 'a vigorous impetus to the realisation of the objectives' of both the church and the British Government. This set of immigrants, later to be joined by Brazilian emigrants, formed the very nucleus of a nascent Nigerian educated middle-class. It is interesting to note that this class of Nigerians imported the western and European forms of the concert and the drama which were to constitute the basic framework of early modern Nigerian drama.[15]

By 1866, the population of Lagos had risen from 25 000 in 1861 to 38 000 and with it came a corresponding rise in the need for recreational facilities in Lagos. In direct response to this need, the cream of the Lagos élite – Bishop Ajayi Crowther, J. A. Otunba-Payne, Robert Campbell, Charles Foresythe, J. P. L. Davis and a host of others – got together on 24 October 1866 and opened 'The Academy', as it was called, 'as a social and cultural centre for public enlightenment, dedicated to the promotion of the arts, science and culture'.[16] Between 1866 and 1910, several groups, after the fashion of 'The Academy', were founded, dedicated in one way or the other to the promotion of culture and the arts. Among the most successful were the Philharmonic Society which was founded by Otunba-Payne in 1873, the Lagos Grammar School Entertainment Society (1872), the Rising Entertainment Society, the Orphean Club, founded by J. Otunba-Payne, the People's Union (1904), the Lagos Glee Singers (1910), the United Native Progressive Society and the Brazilian Dramatic Company under the management of P. Z. da Silva. There were also the Annual Coker Concerts, organised by Robert A. Coker, the 'Mozart of West Africa', which became extremely popular in entertainment circles in Victorian Lagos.

Practically all of these groups organised shows of their own. Quite predictably, the programme format and contents of these performances were based on those of the English music halls that were prominent in England in the late 1860s and the early 1870s – comic songs, love songs, duets, solos, glees and recitations, usually excerpts from plays, novels and comic sketches. Somehow music tended to dominate in these performances.

However, there existed in Lagos at this time other types of entertainment in which drama was fully presented, productions in which music was not the main emphasis. The Roman Catholic Church was the pioneer of this tradition. Faced with the complex challenge of having to conduct church business in Yoruba to a predominantly Yoruba-speaking community and a Portuguese-speaking Brazilian emigrant group, in an English-speaking colony, the French Order of Catholic Priests (Societé des Missions Africaines), which arrived in Lagos in 1867, was compelled to rely on the power of the theatre for a more effective form of communication. So that from 1881 when St Gregory's School was founded by the French priests, to the end of the century, annual end-of-year performances were held. In 1882, Molière's *He Would Be a Lord* was staged, interspersed with farces, songs, recitations, etc. But crucial as these contributions were, they did not, in fact could not, lead to the beginning of a truly modern Nigerian drama. Ironically, the impetus to that came from within the Church.

By 1890, a major schism had occurred within the Protestant Church in Lagos, which led to the establishment of several seccessionist churches in Lagos – fourteen, to be more precise, by 1917. The reason for this development must be understood within the context of the wave of a Yoruba cultural nationalist movement, itself the consequence of the disillusionment and alienation experienced by the educated élite of Lagos. The disillusionment was predictable and perhaps even inevitable. Separated from these men by almost half a century, Frantz Fanon understood better. This period under consideration corresponds partially with the second phase which Fanon identified in the evolutionary panorama of the colonised (native) African intellectual. Wrote Fanon:

In the second phase, we find the native is disturbed; he decides to remember what he is. . . . But since the native is not a part of his people, since he only has exterior relations with his people, he is content to recall their life only. Past happenings of the bygone days of his childhood will be brought up out of the depths of his memory; old legends will be reinterpreted in the light of a borrowed aestheticism and of a conception of the world which was discovered under other skies.[17]

Not only was the call made for independent African churches where Yoruba music and language could be freely used, there were beginning to emerge attempts to blend Yoruba and European materials in entertainments. The lead for such 'innovations' came from Abeokuta and Ibadan, but especially from Abeokuta where, for instance, traditional masquerade songs were re-worked into church songs as a means of winning over converts from traditional religions. It is therefore hardly surprising that the first examples of truly Nigerian dramas came from these African churches. Thus, in 1902, under the joint sponsorship of the Bethel African Church and St Jude's Church, Ebute-Metta, a play written by D. A. Oloyede, *King Elejigbo and Princess Abeje of Kotangora*, was performed by the Egbe Ife at the Bethel African Church School-room. On 22 April 1904 the play received a public performance at the Glover Memorial Hall, thus earning for itself the distinction of being 'the first appearance of a church drama group in a public hall'.

For nearly two decades, *King Elejigbo* was the prototype of most Yoruba drama being written in Lagos, and between 1904 and 1920 some twenty or more such plays were written.[18] Structurally, the plays were similar to the tradition which Hubert Ogunde was to inherit two decades after – the mild satires, the dialogues mingled with songs, the hymn tunes immersed in Biblical themes, the opening and closing glees, the insertions of sometimes unrelated sketches, etc. Under the aegis of the Lagos Glee Singers, headed by Dr Obasa, the tradition grew stronger in Lagos.

It ought to be noted, however, that in spite of all the bustle of those years, of all the hue and cry about the indigenisation of the church, the well-meaning, if sometimes misguided surge towards a cultural nationalism, in spite of all that, the activities around the so-called 'native' theatre[19] were not popular affairs but rather the exclusive concern of only a circle of Victorian Lagosians. A majority of the 'natives' were 'illiterate and uncultivated' and quite naturally, cut off from the cultural life which the élite group promoted and activly supported. In studying the population figures of Lagos between 1861 and 1866, Professor Echeruo concludes that only a tenth of the population could be regarded as 'educated',[20] a generous figure which would normally include such working-class persons as teachers and junior government officials. However, teachers were poorly trained at the time and so were hardly considered educated in the sense in which the word was used at the time. To be educated in nineteenth-century Lagos was synonymous with the acquisition of a Victorian taste, complete with all its vacuity and superciliousness. Numerically, the Lagosians who belonged to this group were infinitesimal – they were the wealthy merchants, those Lagosians who could afford to, and actually did send their children abroad, in some cases, after their own fashion, so they could get into the right professions, law, medicine and the arts, those Lagosians who, suffused in their élite pretensions, associated 'themselves with the usual recreations of a "sophisticated" Europe and so went to the races, to fancy dress balls . . . and to cricket'.[21] It was this class of Lagosians who patronised the theatre and gave it support. It is needless to add, of course, that the theatre catered to their tastes. And yet, ironically, the cultural nationalist movement which provided an important impetus for the founding of this theatre was sometimes initiated and massively supported by working-class Lagosians. For instance, the 1896 call by Lagos teachers for the wearing of native dress was derided by 'educated' Lagosians. The Lagos editor of the *Lagos Observer* saw it as a demand for 'recurrence to primitive quasi-nudity'.[22]

One of the many ways in which the mass population was excluded from these theatres was by charging exorbitant gate fees for performances. For instance, the performances held at St Gregory's School were relatively very expensive, ranging from three shillings (30k) to five shillings (50k) for gate fee with the printed programmes going for three to six pence apiece. Considering the earnings of the average Nigerian worker in 1900, those gate fees were extremely expensive. For instance, under Henry McCallum, who became Governor of Lagos in April 1897, Public Works Department workers' weekly wage of one shilling and three pence (15k) was to be scaled down to nine pence (9k).[23] In 1900, the commencing salary for 'native clerks' was £24 (₦48) per annum, which comes to about ten shillings (₦1) a week. Asking a clerk who earned £2 (₦4) a month in 1900 to pay five shillings (50k) for a performance is roughly equivalent to asking a man who earns ₦100 per month (before taxes) today to pay ₦7.50k for a performance. It is not surprising to read accounts of how some of these theatre houses were attacked and vandalised by those who felt excluded and cut off by the exorbitant gate fees.[24]

So, in effect, the theatre of this period was anything but popular and it relied for its survival on the support of the tiny class for which it catered. Once that support was no longer forthcoming, the theatre was bound to collapse. And collapse it did. According to Echeruo, 'When professional, commercial and later political interests diverted the attention of this elite, the spirit of these concerts began to fade away.' And although the Lagos Glee Singers continued their activities well into the 1920s the combined effects of the coming of the First World War and that of the cinema in 1914 finally dampened the sparkle of the preceding years. It took a Hubert Ogunde to revive that interest some two decades after. But the conditions leading to such a revival manifested themselves long before Ogunde came to the scene.

The ripples of the Great Depression of 1929 were felt in Nigeria, particularly in Lagos, which remained the economic outpost of British imperialism by the early 1930s. The unemployment which ensued from the effects of the depression meant a corresponding gain in strength for the numerous evangelical and spiritualist churches which characterised the period. These churches, through their unorthodox technique of instant results of healing, prophecy and spiritualism, provided solace for the working-class, a majority of whom were then unemployed. It is therefore not an accident that the future growth of a truly popular theatre of some sort should be linked at this time in Lagos with the growth of the Aladura movement.

After a period of initial hesitation about using the theatrical format in its propagation of its brand of the gospel, the Aladura movement plunged into it completely. Driven by a belief in spiritualism as the very essence of religion, and as if aware of the close links between trance, drama and religion, the movement resorted to music, dance and songs 'as a means of impelling its members to express their religious experience'.[25] Although the movement took a stand against the use of the Yoruba talking drum, its methods of basing church plays on stories taken from the Bible and setting them to music and dance was innovative enough to start a new phase in the development of Yoruba theatre. By the mid-thirties, a new kind of drama, Native Air Opera as it was called, had become popular, due largely to the efforts of the church movement – but more specifically, due largely to the efforts of A. K. Ajisafe who started 'to relate church hymns to "native airs" at the United African Methodist Church'. He was followed in that tradition through the years by such renowned theatre artists as E. A. Dawodu, Ajibola Layeni, A. B. David, G. I. Onomole and A. A. Olufoye. This was the situation in the early 1940s when Hubert Ogunde arrived in Lagos as the organist and composer of sacred songs for a break-away church from the parent Aladura movement, the Church of the Lord at Ebute-Metta.

Ogunde's arrival on the scene in 1944 was to determine the course of Yoruba theatre for over three decades. Freeing the so-called 'Native Air Opera' from the strict confines of the church and monotonous church rhythms, Ogunde imbued the 'opera' with a sprinkling of Yoruba music and dances. The fact that the Church of the Lord, which had been founded in 1931 in Ogere by Josiah Oshitelu, was less fundamentalist in its approach than the parent body, was a contributory factor towards Ogunde's innovations. In 1946, encouraged by the warm reception for his first two plays, *The Garden of Eden and the Throne of God*, which was first done as a church play, and *Worse than Crime*, which told the story of the slave trade, Ogunde resigned from the Police Force and decided to go professional. With only £9 (N18) in his total savings after eight years in the Force, he inaugurated the African Music Research Party, marking the advent of modern professional theatre in Nigeria.

From the beginning, Ogunde was actively involved in the struggle for self-rule, an involvement which is not only reflected in the subject and themes of his works, but led to his several brushes with the colonial authorities. Working from the premise that theatre must 'reflect the reality of its society', he boldly retold, sometimes at great risk to himself and his safety, the tragedy, the hopes, dreams, triumphs of his time and age. Not content to confine himself to Lagos, he hit the road and carried out extensive, gruelling tours of the country. Evidently, the tours made quite an impact. One of those who came to see him perform in Ado-Ekiti was a young school teacher. His name was E. K. Ogunmola. Ogunde remembers the details well:

Ogunmola started in 1948. But before he started, the first thing he did was to come to Lagos, I saw him, I did not even know who he was. Then he told me that he had been working at Ado-Ekiti, at Ikare, at Akure and he thought we could do the same thing. . . . So he asked us to help him build costumes for his new play. So we built some costumes and he started from there. And from that time up to the time of his death, he had connections with Ogunde theatre. . . . And many a time, he would come and watch my play and offer suggestions and I would watch his own play and offer suggestions. In fact, I would say that we were together until his death.[26]

So started a long tradition of influences, from Kola Ogunmola, through Duro Ladipo even to the comic Yoruba artists such as Moses Olaiya. For instance, it is not generally known that the group that was later to become the Moses Olaiya company (the Alawada) was in fact, a splinter group from the Ogunde theatre. Nor is it always appreciated that Ogunde had first established most of the theatrical techniques which other artists of the tradition have relied upon.

What is remarkable about Yoruba travelling theatre today is not merely or only the nature of Ogunde's pervasive influence on the tradition, but rather how fully established that tradition had become. It is believed that there are about a hundred Yoruba travelling theatre groups which make up the Association of Nigerian Theatre Practitioners – that is, not counting the groups stationed in the Republic of Benin where these groups perform to Yoruba-speaking Beninois. And as was seen at the 1981 mini-Ife Theatre Festival where some of these groups participated, standards today are high.

Although much remains to be known about the techniques and working methods of these companies,[27] there seems to be a current trend (again after the fashion of Hubert Ogunde) towards film-making. In recorded interviews carried out with scores of these groups, there seems to be a general interest in that direction. Already, Ogunde has filmed three of his works, *Aiye*, *Jaiyesimi* and *Atropin nt'enia*. Both Duro Ladipo and Oyin Adejobi featured in another film, *Ija Ominira*, an adaptation of *Omo Olokun Esin*, Bayo Faleti's novel, and produced by Ade Afolayan. *Kadara* has also been produced by Ade Afolayan. Moses Olaiya Adejumo (alias Baba Sala) has also released his first film, *Orun M'oru*, a commendable film, which justly has been well received. Although Ogunde's films have been uncritically popular with the mass audience of especially Yoruba speakers, they are, to my mind, regrettable departures from his courageous and combative tradition of confronting realistically, without mystification, without recourse to the supernatural, the burning issues of contemporary society. In the world of both films, the diabolical forces of evil, symbolised by witches and witchcraft, are, after a momentary victory, magically destroyed by the forces of good, represented by a well-meaning medicine man. No longer does he ground the problems and implicit solutions of our time on the bed-rock of reality, as he is known to have done in some of his finest works – *Tiger's Empire*, *Strike and Hunger*, *Bread and Butter*, etc., but rather on a supernatural, animistic, intractable world. Whether this trend in film-making will lead

Fig. 19.2a A scene from the comedy The Marriage of Anansewa *by Efua T. Sutherland*

to the abandoning of theatre work by Ogunde and the other artists, and whether the standards of these films will be such as will sustain them and consequently the tradition itself, remain to be seen.

Quite apart from the Yoruba travelling theatres, the other major serious tradition of contemporary Nigerian drama is the literary tradition, by which critics usually mean those works written principally in English. As will be shown later in this study, such a classification ignores a growing body of serious, first-rate and popular works being written in Nigerian languages.[28] Partly because they have been the more visible – considering the factor of a wider readership in Nigeria and outside Nigeria – and partly because they have, in certain respects, been the more artistically enduring, they seem to have received more critical attention than the other traditions of contemporary Nigerian drama.

In discussing contemporary Nigerian drama in English, the year 1960 is taken as a starting point – the year in which Wole Soyinka founded 'the 1960 Masks'. But the facts are not as simple as that. The flurry of activities of the three years preceding 1960 ought to be understood and put in perspective because, in the last analysis, the founding of the 'Masks' depended partly on the events of those preceding years. For instance, before 1960, there were a number of amateur companies in the country. In 1960, John Ekwere revived his 'Ogui

Fig. 19.2b   The final moments of a performance of Wole Soyinka's The Strong Breed

Players' and called it the 'Eastern Nigerian Theatre group'. Then there was the relatively serious theatre work centred around the then University College at Ibadan. The impetus to serious theatre work at the university came from the introduction of drama and theatre courses at the university in 1957 as part of an Educational Theatre programme organised jointly by the English Department and the Faculty of Education. In the same year, a group of expatriates, mainly university teachers and civil servants resident in Ibadan, got together with their Nigerian friends and formed the Arts Theatre Production group which sought to awaken interest in theatre and drama as entertainment and serious art. At about the same time as the Arts Theatre Production group was being formed, the students of the English Department were also forming a Drama Society. A third amateur group, 'The Players of the Dawn', was formed in 1959, drawing its membership from the young university graduates of Ibadan University who were based in Ibadan.

Between these three groups, audiences in Ibadan and environs thrilled to a wide range of plays, from Greek classics, through Shakespeare, Sheridan to old and long-forgotten sensations of London's West End. Said Soyinka: ' "The Players of the Dawn"]have[in spite of the intelligence of the leaders, consistently succumbed to the dictates of the British Council pre-historic strictures and are incapable of seeing theatre as an activity which did not petrify with Galsworthy at the start of the century'.[29] The real impetus to serious theatre may have come from

330

the University's Dramatic Society's production of Wole Soyinka's *The Swamp Dwellers* and an abridged version of *The Lion and the Jewel* in 1958, directed by Kenneth Post and Geoffrey Axworthy, plays which were different from other kinds of Nigerian plays that theatre enthusiasts were used to at the time. The task therefore of initiating what was a new movement was left to Wole Soyinka.

Wole Soyinka's return to Nigeria in 1960 coincided, not unexpectedly, with a new wave of national consciousness, one which permeated aspects of Nigerian cultural life. Driven by that euphoria and by the desire to evolve an authentically Nigerian theatre to express a new national consciousness, Wole Soyinka proceeded to absorb the members of the erstwhile 'Players of the Dawn' into a new group, 'The 1960 Masks'. Beyond completing work on a new play, *The Trials of Brother Jero*, he also produced in 1960 his independence-sponsored play, *A Dance of the Forests*.

The seven years between 1958 and 1965 were very crucial in the history of modern Nigerian drama. They were particularly productive years and marked by an excitement of creative activity. The combined effects of the founding of the Mbari Cultural Centre in Ibadan and the activities of the University of Ibadan Dramatic Society served to popularise the nature of the growing national cultural identity which pervaded the country. In a period of intense superciliousness, laced with the surface individualism of an emerging privileged class at Nigeria's premier and hitherto only university, the more active drama and English undergraduates of those years must have cut a different image for themselves. Inspired by a collective vision, they tried out new ideas and experimented with novel concepts. For instance, it is worthy of note that some of the plays the students presented were joint projects by the students themselves. *Suberu*, for instance, was a collective effort between Dapo Adelugba, Alfred Opubor and Brownson Dede, while the adptation of *The Taming of the Shrew* was written by Ernest Ekom, with some asistance from Geoffrey Axworthy. But even more laudable were the first genuine attempts to take theatre to the people, away from the narrow confines of a pretentious and stuffy university atmosphere. Their audience was a mass audience, their stage, in the words of Axworthy, 'a Town Hall, a Law Court, an open air cinema, a table top of a school dining-hall, or the studio of E.N.T.V. in Enugu'[30] – in short, just about anywhere where their performances could be adapted to the audience and the conditions of performance.

And so it came about that the University of Ibadan remained a vital force in the development of theatre and drama in Nigeria, first through its School of Drama and subsequently as a fully-fledged department of its own. It remained for some time the only training ground for theatre practitioners in Nigeria. For instance, the School of Drama Acting Company which Wole Soyinka set up as Director of School at the start of the 1967–68 academic session, which could hardly get in motion before his detention, served as a laboratory aimed at producing actors in an ensemble fashion. To achieve this, students and actors were exposed to a wide variety of plays, drawn as it were from the world's repertory.

Equally important was the initial, though short-lived attempt made to bridge the gap between the 'academic' and the professional theatre, between the élitist theatre and the mass, popular tradition. The collaborations between Kola Ogunmola and the School of Drama, in the joint stage production of Tutuola's *The Palmwine Drinkard* was a highly imaginative experiment. And then, in the summer of 1971, in what is considered the highlight of the company's life, it spent six weeks at a workshop at the Eugene O'Neill Theatre in Connecticut, rehearsing and presenting Soyinka's *Madmen and Specialists*. Shortly afterwards. Wole Soyinka resigned as director and the Trinidadian technical director, Dexter Lyndersay, took over as acting director of the unit.

Mr Lyndersay's task was to keep the ship afloat against great odds. Obviously, he had inherited an almost unmanageable set-up – a theatre company and a degree-awarding department, without the Rockefeller funds which had come in handy in the previous years but which were discontinued in July 1967, and without the full complement of staff needed to run the set-up. Then came the civil war, which marked the beginning of the government cut-back of funds to universities. Under such trying circumstances, the company foundered and had to be disbanded. Since then Ibadan has never quite been able to attain its former heights.

But in another respect, Ibadan's contributions lay not only in the fact that it provided a forum for the growth of theatre but also the fact that the university helped produce some of the most renowned writers of the earlier period, among them, J. P. Clark, Nkem Nwankwo, the late Christopher Okigbo, and of course, Chinua Achebe. Of these writers, J. P. Clark was to distinguish himself in the theatre.

It used to be fashionable to affirm that J. P. Clark and Wole Soyinka were Nigeria's foremost and best-known playwrights. That may have been correct up until about 1975 or thereabout. That view would be contested today. Certainly, Wole Soyinka remains Nigeria's most versatile and enduring dramatist, standing above the others not only in his prolificity but generally, in the depth of his perception. Clark's stature seems to have dwindled somewhat. For instance, as against Soyinka's fourteen published plays, J. P. Clark's reputation as a major dramatist rests principally on his first four plays – *A Song of a Goat, The Masquerade, The Raft, Ozidi* and more recently *The Boat*, which was produced in April 1981.

By contrast, Wole Soyinka brings to bear on his works a long-standing and ever-increasing experience of practical theatre technique which goes back to his student days in Leeds and his career at the Royal Court Theatre in London. No short summary of Soyinka's works could do justice to his enormous contributions to Nigerian theatre.[31] Without any doubt, the range, the variety and vitality of his writing career in the theatre – the dramatic monologues (*Salutation to the Gut*, 1962); the television plays (*My Father's Burden*, 1961, *You in Your Small Corner*, 1964, *Night before the Hunted*, 1964); the radio plays (*The House of Banigegi*, 1959, *Camwood on Leaves*, 1964); the sketches and revue (*The Republican*, 1964, *Before the Blackout*, 1965, *Before the Blowout*, 1979); the comic satires (*Lion and the Jewel*, 1957, *The Invention*, 1959, *The Trials of Brother Jero*, 1960); the tragi-comedies

(*Kongi's Harvest*, 1967, *The Road*, 1965, *A Dance of the Forests*, 1960, *The Strong Breed*, 1969, *Swamp Dwellers*, 1959; the more sombre works of the post-civil war years, *Madmen and Specialists*, 1970, *The Bacchae of Euripides*, 1973, *The Jero's Metamorphosis*, 1973, *Death and the King's Horseman*, 1975, *Opera Wonyosi*, 1977, and a body of critical and theoretical writing – all these are a testimony to his abilities as a highly skilled and versatile craftsman. And if Wole Soyinka is today increasingly under attack from radical, younger Nigerian critics for not going far enough in his analysis of Nigerian society, he himself must take a lot of the blame for that. For he had himself, by the very stimulus of his example as writer and social critic, indeed, by his courage, set the high standards by which he is now being judged. Among the several writers whom he had unwittingly encouraged by the sheer power of his example are Ola Rotimi and Femi Osofisan, to mention only two.

Playwright, essayist and theatre director, Ola Rotimi is a man of tenaciously stubborn artistic convictions. As a director, he has an eye for detail in the theatre and a sagacious ability to know what can and will work theatrically. Any look at the nature of his theatrical practice must necessarily begin with the Ori-Olokun theatre which he helped to found, 'as an organ in the University of Ife's (then) Institute of African Studies concerned with the practical expression of music, dance and drama in the Nigeria cultural context'.[32] What was unique about the Ori-Olokun was not the fact that it was for a long time the only professional English-speaking theatre company in the country, although that fact is worth noting. Its uniqueness lay in the ideology underlying its objectives, as reflected in its membership, a membership drawn from all walks of life and all classes of society, a membership which affirmed the notion that the struggle for a meaningful cultural liberation is not the exclusive concern of any one select group in society, but rather that of all. In the hands of Ola Rotimi, the Ori-Olokun became a real experimental theatre, providing the much needed meeting-point between the traditional artists and the trained university mind. To date, Rotimi has written some seven major works, among them *Kurumi, If . . ., The Gods are Not to Blame* and *Holding Talks*.

It is, perhaps, also important to add that the last decade, that is, since about 1970, has witnessed the emergence of a 'different' crop of playwrights, inadequately referred to as second-generation playwrights. The finest of this crop of playwrights are set apart from their earlier compatriots not necessarily by any substantial age difference (where it does exist at all) but rather by a temperament and vision, hardened, as it were, by the wounds and trauma of the Nigerian civil war, perhaps. Among these writers are Fela Davis, Comish Ekiye, Soji Simpson, Kole Omotoso, Bode Sowande, Meki Nzewi, Laolu Ogunniyi, Bode Osanyin, Zulu Sofola and Femi Osofisan.

Wale Ogunyemi, by far the most prolific of these writers, is a half-child of both 'generations' being himself a founding member of the old Orisun theatre and currently one of Nigeria's more successful and better-known playwrights. However, his own works did not come to the limelight until about the outbreak of the civil war. The same is true of Femi Euba, who was a part of the '1960 Masks' but whose plays came much later than the early 1960s.

Unfortunately, some of these writers have not been accorded the recognition they deserve, even in Nigeria. For one thing, they have not benefited from the kind of foreign critical acclaim which became factors in the growth and exposure of the first group of writers. In some cases, these writers, out of an ideological commitment, have shunned or, at best, been indifferent to this 'acclaim' by refusing to publish with foreign firms, believing firmly that the production of literature cannot be divorced from its content and over-all objective in a neo-colonialist economy. Others still are more renowed in other areas of artistic endeavour. For instance, Kole Omotoso, who has written two fine plays, *Shadows in the Horizon* and *The Curse*, is a more accomplished novelist than he is a playwright.

This is not the place to embark upon a major critique of these writers. That is work for another time and place. Suffice it to say, however, that some of these writers have distinguished themselves as highly competent craftsmen and deserve to be mentioned if only in passing. Consider, for instance, that Femi Osofisan (to mention only one of them in more detail) is well on his way to becoming one of our finest playwrights. His eight major plays to date, among them *Chattering and the Song, Once upon Four Robbers, Morountodun, Who's Afraid of Solarin*? are some of the finest works to come out of the contemporary Nigerian repertory. Eclectic as he is original, Osofisan has sought to reshape traditional Yoruba mythology and ritual in the light of contemporary realities, to squeeze out of old myths fresher meanings, in the belief that man, in the last analysis, makes his own myth. Not content merely to expose the ills of the society, he has dared to provide us with glimpses of his vision of a new society. It is interesting to note that Osofisan's plays are popular fare at educational institutions across the country.

However, in spite of such popularity at institutions, it is debatable whether Femi Osofisan is eminently a popular playwright, indeed, whether any of Nigeria's literary playwrights can be said to be genuinely popular. The question can be put differently: Can the Nigerian playwright, based in a university setting, writing in standard English, be effective and popular in a society where the mass audience (some seventy per cent of the entire population) is not literate in English? Will such a playwright ever strike a responsive chord in a mass audience, when such an audience comes from his immediate community? Will he be understood and his message comprehended? Do our literary playwrights reach out to mass audiences?

The fundamental questions raised here have been the topics of varied debates among Nigerian, indeed, African writers and critics alike.[33] The views of one school can be summarised thus: why is it that although Yoruba travelling companies manage to draw large audiences, especially in the Yoruba-speaking areas, English-language plays are hardly as popular? Why is it that while Moses Olaiye Adejumo (alias Baba Sala) can quite easily fill a large hall in, for instance, Lagos, our literary dramatists cannot do the same? Even within the English-language plays by Nigeria's literary dramatists, categories have been established somewhat. In Femi Euba's essay referred to above, he posed the question like this: why is it that Ola Rotimi is more able than Soyinka, even at a moment's notice, to fill a theatre hall? Is it not partly because most Nigerian audiences are intellectually lazy and therefore cannot make the extra effort needed to appreciate the sophisticated theatre of Wole Soyinka? Or is this the case of Ola Rotimi writing down to the audience, pandering to its taste?

First, it should be stated from the outset that the issues involved here are far more complex than as presented. Beyond that, certain wrong assumptions must be corrected. First, the contestable view (especially in the absence of empirical data) that Rotimi can fill most theatre halls better than Soyinka can, can hardly apply to all of Soyinka's works. Plays such as *The Trials of Brother Jero* and *The Lion and the Jewel* are immensely popular plays, to say nothing of the *Before the Blackout* series which drew large audiences in Lagos and Ibadan when they first appeared. Neither is the problem simply that of an intellectually lazy Nigerian audience which refuses to do its extra work. Similarly, the problem cannot be reduced to a simple matter of not having enough competent Nigerian directors with the vision of realising these works on stage. The problem seems deeper than these. Implicit in the responses and attitude of most Nigerian audiences to the two playwrights is a critical judgement of some sort, a critical judgement derived from the different stated objectives and practical approaches of both writers vis-à-vis their relationships with their audiences.

Clarification is necessary here. In his rearch for the most appropriate language to use in his work, Rotimi seems to have the Nigerian audience in the forefront of his mind. Rotimi's approach in a majority of his works has been that 'of winnowing, selecting and finding words, phrases and images that run close to vernacular parlance'.[33] When asked specifically for what kind of people he wrote, Rotimi's response underscores the point being made:

English, as you know, is the official medium of communication in Nigeria. Inevitably, I write for audiences who are knowledgeable in this language. However, in handling the English language in my plays, I strive to temper its phraseology to the early of both the dominant semi-literate as well as the literate classes, ensuring that my dialogue reaches out to both groups with ease in assimilation and clarity and identification.[34]

When asked a similar question, Wole Soyinka replied:

. . . quite frankly, I do not think of any audience when I write. I write in the firm belief that there must be at least a hall full of people who are sort of on the same wavelength as mine from every stratum of society and there must be at least a thousand people who are able to feel the same way as I do about something. So when I write, I write in the absolute confidence that it must have an audience.[35]

Even if we ignored the first part of Soyinka's reply, since we know that he has largely written with a Nigerian audience in mind, his response still raises questions. We must admit that Soyinka's belief that at a production of, shall we say, *Madmen and Specialists* at the Mapo Hall, Ibadan, or the assembly hall of Federal Government College, Abakaliki, there could be a thousand people who operate on the same wavelength as his, is a slightly exaggerated expectation. It is quite unlikely to be the case in a predominantly non-literate society where the majority of the people are not equipped to understand, let alone digest the highly sophisticated English language of that play.

Conversely, it may well be an awareness of the predominantly non-literate nature of our society that has determined Rotimi's more persistent tinkering with language. For, while seeking to capture the nuances of Yoruba oral speech processes, he uses the English language in a manner 'which renders his poetry prosaic'. There is a danger, though, that if not properly handled, such an experiment could be flat. This may have caused Dapo Adelugba to describe the result of such an experiment as 'blandness of language' in the unsurer days of *The Gods are not to Blame*.

The solution seems to me to be something of a middle ground between the high 'sophistication' of language evident in some of Soyinka's more complex works and the delicate brand of English which Rotimi has made popular. Ironically, Soyinka tried out such experiments, even with far greater ease, in his earlier works such as *The Lion and the Jewel* and *The Trials of Brother Jero*. In *Brother Jero* he added the dimension of 'pidgin' English, thereby showing, quite early in his career, a brilliant awareness of the use of different levels of English in correspondence with the reality of what exists in the society itself. It is, perhaps, not an accident that these two are his most popular plays with a majority of Nigerian audiences. This adoption of a brand of English with a wider appeal seems a reasonable way out, especially as there is a growing rise of the percentage of persons who are literate in the various levels of English, 'pidgin', standard and colloquial.

Another way to look at the issue is to advocate that the playwrights write in our national languages, as a means of ensuring that their works are accessible to the greater number of our peoples. Once considered an unpragmatic and unrealistic position, that view is fast gaining ground today as more African writers re-examine their positions and their effectiveness as artists. Ngugi wa Thiong'o and Sembene Ousmane have been in the forefront as advocates of the use of African languages in African literature. Ngugi's decision to do a major production in Kikuyu at the Kamiriithu Community Education and Cultural Centre in Limuru, Kenya, was a conscious ideological one. Rotimi has also completed work on a Yoruba version of *Kurunmi*. Any doubts about the possibility that the use of national languages would ensure far wider popularity for literary plays is dispelled by the facts at our disposal. At a production of Akin Isola's Yoruba play, *Efusetan Aniwura*, in early 1981 at the Olubadan stadium in Ibadan, an estimated record crowd of 14 000 people watched a single performance of the play!

But will language by itself do it? When all is said and done, will it ensure that mass popularity of our literary dramatists? Are other factors not also crucial – the factor of the theatres themselves, the adequate styles of presentation, theatre locations, their objectives, their management and operation? While these are all important, it seems that the nerve centre of the issue remains that of relevance. How relevant are our playwrights? For whom do our playwrights write? About whom? The questions are very crucial, especially when it is remembered that the artist, being a product of a particular society, a particular historical epoch, of a particular class, cannot and does not have his meaning alone. He speaks not only for his time and place, but also for his class. If he speaks for his own class alone as happens in some of our contemporary drama, ignoring the creative struggle of the masses of our population, ignoring their hopes and aspirations, it seems logical to conclude that he will remain irrelevant and unpopular at least with that class. Conversely, it would be safe to conclude that if our literary drama sharply reflects the concerns of a mass culture, it will, in all likelihood be patronised. Unfortunately most of contemporary Nigerian drama does not as yet reflect the concerns of the popular rural and urban masses. Clearly, the way out seems a new direction, a search for a new mode of presentation, for a really *popular* theatre.

The kind of theatre we speak of here is not a cathartic one where the masses of the people get a chance to get their bitterness and frustration off their chests. Neither is it the type of theatre where the people are presented with prescribed solutions to their problems. This is, in a manner reminiscent of the best of Bertolt Brecht, a theatre where the people are challenged to look critically at their situation and compelled to want to change it, a theatre which will debunk the myth that reality is unchangeable and the world cannot be transformed. Far from being the passive recipients of finished products, the 'audience' is acutely engaged in the production of meaning. It is a theatre which will have to build on the history of our peoples' songs, their drama, dances, drumming, masquerades, puppets, etc. Because such a theatre will need to provide a means of building a critical consciousness in the majority of the people, it would not portray peasant characters as naive and simple-minded but rather accurately, and that is, as creative participants in the collective struggle for a more humane and just society.

Fortunately, this kind of theatre work is beginning to take place in Nigeria. Two examples will serve to make the point. Since 1977, the drama section of the Ahmadu Bello University's Department of English has mounted three popular theatre workshops in rural areas and other projects involving the performance of plays for audiences in Samaru township, close to the university. Basically, in each of these workshops, short, highly improvised plays dealing with the problems of farmers in Northern Nigeria, among other problems, were presented. A summary of sections of the project deserves to be quoted in full:

> The students were taken to the area before the workshop began and encouraged to talk informally with the farmers and their families. They then spent about a week devising the plays, which were later performed in ... several nearby villages to large and interested audiences. The topics dealt with included the arrogance and frequent ignorance of so-called agricultural 'experts' from the cities; the

337

migration to the towns in search for a better standard of living – and most crucially, the corruption of officials and village leaders in the distribution of government-subsidized fertilizer. ... At all the performances, the *Wasan Manoma* (plays for farmers) inspired a lively response from the peasant audiences, to the surprise of the drama students whose urban elitism had not allowed for the possibility of a peasantry who not only had thoughts and feelings but the capacity to express them forcefully when the opportunity arose.[36]

Also, at the University of Ife Wole Soyinka has demonstrated an awareness of the capabilities of a mass popular theatre as a powerful agent for consciousness raising. And although the efforts at Ife have been far less consistent than that at Zaria, some impact has been registered. During the Road Traffic Campaign in 1980 organised by the Oyo State Road Safety Corps (which was at the time headed by Mr Soyinka) theatre was used to *teach* traffic rules. An adaptation of a Yoruba language play, *Gbekude*, by Adegoke Durojaiye, was taken round urban centres in the state with successful results.

One thing is clear, and that is that there is not a single answer to the many questions posed by the broad problem of how to evolve a genuinely popular theatre, on how, as a medium of social transformation, theatre can be woven into an ongoing process of critical analysis, organisation and struggle. We may cast our lot on the side of the establishment of community theatres in small communities, rural and even urban. Such theatres will be run and managed by such communities. To complement the works of these theatres, the university theatre and drama programmes will have to change radically. The universities must initiate moves towards a meaningful and conscious merging of the best traditions of western-oriented textual dramaturgy and the vibrantly contemporary indigenous theatrical techniques. Beyond merely making their facilities accessible to small regional traditional groups, that is, on an equal basis of exchange and participation, our universities must involve themselves more actively in the creative sturggle of our peasants and farmers by physically going to the countryside. Our drama undergraduates must be made to do a substantial part of their work in rural centres, learning from the traditional artist, while the traditional artist learns from them. And as we implied earlier on, the teaching of national languages must be intensified in our universities.

But finally, when all is said and done, the artist and the theatre can only do so much. The effort is a concerted one. Since it is hardly possible to live in a society and be free of it, all those who have a stake in the progress and future of human society, be they artists, workers, teachers, journalists, farmers, students, playwrights, must be a part of the struggle to evolve a better and more democratic society, a society where art and culture create the basis of the formulation of a common destiny and the collective cooperation in pursuing such a destiny, a truly humane society.

Notes

1 This chapter is a revised version of an earlier paper which appeared as the introductory essay in *Drama and Theatre in Nigeria: a critical source-book*, edited by Yemi Ogunbiyi, *Nigeria Magazine*, Lagos, 1981.

2 See, for instance, George Thomson, *Marxism and Poetry* (New York: International Publishers, 1949), *passim*. See also Yemi Ogunbiyi, 'Nigerian Theatre and Drama: a critical profile', in *Drama and Theatre in Nigeria*: *a critical source-book*, pp. 3–53.

3 Ossie Enekwe, 'Myth, ritual and drama in Igbo-land', in *Drama and Theatre in Nigeria*, pp. 149–63.

4 *Ibid.*, p. 155.

5 Quoted by Meki Nzewi, in 'Traditional Theatre practice', *Nigeria Magazine*, Nos, 128/29, 1979, p. 15.

6 Ola Rotimi, 'The drama in African ritual display' in *Drama and Theatre in Nigeria*, pp. 77–80.

7 J. P. Clark, 'Aspects of Nigerian drama', reproduced in *Drama and Theatre in Nigeria*, pp. 57–74.

8 Hubert Ogunde, at a public lecture at the Oduduwa Hall of the University of Ife, 19 March 1981.

9 Meki Nzewi, 'Some social perspectives of Igbo traditional theatre', *The Black Perspective*, No. 6, No. 2, Fall, 1978, p. 170.

10 J. C. Messenger, 'Annang art, drama and social control', *African Studies Bulletin*, Vol. 5, 1962, pp. 29–34.

11 Ruth Finnegan, *Oral Literature in Africa* (Nairobi: Oxford University Press, 1970), pp. 515, 517.

12 See R. T. E. Ellison, 'A Bornu Puppet show' (1935) reproduced in *Drama and Theatre in Nigeria*, pp. 252–54.

13 I. O. Hagher, 'The Kwagh hir: an analysis of a contemporary indigenous puppet theatre and its social and cultural significance in Tivland in the 1960s and 1970s', Ph.D. thesis, Zaria, Ahmadu Bello University, 1981.

14 See 'Bornu under the Shehus', by G. C. Ifemesia, in Ajayi and Espie (eds), *One Thousand Years of West African History* (Ibadan: Ibadan University Press and Nelson, 1965), pp. 289–98.

15 See Lynn Leonard, 'The growth of entertainment arts of non-African origin in Lagos from 1800–1920, unpublished M.A. thesis, University of Ibadan. Other useful studies include M. J. C. Echeruo's *Victorian Lagos* (London: Macmillan. 1977), and J. A. Adedeji, in *Journal of the Historical Society of Nigeria*, Vol. VI. Nos. 1 and 4, December 1971 and June 1973.

16 Quoted by J. A. Adedeji in 'The Church and the emergence of the Nigerian theatre, 1866–1914', p. 28.

17 Frantz Fanon, *The Wretched of the Earth* (New York: Grove Press, 1963), p. 222.

18 Lynn Leonard, 'The growth of entertainment', p. 165.

19 ' "Native" was in those years, a necessary word. It was used primarily to

separate the indigenes from both the immigrants and the Europeans.'
Echeruo, *Victorian Lagos*, p. 29.

20 *Ibid*.

21 *Ibid*., p. 30.

22 *Ibid*., p. 39.

23 See Segun Osoba, 'The development of trade unionism in colonial and post-colonial Nigeria', in *Topics in Nigerian Economic and Social History*, ed. by Akinjogbin and Osoba (Ife: Ife University Press, 1980), p. 190.

24 Prof. Adedeji quotes an 1896 *Lagos Observer* account of how Catholics 'were labelled "dishonest supernumeraries" and youths who could not afford these exorbitant gate-fees indulged themselves in the unfriendly exercises of throwing stones on the corrugated roof of the building', 'The Church and the emergence of the Nigerian theatre', p. 37.

25 *Ibid*., p. 390.

26 Hubert Ogunde, Ife lecture, 19 March 1981.

27 Fortunately, Dr Biodun Jeyifo of the University of Ife Department of Literature in English has carried out extensive research work on the companies. His findings have been published as *An African Popular Theatre: the Yoruba travelling theatre of Nigeria*, Nigeria Magazine, Lagos, 1982).

28 Also ignored are the less serious plays of the Onitsha market literature tradition, the works of Thomas Orlando Iguh and O. A. Ogali. For an insight into this tradition, see Emmanuel Obiechina's *An African Popular Literature: a study of Onitsha Market pamphlets* (Cambridge University Press, 1973), *passim*.

29 See Wole Soyinka, 'Towards a true theatre', reproduced in *Drama and Theatre in Nigeria*, p. 461.

30 Geoffrey Axworthy, 'The performing arts in Nigeria – a footnote', *New Theatre Magazine*, Vol. XII, No. 2. p. 18.

31 Already, four major critical studies on Soyinka exist and provide valuable information on him and his works: Gerald Moore, *Wole Soyinka* (London: Evans Brothers, 1971); Alain Richard, *Theatre et Nationalisme: Wole Soyinka et Le Roi* (Paris: Presence Africaine, 1972); Eldred Durosimi Jones, *The Writings of Wole Soyinka* (Ibadan: Heinemann, 1973); Oyin Ogunba, *The Movement of Transition* (Ibadan: Ibadan University Press, 1975).

32 From the programme notes of the 1969 University of Ife production of *Kurunmi*.

33 Ola Rotimi in an interview with Mrs Margaret Folarin, in *New Theatre Magazine*, Vol. XII, No. 2, p. 6.

34 Ola Rotimi in B. Lindfors (ed.), *Dem Say: interviews with eight Nigerian writers*, Occasional Publication, Afro-American Studies and Research Centre, University of Texas, Austin, 1974, p. 60.

35 Wole Soyinka in D. Duerden and Cosmo Pieterse (eds), *African Writers Talking* (London: Heinemann, p. 177).

36 Quoted in 'Popular drama work in Northern Nigeria', in *Third World Popular Theatre Newsletter*, Vol. 1, No 1, Jan. 1982, p. 13.

20 Music in Nigeria today*

Akin Euba

This chapter will be divided into two main parts. The first part is entitled 'Traditional music' and this will comprise four sections, as follows: (i) vocal music; (ii) musical instruments; (iii) instrumental music; (iv) social context. The second part, entitled 'New music', will consist of the following sections: (i) music in the Church; (ii) music in the concert hall; (iii) music in the theatre; (iv) music in the night club.

Traditional music

Traditional music is that class of music which was practised in Nigeria before the country came under European influence. In spite of the impact of European culture it has survived till today as the most important type of music in Nigeria.

Traditional music is perhaps most commonly realised as a combination of singing with some form of accompaniment, either by hand-clapping or by musical instruments. This statement by no way denies the existence of other types of music which are performed either by instruments alone or by unaccompanied voices.

Vocal music

There are different varieties of vocal music, among which may be mentioned solo singing, choral singing in unison, choral singing in two or more parts, and singing in which solo and chorus alternate, commonly referred to as the call-and-response technique. In the call-and-response type of vocal music, the soloist's part usually has variety in text or melody or both while the chorus part consists of a simple phrase which is repeated with little change. Song style itself may be divided into two categories: songs in which there are clearly defined melodic patterns, and songs which employ a style which is midway between singing and speaking (sometimes referred to as 'heightened speech', 'speech-song', or 'chant'). The first category may be regarded as denoting song proper and this point is illustrated by the Yoruba distinction between *orin* ('song') and another form of vocal music that is characterised by the verb *sun* (literally, 'to cry'), as for example in *sun rarà* ('to chant *rarà*'). Our use of the term 'song' in this essay embraces both pure song and speech-song types.

Examples of solo song are found in the praise chants of the Hausa and of the Yoruba. In some cases a solo chant is now and then broken by

*This chapter first appeared in *Nigerian Music Review*, No. 1, 1977.

short sections of choral singing (a useful device for creating variety and sustaining the interest of the audience) as in most of the Yoruba chant types such as *ìjálá* (performed by hunters) and *pípè òrìsà* ('the praise-calling of divinities').

Hausa-Fulani choral music is characterised by unison singing and this form of singing is also typical of Oyo-Yoruba communities. Conversely, singing in parts (or choral polyphony) is the predominant form in the eastern sector of southern Nigeria. Choral polyphony is also found, however, in parts of northern Nigeria (for example among the Igede of Benue state) as well as in eastern and southern Yoruba communities (for example, among the Ijesa, Ekiti, Owo, Ife and Ijebu).

Two broad categories of voice quality may be observed in traditional singing, namely the nasalised voice quality and the so-called 'open-throated' voice quality. The first is commonly found in areas having a strong Islamic culture (among the Hausa-Fulani and the Oyo-Yoruba, for example) while the second is found in those sections of Nigeria little influenced by Islam (for example in the eastern states).

Musical instruments

There are many types of musical instruments in Nigeria. They include xylophones, lutes, harps, trumpets, oboes, iron bells, hand pianos, flutes, pan-pipes, slit drums, rattles, earthenware pots, zithers and a wide variety of membrane drums.

Two types of xylophone are found in the country: the fixed-key xylophone and the loose-key xylophone. Examples of the first type are the animal-horn-resonated xylophones from Gongola, Borno and Plateau states, while the best-known example of the loose-key xylophone is the *ngelenge*, commonly found in Imo, Anambra and Rivers states. The keys of the *ngelenge* are mounted on two freshly-cut banana stems, which act as resonators for the instrument.

The class of lutes include (i) *goge*, a single-string bowed instrument with calabash resonator; (ii) *molo*, a three-string plucked instrument with wooden resonator; (iii) *kukuma*, a single-string bowed instrument similar to the *goge* but smaller; (iv) *garaya*, a two-string plucked instrument with calabash resonator; (v) *gurmi*, a two-string plucked instrument with calabash resonator.

All of these lutes are characteristically found in the northern states, although the *goge* also exists among the Yoruba as *gòjé*, where it is used in *sákárà*, a popular type of music.

Harps, too, are typical northern instruments, an example of which is the *gulum*, a three-string harp.

The most common example of the zither in Nigeria is the raft-zither, so called because of its structure. This instrument is known as *molo* and is predominant in the northern states. The raft zither sometimes has a calabash resonator, and one such type, called *molon kara*, is found among the Angas, Yergam and Eggon peoples of Plateau state.

Trumpets are fairly widely distributed in Nigeria and are to be found particularly in the northern and eastern states. One common

Fig. 20.1   Traditional horns blown at a Durbar held in Kaduna

variety of the trumpet is that made from animal horn, such as the *nja* or the *kaho*, examples of which were observed in the area comprised by the former North West state. A well-known trumpet is the *kakaki*, a long metal instrument found principally in the northern states but also among the Yoruba. Some Nigerian trumpets are end-blown (e.g. *kakaki*) while others are side-blown (e.g. trumpets made from animal horns).

The *algaita*, one of the most popular instruments in northern Nigeria, belongs to the oboe family.[1]

It would appear that end-blown flutes are more common in Nigeria than side-blown ones. One of the best-known flutes is the *oja* of the Igbo, a short instrument which customarily leads the orchestra in the Atilogwu dance. Longer flutes are also used, for example among the Naraguta and the Jarawa of Plateau state.[2]

There are examples of globular flutes, one of which (called *adiko*) was observed in Lagos state. An unusual Yoruba flute is a tiny vessel-shaped bamboo flute encased in leather, which is played for Jámújámu, an important masquerade in Ede, Oyo state. It has two finger holes, one in front and one at the back.

Pan-pipes have been observed in Plateau and Kaduna states. Among the Mada of Plateau state, these instruments were customarily used in warfare.

Earthenware pots are sometimes used as musical instruments. The Igbo *udu* is such an instrument and has an extra opening to the side of the main opening. Sounds produced when the player strikes the pot with a fibrous beater on the main opening are modulated by the closing and opening of the side opening with the other hand. The *udu* is customarily played by women.

From the Rivers state comes a set of tuned pots of different sizes and pitches. These pots are not strictly speaking made of clay but of a substance that apparently consists of a mixture of cement and sand. The set is played by one man and the pots are made to sound when the player strikes them at the mouth with a thick fibrous beater, shaped like a fan, held in each hand.

The iron bell is one of the most common and widely distributed musical instruments in Nigeria. It comes in two varieties (single and double) and is known in the northern states as *kuge*, among the Igbo as *ogene*,4E and among the Yoruba as *agogo*.

Hand pianos are identified primarily with the eastern states, but they are also used by the Igede[4] and the Tiv of Benue state as well as by the Yoruba. Their resonators usually consist either of a wooden box or a calabash.

The predominant areas for slit drums in Nigeria are the eastern states. These instruments are also common in Benue state, among the Tiv and the Igede. They are rare in Yorubaland and the *àgídìgbó* (played for the king in Oyo)[5] may have originated from a common source with the Igede slit drum, *ogirigboh*.[6]

Different types of rattling objects are used in musical contexts. The most common are gourds enclosed in a net strung with beads or seeds, such as the sekere of the Yoruba. The *icheche*[7] of the Igede of Benue state and the *chaka chaka* from the Rivers state are identical rattles; they consist of a pair of basket-work containers which enclose rattling objects. Apart from such clearly identifiable musical instruments, other rattling objects are often worn on the bodies of dancers and these also act like musical instruments.

We now come to the membrane drums of which there is probably greater variety than of any other single instrumental type. There are tension drums, goblet drums, kettle drums, frame drums, pot-resonated drums, calabash-resonated drums and pedestal drums.

Tension drums are found predominantly in the northern states and among the Yoruba. There are double-head tension drums as well as single-head ones. Examples of the double-head type are the *iyáàlù* and *kànàngó* of the Yoruba and the *kalangu* and *jauje* of the Hausa. The Hausa *kazage* and *kotso* as well as the Yoruba *kósó* are single-head tension drums. Tension drums are practically non-existent among other Nigerian groups but a single-head variety, known as *idan bupa*,[8] is one of the musical instruments of the Oba of Benin.

Examples of the kettle drum are the *tabishi* (the one which I observed came from the former North West state) and the Yoruba *gúdúgúdú*; each of these instruments has a tuning paste. The *gúdúgúdú* is usually combined with tension drums to form the *dùndún* orchestra.

The *tsintsina* and the *kuru*, from the northern states, are both goblet-shaped, single-head, open-end snare drums. The *tsintsina* has a tuning paste.

The *ganga*, one of the most common instruments in the northern States, is a representative of the category of cylindrical drums. It is a double-head drum with snare and is a counterpart of the Yoruba *bèmbé*.

Examples of frame drums are the Yoruba *orùnsà* (single-head, open-end instruments whose shells consist of the necks of earthenware pots) which are the standard drums used in *sákárà* music.

Some membrane drums such as the *tulu* of Gongola state have shells consisting of whole pots.[9] Unidentified pot-resonated drums from Kwara and Lagos states have also been observed.

Calabashes are sometimes used in the making of shells of membrane drums and examples of such instruments are the *duman girke* and the *dunu* from the northern states. (The striking of sticks on the bare surface of calabashes is also common among the Hausa-Fulani. The calabashes are hemispherical and are placed on the ground in an inverted position. A variation of this idea is the practice among the Hausa[10] and Yoruba of striking calabash surfaces with rings worn on the fingers.)

Pedestal drums, that is drums which have 'legs' or other extensions of the shells by which they are stood on the ground, are found in many parts of Nigeria. Examples are the Yoruba Ògboni drum and a man-sized instrument from Badagry which is used in connection with kingship rituals.

Instrumental music

Instrumental music consists of two main types, namely music for solo instruments and music for instrumental combinations.

While some instruments are characteristically employed solo (such as the raft zither) there are others which may be played solo on some occasions but are used orchestrally as well (such as the hand piano[11] and the slit drum).

Instrumentalists often practise as itinerant musicians and much solo music is realised in this context. Among the Yoruba, tension drum players may be seen on many occasions performing alone and receiving casual gifts by using their drums to praise people. A Hausa *maroki* (praise-singer) sometimes performs solo to his own drum accompaniment.[12]

It is likely that the more common type of instrumental music is that in which two or more instruments are combined. The typical orchestra consists of one or more membrane drums in combination with other types of instruments. More rarely, an orchestra would exclude membrane drums or consist entirely of membrane drums. The unmixed drum orchestra is a common sight in central Yoruba.

Orchestras consisting of one single type of instrument, other than membrane drums, are perhaps less common than those consisting of drums alone. The *apépé* orchestra, made up entirely of bamboo rhythm sticks, may be found among the Ijebu. The Ife have an ensemble of *àbèbè* (leather fans struck against the palms of the hands) which is used in *àgbon* music for the sea-goddess *Òsàrà*. Similarly, devotees of Ifá play an ensemble of bells (*agogo* Ifá). A Kaduna state group has been observed consisting entirely of *shantu* (about eleven in number), a cucumber-shaped gourd with an opening at either end which is struck against the thigh at one end with one hand modulating the sound by opening and closing the other end.[13]

The majority of ensembles employ two or more types of instruments and, given the variety of instrumental types existing in Nigeria, the possible combinations are limitless. Examples of combinations observed are:

1 Igbo ensemble including rhythm sticks and membrane drum.[14]

2 Igbo ensemble including *udu* and *ekpili* (a kind of rattle).[15]

3 Igbo ensemble including slit drums and basket-work rattles.[16]

4 Igbo ensemble including gourd rattles and flute.[17]

5 Igbo ensemble including a two-key xylophone with earthenware pot resonator, flute, single-hole earthenware pot modulated with the hand and membrane drums.

6 Ensemble from Niger state including 3 *kaburu* (large plucked gourd-resonated stringed instruments)[18] *goge* and flute (performing music for a hunters' dance).

7 Ensemble from the former North-West state including 3 *ganga* drums, 5 flutes, *kalangu* drum and rattles (playing music for marriage and birth ceremonies).

8 Ensemble from the former North-West state including small flute, *ganga* drum and *goge*.

9 Ensemble from the former North-West state including goblet drums and trumpets (playing music for hunters' dance).

10 Ensemble from the former North-West state including 2 *goge* and 2 hemispherical calabashes struck with sticks.

11 Ensemble from Kaduna state including pan-pipes (played by dancers), horns and *ganga*.

12 Ensemble from the former North-East state including two calabashes each inverted inside a bigger calabash containing water (both beaten with sticks by the same woman) and two other calabashes inverted and placed on the ground (played by two women).

13 Ensemble from Borno state including two xylophones, two small membrane drums, *ganga* drum and *algaita*.

14 Ensemble from Borno state including a stick placed on the ground and struck with two sticks, *goge*, and calabash disks strung along a stick and shaken from side to side.

15 Ensemble from Borno state including three *garaya* and three gourds scraped with cowries strung across the palm.

16 Ahoada (Rivers state) ensemble including a set of seven tuned concrete pots, membrane drums, bells (played by the dancers) and a bamboo block of the slit-drum family.

When instruments play in ensemble the general principle of organisation is similar to that customary in other parts of Africa. One instrument usually acts as the leader playing a variety of patterns, while the other instruments play patterns having varying degrees of repetitiveness. In other words, each of the secondary instruments has a basic pattern which it either repeats without variation or modifies now and then with minor variations.

It may be observed from the preceding that the principle of ensemble organisation in instrumental music is similar to the solo-and-chorus organisation in vocal music.

Another type of ensemble organisation is that described as hocket, in which a group of melodic instruments, rather than play a continuous melody simultaneously, has different instruments playing different fragments of the melody in appropriate sequence. An example of this is the *sombi* trumpet ensemble of the Plateau state.

In general, when instruments play in ensemble they employ strict rhythm, that is, all of the patterns played by the instruments are metrically coordinated in such a way that one can dance or beat time to the music. Free, that is non-danceable, rhythm is most commonly found in solo instrumental music. Instances, however, exist of solo instruments playing strict rhythm and of ensembles in which one instrument plays in free rhythm while the others play in strict rhythm.

One of the most important aspects of instrumental music in Nigeria, as in other parts of Africa, is the use of musical instruments to talk. Talking instruments are particularly common among Nigerian ethnic groups which use tone languages. In a typical tone language, there is an economy of vocabulary and a single word often has different meanings depending on the tone level or combination of tone levels with which the word is spoken. This dependence on tonality makes ordinary speech in such a language akin to a musical activity and enables musical instruments which can differentiate pitch to act as speech surrogates. Not all Nigerian ethnic groups, or even members of the same group, employ musical instruments for talking to the same degree. Among the Yoruba, talking with musical instruments is probably more extensive in Oyo Yoruba areas than it is with eastern and southern Yoruba.

Since two or more pitch levels are usually recognised in a given tone language, instruments with multiple pitches such as the tension drum, the flute and the hand piano are the most capable in reproducing speech. Talking instruments are now, however, restricted to these and even a single head, fixed pitch membrane drum can be made to talk. For example when using such a drum to reproduce Yoruba speech, the low tone can be obtained by hitting the drum head with a cupped hand to produce a muffled tone; the middle tone can be obtained by hitting the drum head in such a way that it vibrates freely (i.e. to produce the drum's natural pitch); while the high tone can be obtained by applying tension on the drum head with one hand and hitting it with the other hand.

Social context

As is customary in other parts of Africa, much of the traditional music of Nigeria is realised within the context of social ceremonies. This is not to say that music is never performed simply for its own sake. The player of the hand piano (*ubo*) might perform purely for his own enjoyment and without reference to any ceremony. So also might an *ijálá* artist chant portions of *ijálá* to himself.

Nevertheless the most prominent use to which music is put in traditional culture is in the celebration, whether as an embellishment or as an integral part, of social ceremonies. As has been clearly demonstrated by Babalola, *ijálá* is performed mainly on occasions 'connected with the worship of Ògún and the activities of the hunters' guild'.[19] Other occupational groups, such as blacksmiths, farmers and weavers, also sometimes have their own types of music and dance. A type of music customarily associated with butchers in the northern states is that of the *kalangu*, tension drums.

Certain types of music are reserved for the various ceremonies connected with the life cycle, such as birth rites, puberty rites, marriage and death. The *ekún íyàwó* of the Oyo Yoruba (also known as *egbé íyàwó* in Kabba, Kwara state) is a body of poetry which is chanted by brides on their wedding day.

Another type of music that is the exclusive preserve of women is the *shantu* music which is customarily heard only within the harems in the northern states.

The various traditional festivals celebrated all over Nigeria every year usually have specific types of music associated with them. Moreover, music plays a very important part in kingship rituals and in the celebration of religious ceremonies. In some cases, not only types of music but musical instruments are dedicated to specific gods or religious contexts. The *àgbá* Olósunta is a drum which is reserved exclusively in Ikere-Ekiti for the yearly ceremonies connected with the worship of Olosunta, a local Ifá priest who became deified.[20] Among the Yoruba, *igbìn* drums are the special instruments of Obàtálá, the god of creation and *ìpèsè*, the special instruments of Orunmila, the god of the Ifa divination oracle. The *upe*, a trumpet made from gourd, is sacred to Ògún, the god of warfare and of iron implements in Ondo.[21] The drums of the Isoko of the Niger Delta are said to be 'ritually protected' and the *ogri* drum is the central feature of the most important religious ceremony of the Isoko.[22]

Other instruments are reserved for royalty, such as the long trumpets commonly played for emirs in the northern states and which are also played for Yoruba kings (for example, the Aláàfin of Òyó and the Aláká of Abéòkúta), The *ogba*, an ivory horn, forms part of the regalia of an Isoko village head chief.[23]

The preceding represent only a few of the types of ceremonies and social context with which music is associated; many other types, and indeed the vast majority of social ceremonies in Nigeria, utilise music.

New music

Music in the Church

With the advent of Christianity a new type of music was introduced into

Nigeria. Music has always been an important part of traditional religious worship and there is little doubt that among Nigerians, it constitutes one of the elements of attraction to the Church, where music features prominently.

The music used in Nigerian churches was at first little different from that of European churches. It consisted of European hymns translated into Nigerian languages and sung to European melodies. This practice was unsuitable since a text in a Nigerian tone language usually had its own inherent melodic structure and the imposition of an imported melody usually resulted in a conflict with the natural melodic structure of the text, thereby distorting its meaning. Compare, for example, the pattern of speech tones of the first line of the hymn 'Onward Christian Soldiers', in its Yoruba version, with the melodic pattern imposed by the European tune. The first moves from the middle-tone level to the low-tone level and then to the high-tone level, while the second moves from an initial tone level up and then back to the initial tone level.

1. Spoken Version

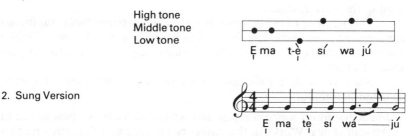

High tone
Middle tone
Low tone

Ẹ ma t-ẹ̀ sí wa jú

2. Sung Version

Ẹ ma tẹ̀ sí wá———jú

In order to remedy this anomaly, Nigerian church musicians began to compose new hymns whose melodies were in agreement with the inherent tonal patterns of the texts. Moreover, these new hymns employ a rhythmic style which is closer to that of traditional music. Further links with traditional culture are evident in some of Nigeria's indigenous church music which is accompanied with traditional instruments[24] and dance; this kind of music may be heard particularly in the non-orthodox churches such as the Celestial Church and the Cherubim and Seraphim Church. The new church music, however, also includes pieces in which strong European influences remain, either by virtue of the use of European instruments to accompany them[25] or in their use of European harmony.[26]

Apart from hymns, church music by Nigerians includes versicles and responses,[27] anthems and cantatas. Moreover, the texts of these works are not always in Nigerian languages; T. K. E. Phillips' cantata, *Samuel*, for example uses an English text.

Music in the concert hall

The most typical form of musical presentation in traditional culture is one which makes little distinction between performers and audience. In other words, although the principal group in a musical presentation often consists of highly trained musicians (whether practising professionally or not), there are usually aspects of performance in which others attending the occasion may participate. An audience in the strict sense seldom exists since all people congregating at a performance are potential performers and if they are completely prevented from joining the performance, it is usually because of a lack of knowledge of the repertoire.

The concept of audience participation is, however, not invariable in traditional culture and there are some pieces specifically meant to be played by a specialist body of performers to an audience that does not join in the performance.

Music written by Nigerians for presentation in the concert hall follows the same pattern as similar music in the western world, from which the new Nigerian tradition was derived. It may be defined as music composed for performance by a body of trained musicians, usually in an auditorium specially designed for the purpose, before a clearly defined audience which, by mutual understanding, is specifically excluded from joining the performance.

This manner of using music is a radical departure from traditional concepts and, as such, has few followers in Nigeria. Its very limited audience usually consists of people who have acquired a taste for western concert music.

Nigerian works for the concert hall belong in four main categories, as listed hereunder.

1 Music based on western styles and which makes no conscious use of African styles. Works in this category are rare and the only one that comes to mind is my own *String Quartet*, composed in 1957.

2 Music in which melodies, rhythms or concepts derived from African culture are deliberately used in works which are otherwise western in idiom and instrumentation. Examples of music in this category are *African Suite* for string orchestra and *Folk Symphony*, both by Fela Sowande.

3 Music in which African and western elements are more or less codominant, often through the combination of western and African instruments or by the use of Nigerian texts. An example of music in this category is Ayo Bankole's *Three Part-Songs* for female choir (whose text is in Yoruba).

4 Music based entirely on African traditional models. Most of the music so far produced in this category properly belongs to and will be discussed under the section 'Music in the theatre'. Examples of such works specifically written for the concert hall (and by this is meant newly composed music and not concert presentations of traditional music) are as yet few. My own *Abiku No. 1* (1965) was originally composed for a dance-drama for solo dancer and has subsequently been performed as a concert piece.

Music in the theatre

New types of music theatre have emerged in Nigeria in the course of the present century and these may be grouped under four main categories:

1 English-language plays which make extensive use of music.
2 The 'folk opera'.
3 Opera based on European styles.
4 Dance-drama.

Plays by Nigerian authors writing in the English language make copious use of music, usually music derived from traditional culture. Examples of such plays are *The Lion and the Jewel*, *Kongi's Harvest*, and *Death of the King's Horseman* by Wolé Sóyinká, and 2*The Gods Are Not to Blame* and *Kúrunmí* by Olá Rótìmí.

The 'folk opera' has been developed mainly by Yoruba composers and is exemplified by the works of Kólá Ògúnmólá (*Palmwine Drinkard* and *Àdììtú Olódumarè*) and Dúró Ládípò (*Oba Kòso* and *Èdá*). The Yoruba folk opera has a Yoruba text and makes use of music either directly borrowed from or based upon Yoruba traditional music. The influences which guided the emergence of the folk opera are more directly related to the European tradition of spoken theatre rather than to European grand opera.[28]

There are other operas, however, which are based on European concepts of opera and which have been composed by Nigerians with professional training in Western music. Ayò Bankólé's *Night of Miracles*, though described as a 'folk-opera' by the composer, falls under this category. The work makes use of a mixed ensemble of European instruments and Yoruba drums. Adam Fiberesima's *Opu Jaja*, while having an Ijaw text, maintains strong idiomatic links with the European grand opera.

Music in the night club

New types of popular music, suitable for use in the night club, have been developed in the last few decades. Some of these new types are adaptations of traditional music. For example, *àpàlà* and *sákárà*, originally used for entertainment at social ceremonies of Yoruba Moslems and now often heard in the night club, evolved from Yoruba traditional music. Other types of popular music reflect interactions between local and western musical cultures. Such western-influenced types of pop music may be divided into three main categories. The first category consists of musical types (such as *jùjú* music of the Yoruba) in which the principal instrument is the western guitar but in which the song texts are usually in the vernacular. In the second category is *highlife*, a type of music which is practised in most parts of West Africa. The classical *highlife* orchestra is essentially the same as the western dance band of the 1950s, except that the Yoruba tension drum is sometimes added. *Highlife* songs are mostly in pidgin English; this musical type reached its peak of popularity in the years preceding and following 1960 but is now practically out of fashion.

Fig. 20.2   Night-club music

In the third category are musical types based on the most up-to-date rock idioms from the west. Nigerian rock musicians sometimes attempt an Africanisation of these idioms through the introduction of songs in Nigerian languages. *Afro-rock* or *Afro-beat*, as these Africanised versions are called, however, retain not only the instrumental style but also the vocal mannerisms of rock music as it is practised in the west.

Summary

Nigeria is an extensive music area, both in its geography and the variety of musical types. Traditional music is a living culture and constitutes the staple idiom of the vast majority of Nigerians. The richness of traditional musical culture may be measured in terms of the multiplicity of instruments and musical styles.

In addition to traditional music, other types have developed, some of them resulting from the interaction of Nigerian and foreign cultures.

Some critics, both within and outside Nigeria, have shown

considerable hostility to the idea of Nigerian musicians using non-indigenous idioms, specifically those deriving from the so-called classical music of the west. This attitude arises partly from an inadequate understanding of the universal functions of music. The critics' view appears to be that what does not immediately 'entertain' or thrill the masses should be discouraged. Or how else can one interpret the fact that foreign idioms in massive (and probably unhealthy) doses are eagerly and unquestionably accepted in the area of pop music?

Hostility towards Nigerian experiments in 'classical' music also arises from a false notion of colonialism. Those practising this music are viewed as having been brainwashed by Europeans. Moreover, there is some anxiety that the acceptance of a new idiom automatically means the rejection of an old one.

Fears of musical colonisation in Nigeria (except perhaps in the area of pop music) are groundless. For one thing, those practising western 'classical' music are in the minority and are likely to remain so. Secondly, the mere presence of foreign ideas in any culture does not necessarily lead to negative consequences. This is easily illustrated by our use of ordinary speech language. Provided a Nigerian is able to speak one of his indigenous speech languages it is an advantage if he can speak English, Russian or French as well. Similarly, provided a Nigerian is able to use and understand at least one of his indigenous musical languages, it is surely advantageous for him to be able to use any foreign musical language of his choice.

Thirdly, present trends indicate that Nigerian society can accommodate foreign musical idioms while at the same time preserving the authenticity, virility and pre-eminence of traditional idioms.

It is worth noticing in this regard that the leading Nigerian composers of music in the western 'classical' idioms – Fela Sowande, Samuel Akpabot, Ayo Bankole, Laz Ekwueme and the present writer – are also among the country's leading spokesmen for traditional music. These men have spent years doing research into traditional music and have published scholarly works on this subject. In addition they have taught courses on traditional music both in Nigeria and abroad and also broadcast programmes on the radio designed to educate the general public about the elements of indigenous musical culture.

Multiple musicality is a positive element and is a phenomenon of those Third World societies which, when bombarded by western musical idioms, were able to accept these idioms without losing their own indigenous idioms. Ironically, such Third World societies are today musically superior to western societies, whose peoples are normally ignorant of anything outside of western music and whose musicians are now groping anxiously for alternative languages of music.

Ideal conditions for creating a multi-musical society exist in abundance in Nigeria and, given the right type of education, most Nigerians should before long be able to accept any form of good music (whether from Europe, China, or India) with the same ease that they accept their own indigenous music.

Notes

1 See K. A. Gourlay, *The Identification and Description of Musical Instruments with Particular Reference to Northern Nigeria*, revised version (Zaria: Centre for Nigerian Cultural Studies, Ahmadu Bello University, Zaria, 1976), p. 31.

2 Notes on *Music of the Jos Plateau and Other Regions of Nigeria.* LP Recording, Folkways Ethnic Library FE4321. Recorded by Stanley Diamond, edited with notes by Victor Grauer.

3 W. W. C. Echezona, 'Ibo musical instruments', *Nigeria*, 84, 1965, p. 46.

4 See the notes on *Music of Dawn and Day: Music and Dance Associations of the Igede of Nigeria*, LP Recording, Love Records LXLP513/514. Recorded and edited by Bjorn Ranung.

5 Samuel Johnson, *History of the Yorubas* (Lagos: CMS (Nigeria) Bookshops, reprint edition, 1966), p. 121; also R. C. Abraham, *Dictionary of Modern Yoruba* (London: University of London Press, 1958), p. 454. I have been able to identify this instrument as a Yoruba variety of the slit drum through the verbal description of Dr Babatunde Lawal who has observed it in the palace at Oyo.

6 The Igede variety is listed in the notes on *Music of Dawn and Day*; according to verbal information from Aliyu Doma, slit drums are found in palaces in most areas of Benue and Plateau states and, among the Alago of Plateau state, they are known as *agidigbo*, which name incidentally is identical with that of the Yoruba hand piano.

7 See *Music of Dawn and Day*.

8 See (i) Laoye I, Timi of Ede, 'Yoruba Drums', *Odu*, 7, 1959, p. 10; (ii) J. W. A. Thorburn, 'City of Benin', *Nigeria*, 10, 1937, p. 68.

9 According to verbal information from Aliyu Doma, such drums are used for ritual music in non-Moslem areas of the north.

10 Mercedes Mackay, 'The traditional musical instruments of Nigeria', *Nigerian Field*, XV, iii, 1950, p. 114.

11 *Ibid.*

12 M. G. Smith, 'The social functions and meaning of Hausa praise singing', *Africa*, XXVII, 1957, p. 37.

13 Mackay ('Traditional musical instruments', p. 115) classifies this instrument as a stamping tube, while Gourlay (*Identification and Description*, p. 41) classifies it as a plosive aerophone.

14 Illustrated in W. W. C. Echezona, 'Ibo musical instruments', p. 46.

15 *Ibid.*

16 *Ibid.*, p. 47.

17 *Ibid.*, p. 49.

18 According to Aliyu Doma, the *kaburu* belongs to the Gwari ethnic group and is found also in Plateau and Kaduna states.

19 S. A. Babalola, *The Content and Form of Yoruba Ìjálá* (Oxford: OUP, 1966), p. 8.

20 J. Ògúnlùsì, 'The Olósunta Festival', *African Arts*, iii, 1, 1969, p. 55; also A. Ajayi, 'Olosunta Festival', *Nigeria*, 84, 1965, p. 19.

21 F. Akínrìnsólá, 'Ògún Festival', *Nigeria*, 85, 1965.

22 P. Peek and N. E. Owheibor, 'Isoko Songs of Ilue-Ologbo', *African Arts*, IV, 2, 1971, p. 45.

23 *Ibid.*

24 See for example a picture of an ensemble including two slit drums, two *udu*, one rattle, one bell and a two-key xylophone, used to accompany hymns with traditionally-derived melodies in an Ibo church. M. Mackay, 'Traditional musical instruments', p. 131.

25 See e.g. J. O. Ajíbólá, *Orin Yoruba/Yoruba Songs* (Ilé-Ifè: University of Ife Press, 1974).

26 As for example in A. T. Ola Olúdé, *Yoruba Hymns and Carols*, whose publisher and date are not indicated.

27 e.g. T. K. E. Phillips, *Orin ní Ohùn Ilè Wa fún Àwon Àdúrà Kúkurú àti Ìdáhùn Won (Versicles and Responses) ati fun Litanì* (C.M.S. (Nigeria) Press, Port Harcourt, 1926).

28 For a fuller discussion of the Yoruba folk opera, see my 'New idioms of music drama among the Yoruba: an introductory study', *1970 Yearbook of the International Folk Music Council.*

Index